THE RISE
OF THE GULAG

THE RISE
OF THE GULAG
Intellectual Origins of Leninism

ALAIN BESANÇON
Translated by Sarah Matthews

CONTINUUM • New York

1981
The Continuum Publishing Corporation
18 East 41st Street, New York, N.Y. 10017

Originally published as
Les origines intellectuelles du Léninisme
© 1977 by Calmann-Levy

Library of Congress Cataloging in Publication Data

Besançon, Alain.
The rise of the Gulag.

Translation of Les origines
intellectuelles du léninisme
Bibliography   Includes index.
1. Lenin, Vladimir Il'ich, 1870–1924.
2. Russia—Intellectual life—History.   I. Title.
HX314.L3569B4713   335.4′0947   80-21485
ISBN 0-8264-0014-0

Contents

1
The Ideology

Solzhenitsyn:

This universal, obligatory force-feeding with lies is now the most agonizing aspect of existence in our country — worse than all our material miseries, worse than any lack of civil liberties.

All these arsenals of lies, which are totally unnecessary for our stability *as a state*, are levied as a kind of tax for the benefit of ideology — to nail down events as they happen and clamp them to a tenacious, sharp-clawed but dead ideology: and it is precisely because our state, through sheer force of habit, tradition and inertia, continues to cling to this false doctrine with all its tortuous aberrations, that it needs to put the dissenter behind bars. For a false *ideology* can find no other answer to argument and protest than weapons and prison bars.

Cast off this cracked ideology! Relinquish it to your rivals, let it go wherever it wants, let it pass from our country like a storm-cloud, like an epidemic, let others concern themselves with it and study it, just so long as we don't! In ridding ourselves of it we shall also rid ourselves of the need to fill our life with lies. Let us all pull off and shake off from all of us this filthy sweaty shirt of ideology which is now so stained with the blood of those 66 million that it prevents the living body of the nation from breathing.[1]

In his *Letter to Soviet leaders*, Solzhenitsyn keeps coming back on nearly every page to an ill-defined but unavoidable concept, a concept which he seems to confront almost against his will: ideology. As word and as object it occupies the central position. With a spirit of decision such as none of his predecessors possessed, not even Zamyatin or Orwell,[2] Solzhenitsyn holds fast to the insight that the essential feature which has remained unchanging since 7 November 1917 is not the nationalization of the means of production, nor the bureaucracy, nor the new class, nor even the party, nor, in a general way, a particular social and economic structure, or political structure but a certain kind of 'belief', an ideology, which is now surely no longer even a belief, but, to be deliberately imprecise, a way of thinking.[3] It is 'that' which he places at the strategic centre of the Communist world. Despite the gaps in his knowledge and the limited nature of his analysis, the simple fact of his having correctly discerned and located the position of ideology is an indication of the quality of his insight.

I

What does *ideology* mean?

Solzhenitsyn uses the word in the sense in which it is used in contemporary Soviet speech. I will follow his example, and use this idea as an empirically verifiable historical fact, and not as an *a priori* concept.

There does in fact exist a Soviet definition of Soviet ideology. It is presented as conforming to Marxism. Thus, ideology in the broadest sense means the entirety of ideas and achievements of a civilization worked out by the dominant class and, deriving from this, the entire society of a given class. In the narrow sense, an ideology is a system of interpretation allowing the justification of particular social situations, and allowing them to be perpetuated, according to the political power of class. An ideology can be true or false. If it is false, it is because it is the intellectual expression of a system of interests which cannot endure the light of day. Only the proletariat – whose interests match those of the whole of humanity – is capable of producing an ideology which is not false, but true.

It is not a science, but it is like a science. Today, there are no more than two ideologies, the others having been overtaken by the movement of history. Lenin wrote in 1902: '*The only choice is*: either bourgeois or Socialist ideology. There is no middle course (for mankind has not created a "third" ideology...).'[4]

A *dictionary of philosophy*, which is a textbook widely available in the USSR, clearly sets out the respective positions of these two ideologies:

The ideology of the working-class is Marxism–Leninism, the ideological weapon of the Communist Party and of the working-class in the revolutionary Socialist transformation of society. The invincible power of this ideology derives from the way it is the faithful translation of the objective laws of the historical development of our age. Contemporary bourgeois ideology, on the other hand, is a reactionary force. It serves the interests of the bourgeoisie in its struggle against the working-class and Socialism. It is a denial of science, it is idealism, fideism, obscurantism, a call to chauvinism and to racism, propaganda in favour of cosmopolitanism; such are the characteristics of modern bourgeois ideology.[5]

So Marxism—Leninism presents a picture of the intellectual world as being divided between two conflicting ideologies. Of course, the false ideology does not vanish spontaneously before the splendour of the true, proletarian ideology. The two ideologies are engaged in a fierce struggle. Marxism—Leninism associates itself with one of these ideologies, and, by a process of reasoning which is an essential part of the doctrine itself, assigns to itself that ideology's criteria of truth. Why is Marxism—Leninism true? Because it is the ideology of the working class, and that class, because of its adherence to Marxism—Leninism, cannot be wrong. But if the working class should not be Leninist? Then that is because it has succumbed to the influence of bourgeois ideology.

Let us ask again, what is Soviet ideology?

To Solzhenitsyn, ideology is not a concept, but a thing. It is a daily reality bearing down on him and his compatriots. It is Marxism—Leninism, *diamat*, as it is taught to schoolchildren, to students, to cadres, to everyone.[6] Censorship and the police make sure that nothing conflicts with it publicly. The ideology is present in every work of philosophy, history and economics. It exercises an indirect control on all literature and all the fine arts. It oversees all the other sciences, whether social or natural, and their results must never be allowed to contradict it. It makes its mark on everyday speech. It informs the whole social body, and, inversely, the social body only exists in so far as it receives this ideological form and gives it shape.

But here a strange fact comes to light. As a system of ideas, Soviet ideology is incredibly simple. The *Dictionary of philosophy*, small though it is, is quite sufficiently large to exhaust it. The *ABC of Communism*, by Bukharin and Preobrazhenski, published in 1919, provides a complete exposé of it.[7] *Dialectical materialism and historical materialism*, published by Stalin in 1938, contains all there is of it.[8] In 1958, there appeared, under the names of a collective of eminent ideologists, a *Foundation of Marxist philosophy*, and, the following year, the *Foundations of Marxism—Leninism*: as far as the claims their titles make are concerned, they are satisfactory. Nothing is added, nothing is retracted, apart from the fact that changes in the team and in circumstances have meant that certain names and events which have come to carry undesirable political associations are not mentioned. The intellectual content is unchanged. Even today textbooks still appear entitled *Principles of scientific socialism*, or *Scientific Communism*, the tenor of which has not altered. Occasionally these books are described as 'popular' or 'elementary' accounts. But there is no higher level.

Can it be that the Soviet ideology is this trivial, uncomplicated system which even the Soviets themselves appear not to take seriously? How can it be at one and the same time both utterly hollow and all-powerful? How can this semi-void make up the vital centre of the whole of Communism? For Solzhenitsyn, with a general's eye for the crucial weakness, points to it as the foundation and support of the whole régime: take it away and the whole edifice collapses. So we are led to consider the problem in other terms. The ideology cannot be reduced to a system of ideas. It *is* the Soviet régime itself. It cannot be defined as or confined to being the catalogue of ideas or propositions which constitute it. It is something else again.

It is a problem which has concerned a number of contemporary sociologists and philosophers. The answers which they have put forward may be divided into two groups.

For the first group, Marxist–Leninist ideology is a particular manifestation of a continuing phenomenon, which has been part of human history for a long while. This is, for instance, the point of view put forward by Mannheim and by non-Leninist Marxists.[9] Regarded thus there can be no opposition between Marxist–Leninist ideology and those other ideologies which have preceded it. They go to make up a series together. Marxist–Leninist ideology is neither more true nor more false. It fulfils the same functions of dissimulation, justification, and so on. Thus defined, ideology is inseparable from political conflict, which has existed ever since man began to live in social groups.[10]

For the second group of writers, on the other hand, Soviet ideology as it has functioned for the last sixty years is a species new to history. It is an unknown animal which has never been classified or described, and which has stunned our century, just as the Aztecs must have been stunned by the conquistadors' horses.[11] It seems to me that this second point of view is more faithful to the actual historical experience than the first, which tends to send *diamat* off into the realms of timelessness, and not to do justice to the numerous witnesses who assert that they have lived under a system such as the world has never known before.

To classify Soviet ideology as belonging to the whole body of ideology in general is not the same sort of intellectual venture as to recognize the irreducible originality of the Soviet ideology, and then to seek historical parallels and precedents for it. In the first instance, the phenomenon is brought into the realm of the known; in the second, one starts by recognizing it as unknown, and then one proceeds to revise the whole of history in the light of this unknown factor, and it is this which forms the basis for an inquiry into its origins, genesis and the conditions necessary for its appearance.

Let us consider this new beast. If we take it in its pure state, as it appears in the works of its creator, Lenin, it presents two aspects which are generally only seen separately, but which here are intimately united: on the one hand it is a faith, on the other, a theory rationally argued and allegedly proved. As a faith, it is more structured than mere prejudices, which are pluralist, vague and confused; than credos, which are partial, fragmented, and do not demand a total commitment; or than political programmes, whose field is limited and which do not demand such a rigid separation between friends and enemies. As a theory, it is distinct from those movements of thought which may well be systematic and explicit, but which do not demand such conformity of behaviour nor the absolute assent of their adherents, and do not, in general, require such a high degree of emotional commitment.[12]

When Lenin writes: 'The Marxist doctrine is omnipotent because it is true. It is comprehensive and harmonious, and provides men with an integral world outlook',[13] we are on the 'faith' side of this ideology. When he writes: 'Since the appearance of *Capital* ... the materialist conception of history is no longer a hypothesis, but a scientifically demonstrated proposition',[14] we are on the side of rationally proven theory. But this is not quite right, either, for in the first passage Lenin thought he was putting forward theoretical evidence, and in the second he was making an act of faith. The two aspects are inseparable.

The result of such a description of ideology is an apparently contradictory *compound*, which has important consequences for the search for its origins and precedents. Because it is a faith, one must inquire into religion; because it is a theory, into rational philosophic and scientific thought. But it cannot be reduced either to the one or the other, and in the course of inquiry, one comes to see that this ideology is their opposite, or, in the Aristotelian sense, their corruption.

The principal error which has impeded and continues to impede an understanding of Soviet ideology arises from the way in which it has been set in a series either of religions or of philosophies.

II

The philosophical descent of Soviet ideology appears perfectly natural for it claims such a descent for itself by explicitly declaring itself to be breaking away from religion. In the textbooks, this ideology lays claim to a glorious genealogy: a large part of classical philosophy (Heraclitus, Democritus, Epicurus, Lucretius); the philosophy of the Renaissance and of the Enlightenment (Bacon, Descartes, Hobbes, Spinoza); the *Encyclopédistes*; and, finally, Hegel and Marx. It lays claim, moreover, to the whole of science, and thus declares itself to be accomplishing the intellectual history of humanity, and gathering together the totality of its 'valid' heritage.

One might well refute such claims, but that does not free one from the need to situate Marxism—Leninism in the history of thought. And one must then beware of a variety of pitfalls.

The most serious of these is to consider it as a philosophy, as false and bad a one as you like, but a philosophy none the less. Thus Losski and Zenkovsky, the authors of two *Histories of Russian philosophy*, each dedicate a chapter to 'dialectical materialism'.[15] It is perfectly obvious that these chapters do not fit into the history of philosophy, and that they are foreign to it. Father Henri Chambre, a meticulous writer, accustomed to treating the written word with all due care and deference, has written a book, *Marxisme en Union soviétique*, in which he examines, by means of official texts, the concepts of right, of 'friendship between peoples' and of political economy, beginning with Marx and noting any subsequent modifications.[16] He reconstitutes a genealogy which starts from Marx or from the Enlightenment, and believes that he can discern a development in, for instance, economics, from the works of Bukharin to Stalin's last teachings. He assumes that there is a similar relationship between Marxism—Leninism and its authors, as there is between Marx and *Capital*. In the same way, he assumes that there is a relationship between the Soviet ideology deriving from Marx and Soviet society itself, analogous to that which exists between French society and the Republican ideas deriving from the French Revolution. This sort of false assumption undermines the whole undertaking, and the greater the erudition, the more the book loses contact with reality. You cannot enter into a philosophical discussion with the ideology, even to refute it, because it is foreign to philosophy, and cannot be refuted by it.[17] Though the ideology, of course, dotes on this sort of 'dialogue' in which it is accorded philosophical status, and, by the same token, legitimacy.

Others, with greater insight, have sensed this division and make a distinction between philosophy and ideology. But even then there are two possible ways of proceeding. Either one must, with one's vision firmly fixed on the catastrophic outcome of the line, demonstrate its illegitimacy. There had been a betrayal at some point in its evolution, which up until then could be deemed healthy, and after which occurred the disastrous deviation. For Kostas Papaioannou, this break came after Marx, that is, with the classic social democrats like Kautsky and Plekhanov.[18] Thus, in his *L'idéologie froide*, one goes from high thought (Marx) to ideology (Stalin). This certainly seems to be the evolution. None the less, it runs the risk of exonerating the philosopher coming immediately before the catastrophic decline from all responsibility for it, and this hardly seems probable. There is no such a thing as an Immaculate Conception in the history of philosophy. Or else – and this is the other possible way to proceed – the descent is recognized as legitimate, but then one is led to regard the history of philosophy as a series of catastrophes receding even further back in time. The sins of the children are visited upon the fathers. Step by step, one can see Hegel, Kant, Descartes, nominalism all arraigned. Russian Slavophiles like Kireevski, or the young Soloviev, were virtuosi of this sort of chain of guilt, calmly proceeding to put Saint Thomas, Augustine and Aristotle all on trial.[19] So one has to go right back to the original philosophical sin, and scrap the whole family tree. In the first approach, one tends to succumb to a vision of a vanished utopian golden age of philosophy, while in the other, one falls prey to a pessimistic belief in the radical corruption of our thinking, which ends with one behaving like Bouvard and Pécuchet,* and regarding Hegel, or Descartes, or whoever, as 'the cause of it all'.

It seems possible to avoid the difficulties of these two approaches

---

Translator's Note: The eponymous heroes of a satirical novel by Gustave Flaubert, in which the *naïveté* and stupidity of two copying clerks provide a vehicle for Flaubert's exposé of the absurdity of intellectual pretentiousness.

by assuming that there is no continuity of *kind* between ideology and the movements of scientific and philosophical thought from which it claims descent. What has occurred is a mutation. There is thus neither a legitimate line of descent, nor even an illegitimate one, retaining, through the process of transformation, the philosophical substance. We are dealing with the appearance of a new species which has made use of portions of old intellectual developments, and it is these which make up the raw material, on which it imprints its own particular form. One can thus avoid any series of accusations, for the intellectual developments are only materially responsible for having borne within them such salvageable elements. They bear no moral responsibility.

What has been said about philosophy holds even more true for science. Marx laid claim to Darwin as an influence. So did Lenin (and so, incidentally, did Hitler). The voyage of the *Beagle* cannot be held any more responsible for the birth of the ideology than can any other single scientific venture, although the ideology may claim legitimate descent from science as a whole.

Establishing a relationship between Soviet ideology and the history of religions is something that can only be done by adversaries of Soviet ideology, since it embodies in itself, and promises for everyone, the end of religion. But, in the generation contemporary with Stalin, the fideist, cultist, dogmatic aspects of the ideology were so patently obvious that the comparison sprang spontaneously to mind, commonly with a picture of a 'medieval', 'inquisitorial', etc. Christianity. Jules Monnerot referred to 'the Islam of the twentieth century'.[20] Raymond Aron suggested the phrase 'secular religion' and he gave one of the chapters in *The opium of the intellectuals* the title: 'Churchmen and the faithful'.[21]

Such analogies do in fact exist, but they are too numerous and run too deep to be examined here. It is not simply by chance that Nadezhda Mandelstam compared Soviet ideology to an 'inverted church', nor that the Church which is thus inverted is moreover likely to be the Roman Catholic Church rather than the Orthodox or Protestant Church.[22] After all, in the story of the Grand Inquisitor, Dostoevsky was aiming primarily at the Catholic Church, but for his readers in our century it is the Soviet régime that springs most readily to mind. None the less, the Grand Inquisitor exchanged freedom for bread, whilst, by a disposition which Dostoevsky might well have thought providential, the Soviet régime has not yet been able to extinguish the taste for freedom in its subjects to anything like the extent that the poverty which it brought about made them lose their taste for bread.

All the same, the ideology is not a religion, not even a 'secular religion'. One distinguishing feature is enough to set the ideology apart from the group of religions with which it is usually compared. This is to do with an act of faith. It is a commonplace that something cannot at the same time and in the same way be known (or seen) and believed. Abraham, we are told, when sacrificing Isaac, 'believed God'. Before the empty tomb, John 'believed'. In the Koran, the word faith means, as it does in the Bible, 'having faith in', 'trusting oneself to'. At the basis of religions of faith, there is a conscious *unknown*. Abraham, Saint John, Muhammed know that they do not know. They know that they believe. When Lenin declares that the materialist interpretation of history is not a hypothesis, but a scientifically demonstrated doctrine, it is doubtless a belief, but a belief he imagines proven, and based in experience. At the basis of the ideology, lies something known. Lenin does not know that he believes. He believes that he knows.

III

And yet, it is not the history of philosophy, but the history of religions which can provide a precedent for the ideology. In fact, the same distinguishing feature which sets the ideology apart from religion, serves to distinguish, within the religions of faith, an attitude of mind which appears to present fairly close analogies to ideology. This attitude of mind is gnosis. It is an imperfect model of ideological thinking, but it is the only one which can provide it with any depth of historical perspective. For though the species may indeed be new, and though it seems to be entirely confined to the modern age, it is useful to relate it, even indirectly, to a phenomenon of which humanity has had a recurring experience. Obviously there is no continuity between the two phenomena. Lenin, and for once I agree with him, would have considered it quite mad to be placed in the tradition of Valentin or Mani, of whom, I am sure, he would barely have heard. *Precedent* should be understood as meaning an analogous structure of thought, an attitude, an arrangement of the intellect, even though what is thought is not related. I will show, later, that another characteristic marks a distinction between gnosticism and ideology. But it is worth considering in some detail the gnostic phenomenon which, though far removed from the area of my inquiry, has none the less suggested to it several influential ideas.

It is possible that gnosticism, as an attitude of mind, is close to all religions, that is, it is possible that they are all susceptible to a 'gnostic' mutation. But as a distinct historical phenomenon, it arose at the dawn of Christianity, and in the midst of Judaeo-Christian sects. Gnosticism did not thrive in a pagan environment, where the divine had not yet been gathered into one godhead, transcendant and separate from the world, and where, as a result, religious adherence was not sealed by an act of faith. It became crystallized in a monotheistic climate, particularly where knowledge had also followed a similar course of being gathered together and unified. It followed late Judaism, nascent Christianity, and, later, Islam, like a shadow, a shadow which was never to leave them.

Gnosticism did not come into being as a unified doctrine, but as a ferment of different systems, maintained by tiny groups along the fringes of the developing orthodoxies (unless it was the orthodoxies which brought into being this fringe of gnosticisms). The burgeoning of socialisms under the July Monarchy can give us some idea of what it must have been like. But from our own point of view (that of seeking forerunners to ideology), certain general themes appear to be of interest.

First of all, an acute consciousness of the fallen state both of the world and of the self, combined with a revolt against that fallen condition. In the world, good and evil (light and darkness) are two irreconcilable elements which have become absurdly mingled in a way which works against the fundamental aims of this world. But our intimate revolt against evil, the bearer of all ills, is 'in itself proof of our primal association with the perfect good which is opposed to it'.[2][3] There is thus good in us, the remnants of a previous condition, which it is up to us to free from the cancer surrounding it, and for which we cannot be held responsible. It follows that the fall and redemption of the world and the fall and redemption of man fit together like a nest of boxes, one inside the other. The world is subject to a past Fall, but the elements of good imprisoned in evil (in matter, in time, in the difference between the sexes, and so on – all of them evil things) will escape and return to that original homeland of which we still retain a shadowy memory. Even in the present world, the elect can perform this act of discrimination within themselves.

There are thus two movements of salvation, that of election, of personal salvation, which can be carried out *hic et nunc*, and that of the redemption of the other particles of perfection scattered throughout the universe, which is brought about at the end of a general eschatology.

The means by which this dual salvation is achieved is, above all, through gnosis, that is, through knowledge. A *theoretical* knowledge of the laws of the cosmos, and of its structure in its entirety, macrocosm and microcosm (man). An *historical* knowledge, bearing on the evolution of the cosmos, its primitive state, the causes and circumstances surrounding and prompting its fall, and the routes of redemption open to it, which in turn make possible a prediction of its final state. A *practical* knowledge of the means which will best promote this twofold salvation and guide the salvatory actions of the elect. On the content of gnosticism there was, however, no agreement, but fragmentation into tiny groups.

Given the inchoate state of Jewish and Christian dogma at that time, it was not easy to define their orthodox beliefs. The gnostics were certain of their orthodoxy, and comforted themselves with a whole body of scriptural texts. For their part, the orthodox attributed to the Christian mystery a true 'gnosis', opposing it to the false gnosticism. Gradually tests were established and the general lines of antignostic argument were laid down.

The gnostics in general were accused of having gone beyond the bounds of human knowledge, in claiming to have pierced the central mystery of the cosmos and of history. By this act, they devalued the majesty of God. In place of a faith in the divine utterance, given in revelation, they substituted a belief greater than revelation, for it laid claim to reason as its base, yet greater than reason, for it presented itself as a transforming illumination: gnosticism was thus in the end belief in itself, a half-conscious substitution of its own understanding for the offerings of revelation.

In particular, orthodoxy accused the gnostics of rejecting the concrete facts of history in favour of an ulterior history which had, in fact, the effect of making concrete history disappear. For instance, the Passion was nothing but the symbol of a deeper reality, the manifest text of a latent text which alone was real and interesting. The cross of Calvary was, *fundamentally*, nothing but a symbol of the cosmic X made up by the intersection of the celestial ecliptic and equator. The whole of Scripture was in this way made the object of a symbolising reading, in which the manifest text (or the literal meaning) dissolved before the latent (symbolic) text, which proved the gnostic system. The material unfolding, within time, of the unrepeatable events of the history of salvation was replaced by a procession of symbols floating in eternity. It was as if real history had been crushed beneath the weight of allegorical over-interpretation.

But it was morality that furnished for Jewish and Christian orthodoxy the surest test. According to the gnostics, evil was exterior to man. Involved in a cosmic struggle whose dimensions totally exceeded him, the question of his responsibility did not arise. He had no free will: he was moved by good and evil powers who fought over him, ignoring him. Sin, if sin there was, was not a question of subjective choice: it meant being placed objectively on the side of the powers of evil. There resulted, for the soul, an objective punishment, even if the soul did not know what the wrong was. As Secundinus wrote to Augustine, 'it is not punished for having sinned, but for not having felt the anguish of having sinned'.[24] There was no sin except through ignorance.

Gnosticism puts an end to this. It awakens the soul, making it aware of its real situation, and enabling it to choose sides. A gnostic morality thus developed. It swung, according to the system, between two opposed but equivalent attitudes: either a strict asceticism, aimed at the extinction of the flesh (that is, the evil within), or else, much more rarely, a licence which left the flesh to its own devices, which is perhaps just as efficient a way of destroying it. But the crucial factor lies not in the conduct, but in the principle behind this morality. This in fact is opposed at one and the same time to the Greeks, the Jews and the Christians, in so far as the criterion of good and evil ceases to be universal and becomes internal to the doctrine. There is no *just* in itself. The *just* is relative to the execution of the cosmic plan as it is revealed by gnosticism, and thus is relative to gnosticism itself. Conformity to the good is thus not marked by the fulfilment of justice, but by the fitting of conduct to the realization of the cosmogonic scheme. This is where gnosticism separates from religion. That is why Plotinus accused it of ignoring virtue.[25]

The most perfect example of the gnostic system is, according to Puech, Manicheism. It inherited earlier gnosticisms, hardened them and shaped them into a coherent system. It was a universal Church whose following spread in a few years from Gibraltar to China. One cannot help thinking of the way in which Marxism—Leninism similarly syncretized, systematized and codified a rich variety of contemporary intellectual movements, in order to spread rapidly throughout the world.

The revelation of Mani is supposed to represent the clear, immediate, total expression of Truth, of full Gnosis, of absolute Knowledge.[26] The system follows the general lines of those which it inherited. It presents itself as a simultaneous understanding of the nature and destinies of God, of the Universe, and of the self. It claims to be a universal science of all things divine and earthly, by which everything, physical phenomena quite as much as historical events, can be explained. Cosmology and theology are welded into a unified knowledge, rational in appearance, and encyclopaedic in vocation.[27]

The general scheme is familiar. There are *two principles* (good and evil, light and shadow, spirit and matter) whose 'mixture' is experienced as being bad. There are *three times*, a past, in which there was a perfect separation of the two substances, a present in which the mixture occurred and persists, and a future, or end, in which the primordial separation will be re-established. To be a Manichean is to confess to these two principles and three times. There follows from it a dualist geography: the two principles are conceived as being two regions separated from each other by a more or less ideal frontier which is constantly in motion, two regions which are symmetrically antithetical: the region of good to the north, the region of evil to the south. Two camps, two regions, three times: we will find similar classifications in Leninism.

But the point at which Manicheism seems to demand, in its own right, that one should draw a parallel with contemporary reality, is over the question of the *new man.*

The universe is called towards salvation, and so is man, who is a part of the universe, and by this token is himself a compound of good and evil. Thus each man contains an originally and substantially pure 'self', which has to be disengaged from its present impure state, in which evil tendencies swamp or threaten to swamp the real self of man. In the language of Saint Paul, there is a struggle going on within us between the *old man* and the *new man.* But for the gnostics, the old man is the soul in its passive and ignorant condition, while the new man is the soul active and saved, the soul to which has been given the understanding to awaken it and to enable it to detach itself from the compound of good and evil.

Man is thus interdependent with the universe. He is moved by it, without responsibility, but, through his capacity for knowledge, he can become the central object of the process of salvation. On him there plays the whole destiny of the world, and even the destiny of God, saviour and source of light, but partially a prisoner of matter, and therefore also needing to be saved. Thus man becomes, as Puech puts it, 'one of the cogs in the salvation-producing machine which is the universe'.[28]

This salvation begins by regaining a knowledge of self. The pure self having thus been perceived, the next task is to bring about its liberation. This entails carrying out, within oneself, the separation of the two improperly mixed substances, and of thus achieving within oneself that 'apocatastasis' which will be definitive for the cosmos and for the whole of saved humanity at the end of time.

Gnosticism, the gnostics assert, has always been present in the world. Throughout history, the Revelationists have followed each other, each bearing in his turn the liberating truth. Others, on the other hand, servants of the lower powers, taught error. A double chain runs through the intellectual history of mankind, dividing it, the twofold chain of the tradition of the light and the tradition of the shadow. Even among those who confess the right gnosticism there will not always be the same degree of understanding. Just as it comprises both morality and dictum, so, among the adepts, there are two distinct and unequal systems of rules of conduct. The ordinary Auditors will content themselves with a lax and minimal régime.[29] But the Perfect, who are in possession of a fuller understanding, are expected to adhere strictly to the conduct which such an understanding entails. The Manichean church is not egalitarian. The followers divide into two classes, according to whether they are capable or worthy of receiving the grace and power which gnosticism is thought to confer in its entirety or only in part. On the one side, the initiates, on the other, the candidates who are as yet imperfectly prepared.

The Perfect could appropriately be termed a professional in universal salvation. The means he employs — rites, fasts, abstinences, mortifications — hardly matter: what matters is that they make up less a morality than a technique, a practical application of the way in which gnosticism embodies and fulfils itself in Salvation.

Thus the concept of sin takes on quite another meaning for the Perfect from that which it holds for the Christian or the Jew. The

Manicheans practised confession. But, said their enemies, what did they have to confess, since they did not admit free will? The self is not responsible for the transgression, but that shadowy amalgam which has its being separate from and exterior to the self. Sin was like a microbic invasion, a sickness, or even an evil spell. But, because it has been enlightened, the soul is not entirely passive. Above it, and immanent to it, there is the 'nous', understanding, conscience. Awakened by gnosticism, this conscience can, thanks to its presence, repel temptation and break down the renewed assault of Evil. As Fortunatus wrote: 'It is because we sin despite ourselves and because we are subject to a substance opposed to and inimical to us, that we attain a knowledge of things. Warned by that knowledge and restored to a memory of the past, the soul recognises its true origins, and the evil in which it finds itself...'[30] Once it has been enlightened, the soul can distinguish between good and evil, and, coming to itself, knowing itself, it automatically separates itself from whatever does not belong to it. It knows at once its duties and its powers. It is assured of victory 'in principle'.[31]

It is clear, then, what purpose confession serves: it serves, through doctrine, to renew self-knowledge. To sin means fundamentally to commit an act of forgetfulness, of unlearning. It means being unwilling or unable to combat evil by appealing to the intellectual resources laid at the disposal of the enlightened soul. To confess is to re-learn, to revise. In such a confession, the concern is less with sin than with error, less with repentance than with self-criticism.

The gnostic temptation draws strength from two powerful and constant tendencies in human nature. It promises knowledge to man who, as Aristotle declared, 'has a natural desire for knowledge'. It is a total explanation, resolving all problems, capable of integrating everything. Transcendant realities, physical phenomena and historical events all find within it a place and an explanation. Even the phases of the moon can be explained as a struggle between the two principles. All the same, as Solignac has put it so well:

This is not a rational science, in the sense of each assertion having been rigorously demonstrated, but rather a superior knowledge, an *intelligence* in which each element is comprehended through its cohesion to the whole. Such a doctrine can only be absolute in dogmatism: it does away with all criticism, since one either 'understands' it, and there is an end to any difficulties, or else one does not 'understand' it, and the whole thing collapses.[32]

This demonstrates how far removed the knowledge of gnosticism is from metaphysical knowledge. In the Greek tradition, knowledge proceeds by degrees, from the sensible to the intelligible, and beyond that towards an inaccessible centre, where dwelt the God of Plato and Aristotle, and the One of Plotinus. The transcendance of the God of Israel preserves this, so to speak, centripetal structure of knowledge. Thus there were several possible kinds of knowledge which could converge on the Centre without ever reaching it. Gnostic knowledge, on the other hand, proceeds from a central vision. From an absolute knowledge, placed at the centre, as if the gnostic placed himself within the Divine understanding, there logically derived particular kinds of knowledge. Nothing can escape from the central vision on the basis of which, in a centrifugal order, a unified and encyclopaedic knowledge is then built up. In one way, the Manicheans were not wrong in feeling that a profound change of state had occurred within them: this total and universal coherence of things did truly make of them new men. Instead of simply being infused with the Light, they were possessed by gnosticism, which assured them that it was the Light. Perhaps, in denying free will, they revealed the psychological truth of this possession. They called their new prison liberation.

But perhaps they did in fact owe to it some sort of deliverance: from internal evil, from guilt, from ambivalence, and from the whole body of suffering and inhibition which goes with it. All of that was placed outside, projected onto an external evil principle, which alone was responsible and which could be mastered rationally.

Several of the characteristics of gnosticism are irresistibly reminiscent of Soviet ideology. I have intentionally isolated and pinned down whatever could foster the comparison: a locked encyclopaedic system of cosmology and soteriology; the over-interpretation of history; a morality deriving from the doctrine, and taking its criteria from it; self-criticism as a way of renewing understanding of the interpretative system; the relativization of man to his contribution to salvation; the division laid down between the militants and the masses; the militant, custodian of knowledge, ascetic, professional, freed from the ordinary tasks of life; and the geo-historical dualism between regions which are ontologically damned and regions which are saved.

But the comparison cannot be taken very far. It is only persuasive so long as one limits it to the general structures of thought, to the state of mind, and perhaps to the psychological disposition. If one starts to look at the doctrines in detail, any similarity vanishes.

The ancient gnosticisms were like inordinately complicated metaphysical novels, with all sorts of celestial characters playing their part. Cosmogonic history unfolded like a serial — and the plot varied considerably from one gnostic school to another. Because it borrowed syncretically from the intellectual movement of the age, it embraced composite and varied materials. As it had an encyclopaedic vocation, it complicated itself indefinitely in order to explain whatever occurred that called for explanation.[33] But this explanation maintained a mythological form, even though it was a mythology which sought to be intellectualist and even rationalist. It is that mythological form which creates an unbridgeable rift between modern ideology and the gnosticisms of old.

In fact, gnosticism remains intimately related to the religion from which it is sprung. Orthodoxy accused gnosticism of replacing faith with a conviction which found its support within itself (and not in an invisible God). But at the same time, gnosticism preyed on religion parasitically, borrowing its vocabulary, its theological constructs and its exegetical methods. More than this, it improved on religion, claiming to be its purest and highest form. Gnosticism was difficult to refute as it appeared to be the same as religion, although in fact it was insidiously different. It was only rarely openly culpable of heresy, and yet it represented a much wider division, a much more fundamental form of subversion. Because of this, orthodoxy feared gnosticism more than heresy, and was pitiless towards it, throughout history, and to the utmost of its ability. It was disturbed by the solidity of the gnostic conviction, which was much harder to eradicate than faith, since constancy even under the most extreme torture was still a way of preferring the self to that which was not the self. Orthodoxy must have felt that the gnostic perversion provided a constant threat to it from within, without even necessarily being aware of it, since gnosticism was not so much a question of dogma as an attitude towards it.

But by the same token, this intimacy with religion could just as easily contaminate gnosticism and surreptitiously lead it back into the fold. For if religion was not always free of gnosticism, gnosticism, for its part, was not always entirely untainted by religion. When gnosticism organized itself into a church, with books and rites and hierarchies, when it became a mass belief, then the perverse aspects became blurred over and it became a parallel religion, another religion. This is what happened to late Manicheism, to the Mandeans,[34] and others. Despite their claim to rationality, the cosmological doctrines were not more susceptible to proofs than dogmas. They had to appeal, whether they would or no, to religious impulses of belief. It was by religious exercises that the Perfect contributed to the salvation of the world, and not by any reorganization of the profane world. Gnosticism did not develop into a political party. It did not seek immediate power.

From Antiquity to the Renaissance, Judaism, Christianity and Islam had to contend with several onslaughts from gnosticism. Sometimes, as with the Bogomils and the Cathars, orthodoxy employed extreme methods. Sometimes, as with the Kabbala, it had to compromise, win it over, and make room for it. The most serious danger lay in not recognizing it, for then orthodoxy ran the risk of becoming insidiously perverted. But once localized, gnosticism did not constitute a mortal danger: it became another religion.

This then is the radical difference between gnosticism and ideology: that the latter can make use of a non-religious argument, and can rely on an absolutely new and scientific kind of certainty.

Modern ideology does not fit into the gnostic tradition. Nor is it clear that there is in fact any such tradition: rather there is a recurrence of similar intellectual attitudes, in different historical circumstances, without any recollection or awareness of continuity.

Ideology could be the form taken by the gnostic attitude in the presence of modern science: such an expression would suggest those chemical reactions which occur 'in the presence' of a substance which, acting as a catalyst, does not take part in the reaction directly, but which must none the less be present for the reaction to take place.

Soviet ideology is not the same as science. It rejects with horror the positivism which denies philosophy ('the denial of philosophy is a subterfuge employed by bourgeois philosophies to introduce idealism into science').[35] It is, it claims, a 'scientific philosophy'. But the meaning of the word science, in the sense in which Soviet ideology uses it ('the discovery and explanation of the objective laws governing phenomena'),[36] is that which emerged under that title in the seventeenth century. This provides a *terminus a quo*: the ideology could not develop until modern science had been created and had achieved some unequivocal and spectacular successes. It is science in this sense which is at the basis of its certainty, and which is invested with a considerable psychological commitment. It is just like a belief, but a belief which no longer has anything religious about it, to such an extent that it even denies being a belief.

The history of ideology could be compared to the different successive *stages* in the lives of certain parasites, which go through a cycle which is apparently capricious, but which is in fact necessary to their complete development. They must, for instance, go through a river mollusc, and then pass into a sheep, and finally lodge, not without deleterious effects, in the body of a human, whence they will return to the river. At every change of location, there is an equivalent change of form.

Before reaching Russia, where it has attained its pure, developed form, ideology has also gone through a historical cycle. It is, moreover, able to recall it, and accords special status to those past episodes which foreshadowed it. We will briefly examine two earlier cycles — the French and German — but only the Russian episode will be looked at in detail. It is impossible to understand ideology as it is manifested in Russia, even in broad outline, without considering those incomplete forms which made up its prehistory and which were necessary to its lodging in its ultimate host. This detour through France and Germany may also serve to absolve Russia of a responsibility with which it too often tends to be charged.[37] For it imported the elements of the ideology from the West. But, despite what certain neo-Slavophile tendencies would maintain today, the West is not solely responsible for it either. Everyone has had a hand in the affair, and now everyone is busy laying the blame at everyone else's door.

2
The French Cycle

At the beginning of the seventeenth century two phenomena coalesced in France, which, although, as we will see, by themselves insufficient, were both necessary to the emergence of ideology — the birth of modern science and the crisis of religion.

Science could be certain, and have its certainties recognized by every reasonable man, but it acted within a field which was no longer that of traditional learning. From Plato on, being learned had meant proceeding from the appearance to the reality, from the phenomenon to the thing itself. But the new science claimed that such a search for ideas and essences was vain. That was not the direction in which certainty was to be found, but rather in the world of appearances and of change, in phenomena whose relationship to each other could be established in laws. There was no other science than the establishing of these laws. Nature did not need metaphysics. Science became autonomous, a closed circle, no longer opening out onto the Divine, but quite the reverse, through a fundamental alteration in attitudes, turning towards the material universe and validating a type of knowledge which the tradition deriving from Plato had always regarded as inferior.

Thus it was that as early as 1630, on the narrow but sufficient basis of the first great scientifically proven law, the law of inertia, what can already be called modern positivism came into being.[1] It was at first accepted by only one section of the scientific community of Western Europe: Hobbes, Mersenne, Gassendi and Huygens. It was not scientism. On the contrary, it was a rigorous limitation of science to the object from which it derived certainty, the phenomenon. The real existed, but it was not the scientist's concern, his realm was merely the organization of appearances into a system of laws. Positive science could offer no guarantee of a correlation between the phenomenon and the real object. But never mind. The phenomenon was enough to interest the scientist. It might be that he was a Christian, but he was not a Christian because he was a scientist.

The new science removed a heavy burden which had lain on the life of the mind since the late Middle Ages. Magic and occultism were discredited. The power of words, of images, of precious stones, of the stars and of sorcerers was lastingly overthrown. Sorcery was no longer to be feared, and sorcerers were no longer burned. The cause of a phenomenon was no longer an occult power, a metaphysical *en-soi*, but another phenomenon linked to it in a constant relationship. *Causa sive ratio*, as Descartes put it. This entailed the destruction of the absolute determinism of magical thinking, which had enveloped man and things within a single system. Scientific determinism was partial: it freed man from total primitive determinism. As a result, gnosticism, which is a pseudo-determinist construct, was buried in the ruins, at least as far as Western Europe was concerned.

With the intellectual field thus cleared, the classical age provided a century of great scope to philosophy and religion. But, although roused and challenged by science, both only put forward somewhat weak solutions.

'Heaven and earth declare the glory of God.' But heaven and earth had been de-realized by the new objectivity of quantitative science. The unreality of the world, which was not the world in itself, but the world as conceived, and which, as such, was not sufficient, that was what inspired Descartes.[2] This world was intelligible because it was the work of the Spirit who was also the creator of our reason. Descartes transposed the traditional order: metaphysics was not the end of science, but its beginning. The phenomenon and the thing in itself were distinct, but God, rediscovered through contemplation of the power of thought, guaranteed the conformity of the one to the other. 'The atheist', Descartes declared, 'can be sure of nothing.'

Armed with this metaphysical certainty, Descartes undertook to reconstruct, according to the ideal, if not according to the Aristotelian method, a physics based on first principles. But this put science in a dangerous position. Gassendi and Hobbes, empiricists, like most of the scientists of the time, were disturbed by the *a priori* generalizations of Cartesian physics. The eighteenth century condemned them.

But Descartes never sought total knowledge. He would not allow that human thinking could coincide with the divine logos. Physics and metaphysics remained separate.

Pascal too accepted duality. According to him, human nature was inexplicable without the Christian irrational. This is the hypothesis which saves the phenomenon, in the type, man, as it appears to us. This kind of scientific reasoning thus provided a kind of fragile bridge, appealing to theology, but not encroaching on it.[3]

Descartes and Pascal render each their due, God and Caesar, physics and metaphysics. A balance was maintained, but by no means an obvious one, since they both have also been interpreted in quite other ways, and been pushed, one towards scientism or metaphysical phenomenalism, the other towards fideism. But it was a balance which could only be maintained through a religious equilibrium. And that was none too secure either.

The controversies of the Reformation, the scandal of the wars of religion, had led thinking men, from as early as the sixteenth century on, to move away from and to lose confidence in the very idea of a dogmatic truth guaranteed by the authority of the Church. A good many, following Montaigne's example, sought to rid themselves of possibly insoluble, controversial questions. They were Christians, but in retreat. They desired certain knowledge, but on a human scale. The new science to some extent answered this need, but at the same time it encouraged this turning inwards and the triumph of subjectivity. The world presented by science had no other existence than in *res extensa*. Uninhabited, said Pascal, this world terrifies. Man, or more precisely, the subject, became the sole frame of reference in which the world could be sited, understood and exploited. There was in some ways a concordance between the setting up of man as the subject of science, and the religious subjectivism which, in Catholic countries, relied dogmatically on an excessive Augustinism.

In the French context, the Catholic Reformation, even at its height, had already lost the exuberant baroque sense of well-being. Bare churches, long faces, and an austere bearing were what was recommended to a still merry court and a still vital nobility. The Jansenist tone predominated. The Jesuit intuition about the freedom of man did not manage to develop into a system of metaphysics. The Society worked above all in the sphere of morality. But there it encountered the opposition of the rigorist. Intellectual religious life got bogged down in the area of moral theology where it endlessly quibbled and debated. The major result was to reawaken the spirit of controversy and of religious persecution. But by mid-century one can observe throughout Europe, whether Catholic or Protestant, a similar langour and similar nervous contractions. Faith was entering the age of doubt. Whence the recourse to tests of orthodoxy — and the host of new persecutions which they entailed: the Dordrecht predestinarian test for the Calvinists, the French Catholic test of the five principles, the test of ubiquitism for German Lutherans, and even the test of the sign of the cross performed with three fingers for the Russian Orthodox.[4] This search for proofs of faith is perhaps a sign of, or an over-compensation for, a secret disaffection from faith.

II

From the point of view that concerns us here, how should one describe that European crisis of conscience which, according to an eminent writer, took place in the last decade of the seventeenth century?[5]

It consisted first of all in the ebbing of the religious flood tide. The century of saints ended in a spiritual stampede.

The Jansenist moral scruple slowly gave up the theological ground of efficacious or sufficient grace for the domain of spiritual and temporal authority. Jansenism became a political party. It set itself up against the ecclesiastical hierarchy as the advocate of religious democracy, and claimed freedom, first of conscience and then of thought. It defended the freedom of the citizen against the absolute power of the monarchy. The scandal of the Revocation of the Edict of Nantes completed the discrediting of ecclesiastical authority, which was compromised by a policy felt to be anti-Christian or, quite simply, inhuman. The Revocation marks an important turning-point. After that, religious opposition doubled as political opposition. The entire politico-religious world was involved in this movement. What is called *the left* in France probably had its birth in 1685. Throughout Europe, religious thinking re-joined the old current of Erasmian liberalism turned insipid, which had been continuing underground, quite as much among Catholics as among Protestants (under the various names of Socinianism, Anti-Trinitarianism and Unitarianism), and which formed the basis for the deism of the Enlightenment. Locke and Newton were Unitarians.

It was a tendency which benefited from the distaste left by the aftermath of the reforms. It also benefited from having kept a sense of Christian freedom which was easily translated into lay terms as tolerance. God was thrown out of the world, a castrated father, a rational postulate of intelligibility, the First Clockmaker who left his children in charge of the machine.

This left the door open, later, to a return to the gnostic way of thought, which was fostered by the subsequent position of religious life. In the absence of a convincing metaphysic, the link between God and man and the maintenance of the Christian tradition had been ensured by the mystic life. Suppressed in Spain at the end of the sixteenth century, orthodox mysticism existed in France, though closely monitored. The condemnation of Fénelon dealt it a mortal blow. Everything in piety which was not reason, conscience, thought, became questionable. As the years went by, mysticism became suspect and even, in a dangerous way, slightly ridiculous.[6] It was reduced to the status of a psychological condition. But this authoritarian destruction of orthodox mysticism left the way open to the heterodox mysticisms and Illuminism with which it had been confused. Fénelon's descendants peopled the English enthusiast revivals, and German pietism; the Savoyard priest could claim to have fathered them all. The Scot Ramsay, whom Fenelon had delightedly converted to Catholicism, ended his career as the founder of French freemasonry. It was then that the esotericism of the eighteenth century was born. The majority of thinking Europeans no longer felt themselves bound to orthodoxy by the ties either of dogma or of mysticism.

Meanwhile, science took a major step forward, perhaps the most important one in the whole of history or science. The discovery of the law of inertia had been sufficient to initiate the mechanist revolution, and here was Newton uniting terrestrial and celestial mechanics at a stroke, and doing it, what is more, by a triumph of the phenomenalist method.

Hitherto I have not been able to discover the cause of those properties... from phenomena, and I feign no hypotheses [*hypotheses non fingo*]; for whatever is not deduced from the phenomena is to be called an hypotheses; and hypotheses, whether metaphysical or physical, whether of occult qualities or mechanical, have no place in experimental philosophy…To us it is enough that gravity does really exist, and acts according to the laws which we have explained.[7]

The triumph of science and the decline of religion put an end to the equilibrium which Cartesianism had managed to maintain between metaphysics and science, theology and physics. Malebranche saw in mechanics the very form of the divine behaviour, realizing through extension and movement, and through an extreme simplicity of means, all the richness of creation. He was led to consider truths of faith as being homogeneous with those of scientific reasoning. 'The facts of religion or revealed dogma are my experiments in theological matters.'[8] Through the infinitesimal calculus, Leibnitz entered into the divine understanding, and became able to evaluate the world as it is. The principle of reason was *sufficient* to explain that things are thus and not otherwise, and the combinative made it possible to comprehend the intimate order linking them together. Leibnitz demonstrated that the universe was sufficient unto itself and that, once created, it was autarchic. But if the universe could conserve itself indefinitely, the Divine Architect became redundant as a hypothesis.[9] Throughout the eighteenth century, Spinoza's metaphysical monism was interpreted as atheist materialism. This was to be, later, the interpretation put on it by the Russian revolutionaries, and, officially, by Soviet ideology.[10]

In brief, metaphysicians at the end of the century believed they had resolved the problem of the unity of truth, which their predecessors in the age of classicism had declared themselves unable to re-establish. The physical debate, or rather, at that time, the mechanical debate, included and absorbed the metaphysical debate, without always giving due notice of the change in emphasis. Given this sort of relationship, the intellectual climate in some measure resembled that of German Romantic philosophy a century later. All the same, this unified knowledge, though descended from the philosophical level, failed to engender a fully developed ideology at any lower level. What we can see forming, during the eighteenth century, are the raw materials for an ideology, and also the types of human ideologists. There was something lacking which stopped ideology from setting, in the way that one speaks of concrete *setting*.

In England, there was nothing left to wait for. The Enlightenment was Whig, certainly, but since the time of the Glorious Revolution, the social consensus had not been called into question. The English revolutions took place in pre-ideological times. At the most extreme, on the left of the new Model Army, one had seen a Christian millenarianism, of the kind which had been rife in the Middle Ages, and which was, as a consequence, deeply religious and without the slightest scientific pretensions. The notions of right, of freedoms (in the plural), and of ownership were the motive forces behind a movement aimed at re-establishing a state of justice which had been momentarily disturbed, rather than re-founding the social body on an *a priori* model in such a way that right, freedoms and ownership all became redundant.

The English Enlightenment confirmed these principles. Their critical aim was directed more particularly at Christian dogma. But not at the established Church, which was itself less concerned with controlling the dominant rationalist deism, than with keeping a check on the vestiges of the religious millenium, that is, the Puritan propensity to restrict, and even to suppress, in the name of the Light Within. The English Enlightenment was sceptical and empiricist. Locke dedicated a fair proportion of his *Essay concerning human understanding* to an examination of language, or, more particularly, an examination of those large words which the enthusiasts tended to resort to. What do you mean? How do you know? This sort of 'tutorial' question serves to place the English Enlightenment fairly accurately. To sum up, there was in England corruption neither of the religious nor of the scientific. The fervour remained, but concentrated in the fringes of society, in the lower classes, where it fostered piety and dissenting revivalism; in the middle and upper classes, a little theology went a long way, and even then it was stabilized by conformity. Science continued on its way, following the strictly phenomenalist method, made even more radical by Hume, without ever being tempted to stray outside its own domain. Politics did not conscript science to serve its own ends. English political society was proud of itself, respected throughout Europe, and, at this period of intense social and economic innovation, biased towards the traditional. The English expected politics to provide tranquillity and security, and that, at the very least, it should foster the happiness of a nation which had never enjoyed itself so much. They did not expect it to provide *salvation*.

III

In France, things were different. To begin with, the Enlightenment made dogmatic pronouncements, and made them against a composite body, which presented itself as an indissoluble unity — the Church and the political order of the *ancien régime*.

From our point of view, there are three themes to be examined: the cosmological theme, that is, Nature; the epistemological theme, that is, Reason; and finally, the political theme.

In the seventeenth-century mind, man, supported by God, stood face to face with nature. But in the eighteenth-century mind, man was part of nature, and nature was the only reality.[11] It was possible, on that basis, to construct a science of man modelled on the natural sciences. Hobbes had already suggested a psychology which drew its inspiration from the physics of impact. From the excitement transmitted mechanically by the sense organ, is born the phantasm; from the phantasm, the imagination, the association of ideas, reflection, which is of the same nature as perception. The will is guided by the mechanisms of pain and pleasure. Thought is an instinct, slightly more complicated than in animals. The new physics severed the Thomist link between God and nature, the new anthropology severed the Augustinian link between the human heart and God. If conscience is nothing but a reflex system, morality is free to shape itself on the basis of a positive science of behaviour. Instead of the old metaphysics of the soul, one finds a natural history of the soul, and a psychology constructed on the basis of external sensation. That was the great achievement of Locke, whom d'Alembert wrongly but significantly praised for having 'reduced metaphysics to what it should really be, the experimental physics of the soul',[12] or at least for having initiated this reduction. It continued with Hume, whose *Treatise on human nature* has as a subtitle, 'Essay in the introduction of experimental methods into moral subjects'. The Cartesian subject was dissolved. It was no longer a bundle of sensations, a flickering mass of inexplicable presences. Intellectual operations were transformed into sensations, as Condillac explained. The very order of our ideas was nothing but a reflection of the biological order of which we are a part, and which makes itself felt through need, interest, utility and our desire for self-preservation. '"Ideas are reborn by the action of the needs which produced them." Ideas form, so to speak, vortices in the mind, and these vortices multiply as our emotional drives grow and are differentiated. Each vortex can be considered as the centre of a certain motion which is continuous from the centre to the periphery.'[13] The same physicist's language — vortex, revolution, attraction — is applied, without any alterations or caveats, to both nature and man alike.

Thus man was caught in a dialogue with nature — of which he was an exceptional representative — with nothing to support himself. Unable to find an explanation of his life within himself, he had to turn towards the external world, and since, in understanding that, he learnt to understand himself, towards the All of which he was a part.

Did this nature have a meaning? The question led to a parting of the ways.

'Nature — vague term', one can read in the *Encyclopédie*, in the short article dealing with the topic.[14] Nature, in fact, in the atmosphere of the scientific revolution, had lost its soul and its unity. It had been broken down into a series of independent phenomena, linked only by mechanical laws, whose study was dependent on separate intellectual ventures. The All, *To Pan* beloved of the Ancients, was nothing but 'the action of bodies upon one another according to the laws of movement'. The scientist's happiness lay in always having things to find out, and from this point of view, nature was an inexhaustible reservoir, full of discoveries, but not to be drained in the vain search for an all-embracing system. That was what was held against Descartes's physics, for his metaphysics were no longer understood. D'Alembert's words well express the moderate opinion of the Enlightenment: 'The physicist's principal virtue would be to have a systematic approach [for you cannot construct a theory without it] , but never to build a system.'

Physics is thus uniquely limited to observations and calculations; medicine, to the history of the human body, its ailments and their cures; natural history, to detailed descriptions of the animal, and vegetable, and mineral kingdoms... in short, all the sciences, enclosed as far as possible within the realm of facts, and of the consequences which can be deduced therefrom, put no trust in mere opinion, unless forced to it.[15]

Voltaire even went so far as to deny the concept of nature any sort of consistency: 'I have been given a title', he makes it say, 'which does not suit me: I am called nature, but I am entirely art.'[16] This is Kantism before Kant.

Because of this, reason is confined within the limits of phenomenalism, and consciously gives up any attempt at total knowledge. Montesquieu, Voltaire, d'Alembert — in short, all the greatest spirits of the age — declared that wisdom, in the intellectual domain, consisted in being content with partial truths, and in putting up with the mental circumcision imposed by science. They were, or at least they would have liked to be, anti-dogmatic. It was this which provided the empirical, and sometimes even sceptical tone of the eighteenth century in France, carried to less cynical extremes than in England, and borne with a stoicism such as Voltaire's Candide inherited from the classics.

But there were others who did go further. They had in common the fact that they had all neither applied nor understood the spirit of Newtonian science. What they took from science was not its method, but its end result, removing it from its context and unconsciously lending it the status of a dogmatic proposition, coupled with a kind of scientific certainty.

For instance, in Meslier and La Mettrie, Descartes's *res extensa* was treated as being identical with matter, and, having become the only reality (a metaphysical proposition which was quietly slipped in), matter gave back to nature the consistency and unity of which it had been robbed by true science. 'There is throughout the universe but one substance in a variety of forms', concluded La Mettrie.[17]

By a natural development, man became, for this erring Cartesian, a machine, according to the model projected onto nature and which was now being reapplied. 'The human body is a self-winding machine'; 'a clock, but an immense one'. And thought? 'I find thought so little incompatible with organized matter that it seems to be a property of it in the same way as electricity, motive power, impenetrability, extension, etc.'[18] This, incidentally, already foreshadows the position taken by Soviet ideology on these matters.

It follows that the whole of the real — which is all matter — can be justified in terms of scientific knowledge. We do not know everything, but everything can be known. La Mettrie wrote:

I am just as resigned to being ignorant of how inert and simple matter becomes active and composed of organisms as I am to not being able to look at the sun without a red glass...One must grant me only that organized matter is endowed with a principle of motion which alone differentiates it from matter which is not organized, and that all animal life depends on the diversity of this organization...[19]

All that remains to be done is to discover the Newtonian law capable of explaining the behaviour of the entire universe, and then that will be that.

So a whole sequence of secondary philosophers exhausted themselves searching for the equivalent of universal gravity in the psychological, the physiological and, soon, in the political arenas — philosophers ranging from Morelly to Listonai, from Robinet to Lassalle, from Azaïs to the Comte de Saint-Simon.[20] Thus attraction awoke, beneath a pseudo-scientific veneer, all the old magical and mystical speculation on the Universal One, which in turn reawakened, in another intellectual domain, illuminist mysticism and Masonic esotericism.

But this extension of the Newtonian paradigm beyond the area of physics to which it belonged, was to have serious consequences. In fact, at the very moment at which nature had been deprived of meaning by the workings of science, it was expected to regulate behaviour and life in society. Although there had been a fairly sober application of the concept of nature to cosmology, an excessive use of it was made in political and moral questions, and this was precisely because the pure sciences had set up some safeguards in the physical domain, while the political and moral arena lay wide open to extrapolation.

It is surely de Sade's greatest achievement to have filled the empty area of the picture with the possible normative meaning of nature. For him, it was evil. Thus *Juliette* declares:

Only through acts of wickedness is the natural balance maintained, only thereby does Nature recover ground lost to the incursions of virtue. Thus we are obeying her when we deliver ourselves unto evil; our resistance thereto is the sole crime she can never pardon in us. Oh, my friends! let us take these principles well to heart; in their exercise lie all the sources of human happiness.[21]

De Sade was alone in this, for almost the whole century felt very differently. 'Oh! Nature,' wrote Diderot, 'all that is good is enclosed within your breast. You are the fertile source of all truths.'[22] Groethuysen has given a useful description of this sense of being at one with a whole full of significance and beauty, a description which characterizes the century:

It is a life in nature, and with nature, seen as being normal and good in itself, to the exclusion of any other. Man determined by nature, living the life dictated to him by nature, in a natural way, fulfilling through his humanity something essential, significant, and fine...Everything works together, through nature, in a whole filled with significance, tending towards a definite end of which every part is a witness...

But if, on the other hand, one considers the life of man, one can see none of the lawfulness which governs the starry sky, or the plants, in the nature of man. This life does not conform with nature. It is against nature. There is thus, on the one hand, in the world, something invested with meaning, whose existence we can remark and recognize all around us and within us, and there is, on the other hand, something absurd and meaningless, and that something is our own, human life.[2][3]

There was profound agreement on this point between Voltaire, Diderot, Rousseau, Buffon — all the major figures. What needed to be done was to rediscover man as nature first created him, man in whom an internal lawfulness would be in accord with the aims of nature. Up to this point, the history of the development of social life, and, in particular, priests and superstitions, had come between man and his natural development. He had rights, and these rights of man were the expression of a teleological organization with which all men had been endowed by nature.

Nature was rational, human life was not. Between man, issued from the hand of nature, and nature itself, there stood an obstacle — society. The social order was defective, and it could be shown to be so by exercising the same reason which had revealed nature to man's understanding. Constraining in the seventeenth century, euphoric in the eighteenth, nature became critical, and, by the same token, reason became practical.

What is needful is that everything in human life should be assembled together in groups subject to the law, that human life should no longer be an incomprehensible *imbroglio* in which the strongest may oppress the weak, in which the chance of birth may decide the fate of a man, in which what is allowed in one province may be forbidden in the next, and in which thousands of men are dependent on one man who is no different from them.[2][4]

To achieve this end, reason should take charge of education and legislation. Thus these thinkers proceeded from a contemplation of nature, to voluntarist action in the name of nature. For Holbach, there was one unitarian scheme of intelligibility which made up the 'natural system' and, on that basis, the 'social system' and 'universal morality'.

After Newtonising psychology — *self-interest* is the gravity of the mental system — Helvétius declared that all men with healthy bodies had equal faculties. All differences derived from education. In consequence, teaching could achieve anything. The state must choose the content and the methods, establish an invariable rule, and draw up a plan of education in conformity with the public good. Thus education became a political question: 'The art of forming men is in every country so closely linked to the form of government that it is not possible to effect any large-scale change in public education without effecting a similar change in the constitutions of the States concerned.'[25]

And thus we are led to political utopias. In 1759, Morelly, an obscure tutor from Vitry-le-François, and nowadays a highly honoured figure in the Soviet Union, posed the problem of 'establishing a situation in which it would be practically impossible for a man to be depraved or wicked', for he would be 'prepared and so to speak forewarned by means of an education according to our principles'.[26] These principles were set out in a brief code, entitled 'Model of legislation according to the intentions of nature'. It was a communism fairly similar to that of the utopian tradition, but none the less sufficiently realistic for the chapter on penal sanctions to envisage, with precision, the establishment of concentration camps.

Holbach, Helvetius, Morelly and later, abbé Mably, did not set the trend. They were on the fringe: the true centre of the century was elsewhere. There was, once again through English influence, and also through a native French tradition of which Montesquieu is the best example, a distrust of fanaticism, a dose of empiricism, a spirit of moderation which placed Voltaire, Diderot and even Rousseau and Condorcet in a different camp from these fire-eaters. They were the fathers of liberalism rather than Jacobinism. The difference does not lie mainly in the opinions, nor the ideas — since the undercurrent of thought fed on crumbs fallen from the table of the great. The difference is one of intellectual style. Granted Rousseau may be ambiguous. He was claimed by the terrorists of '93. But he did not belong to their world. He was quite clearly a philosopher in the eternal meaning of the word, and the majority of *philosophers* in the philosophical party equally deserved that title. As for Morelly, he was on a footing with Marat.

At the end of the century a group of proletaroid intellectuals did in fact emerge. The group's cohesion lay in a shared doctrine, or stock of ideas, notions and terms. Separated from society, they were no longer quite worldly, and, in fact, they were beginning to frighten the men of the world. They were no longer addressing themselves to these men of the world. They were militants, and their group became a political party. They took as their aim the recasting of the social body, according to the natural order. From an internal conviction that such an order existed and was realizable, sprang the revolutionary fervour. For them, from the start, the revolution was total, cosmic, bringing about a universal regeneration. And it is in the light of this concept of revolution that one must understand the series of events which took place from 1789 onwards. The French Revolution was not fated. At each moment, it seemed to be an accident, an unexpected skid. But the fact remains that all these chances and contingent happenings were capable of being subsumed, right from the start, into the totality of the Revolution. 'It is a revolt! − No, Sire, it is a Revolution.'

The Jacobins seized power in 1792, and held it for about eighteen months. The paroxysm took place in 1794. After that, the revolution gradually subsided. Lenin, like all of those in the Russian revolutionary movement, had the highest regard for the Jacobins. It would be worthwhile briefly to consider the French Revolution, from the point of view of the Russian Revolution. What are the parallels, and what the contrasts?

For the first time, there appears in embryo what will eventually become the party. The debating societies, the Jacobin clubs, the popular societies set up a network through which they communicated with each other, spreading information, orders, programmes.[27] They made up an apparatus of power which duplicated the legitimate institutions and set out to control them, to purify them, whilst waiting to replace them. The true political life was carried on inside them. Power was gained and lost between the closed walls of the clubs. Within the clubs a new political technique developed, a technique which had already been tried out in the lodges and societies of the *ancien régime*, and which applied equally well to the legitimate public institutions: the whittling away of majorities, the art of putting the right motion, the manipulation of minorities, infiltration, obstruction, purges, etc. All this, comes the reply, is the daily bread of democratic life. True, but the difference is that these normal manoeuvres were carried out under the cover of a coded language, and their aim was less political administration than the establishment of a utopia. In fact, politics was overloaded because of the way in which it was held to be the arena for universal salvation; the whole social body, including private life, came to be absorbed into the sphere of power in so far as the totality of human problems was seen as being reducible to the political problem.

Within the party, the individual underwent a process of desocialization. Lawyers, journalists, businessmen, clerks, priests — all such classifications ceased to apply. Their nation, their setting, was the club with its particular sociality. That was the site of their social identity.

Their chief means of mutual recognition was through language. One can perceive in the stuff of their language fragments of the doctrines of the century, demoted to the level of slogans, which might serve to provide material for rhetoric. Linguistic inflation, the flattening of personal language into language that is formulated and impersonal, its political codification — with key words like Fanaticism, Moderationism, Federalism, Despotism, etc. — the use of this language for political ends, all this seems to foreshadow the modern logocracy. It gave to the debates of the Convention a similar impression of unreality and terrifying unreason. This sort of language has a deadening and paralysing effect. People, Liberty, Fatherland, were all such highly charged words that they paralysed potential opposition, whilst any such opposition, honouring other realities beneath these names, feared being convicted of despotism or suspected of being in league with Pitt and Coburg. It was a legitimizing language, and it was that which sanctioned the Terror.

Lenin praised the terrorist boldness of the Revolution. Yet 20,000 executions do not amount to much. It is true that there were over 300,000 suspects in prison on the 9th Thermidor, all of whom were doubtless destined for extermination;[28] if that had happened, the slaughter would have achieved Bolshevik proportions. The killings were abstract, involving not people, but 'monsters', 'thieves', 'enemies of the people'. 'It is less a question', said Couthon, 'of punishing them, than of wiping them out.' 'There must be no deportations, the conspirators must all be destroyed', said Collot d'Herbois.[29] It was a Manichean attitude, separating the camp of the good from the camp of the wicked which, according to the laws of Prairial, was likely to comprise almost the entire French population.

Finally, there appeared that human type — the ideologist. Sincere, disinterested, loving neither women, wine nor money, without friends, an indefatigable member of societies, good at manoeuvering, believing all that he said, seeing traps and plots everywhere, the high priest of language, above all else impersonal and abstract, Robespierre irresistibly prefigures Lenin.

But Robespierre fell, and from the Bolshevik point of view, it is easy to see why.

The party lacked cohesion. It was split. It never became hierarchized, monolithic. It was never able to impose on its members any discipline or appropriate training. This was because the doctrine, of which the party was the guardian, was not coherent either. Virtue, People, Liberty, were all moral principles. The revolutionary doctrine was not unified. It was drawn from several themes which were ill-coordinated and often quite simply contradictory. Equality, for instance, was conceived of through ownership which protected the individual and gave him independence from the party itself. Utopia presented itself as utopian. It was not the product of a natural development. It remained an ideal to be accomplished. It was thus dependent on virtue rather than on science. The concept of nature was not sufficient to furnish any kind of historiosophy. Nature, after all was said and done, remained an object for contemplation. It held sway, at the time of Thermidor, in the charming faces of Mme Tallien, Joséphine and Mme Recamier. France was saved by the boldness of some and the chastity of others; it was saved by its women, at once the signs and the agents of the breakdown of ideology.

There was a shift.

The Jacobins, to return once again to the categories of Leninism, were leftist. They believed in the people, in popular representation or control. They harboured a certain anti-intellectualism. They were unable to keep a secure hold on the state. Hoping for a pause — a *NEP* — they were incapable of controlling it: civil society, after Thermidor, escaped from them and crushed them. After they had lost power one can discern an attempt to reform all knowledge, to reshape grammar, psychology and the natural sciences into one single science, and to unify all systems of education into a pyramid crowned by the *deuxième classe* of the Institute, being an *analysis of human understanding*. This generalized Condillacism was the work of Volney, Cabanis and Destutt de Tracy, who called themselves *idéologues*. They looked around for a weapon and dabbled in the plots which brought Bonaparte to power. Unfortunately, he proved a Plutarchian hero, fed on Corneille. He suppressed the *deuxième classe* of the Institute, reintroduced Latin and Greek, and signed the Concordat.

That is why ideology, having undergone a 'French cycle' for a century, still had to pass through a German cycle before reaching its fully developed state in Russia.

3
The German Cycle

The ingredients whose presence, fusion and action were to give rise to ideology — that is to say, religion, philosophy, science, gnosticism and the revolutionary spirit — occurred in France at various times, but never together, and never in such a pure state as to enable their combination.

In Germany, on the other hand, they coexisted, and the fusion took place in the crucible of thought. Of thought alone, though, for Germany lacked the Revolution, the moment for the Master-Work, and so left it to Russia to reunite the French political model and the German intellectual model and so achieve ideology.

The German stage provides a more direct introduction to our subject than the French stage did, since the conditions which prevailed in Germany, in relation to France, were close to those which prevailed in Germany in relation to Russia, particularly in the way that it was from Germany, and in the German form, that the intellectual materials which went to construct ideology in its Russian form were imported into Russia.

I

The religious crisis and the arrival of modern science took place in Germany as in France, but under very different conditions.

In an ironic twist, Lutheran spirituality, which in fact subjected dogma to emotional and personal considerations, also actually encouraged speculation.[1] It was not a spirituality to promote a calm and tranquil contemplation of divine matters. Rather it established distress and anxiety as a permanent state. The Lutheran *simul peccator et justus*, as well as the tendency to make spiritual torment a criterion of faith, was without doubt an influence on Dostoevsky. The profoundly corrupt and sinning individual, with no ontological stability, was as it were obliterated in the event of justification, during which, in a 'forensic' way, Christ the Saviour, the 'Christ within us', took the individual's place. But how was one to confer a rational status on something that was presented as an existential, ineffable experience? Thus the subject who had been forensically saved by Christ was tempted to explicate this event by means of an equally forensic doctrine, capable of giving support to the individual and of satisfying his natural wish to understand. This resulted, in the end, in the duplication, on an objective and discursive level, of the ineffable justification, and, by the same token, in the relief of the agony of the 'mystic cross' by seeking explanation of it in a universal tragic fatalism, the principle of which was inherent in the world and in history, and which was rationally comprehensible. And that opened the door to a whole new gnostic invasion.

There was, in fact, in the Germany of the sixteenth and seventeenth centuries an extraordinary growth in Illuminism, and theosophism, mixed with alchemy, astrology, parapsychology and occultism. Paracelsus, Valentin Weigel, Boehme, 'The father of German philosophy', Alexandrian hermetism, the neo-Platonic tradition, were oddly combined with medieval Rhenish mysticism, the Jewish kabbala and the reformed faith.[2]

The new gnosticism flourished no less luxuriously than the old gnosticism of Alexandria. But the gnostic plot underwent a modification which was to prove favourable to subsequent secularizations. God has a future, and this future necessarily passes through the world. Humanity becomes an indispensible route for divine history, since it is only through humanity that the divine can attain self-awareness. This self-awareness occurs within man, and it is because of this that gnosis (or the cognition which is a 'recognition' of an already immanent presence) is salvation.

From this angle, man was less saved than saviour, and God less saviour than saved. This vision, going back to Eckhart and Boehme, was to lie at the heart of Romantic philosophy.

Now, this God tended to merge more or less with the magic cosmos of the Renaissance, with a nature in which everything was in correspondence, in interaction, animated with life and endowed with a soul. This led to a leaning towards the biologically and evolutionalistically oriented pantheism which was to obsess German thought from Boehme to Oetinger's 'organic *Weltanschauung*' and finally to Schelling. All that was needful, then, was a loss of the sense of transcendance, which was still so powerful in Luther, for man to become the sole repository of the Spirit, the subject and object of salvation, *salvandus* and *salvator* indissolubly linked.

This refocusing on the subject — that is, on the subjective — found its religious expression in pietism. Pietism was an international movement, to which, with certain qualifications, one can relate the quietism of Mme Guyon, Antoinette Bourrignon, the Swedish Swedenborg and the English Wesley, and, with no qualifications, some aspects of the thinking of Jean-Jacques Rousseau.[3] But in Germany, where it had its centre, it brought about a radical mutation of Lutheran spirituality. Instead of being faith alone (*sola fide*) which provided justification and a gauge for piety, it was, to the contrary, piety which was a gauge of faith, and which indirectly underwrote justification. The Pietists sought to compete in emotional outbursts, opening the floodgates of the 'hidden waters of the heart', as one of their leaders, Gottfried Arnold, put it. By 1730, the floods had washed everything away.

There are two aspects of this vast and complex movement which are of interest to us. First, the cultivation of feeling and emotion, which occasionally turned into anti-intellectualism. Only the simple, uncultivated man could bear witness to an authentic Christianity, particularly if he was submerged in a mass community ruled entirely along patriarchal lines, in which he would not be seeking to claim any abstract, individualistic rights, in a way which would run contrary to the 'communist' ideal of some imaginary primitive Church. The soul was constantly being invited to merge into the flux of emotions, to live at the level of the sub-rational, in effusions, exchanges, lamentations, autobiography, anguish, mutual confession and commitment to the moment. One had to *express* oneself, whatever the cost. Equally, pietism was linked to the cult of friendship, the cult of the woman devoted to an interior life. All the pathos of the Russian novel has its beginnings here.

Secondly, the idea of total reform — changing the world by changing man — or, as they put it, setting up the *Reich* — the kingdom of God, but it was understood, through the intermediary of a *regnum hominis* — revived a long-standing eschatological millenarianism. This, steeped in a white-hot religiosity, was the German equivalent of the French pre-Revolutionary Romanticism. It infused Central European freemasonry with speculative mysticism and incandescent fervour.

Thus, in Swabia, in a society of enlightened pastors and passionate scriptural exegetists, there developed some of the formative concepts of Romanticism, and in particular the theosophy of history.[4] Bengel and Oetinger lent an apocalyptic significance to the division of history into periods. They believed in the imminence of the last age. Development was not conceived as a linear progression, in the manner of Condorcet, but as a dialectical struggle between the forces of good and the forces of evil. This dialectic was not essentially mythical, but historical, with the contemporary age constituting the final period. They invented the *ruse of reason*, defined as the re-working, in a divine and decipherable plan, of the egotistical and individual actions of man. They mixed objective historical research with prophecy: history became prophecy in reverse, the search *a posteriori* for the traces left by God. They subordinated everything to a *central vision*, in the sense in which Jacob Boehme used the term, in which medicine, jurisprudence, history and theology all mingled together. The central vision was identified as universal science. All men shared in it as of right, and God achieved in it a total consciousness of self. God was entirely in man at the end of time.

But the vision of the end of time was joined with a vision of a new society which would be democratic and egalitarian (ultimate avatar of Luther's universal priesthood), and which would be communist and anomic, for obligation would have been rendered unnecessary by the abundance of goods, and right by the triumph of love.

Modern science was first conceived in Italy, France, Holland and England. Germany, stunned by the Thirty Years' War, only caught up with the West's innovations some two generations later. In the West, science, metaphysics and theology had, from the beginning, joined forces against the theosophical or gnostic ideas of the late Middle Ages. In Germany, on the other hand, the religious climate appealed not only to theology, but also to philosophical speculation and gnostic imaginings, without drawing any distinction between the genres, which were mutually interpenetrating. Then science, in its turn, was invited to join in.

Leibnitz, a disciple of the Paracelsian Van Helmont, a Rosicrucian and having links with both Bruno and Boehme, received Western mathematics, to which he made his own notable contribution, into a matrix of pre-scientific thought.[5] His world consisted in a network of monads in which each element was conditioned by the others according to fixed rules. It was not a mechanical sum of its parts, but an organic whole, in which each monad was, in turn, a dynamic whole, a unique and vital centre of energy. We are clearly close to esoteric intuition, but this time the *central vision*, instead of being glimpsed mystically, as in Boehme, is worked out rationally in a system which makes every element a part of the best of all possible worlds. This system was the divine calculus, perceptible to man by means of the infinitesimal calculus, which enabled him to formulate his own *raison d'être* within the infinite series of the world's development. Analytic reason can, in theory, unfold the universe, get inside the divine understanding, and enter into a comprehension of its total plan to such an extent that even evil can be justified in terms of a consideration of the greatest possible good and of harmony.[6] And here we are already at Hegel's 'rosicrucian' solution, with the *rose* of reason upon the *cross* of the present.

There are a wealth of other things to be found in Leibnitz. He has only been cited here to show that even where he is concerned, and above all after him, the great professorial rationalism was constantly being threatened by a subversive gnosticism which served only to strengthen even further the mass movement towards pietism.

This may serve to explain the relative isolation of Kant, who could be called — applying the later Russian opposition between Slavophiles and Westernists — the most Westernist of German philosophers. Considered in an Anglo-French context, Kant appears to crown the century's efforts to meditate on science and on the relationship between science and metaphysics. It is quite right that he should be placed in a line of descent from Descartes and Hume. But the Kantian question — what can I know? — takes on another meaning when seen in the German context of the rise of a confused exultation and what Kant disdainfully called *Schwärmerei*. In 1766, he published, in *Dreams of a spirit-seer*, a detailed refutation of the revelations of Swedenborg. If metaphysics were possible, he wrote, it would have to be as 'a science of the boundaries which circumscribe human reason'.[7] He concluded by quoting Voltaire: 'As our future destiny will presumably depend on how we administered our posts in this world, I conclude with what Voltaire's Candide said at the end of so many unnecessary controversies: Let us go into our garden and work!', which is the programme for the three *Critiques*.[8] He thought that he had triumphed once and for all, for he wrote at

the end of *Prolegomena*: 'Enthusiasm, which cannot appear in an
enlightened age unless it hides itself behind a school-metaphysics,
under the protection of which it can dare as it were to rage rationally,
is driven out by critical philosophy from this last covert.'[9] None the
less, in 1775, pure rationalism encountered the birth pangs of historicism and the first beginnings of national Romanticism. This
meant that the intellectual instrument refined by Kant was taken up
by other minds, for other ends, in a spirit foreign to that of Kant,
and was turned against its originator. The fusion of modern rationalism and composite gnosticism, the pantheistic reinterpretation of
Spinoza and Leibnitz, occurred in the generation of Herder, Fichte,
Schelling and Hegel.

There is no need to deal so fully with the content of Romantic
philosophy. Suffice it to say that Kant's subjectivized reason, transcending the limits that he himself had placed upon it (those of the
phenomenon), deployed itself over the entire field of knowledge,
with the aim of providing a unifying factor. It was a reason which
was concrete, historical and encyclopaedic. In the philosophy of
mechanics, the whole was left to its own devices. Such a philosophy
could not comprehend it, except by tearing itself apart, and that is
why French thought in the eighteenth century had not initiated any
coherent, global ideology. The new German reason, organicist, evo-
lutionist, historicist, possessed just that totalizing, synthesizing
ability which, throughout the eighteenth century, was sought for
in esotericism.

From Schelling, and above all from Hegel on, one can say that, turn
and turn about, depending on one's point of view, there occurred
a rationalization of gnostic esotericism, or that modern rationalism
was 'esotericized'. They proposed systems which appeared rational
and whose ambitions were total, which insinuated themselves more
or less plausibly into natural and social historical reality. And yet,
from all the evidence, Hegel was not (any more than Schelling was)
an ideologist. The system embraced in its wide net some extraordinarily profound concrete analyses, presented in a style of such
poetic ambiguity that Hegel presents for one's admiration the most
fascinating spectacle of metaphysical thinking since Plotinus.
But ideology is not far away, and it is important to mark out its
boundaries.

As in France, they ranged from religious to political thinking. The
same was to be true of Russia. In all three countries, as we will see,

these two strands appear in the trough following a long period of religious fervour. The generation of German Romantics opposed, with all the strength it could command, the irreligion of the Enlightenment. Generating a conceptualized theosophy or a systematized mysticism, it thought itself ardently Christian. Hegel proclaimed his orthodox Lutheranism.[10] Nor did this generation send out any call for political action. It was even in retreat from the liberalism of Kant. It idealized the Prussian state, or at any rate accepted philosophically the *status quo*. The real still coincided with the rational. It remained content with the freedom to speculate, within the carefully defined limits of the Republic of Letters.

The Hegelian synthesis presented itself as the final accomplishment of philosophy (and of religion, for Christianity could appear to be the popular exotericism of Hegel's philosophy); on his death, the synthesis broke down.

In the same way as the Enlightenment began with a historical critique of revelation, so with the neo-Hegelian movement. Strauss and Bruno Bauer occupy a position analogous to that of Richard Simon and the Spinoza of the *Tractatus* at the end of the seventeenth century. In this regard, Bruno Bauer invented the concept of alienation — the illusion that something exists over and above the consciousness of man, on which man is dependent, while in fact it is something that man himself has created.[11] But soon this idealism came under attack as a philosophical myth, a secularized shadow of the Christian myth. For Bauer, that was the height of alienation. But alienation being total, total freedom was at last possible. Thus Bauer divided the whole of history in two: before, the history of alienation; after, the restoration of man and of his freedom. The turning-point of history was that very century, to which the imminence of total liberation lent a catastrophic air: 'The catastrophe', he wrote in a letter to Marx, 'will be frightful, it will of necessity be a great one... it will be greater and more monstrous than that which accompanied Christianity's entrance on the world scene.'[12]

Little by little, it became apparent that the catastrophe would not only take place within the domain of metaphysics. The idealist myth had to be overcome in order to attain political and social reality. Action should bring about a correspondence between an imperfect reality and the eternal reality of philosophy. Under Hegel's guidance, absolute reason had arrived at a total comprehension of reality; by a 'dialectical' reversal, reality should be the accomplishment of reason.

Philosophy becomes praxis.

But why stop at a philosophy of action?The Biography of the Mind is, in fact, nothing but the history of material men, reflecting on their material alienation. Feuerbach thus quitted the confines of philosophy. Matter alone exists, and men invent religious myths in order to give themselves in imagination what they cannot have in reality. Science makes it possible to abolish alienation. At this point German idealism completed its somersault and returned to the positions of French pre-Revolutionary thinking: anti-religious, materialist and utilitarian. It was, moreover, in the process of integrating Hegelian historicism. Even better, though — by putting idealism on a materialistic footing, this integration came about of its own accord: the Romantic vision of history and historiosophy was spontaneously transmuted into politics. 'The age', wrote Ruge, 'has become political.'[13]

We are, at this point, in the years preceding 1848. German thinking had escaped from the controlled environment of the university, and spread into thick journals. In Paris, Heine, Ruge, Bauer and Marx — a whole young intelligentsia — were becoming politicized through contact with republican and socialist circles under the July Monarchy. The stage was set for the new Marxist synthesis.

Marx had gone through the same stages of development as his friends. He too had arrived at a concrete, historical and, now, politically oriented humanism. But he went beyond them on one point: the alienation of man was not to be found in religion, or the state, but in labour. Thus to Hegelian historiosophy, Marx added the economic dimension, a dimension which had not been entirely overlooked by the Master at Iena, but which Marx placed at the centre. Marx's extraordinary discovery, then, was to revise the ancient spirit of Jacobinism in the light of German philosophy, and thus to propose a new and definitive French Revolution, enlarged, through Hegel, to the dimensions of the cosmos, and anchored, through Ricardo, in the bedrock of economic and social reality. Beneficiary of his inheritance of French, English and German eighteenth-century thought, Marx was able to advance solutions to the more urgent problems of the nineteenth century.

Systematizing and all-embracing, Marxism avoids ideology only because of the Faustian temperament of its creator, the 'red doctor' bohème devoured by an insatiable curiosity. After 1848, Marx discovered English empiricism, and made his goal the founding of a proper science of socialism. He thus abandoned the Hegelian categories. It may be that he felt the scientific failure of *Capital*, and that that is why he abandoned it and returned, in his later years, to the neo-Jacobin utopianism of his youth. But when his friend Engels undertook, in the *Anti-Dühring*, to set out those results of his researches which Marx judged positive into one vast totalitarian system of history and nature, Marx imprudently gave the venture his blessing. And it was in that regressive and simplified form that Marxism spread throughout Germany.

A cycle of thought had been completed. Leibnitz put forward the idea of the best of all possible worlds. Hegel saw it working itself out in history. Marx placed that history in the field of human freedom. But it was in Russia that there was being forged the political instrument and the (so to speak) *party* of the best of all possible worlds.

II

But is it a cycle of thought? Are we not in the process of creating just the same sort of incriminating chain of guilt — *Hegel begat Marx, and Marx begat Lenin* — that we condemned earlier? What in fact happened, though, is that, at a certain point in this pseudo-cycle, there occurred a change of perspective which wrought the transformation from philosophy to ideology. Perhaps the seed of ideology lies in every philosopher, be he a Leibnitz or a Hegel. But it needs an ideologist to seek it out and make it grow.

Among the circle of 'leftist Hegelians', there were several busily at work, cutting down the great Hegelian mantle to make up their own ideological hand-me-downs. Let us consider for a moment what became of the theme of *dialectics*. Hegelian dialectics contained neither more nor less ideological potential than Greek sophism, Thomist scholasticism or Cartesian rationalism. But it is an historical fact that Soviet ideology places dialectics to the fore.

What was dangerous in Hegelian dialectics, when placed in other hands, was its capacity to justify any contradictory event, and its faculty for evading or integrating that contradiction. But at least it was dealing openly with a phenomenon of thought.

Marx, Engels and, at the prompting of the latter, 'the German worker Joseph Dietzgen' undertook to 'reverse' the Hegelian dialectic, by 'ridding it at a blow of all its idealistic trappings'. 'The dialectic of the idea itself becomes nothing but a conscious reflection of the dialectical movement of the real world and, thus, Hegel's dialectic was turned about, or, more exactly, it was turned over from standing on its head to being set afresh on a solid footing.'[14]

There is no question but that, from the point of view of Marx the journalist, Engels the industrialist, and the worker whom they generously include in their discovery, this reversal had the advantage in being a return to common sense. Compared to Hegelianism, Marxism, for anyone who is not a philosopher, is apparently much more 'realistic'.

Let us proceed to the identification of 'matter' with the 'real world'. The crucial point was to have established dialectics as a property of the real world.[15] From that moment on, reason was severed from the subject. The link was broken between dialectics and the intimate, philosophical, even religious and mystical experience in which it had revealed itself to Hegel. Engels wrote:

We considered the ideas produced by our brains afresh, looking at them from a materialistic point of view as reflections of objects rather than considering real objects as being reflections of such and such a degree of the absolute idea. In this way, dialectics was reduced to the science of general laws of movement, as much within the external world as concerning human thought — reduced to two series of laws which, although fundamentally identical, are different in their expression to the extent that the human brain may apply them consciously, whilst in nature, and up till now for the most part in human history, they have proceeded on their way unconsciously, in the guise of an external necessity buried within an infinite series of apparent chances.[16]

This is a fundamental text. It belongs to the 'symbol' of Soviet ideology. And rightly so, for it depicts the first step taken by ideology, that is, the first breaking down of the real, and the first substitution of a new real for the real which has been lost.

In fact, the return to the real, which Engels intended, was compromised from the start by the injection, into the real, of a pre-conceived scheme — self-developing dialectics. Under Hegel, this scheme had been produced by forcing reality into the categories of discussion, but it remained 'controllable' because reality was captured fully formed, at the point of development to which it had been led by the labour of generations of learned men. Moreover, if dialectics did not catch all reality in its net, whatever it did not catch did not, in principle, undergo any deformation. The 'reversal', on the other hand, depicts a reality already subdivided by a scheme of thought which is no longer recognized as such, but which hides itself within that reality, and in effect becomes a substitute for it. Hegel drew into the realm of thought the wonderful catch of the real, where it constituted the life of logic. But now, this life was supposed to exist within the object, even before it was known. Immediately, all the fish die, and all you are left with is the net. The real was reduced to 'general laws of movement'. It was as if it was possessed (or dispossessed) by the logical entities injected into it, and had been rendered subservient to the explicative power of these entities. In other words, it was real and held to be so only in so far as it was replaced by a lining or understudy — like the lining of a waistcoat, or the understudy used to substitute for an actor — and this lining was ideology, or, as Plekhanov was soon to put it, *dialectical materialism*. The only thing worth considering in the world was the world beyond it, which revealed and explained, radically, the new gnosticism.

Thus the return to the real, to 'common sense', the realistic intention, set up an infinitely more 'idealistic' circle than did Hegelian idealism, and led to a kind of logical autism. In Hegel, thought and the reality outside thought each occupied their own positions. The *reversal* made it impossible for thought to see anything in the reality beyond it apart from what it had itself placed there: structures, laws of movement, all were ideas. Hegel was intoxicated with the pleasure of thinking, of contemplating. It was a pleasure denied to Engels, since he had set himself to reflect a scheme which he himself had unwittingly imposed on things. The only satisfaction remaining to him, where exploring the real was concerned, was that of finding in it, indefinitely, the scheme which he himself had placed there. He was like an explorer trembling with emotion at rediscovering his own tracks. Philosophizing, for Hegel, was a question of gradually identifying oneself with the Absolute, which remained the subject. For Engels, it was a question of identifying oneself with matter, but without such an identification being able to promote the least pantheistic exaltation, since matter had been mutilated by the scheme, emptied of its splendid reality, and hidden away behind a screen of thought. It is wrong to chide Marxism for its materialism: it would be far more appropriate to blame it for having spirited matter away. At least the old 'vulgar materialism' left matter in peace.

Marx's demonic curiosity was still essentially philosophical or scientific. Engels himself began with an excellent inquiry into the conditions of English workers. A practical man, and indefatigably dedicated to self-education, he developed a real talent as a historian. His misfortune was to take Marx's schemes more seriously than Marx did himself. He thought it was possible to reorganize the whole of knowledge on the basis of a few pages from the *Manifesto*, the *Theses on Feuerbach*, and a few fragments of theory picked up here and there. Marx did all that he could to encourage him. His last works, the *Anti-Dühring* and the posthumous pieces published under the title *Dialectics of nature*, are afloat on the full tide of ideology. They did not, like the medieval *Mirrors of science*, draw respectfully on a treasure-house of sacred knowledge. Unlike Descartes's *Traité du monde*, they do not reflect the excessive ambition of a young science. They present themselves as a sort of 'revision' of scientific results lifted entire from Haeckel, from Helmholz's popular lectures, and from textbooks on biology and chemistry. These results are expected to cohere to 'the general laws of movement', which means the 'law of the passage from quantity to quality', the 'law of the interpenetration of contraries', and the 'law of negation by negation'. Whatever will not cohere, such as Carnot, or Newton, that 'ass of an inductionist',[17] is eliminated. What does cohere is poured into the mould. Reality is not discovered; it is translated. Dialectical realism wears itself out in words.

Engels is oblivious of the fact that when he employs the word *law*, when he speaks of the 'laws of dialectics', he is using the word in a sense quite other than that of a physical law, which is subject, within set limits, to empirical verification. The dialectical law of the 'passage from quantity to quality' is illustrated by water boiling at $100°C$, and, in the same sense of the word *law*, by the transformation of money into capital above a certain threshold. In the first case, the law can be verified and is concerned with predicting, not what will change, but when it will change: a simple physical law which has no need to be dialectical. In the second case, there is no verification possible: if the quantity of money does not transform itself into capital, one can always say that the threshold has not been reached. In order to illustrate the 'law of negation by negation', he aligns the negation of capitalism by socialism, the negation of butterfly eggs by the birth of the butterflies, which in turn will lay more eggs (*idem* for the barley seed and plant), the squaring of negative numbers, the negation of a by $-a$, and the negation of $-a$ by itself, to give a^2. By *negation*, he means replacement, succession, birth, growth, change, and so on.[18] Just imagine the hoots of laughter Flaubert would have given if he had read the *Anti-Dühring*! It is straight out of *Bouvard et Pécuchet*.*

In the transition from Hegel to Engels by way of Marx, there is a change of style, or rather a change in the way of thinking. The most obvious characteristic is extreme simplification. A similar simplification occurred from Engels to Plekhanov and Kautsky, and then on to Lenin and the codifications of *diamat*. It was not due to a decline in ability or learning. That decline was the consequence and not the cause of this new way of thinking. When a Soviet scholar or French intellectual got embroiled in *diamat*, what he wrote descended to the level of those who earned their bread and butter from that sort of writing. The cognitive activity consists in verifying more and more closely the applicability of the scheme to the whole body of facts provided by reality. which offers no resistance since it renders up to the ideologist only what he himself has put there. This illusory transparency of the world makes infinitely easier a labour which the ideologist believes to be intellectual. Production becomes easy and very soon excessive. There grew up, from the end of the nineteenth century, a doctrinal canon which was continually increasing and having new books added to it. When these Marxist 'classics' made a fairly substantial shelf-full, they took the place of a culture. The study of the 'corpus', the search for its internal cohesion − or rather, delight in that internal cohesion which, in ideology, is not the end, but given as a premise and a starting-point − determined the intellectual horizon of adherents to the doctrine. It is a short chain which links the militant at the base to the theoretician capable of arguing more fluently but not of knowing more. They all share in the pride of possessing that *eureka*, that principle of universal intelligibility. They all enjoy the divine privilege of thinking without effort, and of being able to behold, at a glance and panoptically, the whole world. The price to be paid is the depersonalization of thought. Or, to adapt a phrase of Spinoza's, they do not think, but it thinks them. The scheme is in possession of their thinking.

It is in possession of it all the more securely because the new knowledge is certain. It is certain, because it has received the absolute guarantee of science, as two centuries of continuous progress

* *Translator's Note*: cf. Chapter 1, note p. 7.

had ensured it. The type of certainty that science possesses in its own area (and which had not been shaken by the epistemological debates at the end of the century), is generalized to apply to all the areas of knowledge which are linked by the central vision and unified by the universal principle of intelligibility. But there too, there is a price to be paid. Ideological certainty, modelling itself on what it holds to be scientific certainty, forbids itself any religious act. Gnosticism is unable to develop in mythology, or art, or philosophy, as other religious gnosticisms had done. In order to be certain, ideology must limit itself to the disenchanted world of technical and scientific textbooks. Not even that, in fact, because the scholar's intellectual reward, of understanding the phenomenon and elucidating its law, is beyond the reach of ideology, which contents itself with tucking it away into some ready-made pigeon-hole in the system.

But this is the crucial paradox: at the instant when it dissociates itself from the world, dialectics leads to action on that world. A knowledge which is no longer truly measured by the real − since the real is neither beheld nor contemplated as in fact it is − spontaneously chooses as its aim to act on the real and alter it. 'The question of knowing whether human thinking can attain an objective reality, is not', wrote Marx, 'a theoretical, but a practical question. It is in praxis that man must demonstrate the truth, that is to say, the reality, the strength, the precision of his thinking... All that philosophers have done so far, is to offer different interpretations of the world; what matters is to change it.'[19] And these men of letters, which is what the left-wing Hegelians were, abandoned their books and emerged from their studies to fling themselves into politics.

It is through political action that ideology differentiates itself from the simple, eternal spirit of system. Through political action, ideology acquired its incisive, victorious edge, and the sort of life which left superseded systems behind. And it was in political action that ideology invested its hope of salvation.

Heinrich Heine wrote in 1834: 'The German revolution will not take place any more pleasantly and gently for having been preceded by the Kantian critique, Fichtian transcendental idealism, or even natural philosophy. Through these theories revolutionary forces have built up which only await the day on which they may break loose, filling the world with horror and awe.'[20] Heine imagines Kantians who will 'churn up, with the axe and the sickle, the soil of our European life, so as to eradicate the very last root of the past',

Fichtean armies, 'fanatics of the will', and most frightening of all, philosophers of nature 'who would intervene actively through action in the German revolution and would identify themselves with the work of destruction'.

And yet, in Germany, this was not the destiny of Marxism. Instead of serving as a core for a revolutionary alternative reality, it accompanied the integration of the workers into German society. It was the working-class movement, the leaders of the unions and the cooperatives which halted the ideological drift of Marxism. Their actions did not aim to re-model reality according to the Marxist scheme, but were simply directed at 'the coming of democracy' to Germany, as Bernstein put it. Working-class achievements were not seen as signs of an eschatalogical struggle whose outcome was being debated elsewhere. They were appreciated as being achievements for the workers. The working class was represented by workers themselves, and Marxism was subject to practical verification. There came a moment when Bernstein was able to summon social democracy to reject a doctrine which, because it held on after its scientific (empirical) refutation, preserved a solely ideological function. Living in the real world, social democracy considered Marxism as a barrier and an obstacle. As a theory, it was overtaken and left behind in the normal course of events. As for dialectics, Bernstein said: 'Hegelian dialectics are all the more dangerous for never being totally false: they are as like truth as a will-o'-the-wisp is like light. They cannot contradict themselves, since, according to their own tenets, every thing carries within it its own contrary.'[21]

All the same, Heine had not been mistaken. For another current of thought, which had also arisen from this same movement of German Romanticism, was also undergoing a process of ideologization, at just the same time. Nationalist and racist thought, which had been diffuse in the nineteenth century, received 'scientific' justifications in the twentieth century, was enriched by a political programme, and provided itself with an intelligentsia and some mass support. Hitler carried it to power.

We will not follow this other branch growing from the ideological tree, though, but rather that which came to bear fruit in Russia. But before taking one step further East, there are a few conclusions to be drawn from our swift flight over France and Germany.

In France, the mutual reaction between the religious crisis and modern rational and scientific thought did not result in one *central vision*, but rather in the explosion of a variety of truths. In Germany, on the other hand, Hegel's version of Romantic philosophy proposed a more truly global synthesis than any which had been put forward since Aristotle. It unified Heaven, Earth and human History in Hegel's own distinctive style, the style of a major philosophy. But, at the same time, allowing for modifications and a change of nature, it could serve as a framework for ideology. It communicated to ideology its universal ambition and made it possible for the illusion to grow up that the universe had been completely deciphered, at precisely the point when contact with it was about to be severed.

We can now have a more sure idea of just what the nature of this ideology is. By arranging the elements which fell successively into place, we are able to describe it, so to speak, genetically, and thus we can also have a better idea of what ideology is not.

It is a systematic doctrine which promises salvation by means of conversion; which presents itself as being at one with a cosmic order, whose development is open to our understanding; which declares that it is based on scientific certainty; and which imposes a system of practical politics aimed at totally transforming society to fit with the immanent model which had lain concealed and which the true doctrine had laid bare.

Ideology has nothing in common with religion, except the hope of salvation (and even that it will not admit to), nor with philosophy or science, except rationalism (the application of which it perverts): thus it is not enough to establish a legitimate descent. It also possesses the mental structure of gnosticism, but modified by a kind of certainty which it would like to have for its own, and which it has borrowed from (or rather ascribed to) science. Its field of action is political.

Ideology is a phenomenon belonging to a certain date, whose genesis required an exceptional combination of circumstances. Neither the liberalism, nor the nationalism, nor the traditionalism, nor most of the socialisms of the nineteenth century could be assimilated into ideologies in the restricted sense in which we employ the term. It conforms, in fact, to only two historical developments, and to them alone: Hitlerism and Leninism. Even then, one could claim that Hitlerism, which comprises irrational, semi-religious elements, and which is unstable and ephemeral, presents an incomplete picture of ideology when compared to Leninism.

Finally, if the genesis of ideology (inasmuch as it is a product of a simultaneous corruption of both religion and science — of religion by science, and of science by religion) belongs to the history of ideas, it should also be restored to the context of political history. It appears in an inchoate form in France, and then in a more developed manner in Germany, within the precisely dated framework of the crisis of the *ancien régime*. It depended on the support of a well-defined social group — the intelligentsia. In France and Germany, ideology was broken down or contained by the success of the civil society. Only this last circumstance did not apply in Russia: in every other respect, the same conditions existed.

4
The Religious Education of Russia

Intellectual developments in France and Germany were of course not confined to those we have already discussed: Russia itself is more simple. The culture is more recent, there are fewer writers, and even fewer thinkers. Even more significant, though, is the way in which all these thinkers seem to have been drawn to share in a history whose weight continues to bear down on the entire world. They were drawn irresistibly into that history's magnetic field, and because of that, generations of researchers have pored over the traces, which should long since have vanished, of the progenitors of Bolshevism. It is a history which has been over-studied, and whatever did not at first appear to contribute to the great event of the Russian Revolution had somehow to be found a place and be made, sometimes by force, to contribute.

I

As in France and in Germany, the question of ideology only arises within the domain of a religious crisis. Unfortunately, little is known of the nature of religious education in Russia. Much appears to be known, but what is familiar has been deformed by a variety of retrospective legends. In fact, Russian religious thinking in the nineteenth century invented and refined its own genealogy until it reached the point, at the beginning of the twentieth century, where it was possible to mistake this confection for its true history.[1] Huge efforts of learning were dedicated to the construction of this imaginary history, to such an extent that, if one wishes to reconstitute the true history of Russian religious thought, one finds oneself confronted with the most fragile conjecture.

Let us try, none the less, to paint in the main features of the design.

The Russian people were converted to Greek Orthodox Christianity around 1000 AD. What does conversion mean? The Romantic vision of a medieval 'Christianity' of the masses, living in an 'age of faith', has today been abandoned by the majority of historians. The splendours of the cathedrals, the theological inquiries, the saints, must all be seen as belonging to an élitist, minority culture. The majority lived, just as they do today, in practical paganism, that is to say, in a religious atmosphere which was apparently Christian, but which was fairly far removed from any truly Christian doctrine. If this is true of the West, how much more so of the Russian people, living on the extreme edge of the centres of civilization, still wild from their emigration into the forests and from the Mongols' destruction of urban life. Having received the liturgy and the Bible in its own language, according to Byzantine practice, the Russian people were isolated, since it was not necessary to study the two great cultural languages of sacred and profane literature, Latin and Greek.[2] The Orthodox style, in contrast to the Roman, put the emphasis more on the celebration of the liturgy than on ethical or intellectual education. The Russian people were liturgized rather than catechized. As far as one can tell, the old popular Russian religion (which still, incidentally, exerts a powerful influence, and on the value of which it is impossible to pass judgement) is marked, even more than its Roman counterpart, by ignorance and magic. There was, especially, an invasion of religious culture by Biblical apocrypha, either in the sense of a popular literature stuffed with marvels, or else an apocalyptic literature which demanded, even more than the canonical apocalypses, an ecclesiastical interpretation which was, for the most part, lacking.[3]

If, thanks to the efforts of Protestant Bible Societies, the Russian people had canonical writings at their disposal in the nineteenth century, these were for the most part Evangelical: in other words, a lop-sided canon which spontaneously fostered Marcionite attitudes.[4] Yet again, there are no unequivocal criteria by which one can decide whether the Russian people in the nineteenth century were more or less 'Christian' than the Catholic French or the Protestant German. But one can be quite sure that the notion of *Holy Russia* is no less a myth than the notion of *Christianity* propagated by Novalis, Chateaubriand or Péguy.

Popular religion eludes investigation and, seen from afar, appears endowed with great stability. The Christian culture of the élite was more intimately attuned to the rhythm of the nation. The vicissitudes of history exerted their influence from above. Three such influences, in particular, are notable: the state, Protestantism and Catholicism.

First, the action of the state. The great prince in Moscow had two sources of legitimacy. He inherited the position of the Tartar Khan. The Khan's legitimacy was that of conqueror. The Russian Church instituted prayers for him. His successor, the Tsar of Moscow, saw himself as the conqueror of his subjects. Accordingly, his subjects were his serfs.[5] But he also sought the legitimacy of the Orthodox Emperor, which meant that he had, like the Basileus, to watch over the faith of his subjects, subjects who, as it happened, had received baptism just as the schism between Rome and Constantinople began to widen.

In the catastrophes preceding and following the Fall of Constantinople, and notably as a consequence of the failure of the Florentine Union, anti-Roman feeling ran high through the Orthodox world, frequently being propagated by Greek bishops who had found themselves comfortable Sees in barbarian Russia, free of the Turkish yoke. Russia, after Rome's descent into heresy and Constantinople's fall under Islam, was held to be the repository of the true faith, the remnant of Israel, that is, the new Israel. This oppositional particularism was useful to the sovereign, in that it provided a religious justification for national unity and dynastic loyalty. The monk Philoteus of Pskov, who at the beginning of the sixteenth century invented the idea of Moscow as a third Rome (drawing on the apocryphal Apocalypse of the fourth book of Esdras), hailed Vasily III as 'the sole monarch of all Christians. All Christian authority falls to his monarchy.'[6] The schismatic spirit of hatred for Rome fostered the concentration of power, and favoured its absolutization in the Muscovite autocracy. 'By his nature', wrote Joseph, Abbot of Volokalamsk, 'the Tsar resembles man, but by his dignity he is the equal of the Lord God. He is not simply the servant of God, but His representative watching over the purity of the faith and the security of the Church. It is because of this that the Lord has placed a sword in his hand.'[7] The Tsar's power was a great deal less circumscribed than that of the Basileus. He had a priestly character, and everyone, even members of the Church, had to render him obedience. From that time on, the Tsars considered the Church above all as a means of reinforcing their autocracy and of furthering their own ends. It was nothing new. The same idea had occurred to the Tudor monarchs in England, and at the same time.

Two forces from the West exerted an influence on the Russian Church: Catholicism and Protestantism.

The Catholic influence came through Poland during the seventeenth century, but mainly in an indirect fashion. In fact, in order to confront the political and cultural threat posed by the Polono-Lithuanian West — particularly the threat of Uniatism — the Russian Church was forced to adopt some of the enemy's weapons, the better to defeat him. This aggressive imitation of external forms, so as to concede nothing of the internal essence, is characteristic of what is called the Westernization of Russia. The area of confrontation was White Russia and in particular the Ukraine, which fell fairly quickly under Moscow's rule. An Orthodox academy was founded in Kiev, modelled on the Polish academies, where students were taught to reason according to scholastic methods. For the Russians, this was a first apprenticeship in the rigours of Western rationality. The language of learning was Latin. The catechism was inspired by the Latin catechism of the Jesuit Peter Canisius. Seminaries, which were the first regular Russian schools, were also founded, again based on the Western model, in which the Greek tradition was taught in Latin, following Latin methods, from Latin textbooks. In 1685, the first institution of higher education was opened in Moscow, a so-called 'Greek' academy which in fact maintained the Latinizing tradition of the Academy in Kiev.

For the autocracy, the move towards Catholicism comprised a certain danger: that of importing into Russia, along with their culture and their learning, Roman ideas of the independence of the Church from the temporal sovereign in spiritual matters. And indeed, from the end of the seventeenth century, the patriarchs of Moscow evinced a certain slow movement towards autonomy, which they justified by reference to the authentic Byzantine tradition (and not as it had been falsified by Moscow), but which was in fact due to the Western example.[8] Then came the Petrine Revolution.

Peter the Great, with the help of his bishop, Theophanus Prokopovitch, imposed a quasi-Reformation on Russia from above.[9] Once the peasants had been enslaved, and the boyars and nobles massacred or forced into submission, the Church remained the only Russian institution which was at least partially outside state control. Peter the Great understood that enforced 'Protestantization' would be the most expedient way of dealing with this vestige. Luther had submitted the Church to the Princes. Not long before, Pufendorf, whom Peter the Great had read, had demonstrated that, from a juridical point of view, the state was supreme, and that it was important to the maintenance of peace and security that the clergy should be subject to it. According to the Lutheran spirit, the true Church is invisible, and freedom for a Christian is something within himself. What a gift for an autocrat!

The patriarchate of Moscow was suppressed and replaced by the Most-Holy-Synod, established along Lutheran lines — replaced, that is to say, by a body of ecclesiastical and civil functionaries, nominated by the sovereign to administer the affairs of the Church. The rules for the clergy (the Dukhnovny Regulation, 1720) followed the *Kircherordungen* of the Lutheran states, and, in particular, the statute of 1689 laid down by King Charles XI of Sweden. They contained clearly Protestantizing declarations, such as the principle according to which Scripture alone was necessary to salvation, making tradition superfluous. Although superstition was the apparent target the declarations were intended as an attack on the liturgy and the sacraments of the Church. In the seminaries, the Lutheran scholastic of Gerhardt, the philosophy of Wolff (as expounded in Baumeister's textbook) replaced Saint Thomas and Cajétan.[10] It was also Peter's intention, put into effect by his successors, to mobilize ecclesiastical education to form the kernel or seed-bed of state education. This was the practice in Lutheran Germany, transforming the parish system into a system of schools. But the spirit of the Petersburg empire could find a further use for the system as a system for spiritual policing.

It followed that, at the end of the eighteenth century, the Orthodox Church suffered a serious loss of authority at two clearly defined levels within society — the nobility and the people. One section of the popular masses deserted the patriarchal Church. The *Raskol* had taken away the best of the tradition. If *Holy Russia* remained anywhere, it was in the lost villages of the North-East, which were simply too remote to suffer the terrible persecutions of the central power. Elsewhere there sprang up a multitude of sects, which were not greatly different in their nature from the sects of Protestant Europe. Anti-hierarchical, illuminist, fundamentalist, they provided a channel of expression for popular religious fervour.

Where the Europeanized section of Russia was concerned — what is called 'society' (that is to say, the nobility and the civil service) — the official Church was not taken seriously. Members of the nobility moved in one of two directions. Some, following along the lines of Petrine laicization, turned towards a species of Voltairean Deism, but filtered through the figures of the German Enlightenment and embodied in what might be called a sort of governmental free-masonry. Others sought to satisy their religious needs outside the Church. As if to compensate for the imposition of the dry Lutheran synodal organization, in a form perverted by the aims of the autocracy, Russia was thus exposed, right from the top, to the other side of German Protestantism — its sentimentality and its pietistic mysticism. For the German pietism of Halle University (and doubtless one could trace these impulses even further back), to the religious projects of Leibnitz, Russia was a territory ripe for missionary activity.[11] A Ukrainian Jew, Simon Todorski, converted to the Orthodox faith, having studied at Halle, returned to Russia in 1735 with a Russian translation of Arndt's *Wahres Christentum*, a book which was honoured in the Russian Church right up to the beginning of the twentieth century. Spener, Arndt and Arnold all found a place in the libraries of Russian monasteries, as did Fénelon and the *Imitation*, which pietism held in particular esteem. But the most effective vehicle for the pietism and esotericism of the Enlightenment was freemasonry, which counted among its members anybody who was anybody in Russia, at the court and in the city. The Illuminist Bible, *Des erreurs et de la vérité* by Claude de Saint-Martin, published in 1775, found its way into Russia in 1777, and was soon translated into Russian. The Grand Duke Paul was initiated into the Swedenborgian mysteries of Swedish masonry in 1777, while his wife, the future Empress Maria Fedorovna, had known Saint-Martin in her Prussian principality of Montbéliard.[12] By 1780, freemasonry had converted the majority from rationalism to mysticism. The publisher Novikov undertook to distribute the literature of freemasonry in huge editions. An immigrant German professor, Johann Schwarz, founded the Russian branch of the Rosicrucian Order, whose aim was to spread scientific and philosophical knowledge and to aid moral improvement, in order 'to become without sin like Adam before the Fall'. At the end of the century, his successor, Lopukin, who was godfather to Kireevski, developed a discreetly heterodox mysticism in his brief work *Some characteristics of the interior Church*.[13] One may find in it the characteristic themes of the Fall of Adam, created androgynous, exiled from the regions of Light, of the final regeneration, of the interior Church, true Church of Jesus Christ, of which the established Church is but the exoteric projection, and, finally, of the soteriological deciphering of history. Significantly, this same Lopukin referred to the posture of prayer in use among the Hesychasts, and published, more or less indiscriminately, the works of Paracelsus and Macarius of Egypt, Molinos, Saint-Martin and Gregory Palamas.[14] In effect, one can see the development of an unconscious syncretization of modern European theosophy and Greek patristics, a syncretization which was to exert a marked influence on all Russian religious thinking from that time on.

In this same period, there was also a Catholic counter-movement. Catherine had granted asylum to the Society of Jesus, which the Pope had dismantled in Europe. Jesuit colleges in the Polish territory had been annexed. The Jesuits founded other colleges in St Petersburg and, especially under Paul I, achieved some notable conversions in court circles.[15] Too notable, in fact, and too close to the court not to provoke a reaction. This took the form of a veritable pietist revolution, which swept through Russia from 1815 to 1825. The great Wesleyan and Quaker revival, which had been unsettling England for generations, spread as far as Russia, adding to the shock waves from Germany. It was a reaction owing nothing to orthodoxy, which was far too weakened to participate. It was of purely Protestant inspiration.[16]

As usual in Russia, the instigator was the Emperor. Alexander, through reading the Bible in a French translation, studying the theosophists, and taking charge of the struggle against Napoleon, was converted in 1812. In a letter to his sister, he explained the difference between the interior and exterior Churches.[17] He recommended her to read Arnold, Swedenborg, Saint-Martin, the *Imitation*, Tauler, all the classics of pietism, and not a single author of the Russian Orthodox tradition. Gathered around him were the Moravian Brothers, the Quakers, Jung Stilling, Baader, Mme de Krüdener and other figures of international pietism. The St Petersburg Bible Society, founded by the English, undertook to translate the Bible into vernacular

Russian for the first time. A Bible without notes (*sola scriptura*), in the English fashion, it did not go beyond the New Testament. At the Holy Synod, Prince Galitsyn, with his friends Labzin (a disciple of Schwarz) and Kochelev (old friend of Lavater, Saint-Martin and Eckhartshauzen) had the intention of establishing, along lines which remained unclear, a new state religion. In fact, Alexander could rely on the support of most of the aristocracy, for only a minority of the high-ranking nobles tended towards Catholicism, which they associated with liberal dreams of a monarchy controlled by the aristocracy, on the English model. This was not a notion to find favour with the petty nobility, who preferred equality under a despot to a freedom tied to privilege. The lower ranks were unfamiliar with the teachings of a French-style education, and found the pietist ideas propounded by German craftsmen, merchants, officers and technicians much more accessible.

The pietist revolution did not last long, however. The state awoke to the utopian aspects of the enterprise. Pietism did not encounter any direct opposition (the Metropolitan of Moscow, Platon, was sympathetically inclined towards pietism), but it met rather with the uneasiness of an already established ecclesiastical administration, which the Bible Societies threatened to supplant and make redundant. But could one expect from them the same kind of exemplary docility that the clergy had displayed for centuries? After all, if the Catholic tendency had leanings towards liberalism, the Protestantizing tendency, which was not entirely free of Calvinist elements, might one day have led to democracy. Galitsyn was dismissed in 1824, and the Bible Societies were dissolved.

This outcome had been pursued for some time by a body of old-time archaeo-Petrines, a few retarded *apparatchiki*, like Magnitski and Chirinski-Chakmatov, who had been disturbed by the growing indiscipline spreading throughout the Church and who sought a return to rigorous state control, even if stripped of its mantle of Orthodoxy. Galitsyn's fall was their achievement.

What then was the religious situation in Russia when German Romantic philosophy first made its entrance? In some respects, it resembled the situation prevailing in Germany when that Romantic philosophy first arose. On the one hand, there was an established Church, subject to a prince, and with little spiritual resonance, unable to offer a framework for the intellectual life of the élite. On the other, there was a religious movement in some lay circles who found themselves on the periphery, that is to say, outside the domain of the established Church. Other characteristics were specifically Russian: the abnormal degree of submission to the prince; the poverty, even the indigence, of the intellectual life of the clergy; the limited impact of the pietist revival (which affected only the nobility, and only a very small fraction of the nobility at that); and finally, the marked lack of originality amongst the Russian intelligentsia, who had only just begun their intellectual education and who had to borrow all their ideas from Germany.

None the less — though one must beware of exaggerating with the benefit of hindsight — there was perhaps one strand of living tradition in the Russian Church. At the end of the eighteenth century, on the frontiers of the Empire, in Moldavia, a Ukrainian monk from Mount Athos called Païsi Velitchkovski translated the *Philocalia* from Greek to Slavonic. The *Philocalia* is a collection of ascetic and mystical writings and prayers by Eastern Fathers, first published in Venice in 1782. It must be emphasized that the Slavonic *Philocalia*, as a collection of spiritual and not of dogmatic or metaphysical writings, was parallel to French and German collections made at the same date. The *Philocalia*, which was used in Russian monasteries, did not go against the pietist sensibility which had spread elsewhere. But the presence, or the vestiges, of an apparently traditional Orthodox spiritual life within Russia sanctioned all the subsequent graftings and syntheses of Slavophile Romanticism. It sanctioned, too, all their falsifications.

In fact, the Slavophile theological edifice — and afterwards that of Dostoevsky — did not flourish in this traditional Orthodox soil, which had for some time been pretty well exhausted. It came from elsewhere. And it was afterwards, as a result of its nationalist logic, that Slavophilism took an interest in it, or rather sought to reconstitute it, in order to establish for itself false titles of paternity.

I will not proceed any further with the history of Russian religious education. It is worth noting, however, a characteristic which was to leave a lasting mark on Russian religiosity, and equally on Russian religious thinking, and that is a certain disdain for the correct canonical forms and an emphasis placed on sentiment and emotion.

It is clear that this does not come from Byzantium. The liturgy in a Greek, or Serbian, or even a Ukrainian church cannot match the overwhelming, profoundly moving effect of the same liturgy in a Russian church. This difference derives from Germany, and more precisely, from Peter the Great's quasi-Reformation. A church which has been rendered entirely subject to a prince, which has been enslaved, is not tempted to ascribe any value to those rights it no longer enjoys. It is opened up, by contrast and by way of compensation, to the religious pathetism being peddled by the pietist movements. This pathetism imbued the immutable liturgy of St Chrysostom, and, modifying the chant, gave it a new reality. Just as a new production transforms a classic play, so the Orthodox form was filled with a new spirit. But it would be a mistake — the very mistake, in fact, which was made by the Slavophiles and their descendants — to attribute the antiquity of tradition to this modern feeling.

II

German idealist philosophy was borne into Russia on the tide of the Illuminist revival. In the general reaction against the rationalism of the Enlightenment, against irreligion and revolutionary ideas, the ardently religious German philosophy fitted in with the views of the government and the Church. Schelling — or rather, a popularized Schellingism — was soon taught at the University and in the ecclesiastical academies. A small circle of aristocrats, sympathetic to matters of the mind, congregated in Moscow: Kochelev, Kireevski, Chevyriev, Pogodine and Odoevski. Around 1830, they came into contact with some teachers who were disseminating at the University what Alexandre Koyré has called 'a Schellingism from Prefaces'.[18] These professors had studied in Germany, under followers of the master such as Oken, Klein and Weber. Often they made use of the commentaries in the *Revue des deux mondes* and of Victor Cousin's summaries. Thus was formed the common framework for the attitudes of their generation.

This Schellingian vulgate proved so seductive because it offered an appearance of total knowledge. Up to this point, Russia had had no acquaintance with Western science. All that had occurred had been the importation of various technicians, artillerymen, engineers and architects. A vague unitarian cosmology was more attractive than the prospect of submitting to a long and arduous apprenticeship in the exact sciences. The 'science of nature' was concerned with the 'profound' (crucial word) unity of nature, or in other words, the central vision which would integrate magnetism, electricity (or rather, galvanism), chemistry, followed by physiology and psychology, and finally the Spirit. Having reached that point, the exact sciences, that which Vellanski, for example, termed the 'current tenets of the physical sciences', came to seem superficial and 'unilateral'. This vague organicism, these schemes of evolution in which 'Schelling's ideas mingled in the half-light with notions drawn from Paracelsus, Bruno and Herder',[19] seemed to a whole generation the last word in science. Provincialized gnosticism thus made it possible to short-circuit the long process of cultural acclimitization and to become Westernized without effort.

It did even more: as soon as this provincial gnosticism had been assimilated, it was possible to disdain the entire culture it criticized and apparently to replace, or rather, to synthesize and round off the entire European pre-idealist culture. Before 'Schelling' there had been, in the West, a partial, light and superficial knowledge — three adjectives which applied to the whole of French and English classical culture. This made it possible, as a consequence, to raise the burning, obsessive question of Russian identity and national culture in a rather more advantageous light.

The problem did not arise in the Anglo-French West, where there was a sufficient sense of self and of history to make it unnecessary to question the value of being French or English. It was more of a problem in Germany or Italy, where the absence of a unitarian national state was felt to be a frustration. But in both Germany and Italy, it was possible to summon up a few glorious works of cultural art as sufficient reassurance. In displacing the nationalist centre of gravity from a national state to a national culture, it was possible to discover the necessary element of superiority. In Russia, there existed a national state which had just demonstrated its power by defeating the three great military leaders of the eighteenth century, Charles XII, Frederick II and Napoleon. But it was a state which demanded justification in the eyes of one section of the Russian nobility. If Russia was without memory and without history, and if its culture was, as Chaadaev wrote, non-existent, then the state would be a hollow sham, and its existence indefensible. In short, there was a dire need to define the Russian mission.

This is not the place to go into all the systems built up by the Slavophiles. It will suffice to point out those elements in the teachings of Kireevski and Khomyakov which prepared the way for ideology.[20]

Their fundamental approach was as follows. The direction of their thinking, their problematic, their guiding notions came to them from the European West, including the most important idea of all, nationalism. Thus their problem was to import the concept of nationalism, whilst removing any labels indicating country of origin. They had to appropriate German nationalism to such an extent that it should appear to have sprung from the depths of the Russian nation, as a valid indigenous growth. It was a question of furnishing this cultural novelty with a long-established tradition. Since nationalism is a result of opposition, it had to be possible to oppose Russia to Germany and the European West, by using German and Western arguments, but turned against the West, and making not the slightest reference to their true origins. There is a total lack, among Slavophiles, of quotations and references.

They were thus led to construct a fictional reality, a fictional history, a fictional religion and fictional politics in every field.

I would like to offer a few examples taken from the work of Kireevski and Khomyakov.[21]

One of Kireevski's main themes was the criticism of the rational idea of man and, hence, of all rationalism. He opposed to it the truly integrated personality who was unified around a vital, hidden centre, which none the less remained accessible to whoever sought it. Rationalism destroyed internal integrity (*tselnost'*), hindered true concrete understanding, broke down the psyche into a certain number of separable faculties, which were jealous of their autonomy and quick to fight amongst themselves. The despotism of reason intensified the breakdown of the psyche, just as their social counterparts, Roman law and the external authority of the Roman Church, linked men together rather than unifying them, and intensified the breakdown of the social fabric. It was only the Orthodox believer who understood that the total truth demanded a total life, and who was constantly searching for this integrity. Thus, two types of civilization were contrasted, the one 'interior' (the Orthodox), the other 'exterior' (the Western); the one integral, the other 'logico-technical'. If the West appeared to have overtaken Russia in science and technology, then that was because it had chosen the easy road of purely external development, whereas Russia had chosen the hard path of interior development, which was, by implication, moral and profound, and superior on an absolute level.[22]

According to the commonly accepted account, Kireevski took

these ideas from the Greek Fathers.[23] In 1842, he went to the monastery at Optina to visit the Staretz Macarios, in association with whom he had translated several passages from Isaac the Syrian. There, he found the idea of interior concentration and of integrity. In Maxim the Confessor, too, reason is considered to be only an instrument of knowledge, whereas wisdom demands the whole psyche. Conclusion: Slavophilism was simply the modern continuation of a religious tradition which had been dominant in Russia since the time of Vladimir, and which had been temporarily obscured by the violent reforms carried out by Peter the Great and his successors. Kireevski's wife informed him that she had already read the same ideas in Isaac the Syrian. And indeed, on examining Isaac's writings, he found the core of Schelling's thought, but more deeply and rigorously expressed.

Unfortunately, it has been shown that Kireevski had already arrived at these ideas before he became interested in patrology. And if one opens Friedrich Schlegel's book, *The philosophy of life*, one can find in it, complete, the notion of the focal point of the soul, of the destruction by reason of interior unity, and the parallel drawn between the ensuing conflict and social chaos.[24] The Kireevskian idea of reason animated by faith can be found in Jacobi. Kireevski violently criticized the Roman idea of law and opposed to it tradition which grows organically, like a living being. So saying, he was repeating Savigny. His entirely negative appraisal of Rome, of Roman law, of the Roman Empire, in which he saw the source of rationalism, of capitalism, of the French Revolution and of Napoleonic despotism, came to him from Adam Muller.[25]

According to Kireevski, there were two types of social bond. The first, based on external coercion, is what characterized Latin and Germanic societies; the second, based on accord, harmony, a shared faith and love, was that which bound the Russian people together and to their Tsar.

In 1814, the German theosophist Franz von Baader had distinguished between two types of bond, which existed both in nature and in society: a bond based on love and mutual attraction between parties, and a bond based on coercion which links mechanically the separate atoms of society. Love renders force unnecessary.

This same Baader, who at the zenith of Illuminism had been given the task of drawing up a book of religious instruction for the Russian clergy, at the end of his life wrote to the Minister Uvarov that the

West was declining, either under the mechanical dictatorship of Catholicism, or in the anarchy and fragmentation of Protestantism; that the Reformation was only the continuation, in another form, of the Roman principle; that, with the degeneration of philosophy since Descartes, reason and faith had come into conflict; and finally that Divine Providence had preserved the Russian Church from the destructive influences of Europe. It remained the only power which might heal the two other Christian denominations and promote a spiritual renaissance in Europe: all of which provides the most complete resumé of Kireevski's philosophy of history.[26]

The same plagiarizing and the same falsifications can be found in Khomyakov. He had thought of publishing his principal theological treatise, *The church is one*, in Greek, with a Preface in which he would have stated that this was an unpublished manuscript reflecting Orthodox doctrine, and was thus invested with due authority.[27] It would have been a theological Ossian. According to Khomyakov, the essence of the ancient Church was the identity of unity and freedom, a synthesis expressed in the law of spiritual love. Rome kept the unity, but sacrificed the freedom. The Reformation sacrificed the unity for the sake of the freedom. Orthodoxy alone remained faithful to the primitive tradition, to what he called *sobornost'*, or the conciliatory spirit, that spirit which leads the Church Councils towards unanimity. Khomyakov did *not* say that this idea was directly copied from Moehler, a theologian at Tübingen who as early as 1825 had opposed the 'multiplicity without unity of the Protestants' to the Catholic principle of unity in multiplicity, which harmoniously reconciles individual diversity with the needs of the community: a definition of Khomyakov's *sobornost'* would be identical.[28]

The campaign against Roman Catholicism led Khomyakov to maintain the thesis that dogmatic truth rested with the consensus of the Church, and not with hierarchical authority, nor even in the Scriptures. But, if infallibility belonged to the Christian people as a body, that came to the same thing as rejecting the authority of the Church; ultimately, it promoted a sort of ecclesiological democracy, a development which was paralleled in the evolution of Lammenais's ideas, although they were not, of course, referred to, since a non-hierarchical *sobornost'* is supposed to exist only within the Russian Orthodox Church.

Dogma must not be based on rational deduction. Khomyakov

opposes to the Western theological rationalism (which according to him culminated in Hegel), the 'integral reason' which was prevalent in Russia, and which integrated will and faith. Will and faith do not proceed through demonstration. They are matters of immediate, internal knowledge. This meant literally readapting the criticisms which Jacobi levelled against Hegel (faith is *Unmittelbare Wissen*), and also those of Schelling in his later writings.[29]

It is true that Kireevski and Khomyakov did examine carefully the writings of the Fathers of the Eastern tradition. But they examined them after the system had been built, so as to find for it another frame of reference than its true one. It was a question of putting in footnotes which would refer the reader back to other authors than those whose influence they wished to deny and whose paternity they refused to acknowledge. This led them to read the patristic writings from the point of view of German idealism. The reverse was also possible. In fact, German idealism had deep roots going back to the same neo-Platonism which had fed one part of the patristic tradition. But whereas the Greek Fathers exerted themselves to balance or correct whatever gnosticizing influences neo-Platonism might carry, their attempts must be fruitless if their works are then re-read in the context of idealist esotericism. The impulse towards gnosticism once again came to the fore. Thus the whole of the Eastern tradition was distorted, to the extent that what was central to it was pushed to one side, and what was peripheral was accorded a central position. The Origenist and Evagrian themes of universal regeneration (apocastasis), the Dionysian themes of the negative way (apophasis), which had thus been reinstated in the place of honour, unbalanced the doctrine, because of the way in which German philosophy had made use of them for its own ends and had prepared the Russians to take them up in their turn. This opened the way for the ideologization of theology, in so far as it was asked not to explicate the act of faith, but to provide a *Weltanschauung*. In this way, belief was applied not to the object of faith, but to that conception of the world which was supposed to be guaranteed by revelation and tradition.

There was religious falsification, because the naturalization of a pietist (masonic, idealist) revival in Russia worked through the construction of a false tradition. The Slavophiles read Isaac the Syrian, Jean Climaque and the others, in the same way as (or even because) the German Romantics read Eckhart, Suso or Silesius —

in order to build up a national theology. But the German Romantics were legitimately descended from Eckhart, however distorted their reading of him was, while the Slavophiles were in fact descended from the German Romantics, and not from Isaac the Syrian and Jean Climaque as they claimed. But the historical falsification is even more evident in the setting up of the two fundamental points of Slavophile thought: Russia and Europe.

Kireevski was twenty-six years old when he left his birthplace of Dolbino for the first time and went to stay in Germany for six months.[30] Immediately he set himself up as a judge, not only of Europe, but also of its essence, which he called *Europism*. It was, according to him, in a parlous condition. Europism was made up of several layers: the 'destructive' spirit of the Enlightenment, science 'which does not recognise what is true, but only what can be observed experimentally', the fine arts, frozen in sterile imitation, and a utilitarian morality. On the other hand, the spirit of counter-revolution was falling into mysticism, reverie and systematic philosophical deduction. The only synthesis possible between these two tendencies was a forced and artificial unity. He did not yet condemn Schelling and Schiller: but it was only a matter of time before they too would be sent to join the rest of European culture in the *inferno*.[31]

In 1845, Kireevski made an even more sweeping condemnation. No more Romanticism, and for that matter, no more poetry. Hegelianism was rotting away, religious life was growing cold. European culture was dying, it was dead. As for the United States, they were a caricature of Europe. If Russia, for its sins, had to exchange its 'splendid future' for Europe's, it would be better to become German, English, even French, rather than to 'let oneself be asphyxiated by the tediousness of manufactured relations, in the mechanism of that anxious search for profit'. The West was bad, but the United States, which was the Far West, was even worse.[32]

In 1852, fresh aggravation. Having read European novels, Kireevski attacked European family morality, the dissatisfaction and desolation of European man. He used all the clichés. Italians were lazy, the French light, Germans heavy, the English snobbish. He also attacked luxury in all its forms. 'When luxury first penetrated into Russia', he wrote, 'it came like a contagious disease from neighbouring lands. One gave into it as to a vice, constantly aware of its illegitimate character, not only on the religious level, but on the social level too.' Luxury was a part of Europism. In fact, as one knows, it was not luxury which penetrated Russia, but the condemnation of luxury. There was a Russian pride in not compromising with the material world; in that way it could justify its poverty.[33]

This universal condemnation of Europe was something which Kireevski borrowed ready-made from European writers, from the reviews and novels and essays which relayed these commonplaces. Since Europeans themselves admitted it, thought Kireevski, that was proof that it was true. He accepted in an entirely uncritical way the criticisms which Europeans were constantly aiming at themselves. What he did not see was that this critical manner of looking at oneself is the essence of true Europeanism, and so he made it impossible for himself really to know Europe.

Kireevski thought he was judging Europe from the outside. But he was an outsider only in the same manner as Montesquieu's Persian or Voltaire's Huron, since his criticisms all derived from Europe. All the same, born in Russia, he was not personally a fictional product, and that was what made his criticism hard to refute. Slavophilism was not the product of a straightforward nationalism, like that which, under the Empire, the Germans brought to bear on France. It was fed by the uneasy feeling prevalent in Europe, which it observed and projected onto the Russian screen. At the same time, Russia only turned this nationalism onto Europe to precisely the extent that it too was subject to the same uneasy feeling and was Europeanized in that particular way. Hence the Slavophile vision of Europe proved so seductive for Russia, and for Europe too — a Europe only too ready to take at their own valuation the Muscovite Persian and the Huron to whom it had taught, at Paris and Göttingen, the rudiments of philosophy. The point of departure for Slavophilism was not the love of one's country, but the fear that one may not be able to love it, a doubt, a disdain, a lack of interest in it, and a terrible resentment of that West from which came all values and all instruction. In the grand theatre of European culture, the young Russian intellectuals could only find somewhere for themselves high up in the gallery, in the most remote and least important seats. When they saw, on stage, a satire of that culture, they took it up passionately. Here was Europe condemned and, by the same token, nationalism restored. The distance from the centre, which had caused such suffering, came to seem a boon. Instead of participating in Europism, they demanded that Europe should participate in Russianism.

According to the Kireevskian vision, Europe was the immediate given fact, Russia the construct. The picture presented of Europe was partial and particular, but at several points it corresponded to reality. As a negative version of an ill-understood Europe, Russia no longer existed as itself. It was a painted figure, contrasted point by point with the other, like an allegory of virtue set against an allegory of vice. It represented from the start Kireevski's utopia.

Russia 'had no knowledge of the iron barriers of unchangeable social classes, nor of the privileges enjoyed by some to the detriment of others, nor of the resulting moral and political conflict, nor of disdain between classes, nor of the jealousy of one class for another'. This wonderful state of affairs still existed in the depths, among the people. It had to be located there, since the privileges characterizing some areas of Russian life were obvious and immutable. So it existed in a hidden and mysterious way. The Slavophiles did not contribute to the positive historiography of Russia. They dealt briefly and badly with the statistics published by the Imperial government. They did not go to the bother of stepping down off the verandahs of their fine houses to visit their serfs, the flesh and blood people. Several were fairly harsh landowners. Because the People were not in the izbahs. The People were a spiritual location, the seat of a mystery. They were not in any hurry to get to know them: it was sufficient to sit back and contemplate them. It was enough to proclaim confidently that the old Russian way of life 'has been preserved almost intact amongst the lower classes of the people: it has been preserved and yet at present it exists in an almost unconscious manner — at present it simply makes up part of ordinary tradition, at present it is no longer bound by the hegemony of recent thought.'[34] In other words. it was invisible, and all the more real for that.

If the Slavophile description is false, the theory explaining it is necessarily even falser. Kireevski based himself on a tritely inaccurate description of Europe, and proceeded first to a historical, then to a philosophical, and finally to a theological explanation of this imaginary state of affairs. After that, he cemented his impressions and lent them a coherence capable of weathering the passage of time. Thus he had a theory to fit Roman Catholicism, or the Roman Empire, or Western feudalism. Let us take the theory dealing with the Roman Empire.[35] The West was already entirely dominated by Rome. In fact, 'external ratiocination' was taking over from the internal essence of things. 'This can be seen in family and social life, in the taste for grammar and the law, in the "artificial" harmony which crushed the natural freedom and living spontaneity of the movements of the soul.' Roman religion was a sort of pre-Catholicism: 'a religion which, behind the external rites, has almost forgotten the value of mystery'. What bound the Romans together was, as in modern societies, 'common interest' and partisan spirit. But Roman patriotism was cold and arid, dictated by pride. It had only 'the dry intelligence of the logician and the self-interested intelligence of the man of action'. As one can plainly see, Kireevski was applying to Roman history the categories which Romanticism applied to the West, and more particularly to French classicism. But what is simply a commonly held opinion, neither true nor false when applied to contemporary affairs, becomes an entirely erroneous historical judgement when applied to the Roman past. Kireevski theorized an impression, instead of analysing it, and so entrenched himself in the false.

As for the political vision of the Slavophiles, one theme is paramount: the denial of a business economy, based on contracts and the circulation of money, and the denial of liberal individualism. In this they were no different from conservative Romantic thinking, which, just as much as Revolutionary thought, inveighed against alienation and the religion of money. It has been possible to compare their anti-chrematistic polemic with that of Karl Marx: the same themes can be found among both European conservatives and socialists at this time.

However, there is one characteristic which set the Slavophiles apart from the conservatives, and it is the same characteristic which set Marx apart from the other socialists: in both cases, their protest was not confined to the moral sphere, but also worked as a philosophy of history. In France or England, conservatism did not often take the trouble to theorize. In the spirit of Burke, long-established privilege and the splendour of things past were enough to justify conservatism. Even among the French traditionalists, where Catholicism was enriched by elements foreign to the tradition, that tradition was so scrupulously supervised by the authorities that any strays found themselves swiftly condemned. In Russia, on the other hand, where the lay theologians carried on their cogitations independent of any ties with the Church, even and above all if they claimed to be faithful to the tradition, they turned to the Romantic historiosophies, which were the same ones which laid the groundwork for Marxism.

Khomyakov's historiosophy was dualist. Religion formed the

principal historical factor, but a religion which was itself conceived as springing from nature, or as constituting a natural principle. Thus Khomyakov was not so very far from Feuerbach.[36] There existed two conflicting religious principles, one, the Iranian principle (or religion of liberty), and the other, the Coptic principle (or religion of necessity). The whole of history arose as a result of their conflict, and of the predominance of the one or the other. This religious dualism coincided with a racial dualism: the human races could be divided into Iranian and Coptic. Equally there was a geographical dualism, whose poles were situated in Iran and Ethiopia. Egypt, Babylon, China and Southern India were civilizations of the Coptic type, in which materialism, formalism, the law and the state were predominant. The Greek and Roman worlds appeared, and were explicable by the fact that they consisted of a mixture of the two principles, Iranian and Coptic, with Greece being more Iranian and Rome more Coptic, as was 'obviously' proven by the conventionality and artificiality of Roman law and religion. Christianity appeared as a triumphant resurgence of the Iranian principle, as ancient Judaism had also been, to some extent. But this ray of light was diffused by the thick foggy layers of Coptism: the result was Roman Catholicism. By contrast, in the North and East, Christianity came into contact with the Germans and the Slavs. Unfortunately, the Germans had been infected by Rome, and the Coptic principles re-emerged in idealist philosophy. The best things in England (Khomyakov was an Anglophile) derived from the Slav element. After all, was not the name Angle a corruption of the Slav tribal name Uglitch? For it was the Slavs who represented the Iranian principle in its purest manifestation. One could see it in Greek religion, in the *Iliad*, which was profoundly steeped in the Slav spirit. Troy was a Slav colony. But nowhere did Slavness exist so purely as in the Russian people. It followed, then, that Russian interests coincided with the highest interests of humanity.[37]

Enough of these Russian ravings. What we have here is a gnostic type of historiosophy, with all the classic characteristics: two principles (here, Coptic and Iranian, but equally: matter and spirit, money and gift, law and love); their localized mixing; and their final, healing separation. They are, in short, the two principles and three times to be found in Manicheism, but instead of being presented through a mythology, they are presented through a history which is stated as real, a verifiable object of scientific study. It is at this point that one can witness the transition from gnostic to ideological thinking.

Slavophile thinking was rarely capable of such openness. Indeed, Khomyakov was happy simply to follow Friedrich Schlegel in this regard, who, in his *Philosophy of history*, had distinguished between two types of development, one carnal and the other spiritual, and had related them to two primitive races, the Cainites and the Sethites.[38]

What confuses everything so is the way in which Khomyakov and Kireevski disguise and cover over their gnostic schema with a mantle of Christian tradition. All historical, political and national concepts finished by converging in an ecclesiological dualism.

In fact, the opposition between Iranian and Coptic was a superfluous and unnecessary fantasy. It was an attempt to propound a different opposition, in naturalistic terms, to that between the Christian East and West, or — which is the same thing — the opposition between Russia and Europe. According to the esoteric way of thinking, each reality expresses and masks another, hidden, more 'profound' reality. The pairs which make up rationalism—integrated thought, rural community—capitalism, liberalism—patriarchalism, and even Iranian and Coptic, are finally subsumed into a dualism which makes up Russian Orthodoxy, and, in the same way, Protestantism and Catholicism.

The Orthodox Church represents the historical future of humanity, the perfect society or Christian *polity*. It is also the mystic reality of Russia. That is why Aksakov said that the history of Russia is a holy history. This sort of ecclesiology is, as such, in some ways traditional. But in other ways, it supports the Romantic exaltation of the *Volkgeist*, since the (Christian) People are the creative source of inspiration, the matrix of liberty and the judge of true infallibility. It also supports the old pietist and masonic base, since the true Church is not the visible institution, but the internal, invisible Church,[39] which means straightaway that there is nothing left to prove, since none of the palpable realities (in Russia, of the Russian political system, of the Russian past, of the Russian rural community, all of them things which are in the end subsumed by the Church) are the final realities, which are to be found elsewhere, and which one cannot grasp except in some mystic manner, in a belief in the mystery of the internal, invisible Church. The Slavophile vision of the world, for all that it claims empirical foundations, can always get away from empirical criticism by escaping upwards, in claiming a superior understanding, which one has to believe in before being able to attain it: and that is typical of ideology. But what makes the whole knot impossible to unravel is the infusion of Orthodox theology. German gnosis (in its esoteric masonic form, just as much as in its Romantic rationalized form), from which the Slavophiles derived almost all their own theories, presented itself straighforwardly as being exactly what it was, without any pretence. But Slavophile gnosis wanted to appear super-Orthodox, super-traditional, and to this end produced a sufficient number of texts from the best sources it could find to make it extremely difficult to catch it out. I am a bird, look at my wings... This fiction which refuses to be a fiction, relying on the Fathers and on reality, became a fiction on two levels, and one which it is almost impossible to uncover.

Once installed in the religious heart of Russia, the Slavophile fiction became ineradicable. It gave to what was, in effect, a transitory state of mind, a manner of thinking, all the solidity of tradition, instead of relying, as in Germany, on a philosophy, which would have meant that it too would have passed away when that philosophy had run its course. Of all the visions of the world which sprang up during the Romantic epoch, the Slavophile vision alone anchored itself in a theology, and fastened itself onto a lasting principle – the Church and the Christian faith. Hence its long life. Hence the fact that, even today, it still constitutes the alternative to any position which opposes it, be it Westernist, populist, liberal or Communist.

But even as a theology, Slavophilism still maintained its character as a sect – which enormously aggravated the schism of the Eastern Church – and a dualist sect at that, with all the hatreds and exclusions that that entailed. Having penetrated into the body of Russian Christianity, it managed to turn it, as in some mass manoeuvre, against its own particular enemies. The true heritage of Slavophilism does not lie in its values but in counter-values.

These counter-values are the very ones informing the Russian revolutionary movement. They implied a disdain for the law, as a contract negotiated between free parties and as the normal framework for freedom and the autonomy of the individual. For the Slavophiles, as for the revolutionaries, the law was a superstructure. They also disdained liberalism, that is to say, of political freedom as the condition, basis and foundation of any adequate political order whatsoever. 'Political liberty', wrote Aksakov, 'cannot be called freedom.' And shifting ground – or rather, conflating his grounds – he added:

'True freedom is the breath of the Holy Ghost.'[40] The Slavophile counter-values similarly scorned the West in all its forms: Roman and Germanic, German and French, Catholic and Protestant, modern and medieval. And finally they abhorred capitalism, that is, the way the world works, and, more specifically, the way the world grows richer. The production of goods, especially if they are beautiful luxury goods, the exchange of commodities, monetary transactions, enraged the Slavophile spirit, quite as much as they did the revolutionary one. Anything was better, for Russia, than a Western-style system of law and liberalism and a market economy. Anything, neo-Slavophiles like Berdiaev would say — even the Bolsheviks. For as far as the Slavophile spirit was concerned, the Bolsheviks were compatible with the Holy Ghost, but bourgeois liberals were not.

However serious the consequences of having these themes in common, they were nevertheless not so decisive as sharing a common matrix of thought. The Slavophiles are traditionally reproached for their lamentable anti-rationalism, and, in effect, they discouraged any attempt to deal with the real on a rational level for generations. All that they hated was labelled rationalist — the West, Catholicism, Protestantism, liberalism, and so on. In this way, they seriously disturbed the balance of faculties in a country which was still engaged in its intellectual apprenticeship: they impelled it to live affectively, maintaining it in a sort of emotional adolescence. The pietist currents which in Germany were counterbalanced by solid intellectual institutions and a serious training of the faculties of understanding, when they made their way into this new and almost intellectually virgin country, pushed it, without any difficulty, towards the slippery slopes of facility, and the least effort. Slavophilism thought that it was replacing the law by love; it would be much more appropriate to say that it was replacing thought by feeling.

If that had been all, it would have been a lesser evil. In depreciating reason as an analytical tool, the Slavophiles did not renounce an understanding of the real: but it was an understanding in the form of a total comprehension, which made for economy in proof and argument, since it was given *en bloc*, mystically, like the central vision of esotericists. The grains of Christianity contained in this vision were powerless to put it right, but lent it charm and attraction. Many Russians, believing themselves to be experiencing a conversion to Christianity, were attracted by this lure to Slavophilism. But, although they thought that they were thus escaping the revolutionary spirit, they were in fact trapped in a parallel utopia. Slavophile historical and political falsification in fact presented an imaginary state as an existing state, already achieved by Russia. There was nothing in reality to correspond to what they had to say about the rural community, about the mutual love between the Tsar and the people, about integrality, about conciliarity, etc. But that was none the less what they claimed to see and to be able to verify empirically in the Russian reality. In this way the Slavophiles placed themselves beyond revolutionary utopianism, which considers the future and not the present, and linked up, in advance, without any violence, and with a benign air, to the fundamental falsehood of Bolshevism in power, which demanded that one sees socialism as already existing. There was a similar hiatus between the reality they claimed to see and the real world. The growth of ideology was made easier not by the regression of Russian intelligence towards the emotional, but by the falsehood in which that intelligence was embroiled. In its falsification of the past, through the distraint of history, in its falsification of the present, through the imposition of a vision of the non-existent, Slavophilism, in its extreme and more fevered manifestations, is analogous to Leninism. And those emerging from one falsehood are in great danger of falling into another.

What, then, are the conclusions one can draw about the religious history of Russia?

It seems that in Europe, ideology could only have arisen in a breakdown and distortion of religion.

In England, the religious crisis ended in a differentiation. The pluralism of religious life meant that each group, from the most satisfied aristocracy right down to the most wretched elements of the population, could lead the type of authentically religious life which suited them, either within the 'high and dry' established Church, or within some more enthusiastic dissident sect. Calvinism, by carefully distinguishing between justification and sanctification, which Luther tended to confuse, was oriented towards ethics rather than speculation. It endorsed the Right and did not seek to justify the fact by some referred cosmogony. The recourse to ideology was not urgent.

The united nature of French Catholicism did not permit this flexibility or these adaptations. The partial failure of the Catholic Reformation, the disqualification which it suffered in the last years of the eighteenth century, made the Church lose any chance of containing the intellectual life of the nation. There was soon no religion in France outside the Church. The first outlines of ideology, esoteric speculations, and the revolutionary spirit arose in a very distant time, and without any reference to religion, which was withdrawing into an increasingly restricted area.

In Germany the sequence is a good deal less clear. The Lutheran Reformation, the philosophical and scientific movement, did not curtail the gnosticizing speculations of the late Middle Ages, but, on the contrary, lent them a new vigour and exuberance. There was not a sequence, but a concurrence and frequently a confusion of elements which, in France and England alike, remained separate. Amongst left-wing Hegelians in the 1840s, ideology emerged from Romantic speculation through a process of sifting and separation.

But as far as Russia is concerned, it would be more appropriate to the historical facts to speak in terms of an imported crisis rather than an autonomous upheaval. There was religion in Russia, but there had never been any indigenous religious thinking. The decline in the Church was of very long standing; indeed, it is questionable that one could ever speak of its rise. The Petrine revolution reduced Church personnel to the status of a caste, and its mission to a function within the state. What there was of religious life, whether orthodox or heterodox, fed on the streams flowing in from the West, whether Catholic, Protestant, pietist or Athonite.

The incursion of Romantic philosophy followed on naturally from international pietism. In seeking to explain the rise of ideology in Russia, one cannot speak of a crisis of Christianity, because the Christian tradition in Russia did not provide the conditions necessary for a crisis. Everywhere else, ideology fought against and uprooted religion. But in Russia, as the Slavophile movement demonstrates, ideology began by re-awakening religion. Religion re-emerged in Russia in its fervour, in its thinking, in its intellectual framework, under the distorted form of a religious ideology.

5
Liberalism or Revolution

The Slavophiles were at pains to distinguish themselves from official spokesmen like Pogodin and Uvarov. They did not want to be associated with the state, since they rejected the St Petersburg bureaucracy. The latent anarchism of the Slavophile renunciation of political struggle coexisted paradoxically with their political programme. Their loathing for certain abuses hardly put them in good standing with the Court, and they found themselves the object of much condemnation. For his part, Nicholas I thought of himself as the descendant of Peter the Great, and saw these Muscovite landowners as the offspring of those eighteenth-century boyars and aristocrats who had tried to set up the beginnings of an opposition to the autocracy and the first outlines of an autonomous civil society. The imperial bureaucracy which was attempting to push Russia towards 'development' and which was employing to those ends rational, not to say rationalist procedures, had no love for the dreamy irrationalism of Kireevski and his friends.

Nevertheless, Nicholas I's régime was able to make good use of Slavophilism, at the cost of a certain amount of falsification, though not as much as the Slavophiles believed. While wanting to drag Russia out of its 'under-development', the régime made play with Slavophile themes in apology for what it was substituting for under-development. The disparity between the state of Russia and the state of Europe could redound to the glory of the first and the confusion of the second if it could be attributed not to any backwardness in Russia itself but to an essential difference between the two states. In forcing the pace of progress, in an effort to catch up with Europe the Russian régime had had to accentuate its despotic character, thus creating a new, and this time irreparable disparity: but this could be transfigured by a mythology which denied the actual relations within the state, and put in their place an imaginary relationship based on love. There was no Russian fault which could not be presented as a mark of superiority, and of religious superiority at that.

The collusion between Tsarism and Slavophilism is more apparent if seen from outside than from within. Michelet saw in it the very essence of the Russian lie:

> The tendency of such a State is to become less and less a State, and more and more a religion. Everything is religious in Russia. Nothing is legal, nothing is just. Everything seeks to be holy...What an undertaking! You cannot even organise in your realm the world of civil order, the inferior world! And you aspire to the superior world of religion! Enemies of the Law, you want to place yourselves higher than the Law, you seek the realm of Grace! Unable to perform the works of man, you call yourselves Gods.[1]

The Russian *falsehood*, according to Michelet, is the falsehood of an ideology and a state propaganda which deny reality and attempt to impose on it a surreality. 'Russia is a lie. It is, in its people, a false people. It is, in its aristocracy, its priests and its tsar...(falsehood of falsehoods, supreme lie crowning all other lies...). *Crescendo* of lies, of pretence and of illusion.'[2] Seeing right through the surreality which was presented to Europe as the reality of Russia, Michelet makes the same total denial as Chaadaev: 'I declare, I affirm, I swear and I will prove that Russia does not *exist*.'[3]

That was the position taken by Custine, and by Marx too, who, in a celebrated formula, declared that the Russian empire 'even after manifold worldly achievements, persists in being considered a matter of faith and not of fact'.[4] But this change applied not to Russia, but to an indissoluble complex of state will and mystification.

And it becomes false when applied to Russia. The mistake made by Custine, by Michelet and by Marx was to confuse the two orders of reality, the actual Russian reality and the surreality which had been imposed upon it. In sociological terms, they misjudged the existence and power of the civil society, which had not emerged as being clearly visible, but simply existed and reinforced itself. Russia in the eighteenth century was an aggregate of great estates kept together by the autocracy with the help of an elementary bureaucracy.

It was a society with two classes, nobles and serfs, simpler and more elementary than any other society in Eurasia. There was some differentiation: several kinds of merchant, several strata of nobility, several species of functionary, several cities, the beginnings of an intellectual life. That Russia did *exist*, and its development was halted only by the First World War and the Revolution. Thus there grew up, at the beginning of the nineteenth century, the dyad of the state and the civil society. The state, since Peter the Great, had set itself the task of creating a civil society, but only in order to manipulate that civil society to its own advantage. Since the state existed prior to civil society, and since it was the stronger of the two, the state contained civil society, and so hindered its natural development. But that development proceeded in spite of the state, as well as because of it, and called into question a state which was, in its aims, frequently a party of change, in its form and essence, the party of reaction. The state, said Pushkin, is the only European in Russia. But it was also the very type of the Asiatic.

As for the civil society, by the very act of entering into this dialectic, it belonged entirely to Europe. And the growing awareness which it had of itself is called liberalism.

In a history of ideology, there is no room for a history of Russian liberalism, and I will not discuss it here. In this, I follow the example of most contemporary historians who, writing in terms of the great revolutionary event, tend to pass over liberal Russia rather quickly. That liberal Russia played no part in the Revolution and it is dead. But this silence should not be allowed to disturb our sense of proportion. Liberalism, as the token of the existence of a civil society, was the main current of thought throughout the nineteenth century, which penetrated everywhere and had an effect on every tendency. In so far as the Russian state was linked to the civil society and wished to promote it, recruiting its agents from within it, there existed a body of functionaries in whom the informed spirit of the Enlightenment became progressively filled with this liberalism of government: the liberal model supplied by Guizot, Constant and even de Tocqueville, had been further adapted and interpreted according to the pressures of the autocracy.[5] That sort of liberalism was present in the royal family. Less distorted, more radical, and more truly liberal, that same liberalism populated the reviews, what press there was, university departments and literature. It showed every gradation from total devotion to the autocracy — justified

along the Hegelian lines of the identity of the real and the rational —
right down to the most open and intransigent opposition.

Liberalism coincided with a proper historical understanding of
Russia. Liberalism, in fact, could furnish an image of the past freed
from Romantic myths and able to explain the situation in which the
historian found himself. The history of Russia given by Soloviev,
Chicherin, Kavelin and their successors in the 'statist school' des-
cribes the formation of the state first of all followed by that of
a civil society. The specific nature of Russia was the determining
factor in their relationship, dictating both the precociousness of the
state and the backwardness of society, the excessive power of the
first and the weakness of the second. The contemporary situation in
modern Europe demanded a realignment of the realtionship. For
these historians, as for all liberals, there was no question of Russia
aiming for some particular stage of European development. That
was the limited, contradictory goal set by the state. Russia had to
aim for the *spirit* of Europe, and thus for the European methods
and style of development. It was therefore necessary for the state
to regulate its behaviour in accordance with legal procedure, in order
to ensure the support of the most enlightened and increasingly
popular segment of the population.

The Slavophiles were in agreement with the first point, in fact
though not in theory, for instead of talking about representation,
they preferred to dilate on *sobornost'*. With the second point they
were not in agreement at all. They could not see the immense progress made by Speranski, on the orders of the Tsar, in simply collating
the laws of the state and arranging them in some sort of systematic
order. The Slavophiles saw the law as oppression, and preferred a
freely acting state to a state based on law, because it was more compatible with the rule of the Holy Ghost.

The liberal programme did not constitute a doctrine. It constituted a frame of thought within which different political tactics
could find a place. The same liberalism could lead Pushkin to praise
Nicholas, or to damn him, according to whether it seemed to him at
the time that the régime was helping or hindering Russia's chances
of fulfilling the liberal vision. It would be the same right up to the
end of the Imperial régime. Liberals might be adversaries of Marxism,
but there was also a liberal version of Marxism. There was, at the
basis of liberalism, an acceptance of the world as it is. The world
is fundamentally good, especially the Russian world. That one should

seek to improve it necessarily leads to political action about which there might be disagreement as to methods, but not as to principles or aims. Between a minister who has come straight out of the tradition of enlightened despotism — say Kiselev under Nicholas I, or Samarin, or Witte, under Alexander III or Nicholas II — between him and a democrat, even a socialist, there could be, transcending the tension between state and civil society, a shared vision of the common good of Russia, and of the boundaries of the field in which political conflict was to take place. In so far as it thought politically, liberalism did not think ideologically. It sought to modify reality, within variable limits. It did not seek to substitute for it an altogether different reality.

Slavophilism, I have said, was in opposition to the other populist, Marxist, Bolshevik ideologies. But it united with all other ideologies to oppose liberalism, because liberalism was not an ideology.

Liberalism appears unified throughout the duration of its history. Its spirit, though under a variety of forms, remained unchanging for as long as it inspired civil society in its quest for existence and recognition. Historically, it has been described as Westernism, in the form that it took to oppose Slavophilism, though at its inception it was not an opposing ideology, but the opposite of an ideology.

Westernism was primarily a return to common sense. The Slavophiles had altered reality beyond all the limits of plausibility. 'They are to blame', wrote Herzen, 'for our having so long failed to understand either the Russian people or its history.'[6] Herzen's early writings, and Bielinski's too, are full of the fresh air of truth regained. They have the frankness and often the gaiety of Pushkin. They are freed of the constricted, devout spirit of Kireevski and Khomyakov. How can one not subscribe to Bielinski's protest against the false problems and false solutions offered by the Slavophiles:

Russia sees its salvation, not in mysticism, not in asceticism, not in pietism, but in the progress of civilisation, of education, and of humanity. What it needs is not sermons (it has heard enough of them) nor prayers (it has said enough of them), but the awakening in the people of a sense of human dignity...suitable rights and laws drawn up, not according to the doctrine of the Church, but according to good sense and justice, and their application in the strictest possible way.[7]

He finally set out Russia's true problems: the abolition of serfdom and of corporal punishment, the establishment of a lawful state, and the honest application of its laws. The Westernists had no system to oppose to the Slavophiles, and that is why, despite the way they are coupled together in the history books, there is no real correlation between them. At the most, all one can say is that Granovski, the young Herzen and Bielinski all had certain values in common. They all believed in reason and distrusted irrationalism. They did not confuse autonomy of the self with an 'integral personality'. They believed in the universality of right, both of the traditional natural right, and of the right of nature, in the meaning intended by the French *Constituants*. They held no hatred for the circulation of money and for wealth as such. And finally, they conceded the necessity of the state, and, as liberals, the benefits of a constitution, or failing that, the regularity of legal procedures.

Their quarrel with the Slavophiles did not include the national question. They were no less nationalist, and had little sympathy for the West, towards which they expressed equal arrogance and disdain. But whereas for Kireevski and his followers the national question posed itself in religious terms, to such an extent that it was void of any political dimension, for the Westernists it was posed in political terms, and the religious question was deliberately avoided. The truth was, most of them had little taste for religious matters.

Religion is the true focus of disagreement between the two camps. One must also distinguish between the lay spirit and philosophical atheism. Russian thinking had been in need of laicization ever since the wounds of the social body had been justified, exalted and transfigured by religious ideology. Against this sort of cant were raised the voices, not only of Pushkin, but of Bielinski and Herzen as well. Bielinski did not go too far when he declared that he preferred the Enlightenment and asserted that Voltaire was more truly 'the son of Christ...than all your popes, bishops, metropolitans and patriarchs'.[8] Laicism is at one with that spirit of liberalism which can distinguish between levels, is rewarded with realism, and does not support injustice — is even covered with a mantle of religion. Philosophical atheism, on the contrary, was to go hand in hand with the revolutionary spirit.

In fact, one could begin to distinguish, at the heart of Westernism, a tiny and more radical group. The process was predictable. Once the Russian problem had been posed in political terms, it became clear that nowhere in Europe was the liberal programme so far from being realized. It was only to be expected that a small group should succumb to despair, which meant both exasperation with the political attempt and, at the same time, an abandonment of a truly political attitude. And indeed, if any action taken by the civil society proved vain, if it was not possible to find a partner in the state, if the conflict could not be set in any regular framework, nor conducted according to the rules, how tempting it was to adopt the attitude of the great denial, how tempting it was to construct an imaginary world which would form the idealized double of a world which had been decreed to be absolutely bad. At that point, an ideology is needed.

II

This is what happened under Nicholas I. In fact, 'reaction' had been going on since 1815, if by that term one means the refusal of the state to collaborate with the civil society. The generation of the 'forties' can be divided into those with a horror of the active life − feeding the splenetic romanticism of the 'superfluous man' − and those with a dream of the absolute action, a dream that could be fed from the same source as that which nourished the Slavophiles, namely German philosophy. But, as these young men came to it rather late, the disposable stock of ideas had been slightly changed: instead of reading Schelling, Schlegel and Baader, they read Hegel and, in due course, Feuerbach. Even then, their originality consisted in the way in which vulgarized ideas were interpreted by them and adapted to fit the project they had in mind for Russia.

Let us follow this evolution in a few of them.

Hegel's ideas arrived in Russia around 1835, to take root in a circle of young men. Stankevitch, the leading light of the circle, received him as Schelling had been received in the previous generation, with the enthusiasm of revealed truth. 'The chains fell from my soul when I perceived that there is no knowledge outside the idea which encompasses everything... At present I have one goal before me: I desire the absolute union of my knowledge with the world. I want to understand every phenomenon, I want to see its relationship with the whole life of the Universe, its necessity and its role in the evolution of the idea.'[9] The tone is Illuminist, as philosophical enthusiasm still was in Russia at this date. Stankevitch's friend, Bakunin, was studying (or rather, was running through) Hegel at the same period, with the same romantico-religious exaltation.[10] He was seeking a total gnosis, in which Fichte would be combined, without the least scruple or rigour, with the Master of Iena. In 1840, on arriving in Berlin, a beating heart before the new Athens, he was converted. But to action, not to philosophy. 'The true life lies in action, and action forms the only true life.'[11] Political action, be it understood, revolutionary action. In 1842, in an article which appeared in the left-wing Hegelian review, *Die Reaktion in Deutschland*, he launched philosophically (but only philosophically) the two constant fundamental tenets of the Russian revolutionary movement — the idea of maximalism and the idea of the party.[12] Bakunin was to change as his amorphous work extended in a variety of directions, but these two points remained consistent and secure.

According to the policy of maximalism, the reactionary was to be preferred to the 'conciliator'. True reactionaries are consistent. They 'perceive the absolute character of the opposition; they see that the positive and the negative are as easily united as fire and water.'[13] The negative, in Bakunin's jargon, is the revolution. Having perceived this, the reactionaries 'maintain with all their force and fervour a radical irreconcilable opposition'. In other words, they push things to the point of the liberating explosion and make possible the rise of the revolutionaries. From this point of view, how very much worse are the 'conservative conciliators' believing in the just mean and in the reconciliation of the irreconcilable. Bakunin refers them to Hegel's *Logic*: the meaning of the negative is the destruction of the positive. The conciliator is to be hated because he does not understand the terms of the struggle, terms on which the revolutionary and the reactionary are in agreement: 'It does not consist simply in opposition to the established powers, any more than in any specific constitutional or politico-economic change, but in the total overthrow of the whole world structure, heralding an entirely new way of life such as has never been seen before in history.'[14] The stake is nothing less than the end of this world, and the apocalyptic birth of an earthly Jerusalem. That is why, in our first glimpse of the party, we see it modelled on a sort of church: 'Democracy [that is to say, the post-revolutionary state] is a religion and, having achieved it [the party] will become religious, which means that it will not only be informed by its principle in all its thoughts and judgments, but also that it will be devoted to this principle in fact, in the least manifestations of its life, and it is thus that the party will conquer the world!'[15] The idea of the party is thus conceived as the prime mover and instrument of salvation, as the present kernel of a future reality, as the achieved microcosm of a radically different nature. It demands, by this token, the total devotion and absorption of its members right up to 'the least manifestations of its life'. It leads a separate existence up to the time when the transformation occurs, and reality changes.

In essence and in principle, the democratic party is universal and all-embracing, but in its existence as a party it represents something particular, and negative. It does not yet exist in all its affirmative richness, but only as a negation of the positive and, because of that, it must perish when the positive perishes, in order to rise again, regenerated, as the living fulfilment of itself. And this internal transformation of the democratic party will not consist only in a qualitative change, that is to say, it will not only mean an enlargement of its present particular, and necessarily bad existence — God forbid, for that sort of enlargement would only lead to a general mediocrity, and the end of the whole business would prove to be an absolute general mediocrity — but would also entail a qualitative change, a new vigorous, invigorating revelation, a new young world in which all present dissonance would be resolved into a harmonious unity.[16]

Beneath this vaguely Hegelian pathos, Bakunin was presenting Russia with the formula of the revolution as a complete recasting of the world. Hence his instrument, the party, would be troubled, just as the intelligentsia (which Bakunin dreamt of transforming, as a body, into the party of revolution) was troubled, in a state still far removed from reality, except with regard to the uneasiness felt by this generation without responsibility, which refused and had been refused any involvement in social and political life. But in waiting for his dream to be realized, Bakunin fleshed it out and completed it with material wrenched from Hegel.

It should be noted that the principal borrowing (as in Marx, as in Lenin, regardless of the distortion which it undergoes) is the notion of dialectic. It is a dialectic in which the negative movement pre-dominates absolutely: 'Opposition is not a balance, but a preponderance of the negative which makes up the prevailing moment.' This is no longer Hegelianism, since any conciliation of the opposites, any synthesis, is impossible. But, to hell with Hegel!: 'The negative, the drive towards the obliteration, the eager destruction of the positive', that is what matters, and never mind the future. The Spirit will provide. The thing is to 'deny' the present. 'The spirit of destruction is at the same time a creative spirit.' It follows that the

revolutionary spirit has no need to rely on a pre-established programme. It is spared the construction of a utopia, since it is only after
the destruction that the 'new, vigorous, invigorating revelation'[17]
will take place.

Until then, destructive action will be enough.

Bakunin was moving out of the Russian orbit. He had left his
friend Bielinski behind. But Bielinski too was a convert. He gave
himself up to Bakunin (to Hegel, as he thought) with a perfect abne-
gation of the will. The Hegel preached by Bakunin in 1835 was still
that of pure and simple acceptance of the real and of reconciliation
with the concrete. But in Russia the real was Nicholas I. Soon
Bielinski could not hold with the notion. He could not draw the equation between Nicholas and the incarnation of the Idea. A less able
'dialectician' than Bakunin, he was not capable, as his friend had
been, of giving his idol a swift half-turn to the left. So there was no
rest for him in Hegelian quietude. His true anxieties were moral,
and he could not find any real morality in the Hegelian *Sittlichkeit*.
So he rejected Hegel as a 'bossy old fool', and even sent the whole of
philosophy packing. His ideal from then on was French-style socialism, and the practical 'negators', Voltaire, the *Encyclopédistes* and
the terrorists of the Revolution. Truth to tell, Bielinski was no
longer entirely sure where he stood. The 'Father of the Russian
Intelligentsia' (which is how he was addressed by Alexander Blok)
could be claimed equally by descendants who were at each other's
throats.[18] His tentative leaning towards speculation, and the violence
of his moral demands preserved him, more or less, from ideology. His
political protest was radical, but it sprang from a spirit of revolt,
seeking the re-establishment of justice, rather than from a revolutionary spirit, which seeks the coming of a new reality, beyond justice.
He recognized the substance of actual reality, and towards the end
of his life pushed realism to the point of justifying the bourgeoisie
and capitalism: an exceptional standpoint in Russian thinking. On
this point, Bielinski belonged to the liberal tradition.

But, if ethics saved Bielinski's politics from ideology, they steeped
his aesthetic in it. It was Bielinski who first perceived that the
national genius, which the Slavophiles had assigned to some arbitrary
historiosophy, should in fact be sought for where it actually was, in
the youthful works of Pushkin and Gogol. It was for the literary
critic to make out its meaning. Through his intervention, the values
of human and Russian life, implicit in the works of literature, would

serve as a paradigm to the whole nation. Thus the fruits of culture were not the private property of a few: they should be shared equally by everybody. Bielinski thus originated the extremely dangerous principle of the responsibility borne by the writer towards his public, a principle that has poisoned Russian literature ever since. It infected the writer with guilt about his own salvation, and gave the public, or rather any politicized section of the public, the opportunity to blackmail him into expressing the proper feelings. The autonomy of art suffered a serious blow. And that is why moral blackmail could be so easily replaced, in the generation immediately following, by ideological blackmail. The writer, under pain of public opprobrium, had to conform to the demands of the revolutionary party's programme, and, even more catastrophically, to its doctrines.

In 1844, Bielinski congratulated himself on 'the beginnings of the happy reconciliation of philosophy with the praxis deriving from the left-wing Hegelianism of today'. As a philosophy, it is neither bookish, nor scholarly: 'It must be as cold, severe and sombre as reason, but it must also, at the same time, be as inspired as poetry, as passionate and full of sympathy as love, as vibrant and sublime as faith, as powerful and heroic as a daring exploit.'[19] Rational, an object of belief, placing value in action: the very picture of the future ideology.

During this period, Herzen was in exile, far from Moscow, far from his friends and cut off from their development. He was still at the stage of Schelling, of Romantic religiosity and the new Christianity of Pierre Leroux. Suddenly, he heard mention of a book and sent off for a copy: 'Imagine my joy, that in all essentials I am in agreement with the author to a remarkable degree.'[20] The book was *Prolegomena zur Historiosophie*, by a young Polish Hegelian called Cieszkowski.

Hegel, claimed Cieszkowski, had given humanity sufficient self-awareness to understand the laws governing its development in the past. And if humanity can know its past, its present and the laws governing its evolution, then it is capable of knowing its own future, not through prophecy, but through prevision. But it is up to humanity to attain this prevision. Historiosophy 'becomes the objective, effective realisation of known truth'.[21] In the state of self-awareness, there is no more distinction to be made between facts and actions: 'The *praxis* formed by fact is unconscious and thus *pre-theoretical* whereas that formed by deeds is conscious and thus *post-theoretical.*'[22]

When awareness is fully attained, it creates a 'point of inflection' in external reality, by means of which facts are converted into acts. The decisions of humanity thus become 'completely identical with the divine plans of Providence'.[23] Hegel had discovered through speculation the logic of historical events. It was now a question of applying this knowledge practically. And this was the decisive formula: 'We think we have satisfied these two opposing demands: letting experience follow its most natural course, and, at the same time, applying, in a systematic way, the rigour of logical deduction.'[24] This formula in fact provides a perfect example of the incompatibility of a utopian policy and an ideological policy. According to the latter, there is no question of achieving an ideal. One must put one's trust in the self-development of events predicted by the theory, and simply commit oneself knowingly to the cause. The more voluntarist policy amounts to a policy of *laissez-faire*: and that is the 'realist' illusion which dominates Leninism.

Cieszkowski conceived his book simply as a scholarly exercise, and never thought of applying his theories in practice. There were huge family estates in Poland awaiting his return from his studies. But read in a forgotten corner of the Russian Empire, his book was to have a profound effect. Even without having read Hegel, Herzen understood that there was a need to go beyond him. Through action. 'The future fate of philosophy in general', he read, 'is to be practical philosophy or, to put it better, the *philosophy of praxis*, whose most concrete effect on life and social relations is the development of *truth in concrete activity*,...Thus, it is now that its normal influence on the social relations of humanity will begin so that absolutely objective truth is developed not only in the merely passive but also in self-created reality.'[25] This foreshadows Marx. Thus Herzen could declare that Hegel provided 'the algebra of the revolution which will liberate man completely and will not leave a single stone standing of the whole Christian edifice',[26] which accords better with Ruge and Moses Hess and the young Hegelians' philosophy of action than with the spirit of the Master of Iena.

Returning to Moscow in 1842, Herzen heard in the plaintive song sung by a *mujik* at the side of the road 'the struggle made by the spirit to leave the heavy confinement of the proletariat and to enter the kingdom of God'.[27] More straightforwardly put, he had become a socialist.

Herzenian socialism is related to a stage of European socialism which Marx and Engels were engaged in going beyond. It is a criticism, not of the capitalist method of production, but of the harm inflicted by the bourgeois life on the personality and on aesthetic values. He read French journals, which were full of arguments between liberalism and socialism, but applying to an economic and social state which Russia could not conceive. Herzen was thus a liberal through his liberal maximalism. But one can see him in exile, discovering France, for whose *salons* he had little regard. Like any Russian traveller in the nineteenth century, he was filled with horror and disgust for French, English and German Europe, for a developed, bourgeois, well-regulated, liberal Europe. The sight of it filled him with nationalist resentment, and he slipped naturally into the matrix of Slavophile thinking. He saw in Europe a reincarnation of the decadence of the Roman Empire, in the Slavs, the barbarians who would destroy it to give it new life, and in the socialists, the first persecuted Christians. Through a repetition of the geographical Manicheism of the Slavophiles, Herzen was led to identify liberalism with the West and socialism with Russia.[28] We are presented with a restored Messianism. The new socialist reality was shadowed forth luminously in the same imaginary place that the Slavophiles saw surrounded in a nimbus of Christianity: the rural community. The community provided the framework in which would occur the osmosis between the intellectual values borne by the élite and popular spiritual values, and in which their mutual conversion would be carried out. Russia is essentially socialist, just as it is essentially Christian. Thus populism was born, and thus was fulfilled the prediction made by Michelet: 'This is the nature of Russian propaganda, varying infinitely according to peoples and nations. Yesterday she told us: "I am Christianity." Tomorrow she will say: "I am socialism."'[29]

The recovery of the nationalist theme, the transferral to the left of any potentially rightist values, the transfiguration, this time in lay terms, of Russian backwardness into a decisive advance on Europe, should have ensured the success of populism. It is hardly less far removed from reality than Slavophilism, since the peasant community, which, incidentally, Herzen took no more trouble than Kireevski to study properly, was in itself no more the bearer of the socialist utopia than it was of the Christian utopia. Like Bielinski and Bakunin, Herzen launched an appeal for praxis. Instead of dreaming passively, like the Slavophiles, of the emergence of an immanent but invisible reality, instead of wishing, like the liberals, to alter reality within the limits of the possible and the reasonable — he exhorted an active devotion to the new reality, of which Russia alone contained the seeds. He liberated revolutionary aspirations.

Bakunin, Herzen and Bielinski all made use of dialectics. But they were not materialists. Herzen, following the contemporary fashion, had studied the natural sciences.[30] In his *Letters on the study of nature*, he protested against philosophical imperialism. He wanted to base speculation on empiricism, and logic on history.[31] He was not far from wanting to put dialectics back on its feet, like his contemporary Marx. All the same, he remained faithful to the Hegelian speculative ideal.[32] Now, at the moment when political action became possible, during the middle of the century, one can clearly remark an eclipse of the dialectical theme, while the materialist theme moved to the forefront.

Bakunin, Herzen and Bielinski were all, of necessity, cabinet revolutionaries. They envisaged the future progress of Russia as a tumultuous, dramatic or, to use their own terms, a dialectical process. Dialectics was a convenient way of thinking about Russia in the most generalized manner possible. It made it feasible to hold together the lamentation of the present with the exaltation of the historic destiny of the motherland. It permitted, within the heart of speculation, a little thrill of action.

The revolutionaries of the 1860s found themselves in a very different position. Chernychevski, Dobroliubov and Pisarev judged the moment ripe for action. They were mistaken, but they had conceived the idea of forming the first secret societies. They were, first of all, militants. For the most part of modest parentage, they had felt in their bones the sordid harshness of Russian life. They belonged to less Europeanized and also less sheltered environments than their predecessors. The sons of priests and of petty provincial nobles, the revolutionary break with established morality, with a code of behaviour and with religion, exposed them to fierce psychological conflicts.

Their parents did not own libraries and no one dreamt of offering them a trip to Germany. What they learnt was the summary materialism which followed the great idealist syntheses: Vogt, Moleschott and Büchner even more than Feuerbach.

There was no need for them to be converted to action. They were already converts. They had no need to think in general terms of the historical development of Russia, nor to convince themselves that praxis was the last word in speculation. They were already committed. What they did need was a system which was able to justify their action in moral and political terms. Politically, there was no problem. Russia needed change, and the formulae of socialism had already been prepared by the West and naturalized by Herzen. They needed a straightforward, obvious doctrine which would make it possible to overcome the isolation, hesitation and guilt of the terrorist intention. Materialism was just right.

6
The Intelligentsia

Bakunin, Bielinski and Herzen were all exceptions within a group which they neither reflected, epitomized nor represented — the nobility and, what almost amounts to the same thing, the upper levels of the bureaucracy, that is, the élite of the civil society. This group was not defined by any conscious body of doctrine — for all there seemed to be some sort of understanding between it and liberalism — since it was possible to belong to it without being a liberal. It had no existence beyond its relationship with the state on the one hand, and with the economy and property on the other: its essence was social.

But, from 1850 on, there developed a new group, whose essence is inseparable from the ideas which it made its own, and of which it was the bearer and the disseminator: the intelligentsia.

The word is German in origin (*Intelligenz*) and was Slavized by the Poles, but it was the Russians who launched the term on its worldwide career.

Retrospectively, one can see that the same sort of thing must have developed earlier in France, at the end of the *Ancien régime*, and in Romantic Germany as well. The worlds of the intellectual societies, of the journalists of the Hegelian left, of the republicans of the July Monarchy, deserve, by analogy, to be called intelligentsias. While, in the twentieth century, the phenomenon has taken on global dimensions: it can be found in Latin America, in Africa, in China, in the Arab world. For the last thirty years, the intelligentsia, which in the developed nations of the West had been in eclipse (in the France of the Third Republic, in Wilhelmine Germany), or had never developed (in the United States, or Japan, or England) has undergone the most remarkable extension.

If the term is familiar to us in its Russianized form, that is because it has nowhere shown such clear characteristics as in Russia, to the extent of representing a generalizable type. The Russian intelligentsia can serve as a paradigm.

There seem to be three conditions, or pre-conditions, necessary for the development of an intelligentsia.

The first pre-condition is the existence of a national, organized system of education, with total state control of all the parallel strands of education.[1] It is this circumstance which explains why Russia, the most 'backward' of European nations, engendered the social type which has dominated the twentieth century in the same way as the bourgeoisie dominated the nineteenth. In fact, the construction of a system of education was, for the Tsarist government, the cheapest and most effective form of investment to wrench Russia out of the state of under-development which was beginning to threaten the international position of the Empire. State education was the key for the constitution of a military and bureaucratic organization capable of standing up to the threat posed by the European West to Central and Eastern Europe, and because of which Poland and the Turkish Empire would eventually perish, due in large part to that very Russian Empire.

The building up of a system of education was envisaged by Peter the Great, planned under Alexander I, and brilliantly executed by Nicholas I. During his reign, the nobility and a part of the non-servile classes were properly schooled. The Russian gymnasium bore comparison with the French *lycées* of the same date. The university, founded according to the German model, and whose staff had for the most part been shaped in Germany, was not entirely unworthy of comparison with its model. Of course, this system of education did not include the great majority of the population, and only admitted the élite of civil society. There were only about 20,000 schoolboys and 4,000 students in the whole of the Empire.

But the very aim of state education provided the possibility of conflict. The formation of a dominant élite was meant to be a substitute for the insufficiency of civil society. All the same, it could itself serve to reinforce, develop and make 'conscious' that same civil society. In France and in England, the civil society was in charge or at least had close control over the education of its children. In Russia, the nobility sought that same measure of control, as soon as it had the strength and the capacity. But in vain, for the state maintained a tight hold on education, which it intended to make use of to its own exclusive profit. Thus the system of education became part of the field of conflict between the state and civil society. It was desired and maintained by the one, and drew its recruits from the other, and ended by delivering these recruits back to it again, primarily for its own benefit. It formed generations of young men, torn from their own particular traditions, set in a uniform mould, who left the educational establishments as part of a new social stratum, with its own subculture, its own separate habits and ways of behaving, outside any of the recognized castes of Russian society.

The second pre-condition is the incapacity of the civil society to impose on its young its own values and *raison d'être*. Under Nicholas I, the nobility grew progressively weaker, losing confidence in itself and abandoning its *esprit de corps*. It tended to fuse with the mass of young men educated successively at the gymnasium and at the university. Few of the nobility still followed the ancient *cursus* of the nobility, the regiments of the Guard which led to the Court and to the important posts, the corps of Cadets which led to the regular army, and then, at about forty, to a return to civilian life, and the cultivation of the family estate.

The majority had to bow to the new system of exams and diplomas. Impoverished, they had no choice. Thus they merged with the students, who came from every class and rank, to make up, with them, one single class, a Russian Third Estate, made up of the new liberal professions, of teachers, journalists and technicians. Within this class there crystallized the intelligentsia. It did not matter whether noble or common origins predominated within it: that sort of distinction no longer applied, since it was not being noble or common which gave the class its tone, but the intelligentsia as such.

The third pre-condition is in a general sense the crisis of the old régime. In Russia this had been taking place since at least 1825, that is to say, since the Decembrist affair brought to light the weakening of the political consensus. A part of the nobility was not satisfied with the political developments. The state had no more confidence in them and no longer associated them with its actions, preferring to govern through government departments. The discovery of Europe, that is to say, of the staggering gulf which separated it from Russia, nourished a sense of national disquiet amongst the nobility, and a loss of confidence in the capacity of the state to fulfil the destiny of the Motherland. To the civil society, educated in a European fashion by the state, but rendering back to the state the fruits of that education, it came to seem increasingly irregular that the great majority of the population should be reduced to a condition of slavery, and that the rest should be deprived of the most elementary legal guarantees. This latent crisis became acute when, on the death of Nicholas I, it reached the political arena. What occurred between 1855 and 1861 bears out yet again the truth of de Tocqueville's remark, that the time of danger for an authoritarian régime is when it sets about reforming itself. The crisis at the beginning of the reign of Alexander II is similar to that in England around 1640 and in France around 1789. The sacred union of men of good will, as much within the government as in society, agreed unanimously on the reforms to be carried out, but started to disintegrate as soon as the reforms were applied. It was a classic process of radicalization. A left wing was formed, and then an extreme left whose excesses the government was unable to curb. If the government failed to accede to the perpetual and increasingly radical demands with which it was met, then it was pushed towards the right. Realignments took place within the opposition. Those who hesitated to follow the move to the left were despised as objective allies of the régime. Between 1861 and 1862 the whole of the educated public had to choose sides: either they accepted the reforms, even though criticizing them and demanding that they be widened, or else they rejected them totally in the name of the revolution.

This kind of polarization is characteristic of the revolutionary process. The displacement of the centre of gravity towards the Independents, at the time of Cromwell, or towards the Jacobins in 1792, are typical instances. But in Russia there was no revolution. The state remained firm, in total mastery of concession and repression. When it thought the time for repression had come (in 1863), everything settled down again. There was not even a revolutionary situation. The peasants, even if they had followed the revolutionaries and risen – which they had no thought of doing – would only have created riots, or at the very most an uprising. They were not capable of making a revolution.

The civil society was too weak in Russia to assert itself decisively against an all-powerful state. It had no means at its disposal for imposing the substitution of the new principle of a national sovereignty, for the traditional principle of monarchy by divine right. In 1905, all the classes of society, including the peasants, would start the ball rolling, in a precarious alliance, to overthrow the Imperial régime. Even then, the Imperial régime managed to keep going, and hung on until February 1917. In 1861, it was still in full force.

This meant that the revolutionary process occurred as it were in isolation, solely within the civil society (for the obscure peasantry remained outside it), and, more particularly, within the most enlightened sector of the civil society. It ended up by separating out from it the most radical section, which refused to get involved with, to compromise with, or quite simply to deal with the state. This was a great loss for the state, since the ruling stratum was numerically weak, and was thus condemned to isolation, and sometimes to obscurity, cut off from the world from which it normally drew its recruits, that is, the educated stratum. But it was an even greater loss for civil society itself, for it was thus divided, competing with itself, and eventually condemned to death by that separate sector of itself, the intelligentsia.

In order for the intelligentsia to take form and maintain its stability, the three pre-conditions mentioned above were necessary, but they were not in themselves sufficient. There was a fourth condition which had to be satisfied, namely, the presence of ideology, in the sense in which I have attempted to define it. The function of ideology is threefold.

1. It defines the contours of the intelligentsia. Social origins were of no importance in order to belong to it. It could hardly have been more composite, made up from all the school and university classes of the Empire. In the 1860s, the nobility were numerically in the majority. But there were also the sons of priests, of clerks, of shop-owners, and even of peasants. This latter group tended to call attention to its origins, as they fitted well with the values of the group, whilst their noble comrades tried rather to gloss over their origins: but this inverted hierarchy did not reflect any social relationship that existed in the society outside − it simply mirrored the ideas current within the group. To speak, as Lenin does, of the social evolution of the intelligentsia (proceeding from noble, to common, to proletarian) is meaningless, since the principle of cohesion is a purely intellectual one. *Ubi doctrina, ibi patria.*

In the intelligentsia, the only superiority possible was in terms of the assimilation of the doctrine. Allegiance to the doctrine was a desocializing process: it did not matter who one was or where one came from. On the other hand, imaginary social allegiances could be attributed to friends and enemies. Whoever did not belong to the intelligentsia was marked out socially as second rate. It was, for instance, because he had 'bourgeois' ideas, that he was a 'bourgeois'. In the same way, having 'proletarian' ideas made you a part of the proletariat, or any other class with which the intelligentsia had decided to identify itself. It was a question of ideal belonging, since real belonging was of no interest to the intelligentsia.

As Wladimir Weidlé has remarked:

By virtue of a tacit convention observed by this new 'clerical estate', no one was thought eligible to belong to it who was either a priest, an officer, or a civil servant, however brilliant and well-informed such a person might be; equally barred, as a rule, was anyone whose opinions seemed in the least reactionary or conservative or even merely moderate, susceptible (if they were known there) of being approved in high places. There might be a considerable difference between a university professor, elegantly critical and liberal, and a bomb-throwing terrorist who was a candidate for the gallows; but to be admitted to the bosom of the new élite, the condition that was at once necessary and sufficient was at least a minimum of subversive spirit.[2]

It was on the basis of shared values that this new group arose, with its particular customs, its mutual signs of recognition, its style in dress and in social behaviour. Ruptures and dissent occurred within it for the same reasons as adherence and allegiance – on grounds of doctrine.

In this way, the intelligentsia became divorced from its social origin and function: levels of education, and qualifications, and even the simple fact of being an intellectual did not automatically confer membership, nor did their absence prevent it.

2. Ideology also ensured the coherence of the intelligentsia *vis-à-vis* the state. Ideology offered it a programme, which might change, but which would admit no compromise. In fact, it proposed a complete new social system, entailing a new political régime, new relationships between its citizens, and a new culture. It armed the intelligentsia with moral justification, and thus facilitated the moral and legal transgressions which the installation of a new system renders inevitable. It has been suggested that there is an equation between the radicalism of a political programme and the frustration it encounters.

The Russian régime being what it was, one could predict that the Russian intelligentsia would be maximalist in revolution. Though the régime did, with some ups and downs, progressively improve, the revolutionary programme did not become any less extreme. This was because the ideology had created a fossilized image of reality in Russia, an image in which the régime was cast in a demonic role. As it represented absolute evil, it was permissible to use against it those means which the régime itself employed, but which were qualitatively transformed because of the ends to which they were dedicated.

In their relationship with one another, the Russian state and the revolutionary intelligentsia made a pair, and tended to become each other's doubles. The intelligentsia formed itself into a system of police, in just the same way as it believed the state to be organized, while the state, for its part, tried to set up a police force modelled on what it thought the party to be like. The state changed, and so did the intelligentsia, but where they came into contact, they were almost fated to show each other their most archaic aspect, and an aspect which, weighed down with illusions, was incapable of changing.

3. But the most important function of the ideology was to protect the identity of the intelligentsia with regard to the civil society. The intelligentsia had seceded from civil society but it was always in danger of being reabsorbed by it. There was no unemployment amongst intellectuals except where it had been deliberately chosen. The universities were not producing a superfluity of students. The impression was current at the time, but false, because if a student wanted a post, he had no trouble at all in finding one. The rapid economic expansion meant that until the outbreak of the First World War there was a chronic shortage of industrial and commercial management personnel, as well as of engineers, teachers and lawyers. A militant student could be arrested and sentenced; once he had served his sentence, any career was still open to him.[3] It was not even expected that he should become a reactionary; in fact, that would have damaged his social standing. Ideology blocked that sort of 'reformation'. It provided the intelligentsia with reasons for preferring its own particular way of life, which was frequently rough and ascetic, to the way of life of society 'outside'. It saw an entry into normal society as being a betrayal, villainous, dishonourable.

A young man wishing to leave, to make a good marriage, take up his inheritance, or follow a particular career, ran the risk of being treated to sarcastic remarks, of being despised, and being accused of careerism, *arrivisme* and *embourgeoisement*.

In the political arena, this circumscription of the intelligentsia in relation to the civil society proved essential. In fact whilst the crisis of the Imperial régime remained latent, the intelligentsia and the civil society were always united in opposition. Both wished by their very nature, if not actually in fact, to put an end to that régime. Thus both of them were, in a general sense, 'objectively' revolutionary. But what the civil society was aiming for was what had been achieved in England and France, and even more in the German society of the nineteenth century. Its goal was limited but concrete, and it corresponded to things existing in reality. It wanted to fulfil itself along the lines of its own spontaneous development, and a diffuse liberalism was sufficient as an expression of that desire. The ideological intelligentsia aimed at setting up the perfect society promised by the doctrine, but which had nothing to correspond to it anywhere. Its goal was abstract, but unlimited. As there could be no common ground between the finite and the infinite, any concession which would have satisfied civil society, and which the intelligentsia would have welcomed even more energetically, would have immediately become valueless if wrested from the state. Thus society was successively both ally and traitor; ally inevitably, since the intelligentsia did not have the means, on its own, of obtaining such a concession, and traitor necessarily, because it did not follow the intelligentsia in the demands which it immediately made, and which, according to the logic of its maximalist programme, served both to reveal that programme and to unmask the treachery of society. Ideology controlled this double movement, by defining alliances as a function of the political struggle, and then, whatever the outcome, by indulging in divine discontent. It defined where and when the intelligentsia should establish contact, and when it should break contact with society.

Ideology fulfilled the same delimiting function towards those classes with which the intelligentsia had a *projected* relationship. In effect, ideology, whilst objectively defining the limits of the intelligentsia, subjectively annulled it. Because of ideology, the intelligentsia never acted in its own name, but always in somebody else's. It was supposed to represent the higher interests of the people

— firstly, the peasant people and then the working people. More, it was supposed to efface itself, and devote itself entirely to the peasantry, and then to the proletariat, inasmuch as those two social groups played an important part in the ideology and in the plan for reorganizing society promulgated by the intelligentsia. Those classes were more than allies, since, according to the ideology, the historical initiative belonged to them, and it was the intelligentsia which, abdicating any consistency and ontological reality, allied itself to them. The intelligentsia thus went before these classes, to try to detach them from civil society and to convert them to ideology. Such was the object of the movement 'towards the people' in the 1870s, and subsequently of the dogged and continuous work of penetrating the young Russian working class at the end of the Imperial régime. None the less, whatever position these classes might have held in the thinking of the intelligentsia, they normally felt called to join up with civil society again, and had a natural tendency to follow their own destinies. This presented unpleasant difficulties for the intelligentsia, which had some trouble fitting the image of the peasantry of the proletariat, presented to it by the ideology, with the visible reality. But the ideology helped the intelligentsia to resist the spontaneously expressed will of the peasantry or the proletariat. If the peasants or the workers were not acting according to the correct ideological canons, that was because they were subject to outside influences, which could be traced back to the rest of civil society and even to the state.

Here we are approaching the central paradox of the intelligentsia. Once the ideological conversion of the particular classes aimed at has taken place, then the intelligentsia disappears from its own considerations. The ideology has been confirmed by that conversion since, in the ideology, there is no place for the intelligentsia as such. Moreover, when the peasant and the worker in their turn enter the ideology — and in consequence, the intelligentsia — they too undergo the same process of desocialization as their student comrades. They join the egalitarian republic of ideas. This confers on them a class membership of an ideological nature, but it is one which coincides with their natural membership. In fact, just as they leave the working class, they become conscious of their 'proletarian' nature, to which the members of the intelligentsia are ideologically integrated. But there are times when the movement breaks down, and the intelligentsia finds itself reduced solely to its own members. Then, the intelligentsia is nothing more than the intransigent guardian of the ideology; it is no longer conscious of itself as a separate entity, it waits to take shape, in either the peasantry or the proletariat. They, meanwhile, are seen as *prima materia*, raw material, an amorphous mass awaiting transformation at the hands of the intelligentsia. From this point of view, the intelligentsia is no longer offering anything palpable, any sort of social reality: it is pure ideology.

But from the point of view of the civil society, the intelligentsia existed as a particular socially recognizable group. It was a separate part of civil society, achieving internal coherence through ideology, but isolated from the state by the political struggle it sought, and cut off from society by the aims which it set itself — and alienated from both state and society by a vocation both deliberately exclusive and permanently cloistered.

The existence of the intelligentsia complicated the task of the civil society in Russia. In seventeenth-century England, an extremist wing of the civil society played its hand and lost during the revolution, but it was not an intelligentsia. It did not owe its existence to the state, and had not been educated by it. It did not impose itself on civil society. It thought in religious terms, not ideologically. It did not, therefore, remain shut in on itself, but was bound by numerous links to the rest of civil society, with which it was in constant relation. In effect, it had never ceased to be a part of it. In Revolutionary France, the Jacobin wing possessed many of the same characteristics. To be sure, its enthusiasm was less religious than rational, and was thus an embryonic ideology. But it did not yet possess a sufficiently powerful intellectual coherence to hinder the movement towards the civil society, with all the ensuing positive effects. Even the most terrorist of Jacobins did not stop dealing with the civil society, even if only to acquire goods and despoil their enemies. Once they became landowners (and their ideals did not forbid them from doing so), then they rejoined the civil society as of right, and found it in their interests to conserve it. Before they could destroy civil society, the Jacobins had been destroyed by those amongst them who had rejoined that society or who wished to rejoin it. The proto-intelligentsia lost power, and very soon lost its autonomy. There were a few occasions on which one can now see it might have had a chance of re-forming — in the Paris of *Les* *misérables* or of Jules Vallès.* Democracy finally broke it up.

The term 'intellectual', which does not correspond exactly to the Russian *intelligent*, was forged during the Dreyfus Affair. But the 'intellectual party' never created a hegemony, not at least prior to the Front Populaire. Besides, intellectual dissidence within French democracy at that time was divided between left-wing and right-wing extremism. Until the Second World War, French culture was essentially literary and artistic — not ideological.

With regard to the Hegelian, left-wing, Marxist-inclined group, it is certainly possible to speak in terms of a German intelligentsia. But even there its links with the state were weaker than in Russia (for the German universities enjoyed true autonomy), and its links with civil society much tighter. As in Russia, in 1848 there was an unsuccessful revolution in Germany. It happened within a more modern society, which Napoleon had already partially liberated from the old régime. The triumphant nationalism that freely took on an ideological appearance in what remained of the intelligentsia, tended of its own accord to weld itself to the civil society and the state. Once the Romantic era had passed, German culture to some extent abandoned the arts, and ideology too; it became learned and scientific. The destiny of Marxism demonstrates the point even better. Marxism succeeded, much earlier and much more completely than in Russia, in embedding itself in the working class — not in order to make the working class rise up against the civil society, but on the contrary, to enable it to enter it. Social democracy became the left wing of the German democratic movement, as an integral part of an enlarged civil society. It sought to take over the leadership of it, rather than to destroy it.

Of the numerous factors which, in France and Germany, made possible the absorption of the intelligentsia into civil society — if it had ever been separate from it — there is one which should be regarded as paramount. Neither in France nor in Germany could an ideology have been established as simple, as complete, as fortified and as organized as the Russian ideology. The cultural environment, more various, more vigorous and more diverse, did not allow it, and was able to combat it and eliminate it. In Germany, it was a question of waiting until the defeat, the breakdown of the Bismarckian balance, and the Russian Revolution, before the re-birth of an

---

* *Translator's Note*: Late nineteenth-century radical French polemical writer and novelist.

intelligentsia which at times drew its inspiration from the Soviet source of ideology, and at others, succumbed to more or less isomorphic counter-currents in the reverse direction. In France it was a question of waiting until the Second World War. The worldwide development of the intelligentsia, at the present time, is a complex phenomenon. In certain cases (in Latin America, in Africa, and so on), it is possible, it seems to me, to make use of a schema analogous to that which applies in the Russian case. Elsewhere, one must take account of new factors, such as the hasty installation of secondary and further education, and the opening of the schools, universities, the world of journalism, etc., to the masses. But in any case, the adopted ideological model — reproduced almost without alteration — is that which Russia prepared in the nineteenth century, and offered to the world in 1917. It had proved itself. Everywhere, ideology, and specifically the Russian model, cuts out and sets apart a portion of society. The intelligentsia does not produce the ideology, but rather is a product of it.

Civil society in Russia suffered, with regard to the state, from a congenital weakness. It had been engendered by it. None the less, the very realization of projects for the development of the bureaucratic state, including public education, benefited the civil society first of all. Once the handicap of serfdom had been lifted, it rapidly developed along the same lines as civil societies in Western Europe. So that, just like them, it demanded an increasing share in the conduct of affairs and, in the end, the liquidation of the old régime. In this political struggle, it found itself competing with the intelligentsia, whose aims it knew, and knew to be incompatible with its own. It thus found itself obliged to fight on two fronts. If at times it agreed to compromise with the intelligentsia, at others it defended itself against that same intelligentsia by seeking the protection or accepting the leadership of the state. This was one consequence of the minor political crisis of the 1860s. Whereas in France the radical elements were revealed in the course of the revolutionary process, in Russia they were gathered and welded together at the start, before the revolution began. In France, the *Ancien régime* was only overthrown because the civil society called on reinforcements from the popular classes — the peasantry and the urban mob — dangerous allies, certainly, but natural ones. In Russia, an appeal to these same classes was made even more dangerous by the fact that, long before the beginning of the revolutionary process, they had been cultivated and perhaps even organized by the intelligentsia, which had turned them quite as much against the civil society as against the state.

This triangular situation (state, civil society, intelligentsia) was never resolved. Any one of the three partners was weakened by a possible coalition between the other two, but was at the same time strengthened by their latent division. This triangle rested on the mass of passive subjects. The régime (the state) wanted to enlarge the civil society by adding to it a part of that mass of passive subjects, and that was also the aim of the civil society. But the intelligentsia wanted to add that mass to itself and make use of it.

It is possible to mark some of the stages of this long struggle.

1. From 1863 to 1874, roughly, the intelligentsia, still in its cradle, vegetated in obscurity and anxiety. The state and the civil society were getting on fairly well together, to their mutual profit. The spread of publicly admissible political positions of good standing was fairly wide, ranging from strict conservatism to a fairly advanced liberalism. None the less, the end of Alexander II's reign found a renewed impatience amongst the liberal left wing, which allowed itself to be to some extent seduced by the chivalresque manifestations of the populist intelligentsia, or which thought of using the latter's terrorist acts as a means of pressure on the government in order to wrest from it a major constitutional concession.

2. The assassination of Alexander II in 1881 threw the intelligentsia back into the outer darkness, and reduced a compromised civil society to silence. There was thus a final moment of glory for the Russian Imperial régime. But to the extent that it remained faithful to the modernizing spirit of Peter the Great, and could accomplish its plans for development without obstacles, the civil society developed at an unprecedented rate. Public education became a mass affair, though that did not work to the advantage of the intelligentsia, which was not up to ideologizing systematically the entire student body, most of whom were left free to pursue a normal career.

3. The beginning of the reign of Nicholas II (1894–1905), thanks to the relaxation which had followed the death of his father, exposed the state of relations between the intelligentsia and the civil society. The former seemed discomfitted. For some time it had enjoyed a cultural monopoly, and had exerted an intimidating influence on

literary, philosophical and artistic affairs. It had constituted a second censorship, much more efficient and awkward than the government censorship for those who did not share its values. Civil society regained its cultural autonomy. Poetry, philosophy, painting were emancipated, and regained the status which had been theirs before 1860, that is, before the birth of the intelligentsia. They escaped from its terrorism. But even more, the intelligentsia found itself threatened in its heart, in what bound it together, in the ideology. That, in effect, was what the revisionist crisis of Marxism really meant. All the same, the defeat was not total. The intelligentsia found amongst its number men capable of saving the ideology, then its values, and finally its identity. From that moment on, Russia lived under a régime of two cultures. The culture of the civil society was complete. It had its base (let us say the non-ideological technicians) and its aristocratic heights, with the poets and philosophers of the silver age. It had its national tradition, symbolized by Pushkin, and its foreign ties. The culture of the intelligentsia, structured around the ideology, also had its base (the 'proletaroid' intellectuals) and its heights, the 'theoreticians' of the ideology. It had its national tradition, deriving from Bielinski, and its foreign ties, centred on German social-democratic culture. The culture of the intelligentsia and the culture of the civil society held each other in mutual contempt. In the refined atmosphere of Moscow or St Petersburg, it was not possible to think of Chernyshevski, Plekhanov or Lenin as having any sort of culture at all. Each of the cultures was expanding rapidly, convinced that time was working in its favour and against the other. For the thinkers of the silver age, the populisto-Marxist tradition was an archaism which the general progress of the country would gradually eliminate. But the culture of the intelligentsia was easily assimilated, as, by definition, was the ideology, and they profited by the education of the masses. They could prove attractive at a time of political crisis.

4. This political crisis began in 1905, and seemed to follow a revolutionary scenario along Anglo-French lines. The different social groups went into action one after another and mounted an attack on the old monarchy. As we now know, the revolution failed. Until the First World War, the three protagonists maintained their separate positions and followed different paths of development.

The state, after the initial impact of the attack, managed to re-establish itself and to halt the revolutionary process. But it did not succeed in regaining the kind of control over the whole of Russia it had had under Alexander III. Stolypin's reforms were the last occasion for forestalling the civil society, by an initiative which should have benefited it — and the state too — but which it was not yet equal to. For the last time, the state justified itself in the spirit of the enlightened despots by substituting its action for the passive inaction of the civil society. After that, it declined. It was capable of impeding, slowing down, halting things; it was not capable of innovating, still less of taking its place at the head of a new project for society, as the Bismarckian state had seemed to do. Its personnel became more and more mediocre. Worse, they became susceptible to ideas emanating from the most marginal sects of the sub-intelligentsia, such as Rasputin and the Black Hundreds.

Meanwhile the civil society was making great strides. It took over the territory abandoned by the retreat of the state. It increased considerably in size. It was able to build up a political machine on a national scale, which was appropriately pluralist and expressed every shade of liberalism, from a fairly vigorous radicalism to the most prudent conservatism. In the economic domain, it took the initiative and left the tutelage of the state. It managed to align itself with important parts of the peasantry — the landed peasantry and the cooperative peasantry. It did not make great efforts to conciliate the working-class élite, nor to organize it.

Civil society needed time in which to absorb the huge, impoverished and uneducated peasantry, and the proletarianized masses gathering in the towns. It was also necessary that the civil society should be able to bring down its rival group, the intelligentsia, which was then working to organize those same classes towards its own ends.

And that it could not do.

As a result, during those years, attention was re-directed onto the intelligentsia so that it became in its own right a subject of study and discussion. Ivanov-Razumnik, to take a typical example, gave a picture of it befitting its legend: the intelligentsia was the conscience of Russia. Conscience in the Hegelian sense, as a social body capable of conceiving the real and of having a conception of itself. A moral conscience, since, in so doing, it was fighting for the good and against fundamental injustice. The history of the intelligentsia became confused with the history of 'social thought'.[4]

More interesting are two attempts to approach the intelligentsia as a social embodiment of common rights, reduced to the ordinary condition of one social class amongst others.

Makhaïski had worked through Polish nationalism, and then orthodox Marxism, before reaching any doctrines of his own, between 1903 and 1908. In *The intellectual worker* (1905), he maintained that knowledge was a means of production and that therefore the intelligentsia was an exploiting class. This new class held itself in place by allying itself with the other working classes, subjugating them to its own capital, which was knowledge, and using them as a manufacturing mass in order to obtain its own ends. Social democracy was the class ideology of the intelligentsia. The notion of a 'classless society' was opium for the exploited working class. In fact, the new class aimed to maintain a statist dominion over the working class, to establish a hierarchical system to its own benefit, and to assume control of the best positions. At first sight, Makhaïski appears to be adopting the cynical, realist point of view of a disciple of Pareto, or, even more, to be expressing a legitimate sense of mistrust about those militants of the social-democratic party who were transferring to the working class those methods of manipulation which their populist elders had tried out on the peasantry. In this way, *Makhaevchina* could be seen as a defensive reaction on the part of the autonomous syndicalist worker, resisting revolutionary penetration. It would have been normal for it to express itself in Marxist terms: the intelligentsia appeared as a parasitic class appropriating to itself the surplus value.

In effect, there were some anarcho-syndicalist aspects in Makhaïski. But they were nourished by an inveterate Bakuninism. He wanted to answer the 'conspiracy' of the intelligentsia with a conspiracy of militant workers, of super-revolutionaries, hidden behind the revolutionaries — to such an extent that his cure came to resemble all too closely the evil he sought to denounce. Makhaïski was an intellectual rather than an enraged worker, who had discovered his own demagogy and hoped to cure it by exorcizing it. His ideas were to encourage Bolsheviks disturbed by scruples, who, following his example, elevated the negative projection of themselves to a power greater than their comrades.[5]

In the celebrated anthology *Vekhi* (*Landmarks*) one can find a certain number of the dissidents of the intelligentsia who took a look back at the moment of regaining civil society. 'The sad task has befallen me', wrote Bulgakov, 'of having to express the opinion that the Russian revolution was a creature of the intelligentsia. Its spiritual direction belonged to our intelligentsia, to its conception of the world, its habits, its taste, its social customs. They, the *intelligenty*, naturally cannot see this, and each one, according to his own catechism, will point to this class or that as the sole instigator of the revolution.'[6]

Of course, he went on, these social groups, the peasantry and the proletariat, could have started to move on their own account, but it was the intelligentsia which provided them with the

ideological baggage, the spiritual armament, and also with the advance-guard of fighters, the armed terrorists, the agitators, and propagandists. It gave a spiritual form to the instinctive aspirations of the masses, filled them with enthusiasm, and acted as the nervous system and the brain for the huge body of the revolution. In this way, the revolution is the spiritual offspring of the intelligentsia, and, as a consequence, its history is embroiled in the historical fate of the intelligentsia.

In *Vekhi*, Berdiaev, Gerchenzon, Struve and Frank dissected it, criticized it, and deplored it. Izgoev sketched out a sociological inquiry into the student body. *Vekhi* was, in effect, a landmark between the old literary intuitions of Dostoevsky and Turgenev, and recent works of the American school of history, which have provided a complete sociology of the world of the intelligentsia.[7]

Yet just as the intelligentsia was beginning to be taken up as an object of study, at the very time when it was being called upon to become self-aware, the intelligentsia was without doubt in the process of changing and disappearing.

In two ways.

On the one hand, it became integrated into the civil society. There was a very rapid increase in the number of students, which accelerated after 1910 (70,000 in 1913), though one cannot really speak of inflation. In an economic world which was taking off, in a society in the process of modernization, and where the third economy was becoming more than proportionately large scale, there was room for everybody. The integrated intelligentsia, that of the liberal professions, lawyers, teachers, engineers, willingly specialized in politics, as did their counterparts in Western democracies, but in *Cadet*, that is to say, liberal politics. There existed, to be sure, a minority of bomb-carrying, gun-toting students, who resurrected the ghost of the 1870s. In fact, though, they did not represent the student body as such, as the homogeneous nucleus of the intelligentsia. The students, who had been officers or officer cadets during the war, were the last opponents of the Bolsheviks.

Nothing gives a better indication of this integration than the semantic alteration in the use of the word intelligentsia. It lost its ideological connotations and took on a wealth of sociological associations. It designated a socio-professional group, at most, that of the white-collar workers. The intelligentsia rediscovered, *mutatis mutandis*, the function intended for it by the Enlightened State, when it first engendered it at the beginning of the nineteenth century as a group specialised in certain tasks, but in no way posing any sort of threat. The difference was that this group neither replaced nor duplicated the civil society, but was now generated by it, as part of the general process of the division of labour. On the other hand, it did become integrated with the revolutionary parties.

When speaking of the intelligentsia, it is important to distinguish between the ideological core and the outer fringes. The intelligentsia was not a political party. Only the core organized itself into a party. But it needed an outer layer which was under its influence if not its direct domination, and which enabled it to influence society 'outside'. The core had an instrumental attitude towards the humanitarian values of the intelligentsia. But the fringes sincerely believed in them, and indeed had to believe in them in order to have the influence the core wanted them to have. The core could be spontaneously integrated into the revolutionary party, but, after the seizure of power, the fringes had to be destroyed.

The revolutionary parties were sociologically derived from the intelligentsia, but they had for some time been recruiting numerous peasants and workers from the classes they sought to win over, as well as a number of marginal *déclassés*. The ideology finished its work of desocialization and homogenization. The intelligentsia lost the contours it had had during the 1860s. The institutionalization of the parties was sufficiently powerful to wipe them out altogether. It was a process which worked all the better, the more revolutionary the party and the more perfect its ideology. The socialist-revolutionary mass party, which was weakly centralized and with only a vague doctrine, touched the liberal world with its right wing. The same with the Menshevik party, locked in its German-style social-democratic position, and perpetually tempted by revisionism. But in the Bolshevik party, the ideology surrounded the militant with a protective barrier, in the shelter of which he could be purged, bathed and re-born as a *new man*, a being apart, with neither father nor mother. Although the leaders belonged by family and education to the intelligentsia, they showed no solidarity towards it. On the contrary, Lenin felt a deep-rooted hatred of the intelligentsia, in the same way as the old intelligentsia harboured a loathing of the civil society, because they had become identical, and liable in consequence to the same treachery.

When the Imperial régime and the revolution came face to face, one can say that the intelligentsia was in the process of disappearing because of the action of two entirely unrelated mechanisms. Either its members, deserted it, left the magic circle of ideology, and, taking root outside it, found their true social reality. Or else, within the circle, the ideology carried out its work of dissolving the original social characteristics, including those of the intelligentsia, in order to endow them with a new identity which existed only in and through the ideology.

It is clear that the intelligentsia could not, by its nature, be a permanent social type. It was, in Russia, a transitory moment in a process which had paved its way with historical pre-conditions, which was crystallized by the ideology, and was finally dissolved by that same ideology. Ideology engendered it, and ideology destroyed it.

7

The New Man

Chernyshevski and Dobroliubov hated and despised the Romantic generation.[1] They charged it with narcissism, and with pandering to states of the soul. The melodious laments of the literary heroes of the forties, torn between an inaccessible ideal of action and idleness in fact, they saw as pure cowardice. They discerned, in the taste for complexity, whether psychological or social, an alibi for doing nothing. What their elders called dialectics, they called phrase-making and hot air. The 'fathers' were rich, but progressive; cultivated, but revolutionary: the 'children' saw in the riches and the culture, of which they were for their part bereft, an unnecessary luxury, a contradiction with progressivism, and an obstacle on the road to revolution.

In order to overcome this difficult division of the spirit, the new generation undertook to 'simplify' itself. Chernyshevski developed his ideas in a dissertation on 'practical philosophy' which summarized the accepted ideas of the sixties in a satisfactory way.[2] He undertook to correct a little book by Lavrov, bearing on moral problems, which relied on a moralized positivism. Lavrov, aware of Western currents of thought, looked towards Jules Simon, Proudhon, Mill and Schopenhauer. Chernyshevski brusquely despatched him back to 'science', that is, to contemporary German scientism.

Science, as he understood it, demonstrated things apodictically. It fulfilled the need for certainty, not only as to the natural order, but also as to the moral and metaphysical order. There was not, in fact, any hiatus between these different orders, since man belonged entirely to the material order. 'Philosophy sees in him the same thing as medicine, physiology, or chemistry.'[3] If there were any nature in man other than his material nature, it would not fail to manifest itself. Which it does not do. 'This proof', he insisted, 'cannot be called into question.' Man eats and thinks: there is more mystery in that than in 'the wood burns and is consumed not'.[4] Materialism (he called it *monism* because of censorship) has been glimpsed throughout the ages by men of genius. 'But it is only in the last few years that our knowledge has made sufficient progress to be able to demonstrate scientifically the justification for this interpretation.'[5] Our chemistry and physiology are in the age of Copernicus. Scepticism is no longer acceptable, nor yet is credulity, both of which demonstrate an insufficient knowledge of the ideas developed by contemporary science. What that science proposes will henceforward be as certain as 'the revolution of the earth around the sun, the law of gravity, and the action of chemical affinity'.[6] It has been verified, proved, demonstrated. 'There remains no possibility for someone who has once entertained [the new ideas] to go back on his tracks.'[7] In the behaviour of the young men of the time, there was no search for truth or quest for wisdom. They already possessed it, ready-made and self-evident. 'The essential character of the philosophical concepts of today is their unshakable certainty, which excludes any insecurity of conviction.'[8] It is easy, in the light of this, to understand his cutting tone, contemptuous of his adversary and of whoever dared to hesitate. Research was not judged to be a merit, but cowardice, stupidity or ill-will. Ideological certainty was rock solid. Its propositions imposed themselves. Something cannot be both seen and believed at the same time. Religious faith deals with the invisible. But ideology deals with things which are visible, tangible and open to the senses. To refuse them is either folly or wickedness, since they are not a question of belief, but of fact. A character in Chernyshevski's novel, *Que faire?* (*What's to be done?*), encounters the ideological hero, Rakhmetov:

> The subject of the conversation matters little; what he said every time was,
> 'It has to be,' and I would reply,
> 'No.'
> He said, 'It's your duty,' and I replied,
> 'Not in the least.'
> After half an hour he ended by saying,
> 'I can see it is useless to go on. Are you persuaded that I am a man who deserves to be trusted?'
> 'Yes, everyone has told me so, and I can see for myself that it is true.'
> 'And yet despite that you stick to your own point of view?'

'Precisely.'
'Do you know what that means? It means that you are either a liar or a scoundrel!'

'He spoke,' adds the author, 'in a perfectly impersonal tone, like a historian seeking, not to wound, but to establish the truth.'[9] Here is the root of the ideological insult, of the 'renegade' Kautsky and the 'Hitlerian' Trotsky. It is a result of the exasperation felt by the ideologist before someone who will not accept what is, for him, patently obvious. Ideology is not a commitment made in full consciousness of risk, and based on the recognized authority of another. It is a recognition verified by personal experience. It is not a faith. It is pseudo-empiricism.

It was in scientific certainty that Chernyshevski saw the guarantee of action: 'When the time comes, the representatives of those who today aspire to transform the existence of Western Europe, remain unshakably attached to their philosophical convictions, and that will be the signal for the coming victory of the new principles in the social life of Eastern Europe.'[10]

Science included anthropology, psychology, morality. There was no free will. 'All the phenomena of the moral world proceed, the one from the other, from external circumstances, following the laws of causality.' Desire was a 'subjective impression'. The will was 'a link in the chain of phenomena and facts joined together in a causal relationship'.[11] Man was thus without responsibility, since he was prompted to act, either from the outside by material circumstances, or else from the inside by his emotional balance, which pushed him spontaneously towards whatever was agreeable, and away from whatever was disagreeable.[12]

Man was an egoist. If one considered an act or a feeling which appeared disinterested closely, one could see that it was based on some notion of interest, of pleasure, or of advantage: of egoism. Chernyshevski offered the following examples: Empedocles threw himself into the crater, but in order to make a scientific discovery; Newton remained chaste, but that was so as to have more time to devote to his research. 'The same can be said of men in politics.'[13] What then was the good? It was the useful. How can one establish a hierarchy of good actions? 'Nothing easier': at the top, the interests of humanity in general, then of the nation, then of numerous classes, and then of less numerous classes. 'This gradation cannot be called in question, it is simply the application to social problems of the axioms of geometry.'[14] Such was scientific morality. It was simple and it was complete. It offered 'a ready-made theoretical answer to almost all the important questions of life'.[15] Its nature ensured that a man was able to follow it, since all he had to do was to make an elementary calculation as to the degree of usefulness. 'Thinking means discriminating with the help of memory between the different combinations of sensations and images prepared by the imagination, those corresponding to the needs of the thinking organism at a given moment; choosing the means of acting; and choosing the images by means of which one could arrive at a particular result.'[16]

And yet, man acts wrongly. He does not follow his own interests. The peasant masses in Russia do not rise up to seize the land, associate in *artel* and *mir*, and apply a populist programme. They do not see where their interest lies. They have not received a suitable education. On the contrary, they have been perverted by the external conditions, by the domestic and social horrors of Russia. *What's to be done?*

This was the title of the novel which Chernyshevski wrote in prison, and which served as a guide to the perfect life for three generations of revolutionaries. It is a novel about education. A young girl, Vera, brought up in a family of villains, becomes emancipated through contact with an 'advanced' student. A prostitute is redeemed, under the guidance of an even more advanced student. Vera goes from the first student to the second during the course of her development. And they all have their eyes fixed on a youth who stands as the living embodiment of the fullest possible development: Rakhmetov is the ideal *positive hero*.

Chernyshevski has constructed a fictional form for his scientific anthropology. Since, being in prison, he could not apply it in reality, he applied it, so to speak, in fiction. This other reality is built up by the 'images prepared by the imagination', without real reality interfering. That way everything can proceed in accordance with the theory.

There exists an entirely satisfactory state of being. Science proves that it is coherent, desirable and possible. Thought, clarified and guided by scientific discoveries, can conceive this world in every detail, with an absolute degree of certainty. This world is not a utopia, since it corresponds to the most fundamental spontaneity of the human being guided simply by the rule of pleasure and self-interest.

It does not demand virtue, nor any sort of self-discipline — only fidelity to one's nature, to one's impulses, and to one's clearly understood interests. For the man awakened by science, this world exists as a precise vision, like a plan laid out in front of him.

But the same science which presents him with the perfect city, also shows him the historical obstacles in the way of its emergence in this world. The conflict between the two cities is much more than a moral struggle. It is an ontological struggle in which that which has no right to exist (because it is not natural, because it does not conform to the plan, and to the rule of interest) is hindering the existence of that which ought to exist. The Russian population could be divided according to its degrees of knowledge, and according to the degree of resistance to that knowledge. Thus the heroes of *What's to be done?* go in stages like to many steps up the ladder of perfection, which the heroine Vera scaled one after another.

The frontier between the two cities is present within each individual, for each man bears the marks and distortions left by his education. He is not immediately prepared to live according to the simple rule of rational calculation, and is not ready for the happy life. The student Kirsanov has just taken the painful decision of allowing Vera to leave him for Lopukhov. The struggle was hard, but full of internal satisfaction. For one must struggle against oneself in order to attain happiness. Lying on his couch, Kirsanov thinks to himself:

Be honest, that is, calculate properly: don't forget that the whole is greater than the part, which means, for you, that human nature is worth more than each of your own aspirations taken separately...One single, elementary rule, that is the code of laws for the happy life. Yes, happy are they who are born able to understand this simple rule. As for myself, I am fairly happy in this regard. Doubtless I owe a great deal to my training, more probably, than to my nature. Little by little, this will come to be the general rule, laid down by education and circumstance. How easy it will be for everyone to live, as it is for me now.[17]

Two tasks present themselves to the new man: to re-educate himself and to re-educate society, in the spirit of the new science.

Chernyshevski gave a full-length portrait of the perfect hero who had accomplished the first of these tasks: Rakhmetov. Rakhmetov was the 'saint', the model for Plekhanov, for Lenin and the Bolsheviks.

He is worth considering in more detail. That is what Chernyshevski himself desired. His novel bears the sub-title: 'A tale of the new men'. Chapter XIX: 'A man unlike other men' goes to the heart of the message.

Rakhmetov is descended from a rich landowning family of Tartar origins. In Russian literature, to have Tartar blood is often a mark of an energetic, strong-willed, tough character, a stranger to the nonchalant bonhomie of the Russians. It is also a sign of a fundamental strangeness with regard to people, a tendency to be a lone wolf. At fifteen, Rakhmetov broke with his family, after an 'oedipal'-seeming conflict. Brutal father, delicate mother; falls in love with a concubine of his father's, etc. It was then that he fell under the influence of Kirsanov who was to him 'what Lopukhov had been to Vera', the initiator, the one who introduced him to the new life.

It is worth emphasizing that his regeneration is in the first place intellectual. Since there exists an absolute truth, guaranteed by science, the culture of the past has no value except in so far as it contains elements of that truth. That is why, in his philosophical dissertation. Chernyshevski proposed throwing overboard almost the whole of inherited and contemporary culture:

The specialists who are committed to the concepts of contemporary science find that, in books like the ones written by those gentlemen whom everybody refers to, and by their predecessors, there are really too few fragments of learning to be picked out, and that reading them is a pure waste of time, with the only result being to clutter up the brain. One could say the same of moral science. The contempt they have for the anthropological principle [Aesop's term for materialism] deprives them of all merit.[18]

The arrogance of the ideal hero, in the novel, is identical. '"In each subject," he declared, "the fundamental works are not many; all that the others do is repeat, pad out and play about with what has already been demonstrated more fully and more clearly in these few fundamental works. So one should only read these. Any other reading is a useless waste of time."' There can be mixtures: in the same work, absolute truth cheek by jowl with flagrant error. The task for the mind would in that case be to separate the true from the false without wasting any more time. It can also happen that the mixture itself proves interesting, as a very general image of the world, in which good and ill can also be found side by side. In this way, Rakhmetov, going through Vera's books, and having swept aside

Macaulay, Thiers, Guizot and Ranke, suddenly came across the works of Newton and picked up a particular volume: *Observation on the Prophecies of Daniel and the Apocalypse of St John*. In effect, it is 'a classic example of a mixture of idiocy and intelligence'. 'It is a question', he goes on, 'of historical importance and general application, for this "mixture" occurs in all events without exception, and in nearly all books and nearly every mind.'[19] Being able to separate the true — or the good — from the false — or the evil — with infallible discernment, is the first result of intellectual illumination. On the evening of his meeting with Kirsanov, having wept and cursed 'that which is condemned to perish', and blessed 'all that is called upon to live', the young convert asked his mentor: 'What should I begin my reading with?'[20] Kirsanov initiates him by giving him a list of titles. Having bought the prescribed books in the French and German bookshops of the Nevski Prospect, the Admiralty and the Bridge of the Police, Rakhmetov shut himself up for three days and nights and read without stopping.

What did he read? Feuerbach, 'the father of modern philosophy'; the materialist trinity of Vogt, Büchner and Moleschott; and doubtless others which are not specified. As soon as he was possessed of the theory, he turned towards action. This hunger for reading did not last beyond 'the first few months of his regeneration'. When he judged that he had acquired 'a systematic way of thinking suitable to the principles which seemed to him correct', books lost priority: 'I am ready for life.'[21]

Thus, knowledge opens the gateway for salvation. But afterwards, one must train all one's faculties to bend one's body to the science thus acquired, and to dedicate to it the powers which will make it effective. Rakhmetov submits to a diet based exclusively on meat (doubtless under the ultra-materialist influence of the later Feuerbach). That, combined with gymnastics, soon transform him into an athlete of almost superhuman strength. He practises a strict and at times penitential asceticism, aimed at forging his will, making him insensible to suffering, and freeing him from set habits. In fact, the will must bend easily and effortlessly to the 'code for a happy life' dictated by the new science. That is why the efforts of frequently heroic self-discipline are not attributed to merit but to calculation. They are not sacrifices, but simply detours in view of a more substantial gain. Asceticism is a form of rational hedonism. The essential thing is to be free of ties. Rakhmetov accidentally falls in love. He catches himself up: 'I must curb this love: it will tie my hands. They are already tied and they will not easily be undone. But I will manage it. I must not love.' It is a question on which he is very strict. One must, in fact, be at the disposal of humanity, and act as an example to it:

I do not touch a drop of wine. I never touch a woman... It must be so. We are asking for a total enjoyment of life for men, and our lives must bear witness that we do not ask it to gratify our own private desires, that it is not for us, but for men in general. What we say comes from principle, not prejudice, from conviction and not from personal convenience.[22]

So no sentimentality. Rakhmetov is simple, ordinary, deliberately banal. Chernyshevski is clearly repudiating the flamboyant revolutionary typified by Turgenev in *Rudin*. Rakhmetov is organized and precise, conducting his life according to a regular timetable. He dresses like everyone else. He speaks as little as possible, without taking any trouble, like a scientist demonstrating something, and not an orator aiming to convince someone. He speaks 'without any personal feelings', revealing his point of view but not imposing it. If, in fact, the one he is speaking to does not yield to the demonstration, then it is because he is not ready, not 'developed', and there is no point in trying to force things.

Rakhmetov's friends are filled with a reverential fear of him. He instils fear by his very perfection. But his ideal is shared by many. From the outside, they appear strange. Are they not just like a new 'sect'? They form a united group, strong in their shared knowledge, behaving according to the same morality, animated by the same love for what they call their 'fiancée'. This fiancée appears in dreams or visions to Vera Pavlovna. It is the revolution, though it can have other names, such as the love of man, or equal rights. Once, after having shown her the history of men from the beginning, it revealed its first manifestation on earth, in Rousseau's Nouvelle Héloïse.

It is since then that my kingdom has existed. I do not yet reign over a great many subjects. But my kingdom is growing rapidly and you can already foresee the time when I will reign over the whole of the earth. Only then will men become fully aware of my beauty. Now, those who know are not numerous enough. But their mission is to make others know, and to save themselves so as to make others know.[23]

In other words, the world is a school. Those who have been freed by knowledge must spread that knowledge and free others in their turn. Their type is 'recently formed'. They have had fore-runners, but these felt themselves isolated and helpless, and gave themselves up 'either to dejection, or to exaltation, to romantic flights of the imagination which deprived them of the essential characteristic of this breed of men, namely, sang-froid and a practical mind, and lucid, passionate activity'. Six years earlier, this type had not existed. In a few years to come, people would be calling to them: 'Save us.' For 'society must be re-educated, so much is certain'.[24]

'He who has re-educated himself, re-educates others.' Thus the standard of the New Man will soon be the universal norm. 'The golden age will come, the iron age will pass.' Even today society, the world, contains the seeds of its own salvation. These new men are few in number, but they brighten up lives which, without them, would shrivel up and crumble away. 'They are (in the masses), like theine in tea, like the bouquet of a full-bodied wine, they are what gives it its strength and its savour, they are the flower of the best, the driving-force behind the driving force, the salt of the salt of the earth.'[25]

Chernyshevski is crucial to the history of ideology.

Through Bakunin, Bielinski and Herzen, Russian thinking had been turned towards action. But, without discovering a point of application, it found itself suspended. Increasingly radical, since it found nothing to stop it in reality — which kept on slipping away from it — the men of the 1840s were in an uncomfortable position. What a gulf between words and deeds! What impotence!

With Chernyshevski and his friends, the situation was reversed. It was understood that action came first, that one was militant, so that action then turned towards thought to find the goal, the means and the moral justification. Speculation, which had flowed fairly freely in the first generation, suddenly dried up. In effect, there was no quest, but adherence to a truth which imposed itself without any debate. The philosophical moment lies in the decision to seek for the truth. The ideological moment lies in establishing that truth as fact. After that, all that remains is to draw the consequences. Chernyshevski's distinctive tone, all arrogance and brutality, comes from an intuition of the simple, the obvious (a single time, a single principle, and an elementary one...these phrases constantly recur), from the joy felt at this *eureka*, and the irritation experienced towards the deliberate, interested blindness of those who refuse to see.

The extreme poverty of the Chernyshevskian gnosis is striking, if one compares it to the luxuriant idealist gnoses flourishing in Russia at the beginning of the century. Baader, Hamann, Schelling and Boehme all fed the Slavophiles and Herzen too, who delighted them in his youth. The imaginary religiosity of mystic free-masonry still lived in them. But Chernyshevski hated religiosity, was suspicious of sentiment, and stigmatized the beautiful soul. Of course, the 'fiancée' can be seen as a gnostic myth. But how impoverished! It is a Fourierist phalanstery,* activated by technological progress. Paxton's Crystal Palace, decorated by the illustrators of Jules Verne: that is the scope of its utopia. Science, taken seriously, clips imagination's wings. All it allows is extrapolation. Moreover, imagination is unnecessary, since matter itself, through its own impetus, has taken charge of the future of mankind. The movement is everything. Action accompanies it, but must not anticipate it beyond a certain point.

But, although cut off from the abundant mythologizing which usually accompanies it, Chernyshevskian gnosis still manifests its typical structure. The world is presented as a mixture of good and evil elements, with the evil imprisoning the good. Salvation is obtained through knowledge. This knowledge is by nature rational, and is complete, powerful and absolutely certain. It gives the true picture of the world, and the key to destiny. It shows that the world can be saved, that all it needs is to be arranged in a different way, with the good elements — which represent the future, progress, life — separated from the bad elements, which belong to the past, to reaction and death. As in Mani, there are two principles and three times. The agents of this separation are the New Men. Awakened by knowledge, they have access to a new life. Rakhmetov is the modern (thus, 'scientific') type of the Manichean Perfect. Awakened by his gnostic initiation, he has become part of the saved and saving section of humanity. Having conducted the separation within himself, he lives the ascetic life of the elect. He is chaste. He is maintained by the community, who feed and clothe him in exchange for his permanent active militancy. He practises a morality which is not the common morality, but which is internal to the gnosis itself,

---

*Translator's Note: A socialistic community as envisaged by the mid-nineteenth-century thinker, Fourier.

and which only the gnostics who have understood it practise amongst themselves. Others are irresponsible, directed from the outside. His task consists in putting forward the gnosis, in resolving difficulties in the strict application of the doctrine, in setting an example, and in drawing the awakened and the initiated up to his heights.

Yet in one way he differs from the Perfect. He has no rites, no transcendance. The cosmic mixture of classic gnosticism referred back to a metaphysic which engendered religious acts. Materialist cosmology makes man one with the universe, but an immanent, mechanistic universe, as revealed by science, from which there is no escape. Rakhmetov did not prevail through rites and prayers. His field of action was society, and his technique, politics.

At the centre of Chernyshevski's preoccupations lies the problem of morality. In order to ensure a certain innocence in revolutionary action, he went to Europe to seek the most strictly deterministic materialism possible. Man is acted upon, therefore he is not responsible. If he acts consciously, it is in recognition of the necessity for his action. Freedom is necessity understood (the definition is Lenin's). The question of freedom becomes displaced and depends on knowledge. Knowledge being certain, the conscious act is unequivocally directed by it. Human action rediscovers, in knowledge, the innocence it had possessed when it was unconsciously determined from without. Whether conscious or unconscious, man unloads his responsibility onto something other than himself. Where then can there be any fault? Only in the case of a man awakened to knowledge, who does not submit to its injunctions. The fault may be weakness. If that is the case, then it is because the training has not been carried far enough to quell completely the mechanisms normally at work in the unregenerate world. But, more generally, the moral fault can be reduced to a fault in logic. The awakening cannot have been complete, or the recovery quite finished, since the knowledge has been badly understood or lost sight of. Sinning means refusing to learn, or understanding badly, or forgetting. It is not a question of repentance, but of self-criticism; nor is it a question of being forgiven, but of going through a sort of exam to see whether the poor pupil can 'keep up', if he should be allowed to try again, or if he should be expelled.

The resolution of the moral problem was crucial for this generation. There was a clear and obvious need for action. These young men had emerged from the obscure depths of Russia. They had been brought up in submission to the Church and to the Tsar. There were only a handful of them. How were they to overcome the crushing sense of guilt which had paralysed their elders, even though they had been better equipped? How could they act without being tripped by the obstacle within?

Man naturally desires to know: now he knows. It seems as if the conversion to certain knowledge and introduction into the circle of revolutionary Perfects engenders such a joy that it overshadows the problem to which conversion had been the solution. In order to act, it had been necessary to conceive the perfect life. But the conception of the perfect life tends to be self-sufficient, and to possess criteria which are not those of political efficacy. Through an initial break with reality, politics becomes a by-product of the doctrine, although the doctrine had been shaped so as to make the politics possible. All the same, in 1860, neither doctrine nor politics had yet been defined. The doctrine was assumed to exist — since it was Science — but it had not been worked out. The guarantee that it was true was enough for the time being. Chernyshevski's political programme was vague and eclectic. He was still in a line of descent from the Enlightenment. His anthropological principle derived from Holbach. Lenin praised him for his resulting 'anti-feudalism': violent hostility to serfdom, advocacy of education, self-government, liberty, defence of the peasant masses.[26] Chernyshevski was a defender of the rural community, and, as such, an ally of the Slavophiles, a left-wing Slavophile, rather like Herzen. At the same time, he was a partisan of 'bourgeois' progress and of capitalist development as long as they did not damage the chances of the rural community. He was also a Westernist. He was thus far removed from classic populism, for whom public enemy number one was less Russian backwardness, than 'capitalism'. Chernyshevski was the undisputed master of the younger generation, not through the programme, which could change, but because of his conception of political action: it represented salvation. Before being able to reply to the question *What's to be done?* the young man desirous of entering the true life must first enter the revolution.

That is why a type of ideological revolutionary developed in the 1860s, before an ideology had been worked out — the conviction that it could be was enough — or any coherent political programme. For a few years here and there militants sprang up without any doctrine and without any programme, practising action for action's sake, and combining the most aggressive confidence in themselves with a momentary ignorance of any doctrinal reasons which could justify it.

8
A Dream of the Party

Chernyshevski had formulated the individual ethos of the revolution. The revolutionary life, in Russia, became an *imitatio* of Chernyshevski and his hero Rakhmetov. Just as in Jacobin France, the ideologist, as a type, preceded the ideology. In the Europe of the Restoration, there existed a model of the secret society in the Carbonari, a model which Russia had imported early, since Carbonarism was one of the characteristics of the secret societies which were formed under the Imperial régime, when the civil society was still too weak to carry out its revolution. Young men, with the example of the Jacobins before them, wanted to substitute themselves for this ineffectual civil society. Not so the *party*, the invention of which is a specifically Russian achievement, and which saw itself not as a substitute for the civil society, but simply as the offshoot of the ideology. None the less, it did not wait for the ideology to be complete and fully rounded off before attempting to establish itself. In fact, the party was dreamt of long before it had any actual existence. None the less, from the time of its 'oneiric stage', it took on definitive characteristics. 'One must dream', wrote Lenin.[1]

The Party was dreamed by two men together, one a young delinquent called Nechaev, and the other an old man infatuated with him, Bakunin. In contrast to Herzen, who said he still believed in the revolution but no longer loved it, Bakunin had kept his revolutionary fervour in the simplest possible formula: destroy, deny, denounce, that was enough. The dialectical rhythm would do the rest. Then, in 1869, in his Swiss exile, he met a young man of twenty-six. It was love at first sight. 'They are wonderful, these young fanatics', he said; 'believers without any gods, and heroes without any fine phrases.'[2] Fine phrases — for a long time that was all the old man had produced.

Nechaev told him that he was the head of a powerful, disciplined organization, ready to give the decisive thrust to the peasant revolution in Russia, according to a programme which Bakunin recognized as his own, and which he summed up in the following words:

Total destruction of the State-legal world and of all the so-called bourgeois civilisation, by means of a popular, spontaneous revolution directed by an imperceptible and anonymous collective of partisans committed to the total liberation of the people from all oppression, securely united in a secret society acting always and everywhere towards the same end and according to the same programme.[3]

This society, this party, was what Bakunin had been dreaming of for thirty years. He knew that there had existed for some years in Russia small groups of violent young men, ready for prompt and summary action. In 1866, they had attempted to assassinate Alexander II. When Bakunin beheld Nechaev, he saw in him the fruit of his long vigil. *Nunc dimittis!* He adorned Nechaev with all the highest revolutionary virtues: seriousness, passion, indomitable strength, absolute devotion to the cause. Of course, none of this had any basis in fact. The action, the holy action which had so fired the garrulous old man with enthusiasm, existed only in dreams. The fantasm is the only reality in the whole affair. Several historians have tried to reconstruct Nechaev as he really was. But he was nothing. Dostoevsky saw very well that the thing was much more serious in intention than it was in action. In terms of hard evidence, all that one has is the body of a student, and the *Catechism of the revolutionary.*[4]

Certain parts of this celebrated text bear the imprint of Bakunin. These parts are the most fugitive. Bakunin the anarchist can be seen above all in the last section, entitled 'The Society's attitude towards the people', which presents his political programme. The party (or Society) has as its goal 'the complete liberation and happiness of the people'. This can only be achieved by means of 'a popular revolution which will destroy everything'. This should not be seen simply as meaning the overthrow of one political régime by another, and the substitution of one state for another state. That, in fact, is 'the classic Western model', and is not one to be followed. The revolution should destroy 'all statism' and suppress all the statist traditions maintained by the regime and the Russian class structure. 'Our mission is total, terrible, general, unmerciful destruction.' Reconstruction will be the future concern of 'the movement and of the popular masses'. That is why, in waiting for this to come about, one must unite with the elements of the popular masses which, ever since the foundation of the Muscovite state, have never ceased to protest, 'not in words but in deeds', against everything associated with the state, nobility, bureaucracy, priests, merchants, rich peasants and speculators. 'We must unite with the tough world of the criminals, the only authentic revolutionaries in Russia.' Along with this *open* appeal to delinquency, another characteristic can be linked with Bakunian negativism: 'The revolutionary despises all doctrinairism, and has renounced all the profane sciences, leaving them to future generations. There is only one science which he understands, the science of destruction. To that end, and to that end only, does he now study mechanics, physics, chemistry, and even medicine. There is only one goal: the swiftest possible destruction of this monstrous régime.' This is a renunciation of knowledge which is outside the Russian revolutionary tradition. Extending utilitarianism to the scientific domain and making the revolution into an absolute but empty value was not something with which the revolutionary could agree. Delinquency and cultural nihilism were doubtless realities of the revolution, but they could not be its principles. That is why Lenin was to be so fiercely hostile to Bakunian anarchism — just as he would be to the moralism of the seventies. The second he saw as an inconsistency — for the knowledge contains the morality, and so the morality cannot claim autonomy — and the first as a contradiction, since the 'gnostic' revolution cannot declare itself to be agnostic. It must have a programme. Even if that programme has to be kept hidden for tactical reasons, it must be there, in principle, if only implicitly. And behind the programme, a whole doctrine.

All the rest of the *Catechism of the revolutionary* belongs to the permanent stock of Russian revolutionary ideas, as it was preserved from Chernyshevski to Lenin.

Little needs to be said about their organizational plans. Secret societies have nothing specifically Russian about them. They proliferated in the Europe of the Restoration. The basic element of the secret society, the circle, had been for a generation past the normal framework for the social life of the young men in Russia. Did it have its origins in the *collegium pietatis* of eighteenth-century Germany? However that may be, as early as 1820, the *krujok* had become an observable fact, in which some young men were grouped around one of their number, some striking personality who gave his name to the group. Thus one spoke of the Stankevich circle.[5] In England, attending the same schools, playing the same games, doing the same sort of jobs, in short social homogeneity, provided the basis for the formation of a group. Ideas counted for little, and were politely avoided. In Russia, social and sometimes even national origins were a matter of indifference. The German circle of piety aimed exclusively at moral perfection, the Russian circle at ethics and a way of life — to which was soon added the political dimension. In the 1860s, the circle changed character. Previously, it had been made up of amateurs from different age groups and different backgrounds; now it became predominantly composed of students. The university offered no official setting for student social activity. The *krujok* became the meeting-point for students who had come from the four corners of Russia, the rendezvous for comrades who felt lost in the big city, and a place to exchange the means of existence, as well as ideas and pamphlets (both frequently subversive). There was no longer any question of struggling towards an elevated and disinterested way of thinking, but rather of parcelling out the developing subculture, of which Chernyshevski and his paper provided the most coherent expression. Once the university realized what was going on, there was a crisis, and it closed for a time, while numbers of students were expelled. Immediately the circles became the matrices of revolutionary action. Thus after 1863 the first terrorist groups took on the same form of organization as the 'friends of wisdom' had had half a century earlier.[6]

The circle became clandestine. In the *Catechism*, the society sought to be secret: 'the workings of the organisation are kept hidden' from any outside eye. Inside it, 'one must exclude any discussion not relevant to the goal'. Such an arrangement was important, since it was aimed at stopping the circle from degenerating into a debating club, following the familiar tendency of the Russian intelligentsia. The only topic of conversation would be 'tasks'. This brought about the introduction of a conventionalized language, whose use was obligatory. It was in these circles that the future *wooden language* was first forged. It created a setting for and *link between* the members, fulfilling, one might say, a 'religious' function. That is why the baring of the soul is made obligatory, with total transparency towards the director of conscience: 'The entire frankness of members with regard to the organiser is a condition of the success of the enterprise.' This is what is left of the *collegium pietatis*:

mutual confession with a view to moral progress.

This is the crux of the matter. Entry into the circle — or the party — is a consequence of a total reorientation of life, of a *metanoïa*, an entry into a new world called the revolution. The revolutionary leaves his father and his mother, he cuts all his old ties: 'He has no personal interests, no private affairs, no feelings, no private property. He does not even have a name. Everything in him is absorbed by one single interest to the exclusion of all others, by one single thought, one single passion — the revolution.'

The vocabulary is easily transposable to a monastic calling. The monk too leaves everything behind, even his name, to devote himself exclusively to the One Who is. One simply has to substitute Bakunian negativity (Destruction, or equally, the Revolution) for divine positivity. The revolutionary renounces self and becomes absorbed in the revolutionary *nada*. That is why mystic accents and vocabulary are so appropriate to this negative mysticism. But this distorted, left-wing mysticism was sufficiently like religious mysticism to impress Dostoevsky who, depicting Stavrogyn to be like the revolutionaries he had known, placed him, so to speak, on the fringe of sainthood. He put atheism (the negation of God in terms of Bakunin's universal negation) at the penultimate stage of the spiritual ascent, and much higher than the calm, oblivious faith of ordinary religion. Blok too was to draw effects of mystico-revolutionary depth from the music of the fires. In the *Catechism of the revolutionary*, this Byronic demonism achieved the final form of its politicization, but as politics it retained the ambiguous moral prestige of the high romantic perversion, and all its power of attraction. Russian religiosity is ready to believe that there is a communion in evil as well as in good, a communion of sinners, just as there is a communion of saints. Which provides a major temptation for adolescent souls.

All the same, if one reads the *Catechism* carefully, one can see that its structure is not that of Christianity in reverse, but of a Manicheism 'the right way round', and in its natural setting. For the Christian retreat is not a break with the world, but a commitment to a law which that world does not keep. It is not a disavowal of civilization and the natural order; rather, it seeks their restoration. The revolutionary, on the other hand, has 'at the foundation of his being…not only in words but in deeds, broken all links with public order and the whole civilised world, with all laws and customs and social conventions and with all the moral rules of this world. The revolutionary is its implacable enemy, and he only continues to live in it so as to be all the more sure of destroying it.' He does not look on the world with a benevolent and forgiving eye:

The revolutionary does not go into the political and social world, into the so-called educated world, and lives in it only in the faith of its swift and utter destruction. He is no revolutionary if he feels pity for anything belonging to that world. He must be able to destroy situations, relations, or persons which are of that world: anything and everything must be, for him, equally to be hated.

Like the Perfect, the revolutionary sorts through the impure mixture, contributing to the destruction of the bad elements, so as to allow the release of the luminous particles which are imprisoned by them. To this end, he must go everywhere, so that no corner of the cosmos escapes the purifying war:

The revolutionary can and indeed often must live in society, passing for something he is not. The revolutionary must penetrate everywhere, into all the middle and lower classes, into the merchant's shop, into the church, into the landlord's mansion, into literary, military, bureaucratic worlds, into the secret police (*The Third Section*), and even into the Winter Palace.

But, though he may go everywhere, the revolutionary does not mingle; his nature is different. He belongs to another society. He is not tied by common morality because there is no common morality. He does not recognize the morality of this 'monstrous society'. He is, on the other hand, tied absolutely to the morality which follows from the doctrine and which is current among those in the know: 'He despises and detests the present morality of society in all its motivations and all its manifestations. For him, something is moral which contributes to the victory of the revolution; immoral and criminal which hinders it.' Chernyshevski's simple calculation — which in him remains buttressed by a general rationale — utility — becomes detached from humanity taken as a whole to become the political calculation (the revolution), directly applicable to the revolutionary alone, indirectly to others, solely according to political dictates. The unity of morality is abandoned, but this does not entail amorality, because in the new society the alternative morality is all the more restrictive.

This alternative morality is described in paragraphs 5, 6 and 7 of the second part. It is a harsh and pessimistic morality. 'The revolutionary is a lost man.' Pitiless towards the state and 'educated society', he should expect from them 'no pity for himself'. How could he? The gnostic is involved in a conflict which is greater than himself, and there cannot be any mediation between two ontologically opposed parties. 'Between him on the one hand, and the State and society on the other, there exists a state of war, visible or invisible, but permanent and implacable — a struggle to the death.' There can be no compromise because there is no middle way. 'Them or us', as Lenin would say.

This morality forbids love and friendship. First of all because the state of war does not lend itself to it. Then also because natural feelings are part and parcel of the world to be destroyed, and so should, like that world, be fought against. 'The ties of kinship, friendship, love, gratitude, and even honour should be extinguished in him by a single icy passion for the revolutionary cause.' Dostoevsky would take up this characteristic. The 'right to dishonour' was one claimed by his demons.[7] This demanded the ascetic training of which Rakhmetov provided the example.

None the less, this morality is not entirely lacking in eudemonism, since the revolutionary is concerned with advancing the ideal world. That is his only compensation: 'There is for him one single delight, one single consolation, compensation, and satisfaction: the success of the revolution.'

This being so, then despite the fact that revolutionary morality applies in two ways, depending on whether it is dealing with the party or the world to be destroyed, in its principle, it is one.

It depends on political calculation. Clearly revolutionaries would free themselves from the common morality with regard to non-revolutionaries, but it is a mistake to believe that, amongst themselves, this morality reasserted its claims. It had been usurped by another morality which dealt only in terms of justice and injustice. Whence the paradox which has baffled so many — that the revolutionary holds the party sacred, and yet apparently behaves towards his comrades with the same cynicism as he deals with those he has vowed to destroy. The only difference being that, amongst revolutionaries, it is a previously established fact that one is behaving thus out of a general principle — although the manner in which this principle is applied may remain undetermined — whilst with regard to the others, it is a question of pure and legitimate duplicity. The first were conjured to observe a pact containing the clause that there is neither truth nor justice (there is only the interest determined by the given moment), and, when finding themselves duped, had the satisfaction of having entered into such an agreement, and not having any grounds for complaint. The others, who believed that there was truth and justice, were rightly punished for having seen them invested in things which were totally condemned.

Paragraph 3, 'general rules of the network', is conceived thus:

Individuals chosen by the circle to become members of a section, undertake, at the first meeting, a) to act indissolubly, collectively, submitting everything to the general opinion and not to leave the section except to go, on the orders of the committee, into a rank further on in the organisation; b) to have in mind only the interests of the society in all their dealings with the world outside.

It is a constitutive pact of the society of *perfects*. These, through this pact, lose their autonomy. They accept that they shall be 'a means or an instrument for carrying out the undertakings and attaining the goal of the Society'. The executants have no need to know the 'nature' but only the details of the action whose execution is entrusted to them. 'In order to rouse their energy, a false explanation of the nature of the action should be given them.' There is no more room for *philia* within the party than anywhere else: 'The degree of friendship and of devotion and the other obligations towards a comrade are determined solely by the extent of their usefulness to the cause of the genuine, destructive revolution.' Another feeling replaced friendship — solidarity. 'That is where all the strength of the revolutionary cause resides.' Friendship is a feeling belonging to the old nature, solidarity to the nature which is fighting it. Friendship seeks the good of the friend, solidarity, the good of the revolution. Solidarity, which is presented as being greater than mere friendship, can in fact be opposed to friendship, which lacks any real consistency:

When a comrade falls into difficulties, the revolutionary, in deciding whether to save him or not, must take into consideration, not his own personal feelings, but only the good of the revolutionary cause. In consequence, he should weigh up, on the one hand, the comrade's contribution, and, on the other, the expenditure of revolutionary forces necessary to save him; his decision will depend on which side the scales finally come down.

Solidarity, although it may be clad in emotional terms, is by nature intellectual. It depends on the consideration of doctrine, of the secrets of the world, and the general situation of the struggle. There is not the sort of equality between solidary revolutionaries that there is between friends. The party is organized according to a hierarchy of knowledge and of observance. The inferior is instrumental to the superior, who makes use of him judiciously for the best results in the cosmic struggle; paragraph 10:

Each comrade should have to hand some revolutionaries of the second and third grade, that is to say, not fully initiated. These should be considered as a fraction of the revolutionary capital placed at his disposal. He should expend his portion of the capital economically, with a care to extract the greatest possible profit from it. He should consider himself as capital destined to be spent for the sake of the victory of the revolutionary cause, but a capital which he may not dispose of alone and according to his own wishes without having the agreement of the whole Society of fully initiated comrades.

The party is constructed hierarchically, in a symmetrical way, and conceives 'monstrous society' as being set out in similar categories for the purposes of destruction. 'The first category comprises those condemned to death without delay.' The party has drawn up a list of them in order of relative wickedness. For just as love does not dictate the choice of comrades, hatred has no part in designating the enemy. Such hatred may be 'partially useful' in helping to stir up revolt in the people. But the initiate holds himself above it. His guide is 'the degree of usefulness which this death would have for the revolutionary cause'. A second category comprises unpopular individuals, provisionally spared, so that their existence might impel the people to revolt. In the third category is 'the rabble of highly placed donkeys'. 'They must be exploited in all possible ways and manners, they must be fooled, misled, and, once in possession of their dirty secrets, made into our slaves.' Then come 'ambitious politicians and liberals of every hue'. One should pretend to follow them, whereas in fact one is 'enslaving them, taking possession of all their secrets, and then compromising them to the hilt, so that no retreat is possible, and then using them to stir up trouble in the State'. Then there are the 'doctrinaires' and other chatterers. They should be provoked into making dangerous public declarations which would send most of them to their doom and 'give to a few an authentic revolutionary form'. Finally, women. The other half of the human race is subjected to a general division. On the one hand, the futile, the stupid, the soulless, committed to a common fate. On the

other, the good and devoted, some of whom 'have not yet attained
an authentic revolutionary consciousness', while others are 'fully
initiated'. These can enter into the hierarchy of the society.

Such then is this little seven-page booklet which was made public
in 1871, during the trial of Nechaev's followers, having been drawn
up in 1869. In the intellectual history of Russia it can be compared,
from one point of view, to Chaadaev's first *letter*.

This *letter* fell like a bombshell of common sense and precision
into the sham debate which the Slavophiles, Westernists and devotees
of 'official nationalism' had patched up between them. It shocked all
parties, who pretended to be replying to each other when in fact
they were trying to reply, without naming him or wanting to broadcast the fact, to Chaadaev. The *Catechism of the revolutionary*
expressed precisely, and with a dangerous candour, the very core of
the ideas which, having first arisen with Chernyshevski, cemented together the first circles of terrorists, Ishutin's circle, and Karakozov's.
Who was the author? Nechaev or Bakunin? Nechaev's role was to be
a vehicle for this fund of common ideas. Bakunin's role was perhaps
to hold the pen — a notion which Nechaev's literary incapacity
renders at least plausible. Bakunin also introduced some personal
notes which meant little or nothing to the young Russians — old
Hegelian reminiscences, negativity, the anarchist programme.
But Bakunin was above all enchanted by the dark Romanticism, the
black Byronic air which lent the whole affair a demonic aura to
which the old aesthete of the 1840s was much more susceptible than
the young brutes who sought to exploit his illustrious patronage.
A lyric impulse uplifted the exile of Lake Leman, an impulse which
prompted him to give a classic literary form to a state of mind which,
in Russia, was immediately concerned with expressing itself in
practice rather than in analysing itself philosophically. But, in doing
so, he ran serious dangers of public exposure.

II

Dostoevsky was quickest off the mark. Ever since the publication of
What's to be done? he had felt that something new had appeared in
the world. In response he had hastily published *Notes from underground*, which marked the appearance of something new in his work.
The revolutionary change had provoked in him a philosophical and
artistic change.[8] The magnificent succession of great novels, *Crime*

and punishment, The idiot, The possessed (which directly reflected the Nechaev affair), and even *A raw youth* and *The brothers Karamazov*, became an ever-increasingly profound meditation on the spirit of Chernyshevski and of Nechaev, its origins and its consequences for Russian history, and its metaphysical implications for the destiny of the world. By a notable stroke of good fortune, the creature had hardly been born before it was described and understood in its innermost recesses. And yet, Western historians like Venturi and Confino charge Dostoevsky with inexactitude and injustice. 'Mythology distorting history, with individuals, such as Bakunin and Nechaev and the others, being replaced by archetypes; facts, by psychological schematisation; chronology, by lists of principles; history by literature or metaphysics.'[9] It is a strange charge. It was a useful exercise to reconstruct what happened, but such was the nature of the event that it emerged as abnormally prosaïc and empty. Chernyshevski's novel is of no literary value. Nechaev was nothing but a young delinquent without any style, a far less poetic figure than the Schillerian brigands which made Bakunin go weak at the knees, or than the least 'horse-thief' of popular Russian folklore. And yet it was this literature, this type of man which usurped — as Dostoevsky foresaw it would — the history of Russia. The only way of coping with the phenomenon was to provide its true metaphysical dimensions, to expose the ineffable depths beneath its insignificant surface.

Dostoevsky presents the *new man* as a being of little substance, without any depth, dedicated in the novel, to the role of ridiculous stooge, relegated to the margins of the plot. It is the sociological *new man*, the figure typical of the Russian intelligentsia, which he characterizes in this way. Thus Lebezniatnikov in *Crime and punishment*, Doktorenko and Keller in *The idiot*, the 'students' in *The possessed*, the seminarist Rakitin in *The brothers Karamazov*. But in an unexpected leap, behold the same 'ridiculous man', still in his sociological garb, projected to the centre of the novel, Raskolnikov, Terentiev, Stavrogin, Ivan Karamazov, and the main plot being that of their damnation (in the confirmation of their emptiness) or of the birth of their new being. This movement is already present in *Notes from underground*, which is the matrix of the second Dostoevsky. He merged a satire of behaviour with metaphysical terror. He mocked the emptiness of the new type of man, and then, becoming serious again, saw a great emptiness opening at the heart of the world, so

immediately and so urgently, that he wrote to the heir apparent*
that *The possessed* 'is almost a historical study'. And indeed,
since then, Russia has not ceased to read her history in its
pages.

Dostoevsky castigated revolutionary doctrine and training, which
he saw as a methodical impersonality, a fundamental error in human
nature, which is woven out of the irrational and based on freedom.
That was fairly easy to perceive. But his genius was needed to depict
the failure of this asceticism without transcendence to which the new
man had bound himself. From behind the bars where they had been
confined, their suppressed impulses came back at them from outside,
in the form of the most fearsome hallucinations. Dostoevsky was the
first to see the revolutionary movement as a forcing-house for
madness. Raskolnikov's and Terentiev's nightmares, Ivan's devil,
Svidrigaïlov's and Stavrogin's suicides followed a precise psychological
logic which he saw to be new, and linked to the revolutionary
modernity. He penetrated that sector of the psyche in which the new
man thought he had triumphed over natural *philia*. Impassivity,
detachment, utilitarian calculation and a declared autonomy all
cover, as Dostoevsky showed as early as *Notes from underground*, a
subterranean dependence on a fellow-being. He conceived of this
dependence from a metaphysical point of view: declared atheism
leads to the most shameful idolatry. Shatov loves Stavrogin: 'Shan't
I kiss your footprints when you've gone?' Pyotr Verkhovenski rolls
at his feet: 'Stavrogin, you are beautiful...You are my idol...You
are the leader, you are the sun, and I am your worm.' But he analyses
this dependence from the psychological point of view as well, as
being the expression of a rather shabby homosexuality. The underground hero vacillates endlessly, with regard to his aggressor whom
he admires and envies, between the most exasperated hatred and
the hope of a mutual tenderness, of loving victory.[10] Love of a
woman, the image of the other, is inaccessible to such men. It is easy
for them to forbid it to themselves, since this false mortification
diverts attention from the inexpressible love they feel for their
fellows. And yet Dostoevsky had not read the letters which Bakunin
wrote to Nechaev, and which are filled with the same loving bitterness and whining resentment as Wilde had for Bosie, or Charlus for
Morel:

---

*Translator's Note: Alexander Alexandrovich, subsequently Alexander III.

I loved you deeply and I love you still, Nechaev, I believed in you strongly, too strongly...how deeply, how passionately, how tenderly I loved you and believed in you. You have managed and found it useful to kill that confidence in me, so much the worse for you. Besides, how could I have thought that a man as intelligent as you and as devoted to the cause as you still seem to me to be even now, in spite of everything that has happened, how could I have thought that you could have lied so impudently and so stupidly in front of me, whose devotion you could never have doubted.[11]

Dostoevsky had glimpsed the general outlines of 'the cult of personality'.

Since Dostoevsky wrote, it has been through him and what he discovered that Russian consciousness has taken the measure of the ideological phenomenon. But it must be added that Dostoevskyism itself was not entirely free from the same poison, and that, as a result, it could not prove an antidote to it.[12]

Dostoevsky accepted the Slavophile inheritance in its entirety. He was filled with the same hatred for the West. He saw the new revolutionary spirit and the importation of corrupt Western principles as being linked together, the one a consequence of the other, to such an extent that Chernyshevski and Nechaev were purely a result of Catholicism, liberalism and of Western socialism, all of which were equally abhorrent. Russia's distress could not come from herself: it came from outside, and Russia itself was free of all responsibility for it. Dostoevsky also inherited Slavophile Christian utopianism, the dream of a good world, so good that it would have no need of laws, property or money, because everything would be regulated by love. Finally, he inherited the conviction which goes beyond utopianism, that this world existed implicitly and even actively in the depths of the Russian people, and that it only needed to be seen for it to reveal itself.

But these hackneyed themes were supported, in Dostoevsky, by a strangely seductive theology, which was to have an enormous influence on Russian thought at the turn of the century, and ultimately on world thought. It spread parallel to Communist ideology, to which it appeared as a sort of Christian double, openly opposed to it and secretly its accomplice. Dostoevsky did not attempt to oppose any sort of corrected reason to the deranged reason of ideology, but rather (and here too he is in the Slavophile tradition) a generalized irrationalism. So he leaves ideologists with the right to be the representatives of reason, contenting himself with the riches of the heart

– without being able to resist the pull towards the voluptuousness of feeling and the delights of hyper-emotionalism. Dostoevsky's Christianity is kin to Kierkergaard's, as Chestov has noted.[13] The two could be taken to represent the two extreme manifestations, transplanted into foreign soil, of the same German pietism. But Dostoevsky's Christianity, lacking in philosophical rigour, is inconsistent in other ways too. It is more Christism than Christianity. Dostoevsky was not sure of his belief in God. His spokesman, Shatov, said he believed in Russia, in Orthodoxy, in Christ, but 'in God?'[14] His Christ-figure is typically romantic, halfway between Hegel's Christ and Nietzsche's, and fairly close to that of Michelet.[15] 'If it were proved to me', he wrote, 'that Christ could not be true, I would rather have Christ than the truth.'[16] Which would mean following an imposter. Detached from the Father and separable from truth, the Dostoevskyan Christ was also separable from the notion of omnipotence. It was an ideal Christ-figure, a beautiful, detached and impotent soul, of which Prince Myshkin stands as a suitable ikon. The Idiot's compassion multiplies the catastrophes which surround him, Tykhon's does not stop Stavrogin committing suicide, nor Zozima's, Karamazov's murder. The Dostoevskyan version of Christianity is tainted with gnosticism in the Manichean autonomy it confers on evil, the condemnation it lays on every viable form of civilization, its ethical anarchism, and the empty angelism of the Messiah.[17] It is opposed to the Greek tradition, because it denies the cosmos. It is opposed to the Jewish tradition, because it rejects the Law, preferring anomy. It is opposed to the Christian tradition, because it lacks the Incarnation, its Christ seeming more a divine emanation. But this deviant Christianity sought to regain its balance in nationalist messianism. The West was doomed, but Russia bore within herself the future of humanity: so one part of the cosmos was saved. Russian man, in spite of all his faults, was closer to God than a German with his 'virtue', or a Frenchman with his 'vices': ethics once again became possible, with Russian-ness as the criterion of good. In the end, the only incarnation of Christ was the Russian people, the 'Russian Christ'.

Dostoevskyan morality appeared evangelical. Traditionally, theological morality distinguished between the Commandments to be found in the Old Testament, and the teachings contained in the New. The first were obligatory, the second were addressed to those who already obeyed the first. In Dostoevsky everything happens as if the

Commandments were optional, and the teachings obligatory. Thus, stealing is excusable, but ownership is absolutely forbidden. Sexual intercourse inspires horror, especially within marriage. On the other hand, continence is obligatory, occasionally tempered by rape. Through his genius, Dostoevsky lent substance to the pietist nostalgia for an actual, present kingdom of grace, freeing man *hic et nunc* from his earthly condition. He set an example of moral Marcionism (by putting the two Testaments in opposition to each other) to which the Russian Church, both through long-standing tradition, and above all through recent influences, was vulnerable. This, with his messianism, was one of the two sources of his anti-Semitism.[18] This led him into a confusion between Christian extremism and revolutionary extremism which has continued to spread ever since.

The theme of the demon is not specifically Dostoevskyan. It too is an import from the West. The generation of Pushkin and Lermontov had meditated on Milton, Byron and Goethe. All the same, in Dostoevsky, the demon was not simply an expression of Titanism, as it was in France, or England or Germany. He was well and truly the devil of theology – not a superman, but an angel. This opened the way for the interpretation of two themes which Dostoevsky presented as examples of his Christianity. First, humility: it is proof of the greatest humility to declare oneself to be the origin of one's sin. One is not a sinner because one has succumbed to temptation, but because one is a sinner at heart. This is what Stavrogin declares, in his confession to Tykhon. Then, charity: it is more charitable to prefer the salvation of the whole of humanity and finally of the cosmos to one's own salvation. Thus with Ivan Karamazov. But to be oneself the cause of one's sin is not the act of a man, but of a devil, that is of an angel, fallen to be sure, but an angel none the less. This declared humility plays the beast in order to be an angel, and so satisfy the most reprehensible kind of pride. This could explain why so often in the Dostoevskyan literary tradition – of which there are still traces in Solzhenitsyn and in Maximov – Russia is freely and gladly compared to a hell. Because even a hell is preferable to our ordinary earth – at least it is an angelic place. As for the act of charity, it consists in depending less on the personal salvation promised by Christianity, than an *apocatastasis*, the *restitutio ad integrum* of theosophical speculation, which comprehends within it both the salvation of devils and the extinction of evil. Ivan Karamazov prefers *apocatastasis* to salvation, so once again playing the angel.

These notions may seem strange. None the less, they do illuminate essential aspects of Dostoevskyan politics. First of all, he dealt openly with the revolutionary theme by means of the demonic theme. The revolutionaries invaded Russia and were driving it towards the abyss just as in the Gospel of St Mark the demons driven out by Christ entered the Gadarene swine. All of Dostoevsky's work after *Notes from underground* can be seen as an attempt at exorcism, an anguished *vade retro*.

All the same, however detested this demonism might be, it is still secretly preferable to the world as it is. In fact, Dostoevsky could not escape a certain fascination with these young men, since, after all they were Russian. Is not extremism in good as well as in evil one of the characteristics of Russianism? Is not this violence in evil, which the revolution foreshadows, preferable, in spite of everything, to the utterly despicable West? The practical 'materialism' of the West is more to be condemned, in Dostoevsky's eyes, than the theoretical materialism of the revolutionaries, since the former expresses a state of satisfaction with the created world which Dostoevsky feels to be totally insupportable.

It follows that Dostoevskyanism is surreptitiously drawn towards the revolution, at the same time as loudly condemning it, because it is through the revolution that the world will be destroyed and *apocatastasis* brought nearer. Dostoevskyanism reproaches the revolutionaries not with making the revolution, but with not understanding what they are doing, and perhaps because of that not making the revolution as radically as necessary. He would always defend them against the 'bourgeois'. In his last years, Dostoevsky felt a reawakening of his sympathy with socialism. Merejkowski, Hippius, Philosophov were delighted with the *depth* of a revolution which the vain and superficial West was incapable of understanding. Blok would be associated with the Cheka's undertakings. Berdiaev would end up in patriotic admiration of Stalin.

The turn-of-the-century expression of Dostoevskyanism was symbolism. It amounted, over and above materialism and populist scientism, to the romantic speculation which had fed the first Russian generation. To Baader and Boehme they added, alas, the theosophy of Steiner. On the other hand, there was an attempt to invent a new religion which was in the way of being Bolshevism with a bit of soul added: this was the *Seekers after God* movement. At the same time, some Bolsheviks were trying to think of a new religion which would complete Marxism: this was the *Constructors of God* movement. In their encounters — which, incidentally, did not amount to anything — one can see recapitulated, in a slightly comical way, a great part of the intellectual history of the nation, at least that which split up in Herzen's youth and tried to come together again on the eve of the revolution.[19]

N.B. In siting ideology in a religious crisis, it was natural to concentrate principally on the fate of Christianity in Russia. One should none the less not overlook the important number of Russian Jews who joined the revolutionary movement — so many that the Russian people, just after the revolution, felt that they were living under Jewish rule, just as earlier they felt they had been living under German rule. It is usual to explain this rallying to the revolutionary cause in terms of Jewish nationalism and a response to anti-Semitism. But this is not enough to explain the transition, so often related in memoirs, from the most pious Judaism to a strict ideology which insisted upon a denial of Jewish origins — that is, a practical anti-Semitism.

It would be interesting to know whether there was a Jewish crisis which corresponded to the European crisis in Christianity. I am not equipped for such an inquiry. All the same, in reading Scholem, it does not seem impossible that there does in fact exist a parallel history. Its principal landmarks would be: (1) the diffusion of the Kabbala; (2) the Sabbatarian crisis and its consequences (all faiths seem to have been shaken in the seventeenth century, Catholicism, Protestantism, Russian Orthodoxy and even Judaism); (3) the growth of Hassidism, with its sentimental and speculative aspects, which is comparable to that of contemporary German pietism; (4) the weakening of orthodox Talmudic Judaism, following the division of Poland; (5) the conditions in which, under Russian rule, the secularization and cultural emancipation of Jewish youth were carried out.

It is up to others to say whether such a parallel has any meaning.

9
A Sketch of the Party

The 'Chaadevaevian' admission revealed by the *Catechism* put the Russian revolutionary movement in an embarrassing position.

Nechaevism was pure activism, without any sort of programme. Nechaev rejected all books. He wrote: 'The thinking capable of serving the people's revolution is worked out solely in revolutionary action and must be the result of a series of acts and practical demonstrations, directed always and in every way towards the sole end which is destruction.'[1]

The cult of action led to a theory of the uselessness of theory. 'We are not going to let ourselves be hamstrung by any of the revolutionary cant which is being bandied about so much just now by these champions of the revolution on paper. We have lost out in words in every time; words are not important to us, except when, immediately following them, one senses or sees the action to be taken.'[2]

But it was an untenable position.

The Russian revolutionary movement was in a dilemma. Either the revolution was one imbued with justice, and so could not recognize itself in Nechaev, who gave off the suspect glow of a sordid delinquency. Or else, charged with a gnostic hope, the revolution had to create a new earth and new heavens; in this case, morality cut itself adrift from the common good to aim at the good specified by the doctrine, a *via positiva*. Without that, the terrorist act would appear, if not criminal, at least gratuitous, absurd and dangerous to the cause of the revolution. So either the revolution had to become moral, or else purify its system and reintroduce positivity: two avenues which the revolutionary movement was to explore, each in turn.

Lavrov's *Historical letters* came out in instalments in 1868 and 1869. They were immensely popular with a young generation preoccupied with finding rules for living: 'Our tears of idealist enthusiasm fell on this book... It gave us an immense thirst to live and die for noble ideas.'[3]

Lavrov's achievement is entirely contained in a chapter in the *Historical letters* entitled 'The price of progress'.[4] A disciple gives us an idea of the grounds for the general enthusiastic response:

Reading this book convinced me that our present social organization, by the mere fact of birth or other circumstances, independent of the will of its individual components, the members of society itself were inevitably distributed in two unequal groups. One of these, numerically very small, was in a privileged position and able to enjoy – to the detriment of the others – all the good things of life. Whereas the second, which made up the great majority, was destined to eternal misery and to labours beyond the scope of human capacity...Mirtov [Lavrov's pseudonym] eloquently pointed out the vastness of this unpaid debt which weighs on the conscience of the privileged group towards the millions of workers of this generation and those of the past...[5]

This was the crux of the matter. Humanity had paid too dearly for the privilege of thinkers who, closeted in the quiet of their studies, talked about progress. 'I would ease my responsibility for the bloody cost of my own development, if I were to use that development to diminish this evil in the present and for the future.'[6] Lavrov played on the sense of guilt of the privileged classes. This feeling was fostered by a number of other things quite unrelated to privilege, but when a young man who feels guilty is at the same time in a privileged position, he tends, not unnaturally, to unload the whole burden of his guilt onto that privilege. This can be seen as a psychological mechanism (a type of 'rationalization'). The end result would be to 'over-determine' a political attitude because of a bundle of confused psychological forces, and so to give it a solidity and a force of conviction far above anything its intrinsic political merit would have earned.

So one must pay one's debt. This is a long way from utilitarian calculation and cold-blooded revolution. Lavrov totally rejected the laws of history and objective development. He set himself up against such 'objectivism' as the defender of 'subjectivism'. It almost seems a replay of old controversies. In the thirties and forties, Bakunin, and then Bielinski, both moved from a cerebral Hegelian love of 'morality' to the sort of Schillerian revolt which they themselves had condemned a few years earlier. Lavrov's approach was more ponderous, and his turn of mind more pedantic. He wanted to refute, point by point, the implacable and amoral determinism of 'materialist' revolutionary circles. He thought that moral values could neither be eliminated nor deduced scientifically, and that the protest against suffering was independent of 'objective conditions'. Besides, there were no objective conditions: knowledge, in these matters, is based on unconscious emotions, or rather, on consciously chosen *ideals*. The 'subjective factor' of which 'developed' men are the bearers, can perfectly well stand in opposition to the so-called laws of history, and change the course of events. From the mass of facts and events the 'subjective factor' selects 'what is important and significant'. The direction of history is thus dependent on an ethical ideal. 'The development of our moral ideal in the past life of humanity is for each of us the *only* meaning of history.' Lavrov defined his ideal in these terms: 'The physical, intellectual and moral development of the individual; the incorporation of truth and justice in social institutions.'[7] What should one do? That is the question which 'critically aware thinking' men should ask themselves. They would change the world gradually, replacing religion with science, and custom with the rational edifice of the law. The populists of the 1870s were conscious of themselves as being these thinking men.

The *Historical letters* were certainly revolutionary. Few works were to recruit so many volunteers for the militant life. But at the same time, they tended towards the anti-ideological pole of the movement. There is very little utopianism in the *Historical letters*. Lavrov put no faith in the Slavophile and Herzenian myth of the peasant community. The fundamental argument is the acknowledgement of an injustice. Society, and notably Russian society, has not respected distributive justice, because the share is not equally divided between those classes which benefit from progress, and the others. It has not respected contractual justice, because the developed classes have not paid their due for benefits received. Lavrov is a revolutionary, but of a classic kind of revolution, aiming at the re-establishment of a long-lost equilibrium, a sharing of wealth that would be equal. This element of natural justice, pre-dating ideology and more fundamental than it, remained a permanent element in populism, and even in Russian social democracy. Until it became weighed down with ideology.

Lavrov arrived in Paris a year before the Commune. Thus he was, at one and the same time, an 'apostle of the Revolution', according to a liberal Russian witness (Stakenschneider) and a 'typical liberal', according to another Russian witness (Sajin), who was a friend of Nechaev's. But in Paris, the new Herzen of the new populism, confronted with the Commune, experienced the same shock that his predecessor had undergone in 1848, and this shock produced the same results. He became disgusted with the West. He became wary of the germs of liberalism which he carried within him. The Paris Commune was, he wrote, a great event in world history: the 'unknown' people (the workers) had attempted an experiment in state organization and had turned towards a federation of self-governing communes. This is just like Marx: he was ahead of him in his vision of the Commune. The Lavrov who, in London and Zurich between 1873 and 1876, composed the weighty deliberations of *Vperiod* was not the same Lavrov who had written the *Historical letters*. All that mattered was the total regeneration of society through the coming revolution. Science must replace religion. Liberty is a means, and happiness is the end. In 1876, Lavrov set out his programme. It could not have been more radical. He would nationalize the press. He would close all schools. The bourgeois world (here he was judging by the Swiss model) seemed to him in complete disarray. In Russia, where the possibility of a social and political revolution was becoming clearer, one must on no account become allied to the liberal movements. Russia would not be parliamentary. The role of the intelligentsia was to separate out a revolutionary phalanx which would prepare, and make propaganda for, the living forces of the people. At that date, he was close to Tkachev. In 1917, he would have been a maximalist or a left-wing S.-R.. He would have opened the door for the Bolsheviks. None the less, even in the most extreme revolutionarism, he would no doubt have preserved his ethical position. He became ideologized, but never to the point of relinquishing that irreducible kernel.[8]

Mikhailovski's case is not very different. He reached his zenith as a publicist a little later. His influence was considerable just around 1890. He propagated, in Russia, the ideas of Haeckel and, in particular, of Spencer, who for some years had been moving to the forefront of the intellectual stage with a fresh assortment of key ideas: evolution, social Darwinism, positivist scientism, all in the context of a victorious capitalism.[9]

Mikhailovski's celebrated article, *What is progress?* (1869), is based, like Spencer, on a certain 'Baer's law': progress, in an organic world, goes from the simple to the complex, from incoherent homogeneity to coherent heterogeneity. Whence a sort of law of three states. Humanity first experiences an individualism without social cooperation (that was the past), then (where we are now), social differentiation and the alienation of the individual in a multitude of autonomous spheres of activity, and finally (in the future), a *subjectively anthropocentric* age. This is characterized by a conscious return to individuality, but within the framework of a fully accepted and desired social cooperation. Within the regained organic social unity, the individual could be, willy-nilly, peasant, craftsman, artist and scholar, according to what was needed and what he was capable of.

This point of view had the advantage of furnishing a certain scientific caution to the old Slavophile themes. In fact, the peasant community might well be inferior in its 'level of development' to Western society, and still be superior to it in its 'type of development', since it allowed within it organic exchanges between men, and since it would only need a little modernizing push to make it the exemplary matrix of the *subjectively anthropocentric* age. This was one of the reasons for Mikhailovski's success.

In a series of articles which he wrote between 1875 and 1876 (*The struggle for individuality*), Mikhailovski acknowledged a loss of confidence in 'formal' guarantees of freedom, and a nostalgia for the medieval forms of social life. In the Middle Ages, human relations had not been reified. Man had an immediate relationship with his fellow. Capitalism, after the atrocities of primitive accumulation, does not free the individual. It must not be given its head in Russia. 'The worker question, in Russia, is a *conservative question*, since the answer is simply to keep the means of production in the hands of the producers.' Mikhailovski was writing thus under the influence of the first book of *Capital*. Having learnt the high cost of capitalism, he refused to pay the price. But while he was thinking about Marx, Mikhailovski was meditating on Tolstoy. Like Mikhailovski, Tolstoy rejected the inexorability of the laws of history, and placed first importance on the 'ethical point of view'. He too took less account of the *level* of development than of the harmony of that development, which could better be seen in a peasant than in an agonized intellectual. What Tolstoy discovered by the light of religion, Mikhailovski proved with the rigour of science. But Lenin was perfectly justified in taxing him with Romanticism and in calling him a reactionary in the 'historico-philosophical' meaning of the word, since Mikhailovski 'tried to measure the new society by the old patriarchal yard-stick and sought to find a model for it in the old order and in traditions which are entirely unsuited to changes in the economic order'. Keeping a measuring rod from the old world in face of the coming world, and thus suggesting the existence of a fixed scale of values, put Mikhailovski out of the running.

Besides, Mikhailovski discovered disturbing implications in organicism. Darwinism appeared to him in a pessimistic light. Evolution leads to the worst and not the best. If, as Haeckel asserted, perfection of the whole entails perfection of the parts, then society is the natural enemy of man. 'I declare that I would struggle against this superior individuality [society] which threatens to engulf me. Its perfection means nothing to me. It is myself I want to perfect.' Developed capitalism offers the perfect model of this sort of organic society. Mikhailovski wants no part of it, preferring a less organized society based on 'straightforward cooperation', consciously accepted. He is thus opposed, not only to Marx, but to Durkheim. At the very end of his life he returned, half consciously, to the earliest from of German Romanticism. Love, he declares, is a nostalgia for completeness. The division of humanity into two sexes, like any division, and in particular the division of labour, robs man of that wholeness which makes up perfection. The Banquet myth is dear to us for two reasons: 'Firstly, it shows us clearly the superiority of hermaphroditism over the diamorphic sexual organism; secondly, because it points out, equally clearly, that sexual love is a form of sickness.' Mikhailovski backtracked swiftly along the course of Russian intellectual history right up to Schelling and Baader.

Scientism, for him, was never anything but a fashionable garment. When the intellectual fashion changed, and the European consciousness of the 1890s turned towards spiritualism, neo-idealism and irrationalism, Mikhailovski's ideas were in perfect accord with this new direction. It was not that he ceased to be 'progressive', nor even perhaps revolutionary, but that he was these things for 'naïve' reasons.

Lavrov and Mikhailovski invented ethical motives for embracing revolutionary action. Whether they appealed to a sense of guilt, like Lavrov, or to vaguely scientist considerations, like Mikhailovski, they were both based on a traditional awareness of justice and injustice. Russian society was sufficiently Christian to have kept this awareness, and sufficiently unjust, by the criteria of the nineteenth century, to make that awareness a particularly guilty one. It was because of Lavrov and Mikhailovski that young Russians entered into revolution: because revolution was the good. But it was not because of them that they stayed there, because the revolutionary good was not that for which they had become revolutionaries. They needed to apprentice themselves to new motives, which were not ethical, but theoretical. Thus from the zero point of Nechaevian nihilism, one proceeds from the ethical to the ideological stage of the revolution, and there, inevitably, one encounters Marxism.

II

Capital met with a response in Russia, a country Marx regarded with horror, earlier than in the countries to which it was addressed, and with which the work was concerned.[10] The first book of *Capital* was translated in 1872, five short years after it had appeared in German, and fifteen years before the English deigned to translate it. The Russian translation was begun by German Lopatin, who had become celebrated in an attempt to get Chernyshevski freed from his Siberian exile, and continued by Danielson, who declared himself a convinced Marxist. The terrorist Kravchinski wrote a novel whose aim was to spread among the workers, in fictional form, the theory of surplus value. As early as 1865, Tkachev called himself a disciple of Karl Marx, whose ideas 'are become common amongst all honest, thinking men'. Mikhailovski, it is true, turned towards Marx only to turn his back on him. Lavrov, the moment he had escaped from Russia, made contact with Marx and filled his *Vperiod* with thoughts on the 'objective laws of development'. In a letter to Marx dated 25 October 1880, the executive committee of the *Narodnaia Volia* told him that *Capital* had been, for some time, the daily handbook of the Russian democratic intelligentsia. It was as much a lie as the phantom organization that Nechaev boasted of to Bakunin, but in both cases, it is the fantasy which is significant. Bakunin himself held the theoretical writings of his great adversary in the highest possible esteem, subscribed in principle to historical materialism, and offered to translate *Capital* into Russian for him.

The facts are all the more peculiar in that nobody — not Marx, not the revolutionaries, not the Russian government — thought that there was capitalism in Russia. The censor who allowed the publication of *Capital*, one Suratov, thought that the work was directed solely against the Western social order, and that the Russian social order could have, in this regard, an easy conscience, since it had never espoused the principles of *laissez-faire*, and since it had 'carefully protected the well-being of the workers'. The imaginary frontier drawn by the Slavophiles between Russia and the West was what lay behind this unknown censor's opening of the real frontier to this quintessence of all the 'poisons of the West', so convinced was he that the Russian soil could not, by its very nature, be contaminated.

On the question of the entry of capitalism into Russia, one must guard against the dichotomy between 'feudalism' and 'capitalism', which has no meaning outside Marxist dogma. In the nineteenth century, the idea of capitalism was not restricted to the rigid terminology of *Capital*. It allowed of wider and vaguer interpretations, all to do with Western modernism. Capitalism was one of the words which the nineteenth century used to describe itself.

By this token, Russia, in so far as it participated in this modernism – and it had been working hard to do so for several centuries – also participated in 'capitalism'. The state pushed it in that direction, and at the same time set obstacles in its path. But there was no system to oppose to capitalism, nor did capitalism present itself as a system either. Such marked intervention by the Russian state can be explained by the need to fulfil military and imperial duties in the difficult conditions of an ignorant and poverty-stricken country. The state substituted itself for civil society, not in principle, but from necessity, and it was afterwards, but only afterwards, that it made a virtue of that necessity. In the second half of the nineteenth century, it was the state itself which laid the emphasis on modernization and on the competition of innovatory initiatives between representatives of the administrative machine and private individuals. The state itself felt that too authoritarian an intervention was merely a temporary measure until a more satisfactory state of affairs evolved. In its state of mind and in its outlook, Russia was closer to Europe than at any previous moment of its history. Of course, there were vast areas which were far removed from modernism. The bureaucratic machine was, as such, incompatible with it, not in its feelings, which were willingly modernist, but in its very existence. None the less, all the travellers, whether they were Russians visiting the West, or French or English in Russia, bear witness that there did exist, between

Western and Eastern Europe, some sort of *continuum*. In this way, capitalism meant the world as it was, or more precisely, the direction in which the world was going, during the second half of the century. It was a world against which a certain part of the Russian intelligentsia had always resolutely set its face. The Slavophile tradition laid down a difference in essence between Russia and Europe. It imposed a geographical dichotomy between good and evil, echoed in the historical sphere, with the good as the Russian past and the evil, the European present. But there was also a part of the state which profited from these oppositions, and which, by its very essence, was destined to become foreign to its own work of modernization. To the extent that the state was successful, Europeanized Russia was bound some day to reject the machine which, in order to Europeanize it, had fixed itself in a non-European mould. The only true frontier between Russia and Europe was the form of its state. Thus there were a good many functionaries who favoured an attitude which delighted in the difference, and lent this frontier metaphysical solidity. The state made use of the Slavophiles, and the Slavophiles put their hope in the state. And when this opposition was carried over into secular areas, the populists in their turn did not fail to look to the state. Herzen and the young Chernyshevski called upon Alexander II to be the Peter the Great who would bring about their utopia. In the same way, the state, which had been sufficiently aware to give a religious colouring to its political antipathy to the European world, managed, confronted with the populists, to give it an economic colouring. It was protecting Russia from capitalism. And that was why it allowed the horror of capitalism to be exposed, in authorizing publication of Dr Marx's great treatise.

Walicki notes that Marxism did more than simply influence populism: it provided its principal frame of reference.[11] Marxism made it possible for the revolutionaries, who had not been able to come to grips with reality, to grasp it in its totality as a unified entity. *Capital* taught them to recognize their primary enemy, and to organize their recognition conceptually, as a coherent body. They still retained the Slavophile habit of seeking in the West the origin of the ill that was overwhelming Russia. They remained determined to derive this ill from some single principle, though it was sought this time in political economics rather than in theology. *Capitalism* was substituted for *filioque*. None the less there is a disparity between the two processes of catastrophe, the one which the Slavophiles derived from *filioque*, and the one which Marx derived from the formation of *capital*.

The first was abstract, evanescent, the other concrete, fed by the very development of reality, daily visible in the world around. The one was without any real force, the other possessed an incomparable dynamism. This was another reason which pushed the Russians precociously towards Marxism: the wicked world, as apprehended by Marxism, is depicted as a permanent assault. This lent revolutionary action a particular urgency. We must act now, because 'capitalism' is imminent. Finally, Marxism gave to the atheist generations a certainty equal to that which the believing generations had placed in the most sublime of dogmas: it was scientific.

The rooting of Marxism is an environment so foreign to that in which it had its birth could not fail to deflect it into directions unforeseen by its founder. In his Russian disciples, Marx found the first 'Marxists' — and it was in vain that he warned them that he himself was not a 'Marxist'. In their hands, *Capital* became a systematic exposé of evil. From that time on they would know against whom and thus why they were fighting. They were delivered from nihilism. But Marxism provided them with a rational tool infinitely more powerful than the primitive materialism of Chernyshevski. Their commitment was first of all an intellectual conversion, before it was a political one. In fact, they used Marxist arguments to maintain a programme opposed to that of the International. They made absolute the Marxist critique of the 'negative aspects' of capitalism and bourgeois democracy. They were not prepared to accept the thesis that capitalism, for all its cruelty, still represented the greatest step forward in human history. Walicki remarks that their vision of capitalism was, by and large, non-Marxist, since they considered it to be essentially a regressive process, but using arguments and a vocabulary borrowed from Marx.[12] The old Manichean turn of mind had subjugated the most powerful of rationalizations.

III

In Tkachev, the Chernyshevskian spirit met for the first time with the spirit of Marxism. Tkachev was of the same generation as Nechaev. As a student, he read Chernyshevski's *Sovremenik*. Picked up in a student riot, he spent the autumn of 1861 in prison, along with some hundreds of his comrades. He was seventeen. In subsequent years, he was frequently locked up. It was then that he made his famous declaration, according to which only the liquidation of everybody over twenty-five would be able to save Russia.[13]

At that time, he was already in possession of his programme, which was not to develop any further. It was, in a word, 'equality in fact'. It must not be confused with political or judicial, or even economic equality, for it is 'an organic, physiological equality, conditioned by the same education and by shared conditions of existence'. Tkachev was peddling a Communism in the old utopian tradition.

'The problem of the distribution of resources would become a fact when all people were unconditionally equal, when there would no longer exist between them the slightest difference, neither intellectually, nor morally, nor physically.'[14]

This egalitarian Communism is not primarily an economic solution. It is 'the final and only possible goal of human society' and at the same time, the 'supreme criterion of historical and social progress'. Because, like a good disciple of Chernyshevski and Nechaev, Tkachev saw the law of history and moral law as one and the same: 'Everything which brings society nearer to this goal is progressive, everything which takes it further away, regressive.'[15]

It was the role of the intellectual élite 'to find in itself, in its knowledge, in its superior intellectual development, in its moral and cultural conditions' the fulcrum from which to overthrow the established power. Tkachev did not lean towards the populist or Slavophile idealization of the people.

'The idealisation of the uncivilised mob', he wrote in 1868, about Reshchetnikov's peasant novels, 'is one of the most widespread and dangerous of illusions.'[16] The masses did not have the capacity, nor even the desire to liberate themselves. They had no knowledge. Those with knowledge were the 'men of the future'. In 1868 he drew up a portrait of one of these which corresponded at every point to the Chernyshevskian model. The man of the future avoided romantic attractions. 'Neither ascetic, nor egoist, nor hero', he was like an ordinary man, with a desire to be prosaic in the way that had already been stressed in *What's to be done?* It was the idea that counted, not the feeling: 'Their distinctive characteristic consists precisely in the fact that all their activity, and their entire way of life, are determined by an aspiration, by a passionately-felt idea.' The subjugation of every part of the person to this idea ensured his unity. The 'realist', knowing and being master of the real, was sheltered from conflict, he was peaceful, serene, discreet and reasonable. From the outside he resembled the bourgeois. 'The realisation of this idea becomes the sole imperative governing their action, because it is merged entirely with the conception which they have of their own personal happiness. Everything is subject to this idea, everything is sacrified to it — if it is appropriate in such a case to talk of sacrifice.'[17] Lying was justifiable if it contributed to the triumph of a more elevated moral principle — that being the programme (and simultaneously the law of history) which had just been sketched out. Thus Tkachev bore within him, intact, the revolutionary ideal of the sixties: the absolute Idea could be laid down. The men of the future knew it, and conspired together to realize it.

And yet, in 1865 Tkachev translated a passage from the *Critique of political economy*, mentioning Marx for the first time in the history of the Russian press, and added that there was not an honest or intelligent person who could have the least objection to this theory. What did Marxism mean to him? To judge from his writings, he drew a very basic economic materialism from it. He sketched out an essay on the history of rationalism: modern thought is a product of capitalism, and rationalism a consequence of the reign of the bourgeoisie. The German religious reformation of the sixteenth century was thus symbolic of the interests of the bourgeoisie. Each time he tried Marxism, he quickly came back to the utilitarianism and summary materialism of his mentor, Chernyshevski. That hardly matters. What does matter in 'Marxism' is its 'great practical value'. Economic materialism is capable of 'concentrating the energy and activity of those who are sincerely devoted to the social cause'. It 'incites them to direct practical activity'. In fact, Marxism lends the Idea greater cohesion. 'The more abstract an ideal is', he wrote about the French Communists, 'the more logical it is. In building it up, man is guided solely by the laws of pure logic. There cannot be any contradictions or illogicalities in it. Everything in it is deduced from an idea, and everything in it is balanced and harmonious.'[18] Tkachev seems to have been one of those revolutionaries for whom it was less important to be a Marxist than to declare oneself to be one; less important to penetrate the inner core of the theory than to guarantee the whole of one's thinking by placing it under the patronage of that theory, and conferring on it the label of a prestigious doctrine which, even without having been examined, has the reputation of being viable, unitarian and scientific. But this is not in fact the case here. Tkachev made use of Marxism in a highly judicious way, though it is more usual to claim the opposite. He is said to have been Jacobin, Buonarrotist and it is certain that he did have links with the Parisian Blanquists. None the less, his thought was entirely shaped by Russia. His terrorist Communism was Jacobin only in terms of a reference to Robespierre and Marat, in a manner quite common in Russia, and through the meetings which took place while he was abroad. But he was certainly no disciple of Marx in his political outlook, nor in his plan of revolution. But his analysis of the Russian situation within the framework of his own revolution was correctly Marxist, and could pass, quite justifiably, as a creative adaptation of the point of view discovered by Marx.

Marx gave him not only a way of conceiving Russian society in comparison with Western societies, but also the *timing* for revolutionary action. The fact that there was no bourgeoisie in Russia — and that there was no proletariat either, in the Marxist sense — did not matter, and was an argument in favour of the possibility of the revolution rather than against it. Russia was situated, with a certain time lapse, on the vector of European history which was being fulfilled along the lines defined in *Capital*:

However slowly and feebly, we too are advancing along the road of economic development, and this development is subject to the same laws, and is being carried out in the same directions as in Western States... There already exist in our country, at this time, all the conditions necessary to the formation of, on the one hand, a very strong conservative class of peasants, landowners and farmers, and, on the other, a bourgeoisie of money, of commerce and of industry, in short, capitalists... That is why we cannot wait, that is why we assert that the Revolution in Russia is truly indispensable and indispensable at precisely this moment. We cannot allow any delay, any sort of hold-up. It must be *now* or perhaps, soon, it will be *never*.[19]

Tkachev, in 1874, shared on a theoretical level what was to be the Menshevik attitude to the Russian Revolution after 1917: Russia was linked, structurally, to the Western type of society; the war was the accident which brought Russia down to an earlier stage of development, and made possible the success of that archaism called the Bolshevik movement. It is because he subscribed to the 'accidental' theory of the Russian Revolution, that Tkachev was able to foresee its advent with such perspicacity in his letter to Engels: 'All it would need would be three or four military defeats, a few simultaneous peasant uprisings in two or three provinces or an open insurrection in the cities, in peacetime, for the government to become totally isolated and be abandoned by everyone.'[20]

The specific nature of the Russian situation, which he was asking Engels to recognize and which he described to him in Marxist terms, revealed two strategic points – the state and the revolutionary party. The Russian state, and here Tkachev was in agreement with what the state said officially of itself, was not a class state. In the West, he wrote to Engels, 'it is not only the military and the police which maintain it, but the whole system of bourgeois society... In our country...on the other hand, the social form owes its existence to the State, a State which is only hanging on by a thread, a State which has nothing in common with the existing social system.'[21] This was pretty much what the liberal historical school, from Soloviev to Miliukov and to Plekhanov, had had to say about the despotic Russian state. 'The State does not, in our country, embody any particular class interest. It weighs on them all equally.' At the time, the Russian state worked to the benefit of the conservatives, the landowners and the capitalists. But it was in essence neutral, and could be diverted towards another end. Thus Tkachev wrote, logically:

Since, in contemporary society in general, and in Russia in particular, material power is concentrated in the hands of the State, the true revolution can only come about on one condition: the takeover of the power of the State by the revolutionaries. In other words, the nearest and most immediate aim of the revolution, is the takeover of this power and the transformation of the conservative State into a revolutionary State.[22]

This takeover would be achieved through violence. But who would conduct it? The revolutionaries themselves. The masses, if indeed they were able to rise at all, would not be making that particular revolution. 'The revolution is made by revolutionaries.'[23] Tkachev took an early interest in the phenomenon of the intelligentsia. He noted that Russian civilization had had the particular merit of producing, at one and the same time, the ignorance of the people and the development of 'sound ideas and concepts in a limited group of our educated class'. He sketched out a Marxist theory of the development of revolutionary ideas in the intelligentsia. Before the emancipation of the serfs, the intelligentsia had been descended from the nobility and reflected the interests of the privileged members of society. But afterwards it was drawn 'from another class of people...intermediate between those who have a solid economic basis and those who by no means possess one.'[24] This foreshadows the Leninist notion of the two generations, nobility and commoners, of the intelligentsia. They must live without any guarantee of employment on what they earn. 'The more he [the intellectual] feels his dependence on others — then the more strongly and clearly does he feel the need for a complete solidarity of human interests.'[25] So he becomes a socialist simply through the circumstances in which he lives. It is from this group that the nucleus of the Party will be recruited, a nucleus formed of *realists* and *men of the future*. These, on entering the organization, break with the intelligentsia, which does not have any particular status simply because of what it is. It is wrong to believe that men of culture create progress simply because they are the bearers of culture. Like Lenin, Tkachev considers the intelligentsia as a reservoir for revolutionaries, but not as a revolutionary class. The intelligentsia spontaneously vacillates between an inflated opinion of itself and self-deprecation. It is by nature vain and servile: 'If they carried you into a black pit and told you: "sing the praises of the perfume of this miasma. Show that what is in black pits is the most healthy and excellent food." you would carry out these orders with cringing humility. *You* show the way of progress!... You go where you are driven.'[26] The Leninist government all too soon proved this prediction correct. It was circumstantial that so many revolutionaries came out of the intelligentsia, but they showed it no gratitude. They entered a world in which it did not matter which class you came from. The populists complained to Tkachev that the élite, once in power, would create a state as oppressive as that which already existed. Tkachev replied that the minority envisaged would not only be made up of repentant nobles, but would also contain *raznochintsy* (people of 'various ranks') and elements drawn from the peasantry. 'And then', he added, 'social origin is not a fundamental problem. Everything depends entirely on the ideas and principles which would guide its activities.'[27]

The soundest sort of Marxist analysis reinforced this careful separation of the intelligentsia and the revolutionary party: in effect, he wrote, the intelligentsia, like Russia itself, was becoming bourgeois. The age of the unemployed intellectual accessible to a vision of the ideal was gone. Now capitalism was saying to the intellectuals:

Develop industry and commerce, rationalize agriculture, teach the people to read, set up banks and hospitals, build railways, etc., and, in return I will guarantee you good, solid rewards, and I will make sure that your work will not be too onerous, I will create conditions suited to your character and I will, moreover, give you a feeling of satisfaction with your work, which will exorcize your melancholy.[28]

And that in fact was what was happening. Members of the intelligentsia, abandoning their 'idealistic principles', were becoming engineers, doctors, teachers. The fulcrum of the revolution was disintegrating. Once again 'the right moment must not be missed'.

So the revolutionaries had to organize themselves securely. Everything depended on 'the strong organization of revolutionary forces, the union of single and isolated ventures into a common, disciplined, solid whole'.[29] The movement 'To the People' was a waste of time. The revolutionaries should put the centre of gravity where it was, that is to say, in their midst and not outside themselves. Nechaev's method was the right one. Tkachev's party corresponded fairly closely to the conspiratorial dream of the *Catechism*. It was resolutely a minority affair. It did not fall for 'the illusion' of a revolutionary movement which would emerge from 'natural groups' through a 'natural evolution', although this was the foundation of the social-democratic Marxist idea. To Lavrov and the naïve propagandists of the countryside, he pointed out that one could not organize the villages, at the same time as preaching to them that all power is evil. 'Whether it is based on federal or centralizing principles...any organization is always authoritarian and therefore anti-anarchist.'[30] That much was common sense. The party was, by nature, weak and few in number. It was like an army in enemy country. 'The problem of unity and organization is a problem of life and death.'[31]

Does this mean that Tkachev completely repudiated his Bakuninian and anarchist ties? On the contrary, he defended them to Engels. The thing was that the people were necessary to the revolutionary break. His conception of the people was far removed from Marx's but anticipated that of Lenin, in so far as he expected from them, not any autonomous constructive capacity, but a capacity for destruction. The people provided the raw primary power, the indispensable *stikhiinost'*. And this is how he envisaged the relationship between the party and the people:

The revolutionary minority, by freeing the people from the yoke that oppresses it and from fear and terror in the face of the old authority, gives it the chance to reveal its destructive-revolutionary force, and, basing itself on this force, to direct it cunningly towards the destruction of the enemies of the revolution. In this way it can destroy the strongpoints that surround it, and deprive them of all means of resistance and counter-attack. Then, by making use of its force and its own authority, it can introduce new progressivo-Communist elements into the conditions of the people's life, and free their existence from its age-old chains and bring life to its dried and petrified forms.[32]

There was another reason why Tkachev maintained a complicity with the old spirit of the Russian *bunt*, and that is that the anarchist myth found itself in accord with dictatorship. In the fundamental directives which the revolutionary state was to obey — after the suppression of economic exchange, the abolition of physical, intellectual and moral inequality, the establishment of an obligatory system of socially integrated education, and the total destruction of the family — we read: 'The development of collective self-administration and the gradual weakening and disappearance of the central functions of State power.'[33] There it is, *the state and the revolution*! The parallel with Lenin occurs spontaneously.

The comparison is so tempting that Soviet historiography avoids the subject. Tkachev's works have not been published in their entirety. Kozmin, their editor, and the author of the monograph on which all subsequent works rely, knew when to stop before he found himself in serious trouble.

The combination of a rigorous realism as to means, and a radical utopianism as to ends, characterizes equally both Tkachev and Lenin, and was something which led them to the isolation of both of them from the revolutionary movement of their time, whose aims were in their eyes too moderate and whose actions were too utopian. This provoked in both of them a similar exasperation. But to overlook the contrast between the two men is to give up any hope of understanding why Tkachev died insane in the asylum at Saint-Anne, and Lenin in power at the Kremlin.

One has to see, in fact, just what it is that the parallel relates to: it relates to Tkachev's *theory* and Lenin's *practice*. That is why the parallel was not visible until after the October Revolution. Lenin's theory contains none of the cynical Machiavellian-seeming elements which make Tkachev's theory so interesting when compared to the political techniques of his great successor. If one reads

Lenin, it is not the party that makes the revolution, but the working classes, the peasant masses, the people — and, if one begins to feel that this might not be so, he slips in a profession of irreproachable Marxist faith. In a word, what separates the two men is an open *avowal* of their beliefs. But it is not enough even to say that, because Lenin, if he had been pressed, would have had nothing to confess. Even in the innermost recesses of his heart, he never imagined that his practice could one day be compared to what Tkachev suggested so openly.[34]

There is, it is said, a progression in the assimilation of Marxism between Tkachev and Lenin. That is undeniable, but not in the way that this is usually taken to mean.

In Tkachev, the synthesis between the Chernyshevskian or Nechaevian *impetus* and the Marxist *Weltanschauung* is incompletely carried out. Marxism is, for him, instrumental in the 'gnostic' plan which he inherited from his first teachers. In order to propel the world into a new age by means of a new species of Perfect, he sought, in Marxism, convenient arguments and analyses and propositions. He maintained, with regard to Marx, a fundamentally utilitarian and empirical attitude, and that is why he made such judicious use of him. He did not hesitate to dissociate the socio-economic analysis from the general aims of the system. He was a good Marxist because he was only partially a Marxist.

In Lenin, on the other hand, Marxist saturation was total. He was only satisfied when he could make his entire argument fit precisely into the framework of, and be verified by quotations from, the works of Karl Marx and Friedrich Engels. Even at the cost of grave distortions of the Russian reality, he wanted to be totally faithful to the totality of Marxism. Now the fact is that this total, blind fidelity has demonstrated that it is capable, not only of containing the whole of the Chernyshevskian stock, but also of realizing it in history. Everything goes to show that if Lenin had been Tkachevian in theory, he never would have had a chance to be so in practice.

IV

For forty years Russian thinking had been obsessed by the value of, and the urgency for action, an obsession which was intensified by the impossibility of acting, and the incapacity for it. The revolutionaries aligned their fantasies, and in terms of what these fantasies were, the government worked out its own counter-fantasies, which were not, for their part, without a certain effect on the way it conducted itself. That is what gives this history its unreality. It is a palace of mirrors, like the fairground booth in Orson Welles' film *The Lady from Shanghai*, where nobody knows who he is firing at, and only the mirrors get shattered and broken. The revolutionaries put down on paper plans for parties to combat the state which were very like the image they entertained of the Russian state, and that state, taking these plans seriously, behaved just as the revolutionaries expected it would, in order to deal with them. For a long time the only material consequence of the revolutionary idea in Russia was the behaviour of the Russian state.

This idea had repercussions in two different directions. There now existed a body of doctrine which was well on the way to philosophical — if not political — unification around Marxism. There existed a type of man with no equivalent in the West, of specifically Russian stamp, that is, the Chernyshevski-style militant revolutionary, who had already been embodied in a number of living examples.

The revolutionary ethos fed from sources other than the doctrinal. Psychological anxiety, the uneasiness of the intelligentsia, Russia's historical ills, all serve to explain the spirit of revolt. What the doctrine did was to propose a global, definitive solution which transformed the revolt into a revolution, and the man in revolt into a revolutionary. Revolt aims at the re-establishment of justice. It appeals to right, and is satisfied when right is re-established. The man in revolt, who wants to achieve justice by violent means, might seek to ally himself with other like-minded people. But the group they form, like Schiller's Brigands, has no desire to transform itself into a party. It does not question the fundamental goodness of the world, all it seeks to do is to re-establish it. Justice is considered as an obligation binding on both the oppressor and on those in revolt, even though the oppressor has put himself beyond the pale. The revolutionary does not ascribe any sort of universality to justice. He makes no appeal to right. He aims at a state of the world in which right would be superfluous and the existence of justice without meaning. He is not seeking justice, but 'social palingenesis' in which relations between things and men would establish themselves of themselves, in perfection. That is the point at which the party comes to seem an imperious necessity. It joins together the men who share this desire and prepares them for knowledge. It constitutes the nucleus of the 'sacred' from which salvation will be propagated. With regard to the world to be regenerated, it is essentially separate from it, and cannot mingle with it. It lays down the tactics for and the successive stages of the salvatory revolution. Justice, for it, is not final: it is instrumental, and reduced to a tactical moment. It can admit into its ranks those 'in revolt' because it needs them to accomplish the revolution. But it sees further than they do, and maintains for the man in revolt the contempt of the gnostic for the uninitiate, of the advanced comrade for the comrade much lower down and, *ipso facto*, junior to him.[35]

Bakunin had vague visions of such a party at the time of his conversion to left-wing Hegelianism. It was sited, logically speaking, at the end of Chernyshevski's moral reform. It was sketched out with precision in the *Catechism* and perfected by Tkachev. Right up to 1875 it was nothing but a project and a vision. But, with *Zemlia i Volia*, the Party made its first entrance into the real world.

Zemlia i Volia was a recapitulation of the whole Russian revolutionary movement. It offered a still imperfect synthesis of all its diverse tendencies, and transformed them into action.[36]

The initial nucleus was of the type of clandestine circle, with a limited scope, of Nechaev's generation. This group, formed in St Petersburg in 1875, was given the name *Troglodytes*, because one of them said that no stranger knew where any of the young men who made up the group lived, or what names they went by. The most influential amongst them, along with Natanson, was Mikhailov. He had already been seen in his first campaign, that same year, in Kiev. There he had encountered the three currents which divided populism at that time, and which came together, without ever thoroughly mingling, in *Zemlia i Volia*. The Lavrists were the descendants of those who, in 1873 and 1874, had 'gone to the People'. 'Opening the eyes of the people', such, said Mikhailov, should be their task. The intention was 'to enlighten all the popular masses' with the aid of hundreds and thousands of propagandists, so that 'a small minority of the people [should] become consciously Socialist'.[37] In the people, 'we must not arouse emotion...but self-awareness'. Bakuninists, on the other hand, relied on feelings and raw revolutionary passion. Rather than enlightening the people, it was a question of unleashing it. As soon as some peasant uprising took place somewhere, it should be fostered and helped to spread, and whatever the outcome, 'the effect would be to concentrate revolutionary passions and to educate the people'.[38] And finally there were the Tkachevists, who were very few in number, and who saw themselves creating a powerful party which, once the actual government had been overthrown, would impose a new order.

The *Troglodytes* managed, during the course of 1876, to organize themselves securely, and to push out tentacles into the provincial towns where they established relations with similar circles in Odessa, Kiev, Kharkov and Rostov. The labels terrorist or propagandist can be applied to a variety of individuals. The propagandist is frequently a student who has not yet broken his links with the world of men. He is, at times, more in revolt than revolutionary. The terrorist lives in a closed world, often in a commune. He is armed and ready for violence. It sometimes happens that for doctrinal reasons, the terrorist by temperament prefers propaganda, or that the propagandist, disheartened, turns to terror. One must be careful not to take as seriously as they did themselves the debate between these two opposing tendencies. Each side accused the other of endangering the revolution, and so of not being revolutionaries. We should not follow their example. Each side clearly aims at total revolution, at a complete change in the way the world is organized. They are not reformists. They may not agree on the techniques of revolution, but neither camp overestimates technique. The revolution which is being prepared in the cosmos surpasses the faculties of the human will, and goes beyond the limits of prophecy. In this sense they were not voluntarists because, though the process in its entirety could be followed, helped along, facilitated, it could not be controlled from beginning to end. Vittorio Mathieu applies to the revolutionary the same distinction that Schiller drew between the naïve and sentimental artists.[39] The naïve artist believes that his skill and knowledge are the cause of the aesthetic success. The sentimental artist knows that they are simply the occasion for this success. He keeps watch for the propitious moment, and holds himself ready to capture success when it presents itself. In the same way, the revolutionary holds himself ready for the event, without knowing when it will arise. In that way his technique is less causal than propitiatory. All the same, between Bakuninian spontaneity and Tkachevian planning, there was a development in gnostic assurance. Both knew that regeneration could only occur after the break and the expected upheaval. But Tkachev believed he knew better than Bakunin what lines that regeneration would follow, and what it would be like. He suspected that the former accorded too great a role to individual feelings, and was never sure that, in him, the revolutionary spirit would not degenerate into naïve revolt or delinquent cynicism. He charged him with being defective in ideology, because he knew that knowledge alone could keep one from this twofold deviation. But despite this mutual suspicion, real political and militant life offered innumerable possibilities for collaboration. And that is why *Zemlia i Volia* was able to function for a few years.

In constituting itself into a party, *Zemlia i Volia* had to construct a definite programme for itself, and this was done in St Petersburg in 1876. It limited its objectives to the short term, with a populist outlook (distribution of land, break-up of the Empire, remittance of social functions to the communes), but it gave a clear indication of the principle: violent revolution, and of the two methods: *agitation* 'aimed at organizing the revolutionary forces and fostering revolutionary sentiments', and the *disorganization of the state*. Between these two poles of organized propaganda and organized terrorism, the short-lived career of *Zemlia i Volia* ran its course.

This is not the place to tell the rather confused story of what happened simultaneously in several cities over the next three years. Suffice it to say that *Zemlia i Volia* attempted to apply, all at the same time, the contradictory practices which had been worked out over the previous twenty-five years, but which until then had been still-born. The spirit of Nechaev walked again in the *buntari* of the Ukraine. A 'traitor', Gorinovich, was shot with a pistol and then sprayed with sulphuric acid. This was a repetition of the killing of the student Ivanov. Another episode, beyond any of Nechaev's fantasies, was more like some Decembrist dream: in 1876, in the Chiguirin district near Kiev, the peasants were called upon to recognize a 'secret imperial Charter' which granted them, by right, all the land, and then to organize themselves to seize the land from the nobles who still held it. Several hundred peasants followed the three *buntari* who had won their confidence. Other *zemlevoltsy*, following their predecessors' example, set up colonies in the Pugachin tradition in the rural areas, or in the working-class urban districts. This was part of the 'propagandist' movement. Less enclosed in their own private world than the terrorists, they ended up by establishing real links with the villages and factories, and by discovering, though without always being fully aware of the fact, the real people, flesh and blood peasants and workers, beneath the theoretical beings which they imagined. Their convictions impelled them to defend unconditionally the interests of the people. But, in so far as they took that defence seriously, they had to pay attention to the real grievances expressed by the people. Frequently, they were living in the villages as doctors or teachers. Sickness and ignorance proved problems intractable to ideology. By trying to remedy them, the ideologists found themselves working for the common good. They experienced another reality as being real. This immersion in reality gently nudged them out of their own unreality. Before the demands of administration, the physiological misery, the concrete exploitation of the poor by the rich and of the weak by the powerful, they could not avoid an appeal to justice and right, and in doing so gradually abandoned their stance as revolutionaries. For years these rural militants maintained positions of the strictest kind of theoretical populism: but at the time this meant being in opposition not to Marxism, but to terrorism, to Jacobinism, and, in a general way, giving due consideration to the people, in their desire for autonomy. They were the first to pose the problem of liberty in political terms. It was from this part of *Zemlia i Volia* that the *Black Partition* splinter group was recruited, which went on to form the basis of the social democrats.

In 1877, most of the *Zemlia i Volia* militants were arrested and sent for trial. This had important repercussions. The accused became the accusers. Public opinion, that is, the opinion of educated Russia, was fired by the heroism of their behaviour. 'They are saints', it was said. 'They were like the early Christian martyrs... They preached love, equality, fraternity.'[40] Russian public opinion of the time formed the peripheral fringe of the revolutionary intelligentsia. It was influenced by the same ideas, but in a dilute form, and without having taken them to their logical conclusion. In fact between revolt and revolution, there was not only opposition but also succession.[41] It was in the favourable soil of the spirit of revolt that the revolutionary spirit took seed, grew and presented itself as a solution. Between the young Marx, a utopian in revolt, and the old Marx, scientific revolutionary, as between the child in revolt and the adolescent revolutionary, there lay a chronological and a logical sequence. Revolution — at one and the same time negation and fulfilment — was the *Aufhebung* of revolt. As a result, public opinion saw in the revolutionary spirit the fulfilment of the spirit of revolt with which it was imbued and which fed as a matter of course on all the injustices of Russian life. It was scarcely aware of it as a negation of that same spirit, because it had not gone through the process which led from one to the other. It related the revolutionary acts on trial to a paradigm of justice — the Christian martyr. For their part, the revolutionaries gladly accepted this assimilation, either simply profiting in good faith from the conservation of revolt in revolution, or else consciously making use of this feeling of revolt in a utilitarian way in accordance with the most advanced 'catechisms'. In each case revolution and revolt formed a mixture, compounded in different proportions, and consistently unstable. But the group on trial embodied the mixture, since it was made up of anarchists, Illuminati (like the 'anthropotheist' Malikov), and the most advanced revolutionaries like Myshkin. This last gave an excellent picture of the true character of revolutionary action.[42] Addressing the tribunal, he elaborated the following points: (1) utopian declaration: 'The essential task of the social-revolutionary party is to build up on the existing ruins of the existing state-bourgeois régime a social organization which satisfies the demands of the people.' Such an organization is the rural commune, in the populist meaning of the word. (2) The revolutionary process as unavoidable destiny: 'It [this organization] can be brought about only through a social revolution', for the power of the state makes any peaceful route to this result impossible. 'In view of the desperate situation of the people today one does not have to be a prophet to foresee that the inevitable result of this situation will be a general popular revolution.' (3) The propitiatory and gnostic role of the party: 'Our only concern is that it [the revolution] should be as fruitful as possible.' To this end, the raw popular force should be put in touch with the guiding intelligence of the party: 'With this aim in view our practical activities must consist in the union and strengthening of popular forces and revolutionary tendencies, and in the fusion of the two fundamental currents of revolution. One of these — that of the intelligentsia — has only recently emerged, but it has already shown considerable energy. The other — that of the people — is wider and deeper and has never been exhausted.' So one must form the party. It is worth noting, in passing, the extraordinary reversal: namely, the fact that the revolutionary spirit of the intelligentsia is systematically subordinated to the construct — or the illusion — of the imminent popular uprising. But the intelligentsia could not be revolutionary unless one could assume a revolutionary people.

The continuing effort in propaganda and in the agitation of the people did engender a reaction, but in 'society', not in the people. It became active during the trials. On the day following the end of one of these trials, 24 January 1878, a young girl, Vera Zassulich, fired at the governor of St Petersburg, in order, she said, to avenge the student Bogoliubov, who had been flogged in prison. The crime aroused even more public sympathy than had the apostles in their villages.

Public opinion, normally discontented with the state of things, assigned to the young heroes a redemptive role, to which pistol shots seemed more directly suited than preaching to peasants. Immediately the revolutionary party saw, in the recourse to terrorist acts, a means of capitalizing on their rapidly acquired political gains. The old Nechaevian stock was revitalized and shone out in all its native splendour. The 'central executive committee', instead of being a magic word striking terror only into the small clandestine circle who uttered it, became a real central committee, able to commit murder anywhere in the Empire, and even in the Winter Palace. Terrorism short-circuited the long detour by way of the people. There was no longer any need to wait indefinitely for the hatred implanted in the people to bear fruit, in order to give free rein to their own. Terrorism was, in fact, the primal truth, the first truth of the revolutionary movement. And to cap it all, Marxism, as we have seen, gave it a theoretical basis and justification: do not let us give the rising Russian bourgeoisie time to smother us: 'Beware!' wrote Kravchinski, the murderer of the chief of police, 'Like a flock of crows which smell a rotting corpse, new enemies are arising on all sides. The enemies are the bourgeoisie.'[43]

But, in order to make the revolution 'as soon as possible', in order to avoid the corruption of the people by 'the development of capitalism and the growing invasion of various poisons of bourgeois life', the party, the majority of which had gone over to terrorism and was once more concentrated in St Petersburg, needed to reorganize itself. In the spring of 1878, its new statutes were ready. They were Nechaevian in style. *Zemlia i Volia* was an organization of 'persons closely linked to each other', of men 'ready to dedicate all their powers, means, relations, sympathies and antipathies, as well as their own lives' to the organization. The members of the organization renounce all private property. They accept the 'control of the activity of all the groups and of each member individually'. The private life of each of them is controlled 'in relation to acts which could be considered of practical importance, in each individual case'. The break with the old man and the conversion to a new spiritual state is thus reaffirmed. 'The end justifies the means', paragraph 9 lays down, 'excluding cases in which the use of certain means may harm the organization itself', which is an exact description of *partinost*'.

The party was centralized. The 'basic circle' was made up of professional revolutionaries. Everyone had the same rights, but had to submit to orders when taking action. The group could force members to undertake whatever work they judged useful. Everyone was bound to secrecy. The central administration coordinated all activities. It gathered 'exact and precise information on the activity of all the groups'. It was in touch with other revolutionary organizations. All members of the party could and should penetrate other organizations, so as to influence and attract them. Organized like this, the party appears as a 'compact and well-arranged organization of prepared revolutionaries, springing both from the intelligentsia and the workers'. It could decide the means of action: closer association with the religious sects, with the peasant groups, and with the workers. The university and the intelligentsia should provide 'the main contingent to make up the ranks of the organization'. Finally, the organization should 'establish relations with the liberals, so as to exploit them for our purposes'.[44]

Zemlia i Volia's new achievement was to realize in actuality what had for twenty years remained a mere project – and following that, to have syncretized, though neither rigorously nor successfully, the diverse movements of populism, anarchism and early Marxism. Finally, to have shown an irresistible tendency towards terrorism. The 'propagandists' ended up leaving *Zemlia i Volia* (which then became *Narodnaia Volia*) and the synthesis broke down. The party had been created for the first time, but the terrorist line quickly led to schism, and then to complete breakdown.

The synthesis was unstable. The elements were juxtaposed rather than combined. The party was Nechaevian in spirit. It formed a separate phalanx of men apart. There was a strong temptation to broadcast, through heroic acts, out-of-the-ordinary exploits showing the new morality, witness to the *new man*. But it was a temptation which had to be resisted. It had to be resisted for political reasons: terrorism was effective to influence society. Through it, they could make the state relax its grip, producing such results as Loris Melikov and semi-constitutional plans of government. But *Zemlia i Volia* was anything but reformist: the party wanted to destroy the state, not to influence it. For that, they needed the battering-ram of popular insurrection, which, in any case, had to be let loose in order to set in motion the process of total renovation. In abandoning 'propaganda', the organization was caught in a political contradiction. And by the same token, it found itself in contravention of its own moral law that everything was subject to the progress of the revolution. It laid itself open to charges of 'romanticism' and 'individualism'. It exalted the self at the expense of the task.

The synthesis broke down. The terrorists were hanged. The propagandists turned towards reformism. In order for them to be united again in a superior, incomparably more stable synthesis, they had to wait for Lenin.

IO
Social Democracy

In order to find our way around the history of social democracy, which has been made even more complicated by the detailed examination to which it has been subjected by historians of all countries for the last sixty years, a useful lead to follow is the career of Plekhanov. Plekhanov (together with Axelrod) was the first to wear the Marxist label clearly and completely, without any qualifications. While contemporary populism, riddled with Marxism, was trying to adapt itself to the new compound, Plekhanov accorded to his conversion to Marxism the significance of a break with populism. Thus he was formally the founder of social democracy. His long-lasting relationship with Lenin, who declared himself 'in love' with him, and was his ally in the crisis of revisionism, made their partial rupture all the more noteworthy. Finally, Plekhanov had the time to reflect, as a *scholar*, on the social history of Russia, and to reach, in practice, positions which one could call, in the academic sphere at least, crypto-liberal. In the Preface to his first Marxist book, *Socialism and the political struggle*, Plekhanov stated: 'A striving for work *among the people* and for the people, a strong conviction that "the emancipation of the workers should be accomplished by the workers themselves" — this practical tendency of the old Populism is no less dear to me than before.'[1]

This, written in 1883, was a clear rejection of the dictatorially aimed terrorism of *Narodnaia Volia*. Deutsch, who founded with Plekhanov the dissident *Emancipation of Labour Group*, consciously desired the title social democracy because, he said, 'in the whole civilized world the name "Social Democracy" was associated then with the concrete, peaceful and parliamentary party whose activity was characterized by almost complete avoidance of all kind of determined, revolutionary methods of struggle'.[2] Social democracy meant moderation. Under a 'socialist dictatorship', wrote Plekhanov, the people could only look forward to the gradual running down of 'economic equality', and they would not be able to participate in the organization of production because of their customs and the low level of their development. 'Or else, they would have to seek salvation through the institution of an *authoritarian patriarchal communism* with the single difference that, instead of the Inca *Sons of the Sun* and their bureaucracy, it would be the socialist caste which would administer national production.'[3]

Thus, no committee, no executive could by right represent the working class and substitute itself for it. The mission of the working class was to complete the Westernization of Russia and finish off the work started by Peter the Great. There was no short cut. Trying to take a short cut would lead to regression. The long route was through the school of the West, and of capitalism. It could be of shorter duration than in Europe, because in Russia 'class consciousness' benefited from Western advances. This is where Plekhanov set himself apart from trade unionism. His 'practical' populism had separated him from the terrorist populism which was betraying its own ends. None the less, he had no intention of letting the people invent or improvise new ways to salvation. Plekhanov already knew what the right way was. Marxism had revealed the plan of history. But he had confidence in the masses, as Marxism itself told him that he should have, to carry out this plan themselves. This is where Plekhanov's stance is ambiguous. He believed deeply that things and men should be left to act for themselves, that natural methods were better than artificial methods. To this extent, he was oriented in the direction of liberalism, trade unionism and non-dogmatic social democracy. But, on the other hand, he only accepted this *laissez-faire* attitude because he was utterly convinced that this meant following the positive laws discovered once and for all by Marx. He was only liberal within the context of an absolute determinism, to which he held all the keys, and in the context of a total belief in the Marxist dogma. It was in the name of a literal Marxism that Plekhanov was opposed, successively, to populist terrorism, then to revisionism, and, finally, to Leninist Bolshevism.

Plekhanov claimed a precedent in Bielinski. Mikhailovski had drawn a parallel between Russian Marxist theodicy and Bielinski's 'Hegelian' reconciliation with reality. Then Bielinski turned against it. But it was the moment of reconciliation which attracted Plekhanov's approval. Bielinski overcame the moralism of Schiller and the abstract rationalism of the Enlightenment. His revolt was a regression into utopianism. This regression was easily explained by Marxism: in Nicholas's time, the objective conditions were not ready for Russian society to bring forth a Plekhanov. In one way, Bielinski the Westernist was the forerunner of the correct Marxism. But in another way, he committed 'the original sin of the Russian intelligentsia'; later Plekhanov similarly stigmatized Lenin's 'subjectivism'.[4]

In political matters, Plekhanov's position was completely clear. He foresaw a revolution in two stages. The first stage would be a 'democratic bourgeoisie', thus rejecting the populist dogma of the bourgeoisie as being intrinsically reactionary. Capitalism already existed in Russia, but its state organization was 'feudal'. The bourgeoisie would be impelled towards liberalism by the logic of its 'class interests'. After that would come the second stage, of the 'dictatorship of the proletariat', which Plekhanov understood in Marx's sense of the term as the government by the immense majority of the population of a tiny minority of exploiters. It would be, as he said, a 'panarchy'.

All this was open to contradictory interpretations. Should one believe that democracy, liberty and the rule of law were provisional attributes of the first stage, or should they be seen as having an innate value? What was to be the interval between the two stages? Would the proletariat exercise its 'hegemony', as Axelrod wanted, right from the phase of 'democratic bourgeoisie'? How should one, within the party, reconcile the two objectives of 'democratic bourgeoisie' and 'socialism'? To what extent should one be allied with the liberals, and to what extent should one be in contention with them?

For, at the turn of the century, what was new in Russia was social and cultural pluralism, and political life. It was a conglomeration of concomitant phenomena which the prevailing Marxism subsumed, inadequately, under the generic term 'capitalism'.

There now existed a society which was more subtly differentiated from the society of two classes — peasants and nobility — of earlier times; a cultural life which was in evidence in a rapidly expanding system of education, an extensive, varied press with a wide distribution and a fundamentally liberal orientation. The intelligentsia lost its strictly clerical appearance and gradually became a socio-professional stratum without any specific ideological commitment. The populisto-Marxist vulgate ceased to dictate despotically to the cultivated public, which was for its part oriented towards the European model. It was influenced by spiritualism, aestheticism, irrationalism and *art nouveau*. It was, like the West, '1900'. And finally, and most importantly, a Western-style political life was beginning to emerge. This was misconceived by the Marxists, who regarded the whole great process of modernization from the narrow viewpoint of the 'development of capitalism': the capitalist class was closely dependent on the state, which remained the chief architect of economic growth. And, as they did not believe in the autonomy of politics, they under-estimated the liberal impulse, which they made into a 'bourgeois' phenomenon, despite the fact that they could see it spreading before their eyes into all classes.

Even in the rural areas, where Socialist-Revolutionary populism played a significant role, it was liberalism which prevailed. Its social bases were the nobility, which expressed itself in the *zemstvo*, and, following on from this, the established, professionalized intelligentsia. Liberalism had at its disposal a political reservoir which enabled it to create, between 1900 and 1905, a true party in the Western sense of the term. While the social-democrat parties were conspiratorial groups organized in order to manipulate a crisis, the *Cadet* party was organized in order to conduct a daily, normal, electoral political struggle. For the first time in Russia, an organized political party set itself aims other than revolutionary upheaval. For the first time, an opposition party set itself to cope with reality and not to change it for a new one.

Now, the two classes which formed the support of the revolutionary projections, given the existence of a political life, were in a position to manifest their true state of mind. The peasantry was supposed to be dreaming of a *bunt*. In fact, the administrative framework of the local power structure and the efficiency of military and police surveillance had made such strides over the previous century as to render a *bunt* highly improbable, though it remained something to be feared or hoped for. After about 1902, though, the peasantry was on the move, and it became apparent that it had abandoned the grand eschatalogical dreams of earlier uprisings. It preferred exerting an insistent, semi-violent, semi-peaceful pressure on the nobility, in order to force it to sell the lands which it still had in its possession. The peasantry organized itself commercially and technically along cooperative and liberal economic lines. The village was sufficiently educated to be able to orient itself politically, and it looked to the *Cadets* rather than to the Socialists. It was the same with the working class. If one discounts the Poles and the Latvians, the history of the working-class movement in Russia really began with the Jews. In 1900, the only organized 'working class' capable of raising funds, of conducting successful strikes, and enjoying a supple and democratic organization, was the Union of Jewish workers, the *Bund*. The mass of Russian workers was far behind. Though it comprised a nucleus of established workers, with sound professional training, it was constantly being overwhelmed and debased by the influx of immigrants from the rural areas. None the less, the Russian workers were able to sustain some fairly important protest movements. The great strike of 1896 was instigated purely by the workers. It threw up an authentic worker leadership, which segregated the social-democrat students into a subordinate position, composing leaflets.[5]

All the same, since the strike was illegal, the growing working-class movement could hardly avoid political involvement if it was to achieve legitimacy. It discovered politics, but liberal politics. When Zubatov felt able to suggest, to the working class, an alternative form of organization to the clandestine political party, it leapt at the idea. Between 1901 and 1903, it could perhaps be said that Russia experienced, if one excepts the *Bund*, its purest form of worker syndicalism, and the fact that the police made great efforts to control it does not substantially alter its true nature. Later, Gapone's success was proof of the feeble influence of social democracy. It was on the eve of the war that the working class became radicalized, and not necessarily in a Marxist direction.

In what way did Marxism take this new Russia into account? 'Populist' Marxism continued to exist. Vorontsov and Danielson, still obsessed by the agrarian question, were harping on the negative effects of capitalism. The famine of 1891, which directly or indirectly caused the deaths of half a million people, seemed to reinforce this catastrophic brand of Marxism. But another, radically different kind of Marxism had arisen. The originator appears to have been a professor at the University of Kiev called Ziber, whose dissertation, *David Ricardo and Karl Marx* was published in 1885, having received the warmest accolades from Marx himself.[6] This brand of Marxism was a resolutely optimistic economic determinism. The forms of social life are the result of natural causes of development. They do not depend on choices made by men. The natural phases, of which capitalism is one, cannot be avoided or shortened. The structure of the state adjusts itself automatically to the social base. Socialism will win, without any revolution, through official inauguration in a congress of economically developed states. The young Struve was fully committed to these ideas. His *Critical notes* (1894) are an apology for the industrial development of Russia (as it had been undertaken by Witte and the Ministry of Finance), in the name of objective science. We must 'learn from capitalism'.[7]

The *Critical notes* were very well received. Struve's reputation was so high that he was given the job of drawing up the manifesto for the first Congress of Russian Social Democrats (1898). In that manifesto, one could read that the working class had as its primary task the struggle for political liberty, a struggle for which the 'weak and feeble Russian bourgeoisie' was unfitted. But why should Struve, who privately declared himself to be much more interested in liberty than in socialism, find himself involved in social-democratic circles which were still ostensibly revolutionary? Because two other kinds of Marxism were making their way in this same setting, under the cover of orthodoxy: economism and revisionism.

Economism? Hardly a faction, or a system, but at the most a timid tendency and a question, shared by a few militants, amongst whom one can, in scrutinizing their writings with philological minuteness, distinguish two or three currents.[8] Briefly, economism sprang from the bitter experience of the strikes of 1896–7, in which the workers proved to have been such bad pupils of their intellectual teachers. 'Propaganda', that is to say, Marxist indoctrination, had failed. The social democrats, declared the 'economists', should join the liberal opposition in calling for what Russia at that time had most need of: a constitution, not a revolution. 'Agitation', that is to say, the call for strikes and for improved living conditions, had, on the other hand, succeeded: let the workers take charge of it themselves, since that was what concerned them most. It would thus be expedient to open the ranks of the directing committee of the *Union for the Struggle for the Liberation of Labour* to a few workers. If Marxism was true (which the 'economists' did not doubt), the workers would work it out themselves, through their own experience. The party must be democratized. It followed that the 'elders' of the party should make room for them. Not unnaturally, the 'economists' provoked an outcry amongst these same elders. Guardians of orthodoxy, they fabricated a repulsive entity which they christened economism, giving it an entirely spurious historical substance. By association, they included it in the condemnation of another tendency, in this case a real one, and one of international dimensions: revisionism.

Revisionism had its birth in the letter that Edward Bernstein sent to the German social-democratic Congress in 1898. There were at least three facets to the letter and to the subsequent controversy. The first was narrowly political. A rift had opened between what German social democracy said and what it did, and this rift was not a healthy one: 'Social-democracy must have the courage to free itself from the phraseology of the past and want to appear in its true colours as a party interested only in democratic and socialist reforms.'[9] It is only by being true to itself that the party will achieve its full potential. For Bernstein, ideology is a parasite on politics. Then he passed historical judgement on the past and the present: 'I have simply denied that the collapse of bourgeois society is close and I have said that social-democracy should not base its tactics on the hope of an imminent catastrophe.'[10] Historical developments have disproved Marx's prognostications. Engels, in his 1895 'testament', had already felt as much. The economic situation of the workers had not worsened. 'It is useless and absurd to try and disguise the fact.' The numbers of the well-to-do had increased. In the political arena, 'we can see the privileges of the capitalist bourgeoisie gradually disappearing before the progress of democratic institutions'. The working-class movement efficiently thwarted capitalist exploitation. So what is socialism? Here, Bernstein reveals the philosophical bases of revisionism. It is first of all a return to the true scientific spirit. 'An error does not become sacred simply because, at a given time, Marx and Engels believed it, and a truth does not cease to be true because an anti-socialist, or incompletely socialist economist was the first to discover it. In the domain of science, having the right opinions creates no privileges and does not serve any writs for expulsion.'[11] Now, Marx had been mistaken. The theory of pauperization had been controverted. 'Dialectics' are a sophisticated catchall. There are contradictions in *Capital*. What is taken to be science, in 'scientific socialism', is a 'litany'.[12] There follows, politically speaking, a choice in favour of reform and against revolution. Socialism is not a breaking away from liberalism, but its fulfilment. Liberalism is a broader social principle than the 'bourgeois liberalism' in which it first made its appearance, and its goal is socialism. 'With growing numbers and understanding [universal suffrage] has become the instrument by means of which to transform the representatives of the people from the masters which they have been, into servants of the people.' Socialism is nothing but an 'organizing liberalism'.[13] It follows that one cannot work out *a priori* what socialism is, since it is dependent on the free operation of social forces. 'Democracy is, at one and the same time, both a means and an end.' Democracy is neither a watchword for further agitation, nor a tactical stage, but a means of achieving more democracy. 'Socialism' is not a state, it is a vehicle, a direction, and there is no point in forcing the pace, since no one knows how long the process should last; 'it was in this sense that I wrote the sentences to which I still subscribe, that the movement is everything, and what is usually called the final aim of socialism is nothing'.[14]

But if socialism is nothing but the spontaneous development of a society in full debate, then the class struggle is nothing but an index of a lack of freedom and democracy. 'Antagonistic class interests will disappear in part on the battlefield of economic competition, and in part – and to an ever-increasing extent – through legislation. Through the conflict of class interests, the collective interest will slowly become clear and the more it predominates, the more democratic the society will be.'[15]

Bernstein has given up the idea of building a different world. It is this world here which is changing and with which we have to cope. Thus, it has a value. The socialist and his adversary are to some extent linked. He rejects the total antagonism of the class struggle and the gulf set by the revolution. In other words, he has rediscovered *the common good*. Immediately, he regains scientific lucidity, historical common sense, patience and political perspicacity. Bernstein is at the jumping-off point for the 'de-ideologization' of the working-class movement. One can already see in him the spiritual effects which go with quitting the magic circle. His eyes are open, his style is relaxed. His book breathes easily. For in his letter of 1898, everything became clear to him. He would develop his ideas further, and with talent, but just as ideology effects a complete change of state, so there is a complete and immediate change on quitting ideology.

The German working-class movement was too massive, too working-class, for its powers to be delegated to a group of ideologists and professional conspirators. The Bernsteinian movement derived in one way from a taking into account and a taking seriously of the working-class reality by a working-class party. As far as this went, it was no different from the social-democratic orthodoxy of Kautsky and Rosa Luxemburg, nor even of Plekhanov who, in faraway Russia, and prior to any working-class movement, had expressed his confidence in its organizational abilities and rejected any conspiratorial manipulation. But Bernsteinism is, in a much more important way, a renunciation of the alternative world of ideology. And that was something which ideology could not tolerate. Nowhere was this refusal expressed more clearly than in the reply to Bernstein given by Rosa Luxemburg:

Relating the great popular mass to a goal surpassing any existing order, to relate the day-to-day struggle to the great reformation of the world, such is the great problem facing the social-democratic movement, which must in consequence navigate between the twin hazards of the abandonment of its mass character and the abandonment of the final goal, of degenerating into a sect and collapsing into a bourgeois reformist movement, anarchy and opportunism.[16]

Bernstein's position was immediately known in Russia. Of course, one could say that the conditions necessary for revisionism prevailed as soon as there existed, if not a socialist working-class movement — which there was not in Russia — then at least a diversified and legal political life — which had existed for some years. Another, simpler explanation would start from an entirely contrary understanding of the situation: that in Russia, precisely because action was difficult, because syndicalist experience hardly existed, and political experience was in its infancy, there remained plenty of time in the socialist parties for debating ideas, and even more so since their membership was made up of intellectuals. The cultural frontier did not exist. Books and ideas passed freely. The prestige of German social democracy was immense: that is enough to account for the early spread of Bernstein's thought. To which one should add one further idiosyncracy of the Russian intellectual scene. Plekhanov remarked that 'even the Europeanisation of our bourgeoisie was being accomplished under the banner of Marxism'.[17] Marxism played, at times, the role of Manchester utilitarianism, as far as the enthusiastic rationalization of the beginnings of industrialization were concerned. In their struggle against populism or against the neo-Slavophilism of the Ministry of the Interior, the *Cadets*, and even some groups within the Ministry of Finance followed the liberal fashion of reasoning in a Marxist way. Marxism laid down iron laws of wages, and attributed to the objective nature of things the horrors of the economic breakdown.[18] It had, moreover, an advantage: it was not overtly 'bourgeois'. It seemed to spring from a socialist tradition. It lent to the Russian intellectual a sense of vision and progressivism which was necessary to his prestige, and useful to the publication of his works.

In 1899 the composer of the social-democratic programme for the first party congress, Petr Struve, also proceeded in his turn to the revision of Marx. Truth to tell, he had only been waiting for the right opportunity, because even when he was drawing up the programme for the congress he no longer believed in the orthodox view, but thought it his duty to keep his doubts to himself. Struve's revisionism is distinctly intellectualist.[19] The Russians had sought for systematic coherence in Marx. If the system is shaken at one point, the whole edifice soon begins to crumble. Struve attacked Marx at the heart of his theory, the theory of value. He took up again Böhm Bawerk's observations on the contradictions between Book I and Book III of *Capital*. In Book I the rate of profit depended on the proportion of variable capital in the total capital, because the exchange value, and hence the rate of profit, are determined by the amount of labour used in production. Now, in Book III, Marx conceded the composition of the rate of profit, which thus ceases to depend on the constancy of capital and accepts that the exchange value is determined by the cost of production, in which the amount of labour is only one element. Marx tried to get out of it by submerging the precise concept of labour value in the indeterminate concept of socially necessary value — but then the explanation became tautological. It was through this crack in ideological coherence that the spirit of Struve followed Bernstein into freedom. After that, it was no longer difficult to demolish the theory of the falling tendency of the rate of profit, of pauperization and, finally, of the revolution. Struve had become a liberal.

Revisionism was seen by Plekhanov as a betrayal. Bernstein's articles in *Neue Zeit* made him ill.[20] His friend Axelrod was thrown into a fit of depression. 'The inner motivation of my idealism, of all my social activity', he wrote, 'has been and is the concept of the infinite progress of human nature...'

And here was Bernstein destroying his faith! Revisionism faced

Plekhanov with the possibility of a reconciliation with this imminent world, and the evaporation of its transcendence: Communism. What is more, the revisionists were now affecting towards him the same attitude of 'scientific' disdain which he had adopted towards populism. The wise and learned were now supposed to be Bernstein and Struve, while he, Plekhanov, was relegated to the same level as the ignorant adherents of a credulous and naïve populism. And the last straw was that Bernstein did not seem to accord to Plekhanov his due rank in the Russian branch of the International.

Plekhanov could not understand why Bernstein had not been expelled from the party immediately. He was amazed that Kautsky, whom he admired so much, did not join him in his characteristically Russian demands for summary justice. How could his dear and much respected comrade Kautsky have allowed such dreadful things to be published? 'Freedom of opinion within the party can and must be restricted, precisely because a party is a freely consenting union of people sharing ideas in common. Once that union has gone, schism is inevitable.'[21] It had in fact been customary in the Russian circle since 1830 to make adherence to the doctrine a condition of membership and a symbol of loyalty. It was a charge which Lenin was soon to level against Plekhanov in his turn.

So Plekhanov set to work. I do not have the courage to give a summary of *Bernstein and individualism, The cant against Kant or Mr Bernstein's spiritual testament, Conrad Schmidt against Karl Marx and Friedrich Engels, Materialism or Kantism, The first phases of a theory of the class struggle, A critique of our critiques*, and so on.[22] They make deadly dull reading. Suffice it to say that, in accordance with Kautskian orthodoxy, he defended the class struggle and the necessity for revolution; that he defended, inch by inch, the front line of 'absolute pauperization', while at the same time fortifying, in the rear, a fall-back position along the lines of 'relative pauperization'. And finally, that he philosophized. Bernstein, having escaped from the Marxist dogma, occasionally reasoned in the manner of the epistemologists of the time, who were neo-positivists and neo-Kantians. But he had not passed from Marxism to neo-Kantism through any apostasy. Plekhanov,and Lenin after him, always saw the abandonment of ideology in terms of a similar sort of commitment to an opposite ideology. This was not the case. Bernstein, having shut the heavy door of ideology firmly behind him, was experimenting with another way of thinking, and if it happened that his thought was coloured by the spirit of the time — that is, if he used neo-Kantian or neo-positivist expressions — he was none the less far from maintaining the same relationship with these doctrines that he had earlier had with Marxism. But those whom he had left behind had no notion that it could be otherwise. And they applied an inquisitorial care to discovering, in his thinking, the germs of an antagonistic system, without perceiving that the novel thing was that these germs were not being developed into a system, because the spirit of system had been abandoned.

What Plekhanov did stick to with all his might, was materialism.

He had written ample dissertations on the subject. The *Essays on the history of materialism* should have appeared in *Neue Zeit*, but, despite Kautsky's promises, this did not happen. They appeared in a German edition in 1896. The book is a substantial history of materialism in the eighteenth century (Holbach and Helvetius), a materialism which he begins by praising but ultimately reproaches for being 'static': 'Metaphysical materialism is only half-way revolutionary.'[23] Then, following Engels, he showed how Hegel introduced the notion of immanence (dialectics): 'The metaphysical method of the French materialists is, to the dialectical method of German idealism, what elementary mathematics are to advanced mathematics.' Restoration historians looked for the laws of history. Finally, he gives an exposé of Marx's historical and dialectical materialism, with examples. The exposé is carried out in strictly orthodox social-democratic terms. It is not 'mechanistic': it gives a detailed demonstration of 'interaction'. There is an order of factors: demand — production forces — production relations — rights, political and moral organization. But through interaction, history is one: 'It is the history of social relations, conditioned at every moment by the state of the production forces.' 'What is called ideology', he concludes, 'is simply the multifaceted reflection of the different aspects of this single, indivisible history.'[24] None of this is original, but it is irreproachable. There is erudition to be found in this Russian, who read a great deal, but only the better to savour the calm certainty of the whole. Any new occurrence, any reading, any history are just so many new proofs. One can understand the change in tone when Bernstein started to disturb the beliefs. There is a certain amount of fury, indignation and bitterness animating the 300 pages directed against the apostate.

The article in *Neue Zeit* ('Bernstein and materialism'), which appeared in July 1898, was also written in the heat of the moment. Everything came bubbling up at once. 'Bernstein had spent long years in intimate contact with Engels, without understanding his philosophy.' 'Marx and Engels were not only materialists in the domain of historical studies: they were also materialists in the concept which they formed of spirit–matter relations.' There follows a demonstration of the agreement between the materialism of Marx and Engels and the 'materialism' of Spinoza (!). Moreover, Spinoza and La Mettrie, Holbach and Diderot shared an equally materialist view. 'I can see absolutely no fundamental difference between Spinozism and the materialism of La Mettrie.'[25] This is a clear example of mental pivoting, by which one turns from a philosophical attitude in order to regard the world ideologically. Then, with everything safely enclosed in its own clear-cut category, there is indeed no longer any difference between Spinoza and La Mettrie. Nothing could be more pathetic than the *proof* which Plekhanov advances of the 'Spinozism' of Marx and Engels. Here is the passage in which his reverence for the Master and his pride in a perfect Westernism stand clearly revealed:

In 1889...I had the pleasure, during the whole of a week, to hold with him [Engels] long conversations on various theoretical and practical subjects. One day, when we were discussing philosophy, and Engels was criticizing, with some vehemence, what Stein had called, highly inappropriately, 'physical materialism', I said to him, 'So good old Spinoza was right, was he, when he said thought and extension were only two attributes of one single, identical substance?' 'Certainly,' replied Engels, 'good old Spinoza was absolutely right.'[26]

Engels's verdict was so crucial that Plekhanov took care to cite two witnesses to this historic conversation: the famous chemist Schorlemmer and Axelrod.

Why set down 300 pages of materialism against Bernstein, when the question that Bernstein raised was a political one: to fit a catastrophist vocabulary to a reformist reality? Perhaps we can find a clue in the numerous passages in which Plekhanov attacks Kant, and even Hume.

Fundamentally, Plekhanov objected to the critical attitude. As an ideologist he rejected it with all his might, because it spoiled the kernel of absolute knowledge from which ideology had to develop. As a revolutionary he rejected it because it spoiled the security of the determinism which justified revolutionary action and conjured away individual responsibility, by placing material nature and man in the same series of determinations. 'Kant would convince us that the category of causality could absolutely not be applied to things in themselves.'[27] Now, things in themselves act on our thought, which is a faithful translation of them, verified by experience. It is essential to affirm the homogeneity of nature and man, to which end Plekhanov once again cites his trusty Holbach: 'Man is the work of nature; he exists in nature; he is subject to its laws; he cannot break away from them; he cannot, even in his thought, stand outside them.'[28] He can apprehend these laws objectively. Materialism assimilates the 'for itself' of technical objectivity, and the 'in itself' of the processes of nature without fear or favour. In this way, the technical expert in the natural sciences is equated with the technical expert in the social sciences (the revolutionary) as both possessing ultimate knowledge ('the object of the materialist's research is nature and human history'). The Marxist, a developed (dialectical!) materialist, is capable of explaining even the Kantian aberration, and the yet more serious one of Bernstein and Conrad Schmidt. And this is the explanation: 'It is in the interests of the bourgeoisie to revive the philosophy of Kant in the hope that this philosophy will help to lull the proletariat.' Did not Kant say: 'I should thus destroy knowledge to make a clear space for faith'? Kant scattered opium on the consciousness of the workers. 'Truly', comments Plekhanov, 'the bourgeoisie is not stupid.'[29]

To a political question, Plekhanov responds with philosophy, or rather, presented with a philosophical question implicit in a political attitude, he firmly put it under ideological lock and key. Having crushed the philosophical doubt beneath the certainty of the system, he returns to the politics which have disqualified his adversary and refutes his arguments by setting them in the context of a politically condemned system: the bourgeoisie. Bernstein's progress from political to intellectual emancipation was retraced in the opposite direction by Plekhanov, who, after an inquisitorial trial, delivered him up to the secular arm of the 'class struggle'.

The circularity of the ideological argument which, after having refuted the objection, proceeds to digest the objector (and often begins to digest him in the guise of refuting his objection) is even more perfect than a trial under the Inquisition. For if a judge in the Inquisition wanted to uncover a heresy, he had no positive theory to explain the heretic. He blamed him on the Devil, his father, from whose temptations no one, not even the Inquisitor himself, could be immune. Ideology, on the other hand, because it is central as of right, must, in order to remain so, take account of this new fact which the dissident constitutes. It has achieved nothing if, over and above the refutation, it fails to reduce the occurrence to nothing, by explaining it away in such a way that the *continuum* in knowledge can be re-established and that, once the operation is finished, nothing should remain to occupy the territory but ideology triumphant.

This method, of which Plekhanov made examplary use (which is why Lenin gave him such high praise), was to be the Bolshevik method *par excellence*. And yet, Plekhanov did not stay with the Bolsheviks. In 1904 he became a Menshevik and even, if one can use the term, a crypto-*Cadet*.

This is not the place to rehearse the history of relations between Plekhanov and Lenin, fraught with incident as it was. There was, on Lenin's side, the veneration of the disciple, on Plekhanov's, the vanity of the master. Lenin rendered the emigré in Geneva the outstanding service of promoting him from the ranks of Marxist philosopher to the position – unsurpassed in splendour for any Marxist – of leader of the party.[30] But Lenin could not dream of leaving the leadership to him. Plekhanov, despite difficulties, aggravation and occasional discord, collaborated with Lenin during the *Iskra* period. *What is to be done?* came out in 1902, and Plekhanov raised no objections. During the famous congress in Brussels and London, when the great schism first opened and Bolshevism first saw the light of day, Plekhanov, though with some misgivings, stayed by Lenin's side.

But by the following year (1904), Plekhanov was keeping his distance from the new 'Robespierre', the new 'Bonaparte' and the new 'Blanqui', to reiterate the comparisons which he drew either openly or in private. At that time he re-read *What is to be done?* and found in it the horrors which had escaped him at the first reading. He saw in it essentially a return to the tradition of *Narodnaia Volia*. How much he regretted not having denounced it earlier! In 1904, he had a prophetic vision, even earlier than the previsions of Trotsky or Rosa Luxemburg:

Imagine that the Central Committee [C.C.] recognized by us all possessed the still-debated right of 'liquidation'. Then this would happen. Since a congress is in the offing, the C.C. everywhere 'liquidates' the elements with which it is dissatisfied, everywhere seats its own creatures and, filling all the committees with these creatures, without difficulty guarantees itself a fully submissive majority at the congress. The congress constituted of the creatures of the C.C. amiably cries 'Hurrah!', approves all its successful and unsuccessful actions, and applauds all its plans and initiatives. Then, in reality, there would be in the party neither a majority nor a minority, because we would then have realized the ideal of the Persian Shah.[31]

It is a premonition of the glorious congresses of the Stalinist era. But, subsequently, Plekhanov was not always so firm in his judgements. The Mensheviks, instead of frankly declaring themselves to be reformists, spent their time proving that they were quite as revolutionary as the next man. To such an extent that, if one reads the social-democrat literature, the Bolshevik–Menshevik split is apparently quite invisible, the declarations of both seeming to such an extent to be stamped with the same die. This is what provoked Ulam to say that the main difference between the two camps could be summed up in the single word: 'Lenin'.[32] Plekhanov himself did not choose between the two camps. In 1908, when he was in close collaboration with the Mensheviks, and because one of them (Potressov) had, in an article, failed to give sufficient prominence to the part played by Plekhanov personally in the beginnings of the movement, Plekhanov threatened to join with Lenin and to denounce them as 'liquidators'. All he succeeded in doing was to discredit the Russian Mensheviks in the eyes of the German social democrats, who knew nothing about Russian affairs, but respected Plekhanov's great name. In 1912, in the Bolshevik *Pravda*, and to the consternation of his friends, he was still castigating the 'liquidators'.

But even before having been cast into the outer darkness as a 'defensist' in 1914, Plekhanov was gradually moving away from the political scene. He took on the status of a scholar and historian. To be sure he remained a revolutionary. He went on defending the theory of the two stages, bourgeois and proletarian, of the revolution. The 1905 Revolution did not seem to him to provide sufficient reasons for modifying this overall scheme. He never tired of recalling Engels's warnings about a premature seizure of power, which would place the proletariat in a position of serious risk. The favoured ally at that time was the liberal movement, which was actively preparing the so-called bourgeois revolution. There was time yet for the second stage. Moreover, in his historical writings, Plekhanov was fully in accord with the conclusions of the liberal historical school. Russia's misfortune was that the civil society had always been crushed beneath a despotic state. Europeanization was carried out, under Peter the Great, by Asiatic methods. The modern age, particularly since the abolition of serfdom, opened the way for development in the European manner. The role of the proletariat was to complete the process of Westernization in Russia and thus wrest it away from oriental despotism. At the end of his life, faced with a brutal return, under Lenin, to an oriental despotism, he was filled with remorse, and wondered about the extent of his own responsibility. However illegitimate his descendants might be, was it not he who had fathered them? 'Did we not begin the propaganda of Marxism too early in backward, semi-Asiatic Russia?'[33] One can already see the Trotskyist justification for the failure of the revolution because of external circumstances and an unfavourable environment.

What binds Plekhanov and Lenin together, hindering the one from making a complete break and the other from outright condemnation, is the doctrine. The conflict of character is secondary. The political antagonisms could have been resolved in a superficial compromise. Right up to the war, there could be no open break with the orthodox Kautskyan line, while Lenin showed formal adherence to the theory of the two revolutions.

But there was this separating them: their internal attitude to the doctrine. Plekhanov believed in it unreservedly. But he believed in it naïvely. To begin with, he thought there was a coincidence between the values and concepts which he made use of in Marxism, and the values and concepts commonly received under the same headings. So it did not occur to him that 'people', 'democracy', or 'proletariat' could have another meaning in Marxism than 'people', 'democracy' or 'proletariat' when used in common speech, or found in dictionaries. He believed in the universality of the value of the truth of Marxism. Plekhanov, unlike Lenin, had never experienced the working class close to, had never participated in a strike, or put his political hopes in a concrete working-class movement. His working class remained a creature of the mind. Since living abroad, he had encountered the working class only in the shape of the duly qualified envoys, suitably attired in frock coats and bowlers, the representatives of social democracy.

But it was this abstraction which, paradoxically, maintained the contact between Plekhanov and the Russian reality. It was his very dogmatism which led him to put his confidence resolutely in the Russian working class, despite his lack of familiarity with it, and to reject any manoeuvre which might lead the party to substitute itself for it. Through a serious assimilation of the totality of Marxism, he had made his own the democratic and 'Westernist' elements of the doctrine. He had made his own one part of Marx's vision of Russia, which was very close to the sort of vision held by, say, Custine or Michelet. The Russian state was the ideal type of despotism. Plekhanov developed this theme at length in his *Introduction to the social history of Russia*. Thus he was in the Westernist movement of Russian historiography, which was for the most part liberal in the tradition of Soloviev, or left-wing liberal like the Miliukov circle. This liberal vision of Russian history was, in its Marxist guise, correct. If doctrine constituted the indissoluble link between Lenin and Plekhanov, it also constituted the insurmountable obstacle. Civil society in Russia had to become decisively more powerful than the state before it could dream of progressing to socialism, or else that socialism would be nothing more than a new form of the sempiternal Asiatic despotism. Plekhanov and Lenin both believed in a revolution 'in two stages', liberal bourgeois and socialist proletarian, but Plekhanov had a much more serious belief than Lenin in the spreading out of the programme over the two stages, because he had a serious belief in the concrete changes which the liberal bourgeois revolution had to introduce into Russian society.

What he awaited, in effect, was the introduction into Russia of bourgeois liberalism, and with it bourgeois economic development, and the maturation of the working class, towards all of which the revolution would constitute a means. Lenin, on the other hand, was entirely concentrated on the revolution as an end, with regard to which the liberal taste of the Russian people, and its desire for economic development were taken up as themes for propaganda and agitation, as political means. Depending upon whether the emphasis is put on 'revolution' or on 'bourgeois' and 'proletarian', Marxism takes on a different meaning. That was why, as he grew older, Plekhanov was led to accept the liberal part of the Marxist heritage. Now it is worth remarking that the liberal part is not separate from the materialist tendency, while the revolutionarist vision has an affinity with dialectics. What safeguards Plekhanov's reasoning to a great extent is this ballast of materialism, an honourable if unremarkable philosophy, allowing a certain contact with the real.

It was because of materialism that he believed in economic forces, in the weight of social classes, in the dangers of making haste, and in the impossibility of going against the objective forces of history and of nature. His materialism, at the moment of his death, took a spiritual turn which was at least a little in tune with the Spinozism which he mistakenly professed during his conflicts with Bernstein. Dying, and seeing his wife in tears, he said: 'You and I, we're old revolutionists and we must be firm. And, then, what is death? Look through the window. Can you see that birch which leans tenderly against the pine? I, too, perhaps will one day be transformed into a similar birch. What's so bad about that?'[34]

A materialism sufficiently imbued with a spirit of pantheism is fulfilled in contemplation of the world as it is, and is almost raised to thanksgiving. For half a century, materialism had fostered the passion for revolution and had justified violent actions. The same materialism, in the elderly Plekhanov, served to explain the extinction of that passion and justified prudence and caution. As long as he was filled with the pride of total knowledge, materialism was a door shut on philosophy, but when his powers began to fail, all that remained of his materialism was a recognition of the magnificence of matter, which served as a stepping-stone to all that the old man was capable of. It served, in fact, as a philosophy.

II
Lenin

History is personal. The outstanding events of history, its turning-points, exist in and are expressed through outstanding personalities. Plekhanov's Marxism, which deviated from Hegel at this point, denied this. It gave to historical development a transpersonal character: the infrastructure, the masses, classes and the ideology of class. 'If some stroke of misfortune had killed Robespierre', wrote Plekhanov, 'his place would certainly have been taken by somebody else, and even if that other had been inferior to him at every point, events would nevertheless have followed the same course.'[1] Lenin was of the same opinion. And indeed, in the past century, one can at a pinch imagine the history of our Western democracies in the absence of all the principal statesmen. One does not have the impression that Chamberlain or Daladier or Hoover had a decisive influence on the history of their countries, nor even, one could claim, Churchill, or de Gaulle, or Roosevelt. But it is impossible to imagine the history of the USSR without Lenin.

It is not possible to assert that the revolution would have happened if Lenin had not made it and kept it going. Lenin was its author, its instigator, its inspiration, and the point of reference for a new type of régime, which has spread substantially unchanged across a third of the world, and which may still spread over the entire globe.

Who is there in history to rival Lenin? Stalin was content to apply the principles of Leninism, with a determination and a logic which were themselves Leninist. Hitler set up a misconceived, unstable and convulsive version of Leninism, which had no lasting application. Is there any need to go on? It is apparent that Lenin fits into no known category. Soviet domination is more extensive and longer lasting than the empires of Alexander the Great or Genghis Khan, but, examined closely, it does not have the structure of an empire of conquest. Like Caesar, or Richelieu, or Thiers, Lenin founded a new kind of legitimacy. But his legitimacy did not rest on the consensus of his subjects. It did not produce a stable, self-regulating system. The consensus was assumed, but it was not demonstrated in any relaxation of coercion. This necessarily remained as strongly in force as on the first day. Should one perhaps move outside the political arena altogether, and compare Lenin to Constantine the Great, who renewed the spiritual foundations of his empire, or to Muhammed and the armed prophets? But ideology is not a religion.

To revolutionary leaders then? Not in any case to Münzer or to the millenarians who, in denying themselves the political dimension, hastened to their destruction. Cromwell had a dexterity, a sense of the concrete situation, a capacity for discerning the possible and the impossible which could be compared with Lenin's corresponding abilities. But Cromwell thought in religious terms. He did not want to be a revolutionary, but the restorer of a violated constitution. He was not in step with the revolutionary party. On the contrary, he brought the extremist wing round to his own view, and once in power he expressly repudiated the idea of a utopia. In doing so, he prepared the way for a restoration. Napoleon detested the Jacobin ideologists, the 'men of blood', and sought a *via media* between the old and new régimes, between a monarchy by divine right and the consignment of power to the civil society. This *via media* was, as with Cromwell, his own personal power. In this way he re-instituted politics as understood by Machiavelli's Prince. But this was not Lenin's way, who hated any *via media*, who was equally opposed to the Imperial régime and the civil society, and who did not consciously aim for personal power.

Robespierre is the type closest to Lenin. One can say of the latter, as of the former, that 'he believed everything he said'. It is a parallel that, following Malaparte, has often been drawn. Their characters were alike. The domination of an ideological party in a revolutionary situation, leading to a dictatorship in fact, but not in intention, lends their careers a similar appearance. But Robespierre fell after a few months and left no legacy of Robespierrism. Lenin's superiority stands out. The astonishing thing is that it does, none the less, contain the two opposite poles whose tension finally destroyed Robespierre, the ideological pole and the political pole. Robespierre was not sufficiently ideological for the politics he had: his party, poorly educated and poorly held together, split and betrayed him. But neither was he sufficiently political for his ideology, since in him the vision of utopia hindered action and fogged his perception of situations. Lenin carried ideology to the point of perfection, but at the same time his political action remained supremely free and realistic. A thousand times more intoxicated than Robespierre or Marat, incapable of perceiving the world as it is, totally dominated by an unreal vision of things, he appeared at the same time as lucid, implacable and cynical as Machiavelli's Prince, as steady in adversity as Frederick II, as assured in scheming as Bismarck, and as decisive and bold as Caesar and Napoleon. How could one be both Marat and Bismarck? That is the mystery of Lenin.

There is another mystery. History, we have said, is personal. But the person of Lenin escapes us. Caesar, or Richelieu, or Bismarck will never cease to fascinate with the inexhaustible riches of their personalities. The best biographies of Lenin do not get inside the person. Both Wolfe and Fischer slip from biography to general history. Ulam does not settle for calling his book *Lenin*, but *The Bolsheviks*.[2] Biography leads nowhere because this exceptional individual cannot be reached as a person. It seems as if it is an unparalleled novelty unique to ideological ages that their history should be shaped by impersonal individuals. In Stalin, or Hitler, or Trotsky, the criminal, or insane, or theatrical aspects of their beings marginally confer on them, so to speak, some sort of personality. It manifests itself on the fringe of their historical activity, like a fantasy in relation to their principal line of action in which they tend, like Lenin, at one and the same time towards all-powerfulness and non-being. In Lenin, even that fringe does not exist.

His father was inspector of public schools in the province of Simbirsk. When he took up the post in 1869, a year before the birth of Vladimir Ilich, there were only 20 schools in this huge, rather remote province. At his death, in 1886, he had increased this figure to 434 (with 20,000 pupils), not including several secondary schools of a very high level. So fate made Lenin the son of a good servant of the Russian educational system, and saw that he was born into the very places where the intelligentsia was forged. Lenin's incomplete provincial education made it impossible for him to enter on an equal footing into the high culture of St Petersburg, which was, at the turn of the century, beginning to break away from the populo-Marxist culture of the intelligentsia. His opinions rather inclined him towards the latter, and his tastes entrenched him there.

Lenin's tastes were entirely unchanging, and can be dated exactly. They were those of the generation of the sixties, just as they had been fixed in those years once and for all. Of modern art he knew nothing and wished to know nothing. A contemporary of Max Weber, of Freud, of English logic and of German critical philosophy, he knew nothing of any of them. He was wary of the Russian literary *avant-garde*, even when it claimed to be revolutionary. 'I simply cannot understand', he said, 'their enthusiasm for Mayakovsky. All his work is cheap mumbo-jumbo to which the label "Revolution" has been attached. I am quite convinced that the Revolution does not need comic buffoons who flirt with it, such as Mayakovsky, for example... People should be reasonable... and not keep asserting that Mayakovsky is three times superior to Béranger.'[3]

His classical culture was strictly limited. Valentinov, who knew him well in Geneva, and has left the most faithful portrait of him, asked him whether he had read Shakespeare, Byron, Molière or Schiller. He had not. Of Goethe, he had read *Faust*, and that was all. Amongst the Russian classics, he had read Pushkin, Turgenev, Tolstoy and Goncharov, but only in the manner in which the critics of the intelligentsia, Bielinski and Dobriolubov, understood them. He adored Nekrassov, the 'citizen poet'. He happily ignored Dostoevsky. 'I haven't got time for this rubbish!' he declared. After having read *Memoirs from the house of the dead* and *Crime and punishment*, he had no desire to read *The brothers Karamazov* and *The possessed*.

I know the subjects of both these malodorous works, and that is quite enough for me. I started to read *The Brothers Karamazov*, but I dropped it — the scenes in the monastery made me feel sick. As far as *The Devils* is concerned, it is plainly a piece of reactionary filth...I have absolutely no desire to waste my time on it. I looked through the book and threw it away. I don't read such literature — what good is it to me?[4]

It was also typical of his type of culture that he had such a taste for folklore. One day in Paris, his housekeeper was humming 'Ils n'auront pas l'Alsace et la Lorraine...' Lenin was delighted: it was the voice of the French people.

Plekhanov was his tutor in Marxism. He was devoted to the man, then quarrelled bitterly with him. But however much he attacked him, he never denied him as an intellectual guide. He admired his unshakeable dogmatism.

Lenin declared to Valentinov:

Marxism is a monolithic conception of the world, it does not tolerate dilution and vulgarization by means of various insertions and additions. Plekhanov once said to me about a critic of Marxism (I've forgotten his name): '*First, let's stick the convict's badge on him, and then after that we'll examine his case.*' And I think that we must 'stick the convict's badge' on anyone and everyone who tries to undermine Marxism, even if we don't go on to examine his case. That's how every sound revolutionary should react.[5]

But before Plekhanov, Lenin had encountered the earlier and even more decisive influence of Chernyshevski, which affected not only his thought but also his character. He read Chernyshevski throughout his youth, and particularly when he was in enforced residence in the country after having been expelled from the University of Kazan.

I used to read greedily from early morning till late at night...Chernyshevski was my favourite author. I read and reread everything he had published in the *Sovremennik*. Chernyshevski introduced me to philosophical materialism... I read Chernyshevski's magnificent essays on aesthetics, art and literature from cover to cover...Chernyshevski's encyclopedic knowledge, the brilliance of his revolutionary views, and his ruthless polemical talent captivated me. I even found out his address and wrote a letter to him; I was very pained when I did not receive any answer, and I was greatly distressed when I heard the news of his death in the following year...It is said that there are musicians with perfect pitch: one could also say that there are people with perfect revolutionary flair. Marx and Chernyshevski were such men. You can't find another Russian revolutionary who understood and condemned the cowardly, base and perfidious nature of every kind of liberalism with such thoroughness, acumen, and force as Chernyshevski did.

He read *What's to be done?* just after his brother Alexander had been executed, knowing it to have been one of Alexander's favourite books. 'I spent', he said, 'not days but several weeks reading it. Only then did I understand its depth...*He completely transformed my outlook.*'[6]

What's to be done? is the most favourable observation point from which to contemplate the life of Lenin. If one cannot lay hold of his *self*, which remains elusive, at least one can say that his *ideal self* is Rakhmetov. Like his fictional model, Lenin set about training his physical faculties. Gymnastics, diet, a regular life, a precisely ordered domestic life, all ensured that the revolutionary had his full forces ready at his disposal. He too took on, through his economy, asceticism and moderation, the appearance, but the appearance only, of the perfect *petit bourgeois*. Like Rakhmetov, Lenin divided literature into *useful* and *useless* reading, and the *useless* he left unread.

This indefatigable autodidact, who, like his teacher Marx, spent a good deal of his time in public libraries, was always ready, like Chernyshevski — and Rakhmetov — to lay down the law in the name of his unshakable convictions and his new-found provincial science. He had no hesitation in writing a long book attacking a difficult Austrian logician, Ernst Mach, whom he was not intellectually equal to reading, but whom he refuted through and through. Later on, when he was in power, he had Mach withdrawn from the public libraries along with Descartes and Kant and certain other 'anti-Marxist' philosophers.

Like Rakhmetov, Lenin lived chastely. No one has ever suggested that sensuality played much part in his union with Krupskaya, to whose exceptional ugliness and mediocrity all the testimony bears witness. Much has been made of an attachment he might have had for a very different kind of woman, Inessa Armand. It certainly seems as though they were on fairly intimate terms at one time, and that Lenin was deeply affected by her death. Some letters have survived: they comprise lengthy political dissertations and instructions for militants. They had discussions on free love. Lenin thought it a bourgeois notion. 'The point is not what you *subjectively*' understand by free love. The point is 'the *objective logic* of class relations in matters of love'. On a novel which she had lent him: 'What rubbish and folly! Collect the largest possible number of 'horrors', tie together 'vice' and 'syphilis' and romantic villainy and extortion of money by blackmail…and the trial of a doctor… In my opinion, imitation is certainly there, supremely bad imitation of the supremely bad Dostoevsky.'[7] It hardly matters what went on, or did not go on, between Lenin and Inessa. But it is worth noting that there was a literary model for Inessa, and that was Vera Pavlovna in *What's to be done?* She too went from a bourgeois life and from a less progressive to a more progressive husband. Towards 1860, it was the fashion to follow not only the spirit of *What's to be done?*, but its plot too. Was Inessa conscious of the parallel? And if she was not, was Lenin? We do not know.

The key to Lenin, as to Rakhmetov, lies in total devotion to the demands of ideology, and complete subordination to the revolutionary practice dictated by it. In Lenin this absorption reached a pitch of perfection. When he dreamt, in the dark of the night his dreams were of revolution. The revolution was the yardstick by which he judged human relations. We can see him in 1907, abandoned by nearly everybody, greeting Valentinov with a 'cold and angry' expression, and asking him:

'Do you *still* belong to our group?' 'Yes.' 'So you haven't left the group yet. I had to make sure of that — if you'd told me that you'd left the group, I would have walked away and had nothing more to say to you. I won't ask you why you didn't sign the protest of the thirty-seven Bolsheviks; I am told that at that time you had some difficulties of a personal nature!' 'At that time my son had just died.' 'Whether that was the reason, or something else is of no interest now; I want to talk about more important things...'

And so powerful was Lenin's conviction, so all-absorbing the logic of the system, that poor Valentinov said no more about it, as if the protest of the thirty-seven Bolsheviks really was more important than the death of his son.[8]

But did Lenin exist outside this polarization? His *ideal self* holds no mysteries, but what about his *self*? In vain did the cult organized after his death seek to raise altars to a 'human' Ilich, a sort of gay and mischievous genie. The legend fell flat by itself. In vain have historians of all persuasions sought to reach some non-political fringe, some nook of his personality which might have escaped the ideological mould. Lenin is absent from the biographies of him, which all develop, as I have said, into political analyses.

Was he Russian in the same way that Gladstone was English, Thiers French, and Bismarck Prussian? He certainly cannot be explained except in relation to the political and intellectual conditions which shaped him and which existed all together only in Russia. But, as a human type, as a character, he evades any sort of national specifications. Dostoevsky charged the revolutionary intelligentsia with becoming denationalized. Lenin could provide a perfect example of that sort of denationalization, appearing to fit so perfectly into the anonymous Europe of the middle class. Besides, he was not interested in national culture. In 1914 he declared that this concept was a bourgeois trick spread by the Black Hundreds and the priests. National culture was the culture of the great landowners, the clergy and the bourgeoisie. The culture of the masses was international. The principal claim to 'the pride of the Greater-Russians' was their contribution to the world revolutionary movement and especially in having as their fellow 'Chernyshevski, the Great-Russian democrat, who dedicated his life to the cause of revolution'.[9]

Nor did he feel any greater interest in 'international' culture. The vicissitudes of exile led him to visit all the brilliant centres of European civilization at its zenith. He disregarded them. In London, he disdained *their* famous Westminster', the Westminster of the class enemies.[10] Similarly Chernyshevski left Russia only once in his life, to see Herzen, and spent four days in discussions in London, and then went home without him. In Salzburg, Lenin complained of a stomach ache, and asked for a hundred roubles from his mother. In Berlin, he went for his daily swim in the Spree. He hated Paris. Trotsky had made friends with some of the young French *Confédération Générale du Travail*. Lenin did not take that trouble, or have that pleasure. Somebody stole his bicycle, there was too much traffic, the library was inconvenient. In Capri he played chess with Gorky, did not agree about Mach, lost, and was cross. He was happy in Geneva. He was even happier in Cracow: 'The women are barefoot and wear gaily coloured dresses — just as in Russia...We are living better here than in Paris.'[11]

Let us look at the man who was to disturb the universe. A broad-shouldered little man, neatly dressed in his anonymous clerk's clothes, with waistcoat, cravat and watch-chain. His family background? Nothing out of the ordinary. One Russian grandfather, his other grandfather a Jew (a fact suppressed in the official biographies), one German grandmother and one Kalmuk grandmother from whom he inherited his cheekbones and his slanted eyes: he was a frontier Russian like so many on the Volga, of mixed blood. Worthy, affectionate parents, and a united family. A lively, studious, headstrong child, giving, by and large, every satisfaction. His style? The style of the journalists of the sixties, fulsome, prolix, solid, lacking rhythm or imagery, and yet not always tedious. His state of mind? Tense, with a slight manic-depressive alternation between hyperactivity and depression. Faults? A tendency to impatience and anger. Health? Good, except for some stomach trouble, migraines and hypertension. Vices? None.

The whole picture is extraordinarily banal, perfect in its prosaicness, and in its range of platitudes. We are still up against the mystery of the Leninian self. The most likely explanation is that the self did not exist, that the doctrinal framework had completely replaced it. What internal catastrophe forced Lenin to secrete this huge and complicated prosthesis of self, this elementary but coherent 'Marxism', which he could not question without endangering his own identity, without feeling a threat which he exorcized by perfecting the system and by annihilating the instigators of doubt? Should one date it from the death of his father, when Vladimir Ilich — he was sixteen — stopped going to church and broke with the family tradition? Or did the break occur earlier? It is hopeless to speculate, we will never know. He did all he could to hide beneath that hard, dead and calloused tissue, which was like the tissue that a burrowing insect can cause in certain trees so that they die of suffocation. It is a fairly ordinary case, a common character which the psychology of his time would have labelled paranoid. What was unusual was that an individual so unremarkable in some ways should possess great gifts, and that such a deficient character was matched with an exceptional historical situation — the flaw in his being echoed the flaw in our world and in millions of human beings.

That is why the historian is going the wrong way about it when he is set on considering Lenin and Leninism all together and attaching some picturesque 'human' details to that perfectly smooth, enclosed personality. The only suitable approach to Lenin is metaphysical, because from a certain angle this personality, opaque in its transparency, by turns amused and angry, and with simple tastes, reveals beneath its smooth surface the disturbing depths of the Void. This is what Solzhenitsyn had in mind when he drew the busy, migraine-ridden, vain portrait of Lenin in Zurich. Thus was he anticipated, not by Chernyshevski, but by the man who, having seen the activity of inconsequential provincial militants, understood what was bearing down on Russia: the author of *The possessed*, Dostoevsky. Now Lenin is not like the princely Stovrogin, but much more like the tiresome, talkative, troubled, petulant Verkhovenski, who was not really bad, but on whom the whole world, transformed by his anxieties and swallowed up in his own self, could not confer existence.

But there is another approach, which is to make an abstraction of the abstract Lenin and to examine what, in him, had been substituted for himself, that is, the doctrine. The gnostic, in the grip of the saving gnosis, felt himself reborn and that he had become another, filled with a new content. It was the same with the Chernyshevskian hero, gripped and possessed by the true knowledge and reborn as a *new man*. The metaphysician can meditate on the havoc wrought in a man thus deserted by himself. The historian should pay attention to what it is that functions in its place, and whose political efficacy has proved unrivalled: Leninism.

12
Metaphysical Leninism

It is too simple to assert that Leninism provided a synthesis of the Russian revolutionary tradition. In one sense, all the elements that we have seen appearing one after another in this history converged in Lenin. The French Jacobins, the left-wing Hegelians and Marx, the Slavophile divisions, Herzen and Chernyshevski, the party projected by Nechaev and Tkachev, *agitprop*, first populist, then Marxist, Plekhanov: these marked his horizon, they were his constant referents, and formed the narrow circle of his approvals. But it is a selective heritage, because Lenin overlooked the portions of true philosophy which existed in Marx, would not accept the religious or ethical elements which persisted among the populists, and because one cannot find in him the sort of intellectual good faith which still informed Plekhanov. Besides, the heritage had been recast in such a way that it is no longer possible to be sure whether he was keeping or betraying the tradition which he had received. There has not been a moderately well-versed Marxologist since Kautsky who has not been influenced by the distortions that Lenin applies to the spirit of Marxism; but it is always possible to claim that Marx did in fact contain whatever has been found in him. In the heterogeneous combination that Lenin yoked together, all the elements which were retained were carried to their most extreme manifestation. What was violent became more violent. What had remained a fantasy or a dream sought to become incarnated in reality.

I

Can one speak of Lenin's metaphysics? He only wrote one book of philosophical intent, and a few articles bearing on the history of his conception of the world, from Marx and Herzen. Moreover, he himself would have energetically repudiated the term metaphysical. In fact, Engels, in the *Anti-Dühring*, declared that the metaphysician considered objects and concepts one after another, as separate objects of study: 'His communication is Yea, yea, Nay, nay, for whatsoever is more than these cometh of evil.'[1] The term, being thus opposed to 'dialectics', connotes something bad, something to be avoided. If one takes *metaphysics* in its traditional meaning, Lenin would still have repudiated it. And in effect, the spirit of speculation was foreign to him. There was only one method worth anything, and that was demonstrative science. The basic principles of his thinking were thus held to be scientifically demonstrated, compelling the assent of all men of good faith. They are not a question of opinion. His 'metaphysics' are thus homogeneous with physics, of which they constitute one of the basic principles.

The science of the principles of physics was not a prime inspiration to Lenin, who did not believe himself to be, and did not claim to be, a universal man. None the less, it can happen that a political attack cannot be dealt with solely in the political arena, and that it has to be traced back to source. Then one can see Lenin fearlessly confronting Hegel's logic, Mach's treatises, and Averanius and Poincaré, and, armed only with Plekhanov, Marx and Engels, refuting them on their own ground. The principal organizers of the social world have the same structure as those of the physical and philosophical world. To be involved in politics, it is not necessary to be a specialist in physics and in philosophy, but it is indispensable that the politics should be verified by the same *science* that underwrites physics and philosophy. Lenin could thus not but concern himself with their fate. Hence a common Western misconception. It is unusual for a political man to be interested in philosophy, so Lenin has been accorded the Periclean aura of the laurel-crowned philosopher, and there have been set about him the venerable shades of Plato and Marcus Aurelius. It would hardly be possible to be more utterly mistaken. Lenin was not interested in philosophy, but he believed in an ideology in which philosophy and politics were homogeneous and mutually guaranteed each other.

He committed himself to an ideology that imposed a vision of the world, and hence, dictated a line of political conduct.

Acting politically was thus a way of furthering the conception of the world, and, by the same token, practising philosophy. All the same, there did have to exist the beginnings of the elements of this conception of the world, which Lenin did not feel the need to elaborate, because they had been definitively established by others, who were there in the background, dominating his intelligible universe.

Hark, Lenin, matter, your God, matter is one. The world is material. The diversity of phenomena is a manifestation of the forms taken by matter in movement. The atom, the living cell, social man and thinking man are all different aspects of matter. 'Nothing is eternal', Engels had written, 'but eternally changing, eternally moving matter and the laws according to which it moves and changes.' Matter is eternal, infinite, all-powerful, predictable to infinity, and substantially one. *Materia sive Natura.*

'The materialist concept of nature', wrote Engels again, 'does not mean anything more than an apprehension of nature as it presents itself without any foreign excrescences.'[2] Matter is endowed with movement. As there is only matter, the movement is internal to it and the origin of the movement lies within matter itself. In this vast cauldron of matter in movement, which is the world, the elements react one upon another. Taking up fragments of Hegel's logic, Lenin wrote:

Movement and *'self-movement'* (this NB! arbitrary [independent], spontaneous, internally-necessary movement), 'change', 'movement and vitality', 'the principle of all self-movement', 'impulse' (Trieb) to 'movement' and to 'activity' — the opposite to *'dead Being'* — who would believe that this is the core of 'Hegelianism', of abstract and abstrusen [ponderous, absurd?] Hegelianism? This core had to be discovered, understood, hinüberretten, laid bare, refined, which is precisely what Marx and Engels did.[3]

Carried away for once by Hegel's flowery style, he went on to note:

A river and the *drops* in this river. The position of *every* drop, its relation to the others; its connection with the others; the direction of its movement; its speed; the line of the movement...The sum of the movement. Concepts, as *registration* of individual aspects of individual drops (= 'things'), of individual *'streams'*, etc. There you have à peu près the picture of the world according to Hegel's *Logic*, — of course minus God and the Absolute.[4]

A lot of different things are subsumed into this same concept of movement. The movement of particles, the displacement of a body in space, the chemical combination of atoms and molecules, the metabolism of the cell, conscience, social life were all so many *movements*. None the less, the sum of these movements did not produce a random agitation 'in one spot'. It was governed by a process which unfolded in history. It came about through contradiction. Any phenomenon contains two opposite tendencies which are linked together and which are at the same time mutually exclusive and 'contend' with each other. In a short passage, Lenin illustrated what he called this 'law' with the following examples: 'In mathematics: + and − . Differential and integral. In mechanics: action and reaction. In physics: positive and negative electricity. In chemistry: the combination and dissociation of atoms.'[5] In synchrony this is called contradiction. In diachrony it has another name: the struggle between the old and the new. The development of nature is carried on through the struggle between what is 'perishing' and what is 'being born'. The struggle leads to the victory of the new, which then is termed progressive. The movement is in fact directed from the inferior towards the superior. The curve is not circular, it is *ascending*. But it is not continuous. There are, necessarily, accidents and hold-ups. But the point is that we are on the brink of a *qualitative change*. The elements accumulate (quantitatively) and then there is a *leap* forward. Example: an electrical current has to reach a certain threshold of intensity before a bulb will light up. Another example: the revolution.

There is only movement. Rest, equilibrium, is only a moment in the movement. Only the movement is eternal and absolute. The unity of contraries, declared Lenin, was momentary, transitory, relative, while the struggle between contraries was absolute and never stopped. That is why whatever is outdated and reactionary (that is, whatever hinders the progressive movement) is eliminated. This general process is called dialectics, and the method for understanding it, the dialectical method. Dialectics are the 'heart of Marxism'.

Man is the pinnacle of matter, and of nature. Thought is the superior product of particular organic matter, the brain. As such it is entirely subject to the objective laws which govern matter. It is not the transcendental subject which would fit matter into the categories which it imposed on it and which would be called laws. That is 'idealism'; 'the recognition of objective law in nature and the recognition that this law is reflected with approximate fidelity in the mind of man is materialism.'[6]

There is no such thing as chance. Nothing is accidental. Everything is necessary. Man is fully subject to determinism. There is thus no room for free will, any more than there is room for an autonomous 'soul'. How then is one to regard the question of the moral responsibility of man and, more generally, the question of his freedom?

In his first work (1894) Lenin was concerned with refuting Mikhailovski. This is what he had to say:

The fact is that this is one of the favourite hobby-horses of the subjective philosopher — the idea of the conflict between determinism and morality, between historical necessity and the importance of the individual. He has filled piles of paper on the subject and has uttered an infinite amount of sentimental, philistine trash in order to settle this conflict in favour of morality and the importance of the individual. As a matter of fact, there is no conflict here at all...The idea of determinism, which establishes the necessity of human acts and rejects the absurd fable of freedom of will, in no way destroys man's reason or conscience, or judgement of his actions. Quite the contrary, the determinist view alone makes a strict and correct judgement possible, instead of attributing everything one fancies to freedom of will. Similarly, the idea of historical necessity in no way undermines the role of individuals in history: all history is made up of the actions of individuals, who are undoubtedly active figures. The real question that arises in judging the social activity of an individual is: what conditions ensure the success of this activity, what guarantee is there that this activity will not remain an isolated act lost in a welter of contrary acts?[7]

Lenin did not change his mind on this point. In 1908, in refuting Mach, he returned once again to this question of freedom, and resolved it in the following way. He began by quoting Engels: 'Freedom of the will therefore means nothing but the capacity to make decisions with knowledge of the subject. Therefore the *freer* a man's judgement in relation to a definite question, the greater is the *necessity* with which the content of this judgement will be determined... Freedom therefore consists in control over ourselves and over external nature, a control founded on knowledge of natural necessity.' Then Lenin added his own commentary, in four points:

Firstly, Engels at the very outset of his argument recognizes the laws of nature, the laws of external nature, the necessity of nature — i.e., all that Mach, Averanius, Petzoldt and Co. characterize as 'metaphysics'...

Secondly, Engels does not attempt to contrive 'definitions' of freedom and necessity, the kind of scholastic definitions with which the reactionary professors...are most concerned...The necessity of nature is primary, and human will and mind are secondary. The latter must necessarily and inevitably adapt themselves to the former.

Thirdly, Engels does not doubt the existence of 'blind necessity'. [Materialism is] 'the recognition of the objective reality of the external world and of the laws of external nature, and of the fact that both this world and these laws are fully knowable to man but can never be known to him *with finality*. We do not know the necessity of nature in the phenomena of the weather, and to that extent we are inevitably slaves of the weather. But while we *do not know* this necessity, *we do know* that it exists.

Fourthly, in the above-mentioned argument Engels...makes a *leap* from theory to practice... For Engels all living human practice permeates the theory of knowledge itself and provides an *objective* criterion of truth. For until we know a law of nature, it, existing and acting independently of and outside our mind, makes us slaves of 'blind necessity'. But once we come to know this law, which acts (as Marx repeated a thousand times) *independently* of our will and our mind, we become the masters of nature. The mastery of nature is a result of an objectively correct reflection within the human head of the phenomena and processes of nature.[8]

Thus it is knowledge which saves man and makes him master of necessity. Now objective knowledge is possible. In fact, it is a function of matter. 'Sensation depends on the brain, nerves, retina, etc., i.e., on matter organized in a definite way.'[9] Matter gets to know itself through matter. That is even how it is defined: 'Matter is a philosophical category denoting the objective reality which is given to man by his sensations, and which is copied, photographed and reflected by our sensations, while existing independently of them.'[10] The self-moving process of matter is at the same time, through man, who *reflects* it, a process of self-awareness. It follows that knowledge is at one and the same time objective — because matter is reflected in itself exactly — and relative, because matter has not stopped moving and reflecting itself. Leninism includes relativism, but it is not a kind of relativism: 'The *limits* of approximation of our knowledge to objective, absolute truth are historically conditional, but the existence of such truth is *unconditional*, and the fact that we are approaching nearer to it is also unconditional.'[11] Relativism leads to scepticism, agnosticism, sophism and subjectivism, all things which Lenin abominated.

When and under what circumstances we reached, in our knowledge of the essential nature of things, the discovery of alizarin in coal tar or the discovery of electrons in the atom is historically conditional; but that every such discovery is an advance of 'absolutely objective knowledge' is unconditional. In a word, every ideology is historically conditional, but it is unconditionally true that to every scientific ideology (as distinct, for instance, from religious ideology) there corresponds an objective truth, absolute nature.[12]

As for the criterion of absolute objective truth, it is practice which will provide it. And Lenin again quotes Engels: 'The success of our action proves the conformity (*Übereinstimmung*) of our perception with the objective nature of the things perceived.'[13] This provides the Leninist with a comfortable latitude for action. His action is sanctioned by absolute objective truth. But, from one moment to the next, he can give it a relativist twist and make a complete *about-turn*: practice then carries it up onto a new, higher level, which approximates even more closely to the absolute objective truth.

As one can see, there is a history of knowledge just as there is a history of matter, and, in fact, they are one and the same. It follows then that this history is subject to the great dialectical law of the struggle between contraries, of the struggle between the old and the new. In the recent history of matter, which is the history of social humanity, there stand opposed to each other the movement towards self-knowledge and a movement which goes against and hinders that knowledge. This latter movement should be given the generic name idealism. For as long as men have existed and they have had the power to think there have thus been 'two fundamental *lines* in philosophy'.[14] 'For the materialists nature is primary and spirit secondary, for the idealists the reverse is the case.'[15] One of these lines goes by way of Plato, Berkeley, Kant and Hume, and comes to a shameful conclusion in Mach, Avenarius and Co. The other line starts from Heraclitus, Democritus and Epicurus, goes gloriously by way of Holbach, Helvetius and Diderot, passes victoriously through the ambiguous Hegel, skirts perfection in Feuerbach and Chernyshevski, and finally blossoms in Marx and Engels. The self-revelation of matter is fulfilled in Marxism.

The struggle is not over. In fact, for dialectical reasons, not all minds are compelled by the splendour of the truth. Worse, the disseminators of error busy themselves confusing the issue and particularly with obscuring the distinction between the two lines. Now, observed Lenin, 'behind the mass of new terminological artifices, behind the clutter of erudite scholasticism, we invariably discerned *two* principal alignments, two fundamental trends in the solution of philosophical problems'. The work of Marx and Engels must be carried on by 'mercilessly brushing aside as rubbish all nonsense, pretentious hotchpotch, the innumerable attempts to "discover" a "new" line in philosophy, to invent a "new" trend and so forth'.[16] There are thus *parties in philosophy*, and, to be more precise, there are *two* parties.[17] The party of the just mean is, as always, the most despicable of all parties. The claim of impartiality is a trap and a revolting hypocrisy. Even if it is sincere, it *objectively* follows the path of idealism. There is 'a *partisan* science'.[18] And at this point we run up against the domain of politics.

Before entering this domain, let us consider for a minute Lenin's vision of the world. It had been conferred on him as a youth, certainly before he began writing, possibly at the time of his sojourn as an expelled student, during which he gorged himself with reading on the family estate at Kokuchkino. One cannot see after that any revolution, or deepening, or development in his thought. Polemics obliged him to return to his reading, to Chernyshevski, Marx, Engels, Plekhanov and others. But they did not oblige him to extend it. The stock of arguments which he had dug out of these writers always seemed to him sufficient. 'You are mistaken, M. Poincaré', he declared with intrepid calm.[19] One should not place Lenin's ideas in the context of the history of philosophy, however simplistic and crude one might think that history to be, because that would be to give credence to the notion of Lenin the philosopher. One would do better to try to find out just where it was he had come across the elements which he had wrenched from philosophy and stuck together in that particular ideology. It most resembles a rehashing of Marx, and even more of the Engels of the *Anti-Dühring*. The latter book contains almost all of Lenin's cosmology, a fact which he would freely have acknowledged. He did not claim to be an original thinker, but rather a disciple able to apply the same principles in different historical conditions. Thus simplified, for the preceding pages have already provided an ample summary of it, the system is striking in its archaism. This monotheism of matter recalls to a great extent the naturalist cosmologies of the Renaissance: a hylozoism, a homogeneous fabric, in which everything reacts on everything, driven by internal movements; a macrocosm containing man as its most developed product, on the way towards some final palingenesis; it could be Paracelsus, but without the religious elements and without the correspondences between the parts being placed in the symbolic register in which they actually exist. The word 'movement' is used analogically to characterize several phenomena which bear no clear relationship to each other. As a way of thought, it constitutes an enormous regression from the phenomenological method and from modern scientific thinking. Nature and Matter are restored to a status from which critical thinking in the seventeenth and eighteenth centuries had already removed them.

But what makes it an ideology is the way in which the kind of consensus required by exact modern science is demanded for the subject of that cosmology. The word *law* is used to designate 'the struggle between the old and the new' or 'the conversion of quantity into quality'. The same kind of assent which reasonable beings accord to the equations of Newton or Fourier, is required with regard to these confused analogies. The two are married together to form a 'single science'. The system constitutes the universal framework in which particular positive laws have to be set. They sit there so well that each one provides fresh proof of the validity of the whole. The discovery of electrons, in Lenin's eyes, confirms Marxism.

Ideology 'understands' science, but science does not understand ideology. What could Mach and Poincaré have said in reply to Lenin? They would not have known where to begin, or on what to base a discussion. 'You are mistaken, M. Poincaré.' But about what? Poincaré would not have begun to understand.

But Lenin understood the blindness of Mach and Poincaré. To be sure he did. He even understood that he himself would not be understood, because his theory anticipates possible contradictions, understands them fully, and explains them in advance wonderfully. In effect, there is a sociology of error and bad faith. And there is also a political policy to be pursued with regard to them.

Let us return to the examination of Leninism.

According to Lenin, Marx extended the universal science of nature (or matter) to social science, to man. Lenin announced his admiration for this achievement as early as 1894. He quoted the Preface to *Capital*: '[From] my standpoint', says Marx, 'the evolution of the economic formation of society is viewed as a process of natural history.'[20] Marx was the Darwin of sociology.

Just as Darwin put an end to the view that the species of animals and plants are unconnected among themselves, fortuitous, 'created by God' and immutable, and was the first to put biology on an absolutely scientific basis by establishing the mutability and succession of species, so Marx put an end to the view that society is a mechanical aggregation of individuals, which allows of any kind of modification at the will of the powers that be (or, what amounts to the same thing, at the will of society and the government) and which arises and changes in a fortuitous way, and was the first to put sociology on a scientific basis by establishing the concept of the economic formation of society as the sum-total of given relations of production and by establishing the fact that the development of these formations is a process of natural history.[21]

The same science which had served to explain non-human matter, from Marx on could also explain human matter. Science was one, since it explained all that could be explained, matter and the knowledge of matter, the object and the subject. It was known, before Marx, that man and the universe were cut from the same material cloth, but it still needed a unitarian law to govern these two apparently separate worlds, which were substantially one. Marx having provided it, the major outlines of the universe stand revealed, and at the same time we can see why they were revealed specifically by Marx, why men are separated into two camps, and into two philosophical parties, those who accept and those who repudiate the scientific conception of the universe, and why they accept it and why they repudiate it. Lenin understands himself, and he understands his adversary: he understands everything. Of course, there remain things to be known. But the nucleus of objective absolute truth has been definitively established. It was for practice to see that this nucleus should grow, without becoming deformed, until it coincided with absolute objective truth.

Marx provided the social and historical world with a complete theory. Leninism is, as far as that goes, nothing more than an affirmation of the Marxist analysis, as it had been gradually codified by Engels, Kautsky, Mehring, Plekhanov, and European social-democratic thinkers.

The heart of Marxist teaching, as it was understood by Lenin, was this: history was a succession of social and political régimes ending in capitalism. In Western Europe, the struggle between the old and new was the struggle between capitalism and the social and political régime which was to succeed it, socialism. In Russia, the struggle between the old and the new was the struggle between feudalism and capitalism on the one hand, and between capitalism and socialism on the other.

One cannot pass from one régime to another without a leap called revolution. The struggle between contraries which prepares this leap is the class struggle. Thus, any right, correct, scientific position in the past was a reflection of the positions taken by the bourgeoisie in the face of feudalism, and today is a reflection of the positions taken up by the proletariat against capitalism. Any theoretical variation can be analysed by means of this rule: bourgeoisie or proletariat. For instance the variation of empirio-criticism: 'Here a division of the philosophers of Russian Machism according to political parties begins... The Machist Mr. Victor Chernov, a Narodnik and a sworn enemy of Marxism, opens a direct campaign *against Engels* because of the "thing-in-itself".'[22]

Social and political conflict is thus the proof of Marxism. Marxism is the objective reflection in the consciousness of men of the emergence of the proletariat. It explains the proletariat, just as it is explained by the proletariat. Its progressive emergence in the history of thought is parallel to the history of the class struggle. The system is closed because any attempt at refutation reveals the influence of the bourgeoisie, and thus is evidence of the class struggle as Marxism itself has defined it. Any contrary argument is thus a fresh proof of the validity of the system. In a word, there is an equation between the self-movement of matter, its self-revelation in Marxism, and the self-verification of Marxism in political conflict.

That is why on the one hand Marxism is certain and on the other it must be defended by every means. The certainty does not lead to serenity, but on the contrary to a violent polemic which knows no rest. To be a Marxist, for Lenin, means waging unceasing war on the enemies of Marxism.

Lenin bludgeoned his first adversary, Mikhailovski: 'Now — since the appearance of *Capital* — the materialist conception of history is no longer a hypothesis, but a scientifically demonstrated proposition ...Materialism is not "primarily a scientific conception of history", as Mr. Mikhailovski thinks, but the only scientific conception of history.'[23] Later, in an article published in 1913, and which, thanks to its compact form, has since served as a confession of faith to the Communist movement, he wrote: 'The Marxist doctrine is omnipotent because it is true. It is comprehensive and harmonious, and provides men with an integral world outlook... It is the legitimate successor to the best that man produced in the nineteenth century, as represented by German philosophy, English political economy and French socialism.' Marx's *'historical materialism* was a great achievement in scientific thinking. The chaos and arbitrariness that had previously reigned in views on history and politics were replaced by a strikingly integral and harmonious scientific theory, which shows how, in consequence of the growth of productive forces, out of one system of social life another and higher system develops — how capitalism, for instance, grows out of feudalism.'[24]

Except that Marxism, which is the most scientific of all the sciences, cannot expect the credence so readily accorded to physics and to chemistry. This too had been foreseen. The same article opens with these words:

Throughout the civilized world the teachings of Marx evoke the utmost hostility and hatred of all bourgeois science (both official and liberal), which regards Marxism as a kind of 'pernicious sect'. And no other attitude is to be expected, for there can be no 'impartial' social science in a society based on class struggle. In one way or another, *all* official and liberal science *defends* wage slavery, whereas Marxism has declared relentless war on wage slavery.

Thus the struggle for scientific truth can never be distinguished from the class struggle:

The genius of Marx lies in his having been the first to deduce from this the lesson world history teaches and to apply that lesson consistently. The deduction he made is the doctrine of the *class struggle*. People always have been the foolish victims of deception and self-deception in politics, and they always will be until they have learnt to seek out the *interests* of some class or other behind all moral, religious, political and social phrases, declarations and promises.[25]

This explains Lenin's distinctive tone. When he is propounding his theories, he speaks as if it were obvious, seeking not to move, but to convince through what he thinks are demonstrations. So there is no eloquence in Lenin, but the authority of an expert who is putting forward facts and proofs. Stalin was struck by this the first time he heard Lenin making a speech:

I was captivated at the time by that irresistible force of logic in them which, although somewhat terse, thoroughly overpowered his audience, gradually electrified it, and then, as the saying goes, captivated it completely. I remember that many of the delegates said: 'The logic of Lenin's speeches is like a mighty tentacle which seizes you on all sides as in a vice and from whose grip you are powerless to tear yourself away.'[26]

That was how he spoke to comrades. But he knew that the scientific truth could not be established without repudiating one after another the liberal, bourgeois treacheries, errors and falsifications. So his speeches and his writings throughout the forty-six volumes into which they have been collected so far are filled with a furious and inexhaustible aggression, and a wealth of invective. That was for the enemy. But it sometimes happens that this aggression whips itself up into a rage, into a frenzy of insults, into a screaming and exasperated fury: that was when he was addressing neither the natural friends of Marxism, nor its natural enemies, but the traitors, those who, by nature, should have understood and who, through bad faith, pretend not to have understood. It is normal for 'official professors' to teach their 'bourgeois science and philosophy' and 'repeat the platitudes that priests have uttered a thousand times'.[27] But what can one say of Marxists who 'try to revise the foundation of Marxism, namely, the doctrine of the class struggle'? What can one say of a Bolshevik who turns from Marx to Mach? There are no words strong enough. Renegade! Toady! Shame! And so on.

But the shame still has to be understood. There is an explanation for the traitor or for bad faith. So, after the flood of indignation, Lenin pulls himself together and puts forward the complete theory of the phenomenon.

Wherein lies its [revisionism's] inevitability in capitalist society? Why is it more profound than the differences of national peculiarities and of degrees of capitalist development? Because in every capitalist country, side by side with the proletariat, there are always broad strata of the petty bourgeoisie, small proprietors... These new small producers are just as inevitably being cast again into the ranks of the proletariat. It is quite natural that the petty-bourgeois world outlook should again and again crop up in the ranks of the broad workers' parties.[28]

Thus knowledge always wins in the end. All the same, the unleashing of aggressive feelings is not an aberration. The class struggle involves the militant completely. His whole being makes up that part of matter which struggles and triumphs over that other part of matter which represents the past. Lenin is included in one of the two *contraries* which are producing the *new*. The thinking man is militant because he is a thinker, and the militant is a thinker by the very fact of being militant.

II

What's to be done? is a novel of initiation, and Rakhmetov, the new man, prefigures a Perfect of a new kind. But this Perfect was in advance of the state of the system, which, during the 1860s and in Chernyshevski's thinking, was still in a sketchy condition. The ideologist preceded the ideology, and the gnostic, as a human type, preceded the gnosis. Leninism was the gnosis for which Rakhmetov had been waiting, and that is why the person of Lenin was the true fulfilment of the fictional personality. The Perfect was now filled with a total gnosis, which set him apart from the common run of humanity, a gnosis which imbued him with a life unlike any other and appeared able to provide him with countless comrades.

Leninism carried out a brutal and simplifying crystallization of the gnostic themes and attitudes which had haunted Russia, recasting them in a system whose structure is by now not entirely unfamiliar to us.

The world, which is homogeneous, is made up of more or less subtle matter, and is the theatre of a conflict which is immanent to it. Through this conflict it is moved through time towards the end of time. The Leninist, like the Manichean, recognized *two principles* and *three times*.

The *two principles*: Leninism is a dualist system. What animates matter is not disorder, but a coupling of forces. The contraries always tend, each at its own level of the material cosmos, to become polarized. At the social level, this polarization relates to the two classes. The other classes tend spontaneously to associate with one or other of the two opposed camps. This polarization is good, because it aggravates the conflict and thus brings it closer to solution. The principle and most important enemy is the liberal, the conciliator, the opportunist who keeps things in the amorphous state of mixture and hinders *movement*. In the Marxism which Lenin inherited, the struggle of the contraries was structural (the classes); it was not spatial, as in the old gnoses, in which the two principles were opposed in space, separated by a moving frontier. But Lenin remedied this lacuna by adding the notion of *imperialism*.

The theory of imperialism was no more Lenin's own than any other part of the system. It derived from Hobson and others. Originality did not interest Lenin. But being integrated into Leninism, by becoming an essential part of it, this theory has achieved worldwide success. The fact that it might be false or inconsistent did not stop it being held to be true, before ever it was examined more closely, not only by the Communists, but by non-Communists too. This was because it fulfilled the important function of giving a geographical content to the social dualism. With imperialism it was not only the classes which were opposed but areas which advanced and retreated along a moving frontier. Besides, *imperialism* provided a convenient reserve position if the class struggle ever happened to be disproved by the facts. If, in such an area, the proletariat does not fulfil its role of *contrary* to the bourgeoisie, that is because it has been corrupted by imperialism, because it has been penetrated by the ideology of imperialism. By that token, the entire region stands condemned. This gave the old Slavophile dichotomies between saved regions and condemned regions a new lease of life. The Slavophile motto, *ex oriente lux*, became the watchword for the Comintern Congress of the Eastern peoples. On the other hand, the English proletariat being *embourgeoisé*, the whole of England was seen to be immersed in imperialism.

Class dualism is the basis of a generalized dichotomy. There are two moralities. Lenin was not immoral:

In what sense do we reject ethics, reject morality? In the sense given to it by the bourgeoisie, who based ethics on God's commandments. On this point we, of course, say that we do not believe in God, and that we know perfectly well that the clergy, the landowners and the bourgeoisie invoked the name of God so as to further their own interests as exploiters.

This morality, which is 'based on extra-human and extra-class concepts', was repudiated. But there was a Communist morality: 'To us morality is subordinated to the interests of the proleteriat's class struggle.' And what is its commandment? 'We say: morality is what serves to destroy the old exploiting society and to unite all the working people around the proletariat, which is building up a new, communist society.'[29] There were also two cultures.

But it would be wrong to suppose, as the leftists of the *prolekult* did, that proletarian culture constituted an absolute innovation, a self-sufficient entity which would succeed as a body to bourgeois culture. In reality, the two cultures had their roots in the distant past and their conflict dated from the beginning of the world: 'Marxism has won its historic significance as the ideology of the revolutionary proletariat because, far from rejecting the most valuable achievements of the bourgeois epoch, it has, on the contrary, assimilated and refashioned everything of value in the more than two thousand years of the development of human thought and culture.'[30] But when this compound condition was ended, when the separation had been effected because the proletariat had taken power, then the victory of truth would be ensured. Hence the fundamental importance of education. The old school claimed to provide a general culture. But this was not so, because 'every word was falsified in the interests of the bourgeoisie.'[31] 'Apolitical' education is a 'bourgeois hypocrisy'. The crucial task is to 'contrapose our own truth to bourgeois "truth", and win its recognition'.[32] It does not amount to anything to combat the bourgeoisie with weapons, it must be combatted 'still more by means of our ideology through education'. For everyone, even the working masses, must be re-educated. And in this struggle 'each man must choose between joining our side or the other side. Any attempt to avoid taking sides in this issue must end in fiasco.'[33] Thus one would arrive at a proletarian culture which was 'the logical development of the store of knowledge mankind has accumulated under the yoke of capitalist, landowner and bureaucratic society'.[34] This dualism does not allow of any exception. There is not a single product of social man, not a painting, not a sonata, not a chemical formula, to which one cannot assign, in the last analysis, a class content. And this social dualism is analogous to the dualism which also polarizes the other areas of matter. One can speak of *their* Westminster (belonging to the class enemies), but of *our* electrons, which can be claimed because they lay another new stone on the edifice of Marxism. The contraries which set in motion material matter are not different in nature from those which aid the transition of social matter from the old state to a new stage of development.

Because, along with the two principles, Lenin also recognized the *three times*. The *past* is not hated so long as it is past, but it is wholly detested in so far as it extends into the present and corrupts it. Lenin detested unreservedly 'reactionary' Russia, and its régime and its culture, which was that of the landowners, the capitalists and the Black Hundreds. If he analysed Tolstoy, it was only in order to mark the distinction between reactionary and progressive, to praise the latter and abominate the former. There was a good and a bad past, a good past which laid the way for the future, and a bad past which persisted for longer than it should have done. From that past there was nothing to be salvaged.

The *future* was being prepared, not decided. The self-movement of matter was enough to ensure that the future would be what it should be. All that had to be done was to clear the path for the future, and remove the obstacles to its arrival. So Lenin did not say much about the third time. *The state and the revolution* was his only incursion into the future. It is not a utopian book. It is put together like a volume of quotations from Marx, to form the basis of a critique of what the past–present seems to hold which is most worthy of enduring: democracy and liberty. Democracy, he demonstrated, is a democracy for the rich, who only decide which oppressors will represent the oppressed in parliament. Liberty is nothing but a formal liberty. In the period of transition from capitalism, repression is still necessary and the state, which is in itself 'a machine for enabling one class to oppress another', still maintains that function, albeit to the benefit of the oppressed of yesterday. Communism alone makes the state superfluous. But what is Communism? Well, it appears here less far-fetched than Chernyshevski's phalansterian fantasies in *What's to be done?* The beginning of Communist society as conceived by Lenin is nothing more than a self-governing bureaucracy.

Accounting and control — that is *mainly* what is needed for the 'smooth working', for the proper functioning, of the *first phase* of communist society. *All* citizens are transformed into hired employees of the state, which consists of the armed workers. *All* citizens become employees and workers of a *single* country-wide state 'syndicate'. All that is required is that they should work equally, do their proper share of work, and get equal pay.

The vision comes down to the fact that 'the whole of society will have to become a single office and a single factory, with equality of labour and pay'.[35] But this poverty of imagination corresponds to the spirit of the doctrine. There is no knowing what matter will do, all one knows is that, freed of restraints, it will do it easily.

'Accounting and control' have already been '*simplified* by capitalism to the utmost', and under Communism they would be reduced to 'the extraordinarily simple operations — which any literate person can perform — of supervising and recording, knowledge of the four rules of arithmetic, and issuing appropriate receipts'.[36] So the curtain goes up on a society which seems to be nothing but an extension of the previous bureaucratic society, with the sole difference that now it all goes like a dream. Kitchen-maids can run the state. Men will live like gods, with no effort. 'Then the door will be thrown wide open for the transition from the first phase of communist society to its higher phase.' But we must not anticipate that phase. 'The Marxists...are opposed to *all* utopias.'[37]

There remains the *present*, where what is dying and what is being born, what is hindering birth and what is hindering death are all sorted out. The militant stands on the bank of the material river manoeuvring its locks and levels.

He feels that his mission is to allow the stream through, and only keep back the flotsam and the foreign bodies. He watches over the purity of the liberated matter. So it must be that *all* citizens become the employees of a *single* syndicate. *All*, one *single* whole, by means of which the *crucial* task (of accounting and control) can be achieved. The criterion for this process is given through doctrinal analysis, but the sorting out is not in fact carried out without a struggle, and that is why the present is the moment of political decision. What will verify the rightness of the decision is the purity of the stream, and the ease with which the matter in movement will move, once the barriers which hindered it have been raised. If, in spite of everything, the stream refuses to go in the predicted direction, then that is because there are fresh obstacles, which have not yet been seen, because *all* have not yet been regrouped into *one*. In which case the political struggle must be resumed.

Man is one with matter and subject to determinism. He does not possess free will. But through his capacity for knowledge he can become a central part of the process of salvation. Ideas are the reflections of matter, but once turned in the direction taken by matter, they can take on an auxiliary, accelerating role. Ideas become a material force, the more so the more directly they are drawn from praxis, and return to it. 'The point of view of practice, the point of view of life, must be the primary point of view, the foundation of the theory of knowledge.'

The knowledge which in Leninism goes under the name of *theory*, allows man the action which conforms to the determinism whose secret he has penetrated. Like the ancient gnosis, *theory* is encyclopaedic. In fact, the world being one and homogeneous, dialectical materialism is its central vision. It has the right to oversee the various sciences and the right to censor their results. If, in the process of the spontaneous development of genetics, or linguistics, or any other specific science, a scientist finds himself in contravention of the science of sciences, then he should bow down before the authority of the one who holds in his hands Movement itself, that is to say, progress, the only conceivable form of salvation. That alone can provide the *meaning* of particular results.

All the same, Leninism is not a gnosis, but an ideology. The most obvious change is the elimination of any mythical and religious elements. Even the great myth of *imperialism* has had to be trimmed down to the proportions of a positive theory, revealing its ideological content only in the way it resists any refutation. Whence the stifling nature of Lenin's style, constantly riveted to his pseudo-positivity, covering the poverty of his intellectual material and the circularity of his arguments with a continuous barrage of insults: he is right because it is the doctrine of the proletariat and the proletariat is only right if it accepts this doctrine. A closed doctrine, able to grind up anything within reach without being able to assimilate it, Leninism remains the same as at its inception, like one of those insects whose carapaces make it impossible for them to grow.

The transition from gnosis to 'scientific' ideology disguises the only element in Leninism which could be considered religious. In this system in which the subject controls all the operations and holds all the strings, there remains none the less that irreducible element of confidence, of self-abnegation and, in effect, of *faith* in an uncontrolled force − time. Lenin offered himself blindly to the future as the source of all good and of all truth. But this truly religious act of *chronolatry* was hidden from him by ideology. He was not conscious of it, and he could not endow it with any virtue or value. It was impossible for him to perceive it.

The elimination of the mythological, the poetic and the religious had another consequence. In the old gnoses, the cosmology of the two principles and the historiosophy of the three times were dominated by supra-terrestrial beings. Man, although situated at the meeting-place between the principles, and at the strategic point of the great universal struggle, still received impetus, inspirations and help from powers outside him. Man, in Marxism, is supreme. In Leninism, there are no more demiurges, either good or bad, no more aeons, no more emanations. It is thus men, 'classes' of men, who have to bear the responsibility of cosmic becoming. Man is, in the last analysis, either the good or the bad demiurge. All men are divided between one role or the other. It follows that the fundamental relation linking men together can be neither love, nor concord, but must be, on the contrary, hatred. Lenin accepts this situation of unmerciful conflict, in which the link between men in the same camp, which is called *solidarity*, can only be appreciated in terms of a state of war, and must thus be subordinate to the higher principle of hatred. Lenin's astonishing aggressiveness, which one might have taken for an aspect of his character, even for his dominant characteristic, comes to lose its personal tenor when seen in this perspective, and must, like everything else, be seen to stem from the doctrine.

So we come to the final consequence. Since the cosmic conflict is finally a conflict between men, then the terrain on which universal salvation will be decided is the political terrain. If Lenin devoted all of his energies to politics, this was not because of any personal preference or particular taste. It was because, in terms of the ideology, politics was the most important thing, the *only thing that mattered*. Whoever has really understood the doctrine places himself in the class struggle and takes an active part in it. Lenin in practice is concerned with nothing but politics, but this preoccupation is sanctioned by the theory. The metaphysic is not the object of systematic development. It remains implicit, which is in accord with the primacy of praxis. It only appears when it is challenged, or when political implications entail theoretical explanations. Then the theory comes out of its burrow, and Lenin theorizes, not for his own pleasure, but because there is a political need for it. The politics are inconceivable without the theory. But they are none too fond of theorization which, once articulated, might get in their way and prove a distraction. At the most, the best theory is merely politics crowned with success. Politics are the ultimate criterion of theory.

The order of the sequence in ideology is the reverse of the order in philosophy. For philosophy, politics, which take account of man as a social being, form the basis, then comes morality to govern the politics, and finally metaphysics as the ultimate object for consideration. But ideology first posits a vision of the world, which contains within it an ethical stance, which in turn leads to politics and defines the requisite action.

The philosopher finally turns from the sublunary world in the natural pursuit of his desire for knowledge. He returns to politics only for reasons of philosophy. The ideologist who starts off in possession of knowledge, follows it by turning away from it. He only returns to the theory when it is duly sanctioned by a political mandate.

The relationship between theory and practice in Leninism is, despite a superficial resemblance, nothing like the relationship between dogma and, respectively, faith and virtue in religion.

In religion, or at least in the Christian religion, faith is a gift, and virtue verifies the authenticity of the gift. Dogma is most often evolved in response to an alteration in the repository of faith. It explicates the object of faith, but as such it does not constitute faith itself and is not necessary to the exercise of virtue. That is why a knowledge of dogma does not constitute a principle for hierarchy among Christians. On the other hand dogma, having been received as a re-establishment of the truth (a *sed contra*), is considered as immutable as the truth that it seeks to account for.

In Leninism, the recourse to theory often occurs, as in religion, after a challenge, a *revision*. Theory, as Lenin said again and again, is linked to practice and vice versa. Knowledge of the theory is thus a principle of hierarchy among the militants. The master of practice must also be the master of theory, which means that, even today, there is no leader who does not also have to pose as a theoretician. Equally, the link between theory and practice means that they regulate each other, and that, when praxis demands it, the theory changes — a change which is, incidentally, accounted for in advance in the theory itself (in the chapter on dialectics). The leader is equipped to decide whether or not the change in theory constitutes a revision. The theory contains a stock of potential variations, or ones which have already been tried, so that one can always produce a new one without there having been revision as such. The leadership decides what should be said and thought at one moment, and then at another, so that there is a sort of orthodoxy which can be dated in time, related to a particular situation, a directive, a ruling power. But there is no dogma. 'Marxism', Lenin was given to saying in imitation of Engels, 'is not a dogma but a guide for action.' Orthodoxy is what the party *says* at the time and in the form in which it says it: it is an *orthoglossy*. None the less, all the variations should be produced within the theoretical framework which provides, for praxis, an adequate combination. Theoretical work consists in making this combinative function, but without transcending or destroying it. The framework is sufficiently comprehensive to provide the praxis with everything it needs and to orient it in such a way that it itself consolidates the framework within which it is working. Thus, in every case, the act can be linked to a justificatory reason, from which in turn the act itself is assumed to derive.

13
Political Leninism

Everything in Leninism — and everything in Lenin himself — comes back to politics. But politics take on quite a different meaning from that of traditional philosophy. Aristotle:

> Such organization is produced by the feeling of friendship, for friendship is the motive of social life…And a state is the partnership of clans and villages in a full and independent life; the political fellowship must therefore be deemed to exist for the sake of noble actions, not merely for living in common.[1]

Politics aim for the common good. But in Leninism the social matter polarized into classes does not form a political community. There is no common good and there is no friendship either. There is hatred and war.

Lenin, taking up some phrases from Clausewitz in 1914, appropriated as his own the famous remark: 'War is the continuation of politics by other means.' But in Lenin it means the complete reverse of what it originally meant. According to Clausewitz, war meant, in essence, going to extremes, and could not be thought of without these extremes being foreseen and anticipated; but such is not the aim of war either in fact or in principle. Because war is the continuation of politics, it retains the aims of politics, namely a negotiated sharing or division between autonomous subjects. Armed conflict is a modality of that negotiation.[2]

The division, if it leads to peace, and if that peace is worthy of the name, defines the common good by that very fact empirically. In Lenin, on the other hand, war, by its very nature, aims at the total defeat, the elimination, the extermination of the enemy, and is necessarily accompanied by a hatred which Clausewitz judged unnecessary. This is precisely because Lenin's war was a continuation of a politics which, in essence, aimed at the total defeat of the enemy and his extermination. Lenin's intention would have been clearer if he had turned the Clausewitzian formula round the other way: politics is the continuation of war by other means.

The goal of politics is the destruction of the adversary: 'If the revolution gains a decisive victory — then we shall settle accounts with tsarism in the Jacobin or, if you like, in the plebeian way... ruthlessly destroying the enemies of liberty, crushing their resistance by force, making no concessions whatever to the accursed heritage of serf-ownership, Asiatic barbarism and human degradation.'[3] And again: 'We would be deceiving both ourselves and the people if we concealed from the masses the necessity of a desperate, bloody war of extermination, as the immediate task of the coming revolutionary action.'[4] Winning means annihilating the enemy, and ensuring that it will never be able to recover. Thus, in April 1918:

The bourgeoisie in our country has been conquered, but it has not yet been uprooted, not yet destroyed, and not even utterly broken. That is why we are faced with a new and higher form of struggle against the bourgeoisie, the transition from the very simple task of further expropriating the capitalists to the much more complicated and difficult task of creating conditions in which it will be impossible for the bourgeoisie to exist, or for a new bourgeoisie to arise.[5]

There is no middle way. 'Either victory over the exploiters in the civil war, or the collapse of the revolution.'[6] In January 1918, however, the civil war had not yet begun. But it existed invisibly: 'In revolutionary epochs the class struggle has always, inevitably, and in every country, assumed the form of *civil war*, and civil war is inconceivable without the severest destruction, terror...'[7] It is not Lenin who wants the war. It exists, in fact, at every moment. It has been declared since the beginning, and social peace is either a delusion or the acceptance of defeat. The war is a war to the death and its conclusion is the revolution. Conducting politics is thus preparing the revolution.

But Lenin sees this revolution in terms of power. 'The basic question of every revolution is that of state power.'[8] This is one of the places in which Lenin is furthest from the populist tradition which emphasized social relations to the point of neglecting and sometimes even disqualifying the political struggle. Some populists envisaged a slow transformation of society to a sub-state level, out of sight and beyond the reach of the state. Lenin put forward the struggle between 'contraries' in the adversary form of two organized, hierarchized, directed armies. The supreme form of this organization is the state.

Making the revolution means overcoming the state. Doubtless such a point of view derives from Lenin's exceptionally trenchant and vivid Manicheism, in which two *continuums* of matter-knowledge and self-knowledge are concentrated on the one side in the state, and on the other in the party, which has a vocation to become the state. The state and its twin, the party, hold in Lenin the position of Archons in the cosmic Manichean struggles. The two camps know what they are doing. They are at their summits highly personalized, in no way innocent, and entirely responsible.

The struggle puts the classes in opposition, but it is decided at the level of the state. As there is no political community, the state is at the service of one class, and its function is not to arbitrate, but to ensure the domination of that class. It has always been the same:

The history of mankind knows scores and hundreds of countries that have passed or are still passing through slavery, feudalism and capitalism. In each of these countries, despite the immense historical changes that have taken place, despite all the political vicissitudes...you will always discern the emergence of the state. It has always been a certain apparatus which stood outside society and consisted of a group of people engaged solely, or mainly, in ruling. People are divided into the ruled, and into specialists in ruling, those who rise above society and are called rulers, statesmen. This apparatus, this group of people who rule others, always possesses certain means of coercion, of physical force, irrespective of whether this violence over people is expressed in the primitive club, or in more perfected types of weapons in the epoch of slavery, or in the fire-arms which appeared in the Middle Ages, or finally, in modern weapons, which in the twentieth century are technical marvels and based entirely on the latest achievements of modern technology...The state is a machine for the oppression of one class by another, a machine for holding in obedience to one class other, subordinated classes.[9]

This oppression is by nature violent, but this is not always apparent to the naked eye. The bourgeois state hides behind a democratic republic, but it is no less of an oppressor for all that: 'Nowhere is

[the] suppression of the working-class movement accompanied by such ruthless severity as in Switzerland and the USA.' As for the Soviet state, it declares openly and without prevarication that it is a dictatorship.

The framework of the struggle is thus the state. Lenin, the strategist of world revolution, is resolutely internationalist. But international society, the seat of the class struggle, is seen as a chain of states. Imperialism might oppose some states, to the greater benefit of the revolutionary movement, but their class nature remains intact. They are united. The task for the revolutionaries, wherever they might be, is to break a link in the chain of states, that is, the particular state under whose domination they are labouring. When this chain is broken at one point — with the creation of the Soviet state — their main task is to see that it does not re-form, and that they do not compromise, by a local tactical success, the strategic victory won over imperialism.

The state crowns the social totality which it represents. Thus the struggle cannot be restricted to the narrow sphere of politics. The revolutionary movement is deployed on the front of the economic struggle. It is not detached from workers' claims, from concern about wages and living conditions. It is deployed on 'the front of the ideological struggle'. It unmasks the bourgeois lie wherever it is to be found, and works to spread the class truth in the class which is prepared to receive it. But this generalized struggle is hierarchized in just the same way as reality itself, that is to say, it cannot be fully comprehended except after the point at which it has reached a decisive conclusion in the seizure of the power of the state. The syndicalist struggle and propaganda must be distinguished from political conflict in the strict sense, as the latter is carried out in normal political arenas, but they are none the less part of the generalized political conflict of which they constitute a specialized branch. Leninism is not Blanquism, as it was accused of being by its adversaries, who, as classic social democrats, thought that Lenin relied too much on political means, in the narrow meaning of the word. The charge was unjust. Lenin, according to circumstances, could put the emphasis on politics, or on the other hand exploit this or that mass movement, or yet again fill in some gap in the theory: each of these actions should be seen as political actions, as moments in the universal political struggle. Leninism is not Blanquism but *politicism*. Everything leads to politics and politics lead to the seizure of power.

This politicism throws light on Lenin's characteristic impatience, his desire to leap across time. Classic Menshevik and Plekhanovian Marxism paid close attention to the maturation of conditions. It wished to wait for Russian society to reach a degree of development which would make it ripe for what was called the 'bourgeois revolution'. Only when this had fully come to fruition could one begin to think of the 'socialist revolution'. If the movement was hastened, if an attempt was made to carry out the socialist revolution before the conditions were right, then it would lead, according to them, to the most dreadful mess — to dictatorship and worse. Now there could be nothing worse for Lenin than the maintenance of Tsarism, unless it were a bourgeois revolution which would lead to the consolidation of a liberal government. As a Marxist, he was forced to admit that the bourgeois revolution was an inevitable stage between 'feudal' Tsarism and socialism, but he wanted the state to be a proletarian state immediately (with the revolutionary party transformed into the state) and insisted that the revolutionary party would be in charge of conducting this bourgeois revolution. It would conduct it in a terrorist, Jacobin, 'plebeian' way, and it would retain the capacity for judging when and in what way it would be appropriate to pass on to the following 'socialist' phase. It would keep power throughout. 'The basic question of every revolution is that of state power', and not that of existing socio-economic preconditions, except in so far as these affect in advance the opportunity for power. It is from a consideration of power, of the possibilities of seizing it and keeping it that one must start, and everything else will follow after. Having judged that the world war offered the chance to make a break in the imperialist chain of states and to seize the Russian state, Lenin decided to begin the process of world revolution. Never mind that the poverty-stricken condition of Russia nullified in advance the idea of socialism, as it had been put forward in the Second International. The crucial thing was to start the revolution.[10] He reiterated Napoleon: 'We'll engage and then we'll see.'[11] But when the hope of world revolution has diminished, the crucial thing is to safeguard the fortress of the world proletariat, the Soviet state, whence, at some future date, the process of world revolution will commence once more. That is when the notion of imperialism, as giving geographical definition to the class war, really comes into its own. Imperialism and socialism face each other as two territories sharing a common, moving frontier, and as two states expanding in competition with each other.

Lenin's politicism is also a species of voluntarism. This is because the two opposed material contraries have a tendency to organize themselves and so are subject to the conscious will of the political actors. Of course, they are bound by necessity, and cannot act effectively unless they conform to the scientific laws governing them. But having a perfect knowledge of those laws, thanks to Marxism, the revolutionary party in power can procure for matter the ideal conditions for its self-movement. It arranges the field, clears away any obstacles, turns things in the right direction, and then everything can proceed of itself very simply, and above all, a good deal more rapidly. Power can arrange a short-cut for the movement of history. So it can never be too soon to take power and the very possibility of taking it proves that the moment to seize it has arrived.

II

'We are marching in a compact group along a precipitous and difficult path, firmly holding each other by the hand. We are surrounded on all sides by enemies, and we have to advance almost constantly under their fire.'[12] This compact group, described with such unaccustomed lyricism, is the political instrument, the party.

The party must be distinguished from ancient and modern conspiracies. These were political in their aim: it was a question of seizing power within a society which remained political even after that seizure of power because its structure remained political. The party was political in its means. But it was different in that for the party it was a question of seizing power in order to change society according to a plan and in such a way that politics would be abolished in society, because society itself would become itself spontaneously self-governing. The aim of politicism was to destroy itself in the revolution which would render it unnecessary and which would lead to the dissolution of the party itself.

The party is the normal product of ideological gnosis. If several men together are privy to an absolute, all-encompassing truth entailing a plan for the reorganization of society and calling for political action, then they tend to join together in a party. This is what the Jacobins did, precisely to the extent that they shared an ideology. So also the numerous groups which formed around the countless ideologies rife in the Europe of the Restoration and the July Monarchy. We have seen how early this generalized Carbonarism was imported into Russia. Decembrism already seemed a local version of international left-wing Romanticism. A steady succession then followed: Bakunin's philosophical version, Bakunin and Nechaev's delinquent version, then Tkachev, *Zemlia i Volia* and all the rest.

The idea of the party was no more original to Lenin than any other part of his thinking. Most of the characteristics of the Bolshevik Party were prefigured in the populist and Marxist organizations of the sixties and eighties. Lenin willingly admitted the fact. He admired 'the magnificent organization that the revolutionaries had in the seventies, and that should serve us as a model',[13] namely *Zemlia i Volia*. 'We need Social-Democrats like Zhelyabov', he also wrote, thus partially rehabilitating *Narodnaia Volia*. And finally: 'The attempt to seize power, which was prepared by the preaching of Tkachev and carried out by means of the "terrifying" terror that really did terrify, had grandeur.'[14] Lenin admired the conspiratorial efficiency of his predecessors. For in Lenin, plotting and political activity are not in opposition to each other, rather political activity emerges from plotting as a generalization of it.

All dualist thinking conceives the world as being divided between two organized but hidden forces. Any gnosis, any ideology, surmises a further world which alone is real, which alone is active. It follows that the party does not come together in order to lay plots, but to resist the plot which threatens it, and whose discovery provides the *eureka* of ideology. The party presents itself as being first of all a counter-plot. One might be tempted to try to give some sort of picture of the whole network of plots and counter-plots which polarized vast areas of the nineteenth century were it not for fear of being contaminated by the contagion of such a story. None the less, one must at least mention the Masonic plot which the Abbé Barruel saw at work following the constitution of the Illuminati at Bavière, and to which he attributed the French Revolution. Such a vision could not have been without its influence on those who, at the French Restoration, founded the *Chevaliers de la Foi*. This formed the kernel of truth for the myth of the Congregation, which in turn provoked the revolutionary counter-organizations of the July Monarchy. The myth of the Congregation also provided fresh impetus to the much older myth of the Jesuit conspiracy, which had been around since the eighteenth century and which had fostered the counter-fantasy of the Masonic plot. The shadowy dealings of the Society, which filled Michelet and Quinet with fear and indignation, flared up again once the Jesuit myth had found highly fertile ground in the imaginings of the revolutionaries. Doubtless Bakunin and Nechaev saw the party as an imitation in reverse of the Society as Michelet, Quinet and other propagators of the myth had described it.

Towards the end of the century, the notion of a Jesuit plot was gradually replaced by belief in a Jewish conspiracy. The forgery on Russian orders of the *Protocols of the Elders of Zion* provoked the counter-plot of the Black Hundreds. And so on. Plots and counter-plots grew out of each other *in contrario*, and described a sort of zigzag genealogy. But it is worth observing that very real conspiracies were plotted in response to purely imaginary plots. The philosophical party really did seek to organize to defend itself against a Jesuitism which had long since been moribund. This philosophical party no longer existed when the *Chevaliers de la Foi* were founded. The Congregation and the Society of Jesus only existed as fantastic justifications for a variety of tiny groups which formed themselves to combat them. It was the same with the Jews. It was not that Jews and Jesuits did not exist. On the contrary, they certainly did exist, but not in the organized, conspiratorial forms conferred on them by the ideologies. All the same, the simple fact that they did exist provided fuel for the fantasies about them and furnished a constantly renewed proof of the reality of the cosmic threat they represented and of the urgency of the measures to be taken against them. Plot and counter-plot are not symmetrical: the latter is real and comes first even though it claims to be defensive and to have arisen in response to an existing threat. Counter-plots are the consequence of ideology. The plot exists only in the light of the ideology and this lends it a horribly offensive appearance. Jews or Jesuits, playing a passive role in the whole business, find themselves attacked as being attackers and are called upon to justify themselves. But their justification, if they are rash enough to give one, is soon exposed and only serves to fuel still further the charges against them.

The idea of the counter-plot is proportional to the idea of the plot. The party is modelled in its ideal form on the enemy against which it would defend itself. If, in terms of the ideology, the enemy is localized, the party can set itself limits in intensity and extent, but if the enemy is total, then the party too must become total. Jews and

Jesuits make up a fairly restricted section of reality and do not in principle demand a particularly vast machine to eliminate them. But to the dualist mind they appear to embody the contrary principle, and these restricted groups are eventually invested with unlimited power which demands counter-measures of almost infinite proportions.

In Russia the enemy was from the start total. The party's mission, as defined by Bakunin, a good generation before there was any sort of party, was 'the complete overthrow of all the structures of the world'.[15] The mission of the ideology was to measure the height, width and depth of the world to be overthrown. With Marxism, which decisively enlarged the scope of evil, the enemy was no longer a group of men. It was in fact the very structure of the whole of society in all its dimensions, its economy, its stratification, its political and cultural life, which were shown to be a conspiracy. This conspiracy reached its pinnacle in *imperialism*: that is why the party, in setting itself up as a counter-conspiracy, by that token made up a counter-society as complete as the other. Everything concerned it and there was nothing to which it was indifferent. Nothing human was foreign to it.

Lenin drew away from the social-democratic interpretation of the party, or rather he drew away from their practice, which tended to confine the action of the party to the socio-professional interests of the working class. The party was not an offshoot of union activity: 'Social-Democracy represents the working class, not in its relation to a given group of employers alone, but in its relation to all classes of modern society and to the state as an organized political force.'[16] The party was working class in its means, instrumentally, but it was essentially pan-social. Class consciousness was only possible if the workers 'learn, from concrete, and above all from topical, political facts and events to observe *every* other social class in *all* the manifestations of its intellectual, ethical, and political life; unless they learn to apply in practice the materialist analysis and the materialist estimate of *all* aspects of the life and activity of *all* classes, strata, and groups of the population'.[17]

He returned to the same themes a little further on: 'We want to know everything that others know, we want to learn the details of *all* aspects of political life...'[18] Lenin comes back to this again and again. The action of the party was as total in every direction as its theoretical knowledge. This is the point at which it would be appropriate to say something about the most familiar aspect of Leninism: relations between the party and the working class.

The party 'represents the working class' in its relations with society as a whole, but it represents theoretical knowledge, ideology, in its relations with the working class.

Marx had made the working class into an elect class. But Messianism was the property of the workers themselves: 'The emancipation of the workers will be the achievement of the workers themselves.' The workers' party, in Marx, is not separable from the working class: 'The Party, in the outstanding historical sense of the term', means the totality of the forces through which the 'self-activity' and 'self-enfranchisement' of the working class manifest themselves. The political struggle is profoundly devalued by the organizing activity of the proletariat within the heart of society.[19] Thus Marxism, even weighed down with Messianism and with the theoretical apparatus to justify it, did not leave the domain of reality, that is, the combative entry of a new social group which was in the process of winning its place within civil and political society, a process which — all eschatology apart — could very well be termed the *class struggle*. That is why Marxism could, for a while, accompany the working class on its way, constituting itself into an autonomous political force within a political, that is to say, an adversary society. Social-democratic Marxism is political in the sense in which politics is opposed to ideology.

Lenin did not see the process of emancipation like this. To him it was not an empirical effort made by a determined group under its responsibility, allowing for attempts, errors and corrections. For him, emancipation was the fruit of the diffusion throughout the interested social body of the liberating doctrine, of the knowledge, of the theory, of 'consciousness'. But the salvatory knowledge does not spring up spontaneously in the social group to which it assigns the salvatory mission.

During a strike which took place in St Petersburg in 1896, Lenin observed that the workers spontaneously turned themselves to a defence of their particular interests and did not lend themselves spontaneously to ideology. In 1902, in *What is to be done?* he concluded from this: 'The working class, exclusively by its own effort, is able to develop only trade union consciousness.'[20] Where did the ideas come from then? From ideas themselves, through a progressive illumination which occurs among specialists in ideas, who could through historical circumstances belong to the 'bourgoisie', but who were *ipso facto* removed from it by those ideas. 'The theory of socialism...grew out of the philosophic, historical, and economic theories... It arose as a natural and inevitable outcome of the development of thought among the revolutionary socialist intelligentsia.'[21] This is the extraordinary shift from the real working class towards the theory of the working class. It is also an unexpected reversal of traditional Marxism. As has been written:

It is no longer the being which determines consciousness, ideas are no longer the 'reflections' of the social situation, but develop spontaneously, following their own logic, independent of any situation of class or anything else, and finishing by determining the being. Even more, the being of the proletariat is in the end determined by the consciousness of the intelligentsia... Since the workers, left to themselves, cannot conceive their own historical situation except in an obscure and inadequate manner, it is the petty-bourgeois intellectuals, turned professional revolutionaries, who must, according to Lenin, form the nucleus of the Party and take on the mission of taking proletarian consciousness and science 'to the proletariat'.[22]

There is a dichotomy between the proletariat and the idea of the proletariat. Like the Platonic demiurge, the party, its eyes fixed firmly on the *idea* of the proletariat, reshapes the working class in order to make it fit with its ideal model.

So Leninist Manicheism works in two stages. On the one hand, there is no solidarity by right or in fact between social groups; the proletariat recognizes no obligation towards the other classes, whose fate, whether for good or ill, will be decided automatically by its victory, the victory of socialism. But on the other hand, the party is no longer committed to the proletariat. It does not 'represent' it through any democratic delegation, but through some mystical delegation. It is only committed to the higher interests of socialism, as defined by the ideology. It is interested in the working classes only in so far as the working class is supposed to play a particular role in the terms of that ideology. If the working class shows itself incapable of carrying out the job to which it is destined, if in some way it betrays the 'proletariat' and 'socialism', the party will treat it exactly the same as the 'bourgeoisie' or any other enemy class. The party would then be careful to proclaim that Rome was no longer Rome; that the proletariat was located in its entirety within the party, and that the working class, whose soul had transmigrated through metempsychosis into the party machine, had received in return a *petit-bourgeois* soul.

As we know, it was Leninist practice to view with suspicion any organization, whether Soviet or union, which the working class might have formed for itself. The working class was one of the fields in which the two rival ideologies confronted each other. It was fundamentally passive and took its direction from others. '*All* worship of the spontaneity of the working-class movement, all belittling of the role of the "conscious element"...*means, quite independently of whether he who belittles that role desires it or not, a strengthening of the influence of bourgeois ideology upon the workers.*'[23] Before and after the seizure of power, the working class is the *prima materia*.

Relations between class and party were such that the latter could preserve more or less intact the conspiratorial structure it had inherited from preceding generations.

Lenin was short and to the point on the internal organization of the party. These were areas which had already been worked out by the populists. The spirit of the *catechisms*, of Bakunin and Chernyshevski had become second nature. That went without saying. It would not be politic to dwell on it. The party was stable, centralized and selective. 'The only serious organizational principle for the active workers of our movement should be the strictest secrecy, the strictest selection of members, and the training of professional revolutionaries.'[24] The party has as its nucleus men whose profession is revolutionary action. These men have to be trained: 'Such people must *train* themselves patiently and steadfastly to be professional revolutionaries.'[25] Within the party the social distinctions abandoned by the *new man* on entering the organization disappear. Before the common characteristic of professional revolutionary '*all distinctions as between workers and intellectals...must be effaced*.'[26] The party is above classes and perfectly homogeneous.

One thing unites the party and welds it together: 'something even more than "democratism"...namely, complete, comradely, mutual confidence among revolutionaries'.[27] There is no need for elective procedures, which spark off *movements* and faction, since the revolutionaries are bound together in a single and infallible doctrine. The party is its guardian, and that is why it does not allow freedom of criticism. Can one criticize what, being scientific, compels the assent of all thinking men, except those of bad faith? 'Those who are really convinced that they have made progress in science would not demand freedom for the new views to continue side by side with the old, but the substitution of the new views for the old.'[28] Proletarian science creates unanimity, it seals the unity of the party.

The innermost core of the party is thus not the stable band of professional revolutionaries, but something even more intangible than that — ideological knowledge. And this is the third and last stage of Leninist Manicheism. The party member is not committed to the party for the same reason as the party is not committed to the proletariat, nor the proletariat to the other classes of society. He is committed to socialism. Now, at every moment the party is being undermined by the same hostile force which, on the outside, is fighting it for possession of the working class: bourgeois ideology. That is why freedom of criticism is not possible: it means 'freedom for an opportunist trend in Social-Democracy, freedom to convert Social-Democracy into a democratic party of reform, freedom to introduce bourgeois ideas and bourgeois elements into socialism'.[29] The 'total trust' is conditional. Suspicion, falling on a comrade, breaks the solidarity and *ipso facto* expels him from the ranks of the party. Suspicion can relate to any point of the unitarian field of doctrine, since any metaphysical (theoretical) error extends into political error, while political error has its roots in theory. Both are due to the one cause: penetration by bourgeois ideology. Thus the party as a whole is in this respect a *prima materia* penetrable by one or the other ideology. One militant, alone among all the others, can become the sole repository of true knowledge. There is then no remedy other than a struggle within the heart of the party. If the knowledge is disseminated correctly (through persuasion, criticism and self-criticism), unity will be maintained. If not, a split will occur. The whole history of the Bolshevik Party, through all its countless purifications and divisions, bears witness to the fact that, for Lenin, it was important to sacrifice the size and influence of the party to its essence, that is to say, to 'monolithic' unity, programmed by ideology, like a cell by its genetic code. Once the party has been achieved, once ideology has found its point of incarnation, even if it were only in one place (and there were times when the party was almost reduced to being Lenin alone) then everything becomes possible, because the crucial element, the *logos* of the new world is there: 'Give us an organization of revolutionaries, and we will overturn Russia!'[30] And after that the entire world.

With the setting up of the party, the cosmic struggle has found its centre. All around the party enemies and allies fall into place in concentric circles. The central position of the party makes it possible to set the political universe into a logical order.

III

The heart of the enemy world is as intangible as the heart of the party. It is structural: it is *feudalism* in certain areas subordinate to the main conflict (notably in Russia), it is in a more general way *capitalism*, and finally, it is *imperialism*. Imperialism constitutes the natural enemy of the party, its *raison d'être*. It is, to be sure, the object of sustained hatred, but the hatred has become routine, almost professionalized. It is ideologically coherent and manipulates men, so it is not a question of hating this or that employer, or statesman, or even a particular and influential member of the enemy's police: they are doing their job, and the feelings one might have for them should be directed at the structure. Hatred of individuals is for the men in between, whose social or intellectual condition puts them in a position to choose sides, and who, in refusing to do so, hinder the development of the struggle and confuse the understanding one should have of it. On the fringes of the bourgeois camp stand the *liberals* and, in particular, the *liberal intelligentsia*. Lenin unfailingly expresses his contempt for them. If he praises Herzen, for instance, it is for having broken with 'one of the most repulsive exponents of liberal servility' (the honest professor Kavelin).[31] 'The liberal utopia', he wrote, 'consists in the belief that it is possible to secure improvements...peacefully and harmoniously, without offending anyone,...without ruthless, consistent class struggle.'[32] *Liberalism*, in his vocabulary, is opposed to *democratism*, which means being revolutionary: 'the utopia of the liberals corrupts the democratic consciousness of the masses'.[33]

Closer to the party, on the outer fringes of the proletarian camp and thus infinitely more detestable, is the opportunist. *Opportunism* is liberalism in the working-class movement. Thus this term too is opposed to *revolutionary*. All the European social-democratic parties, including the Russian one, recognized 'the fundamental division between the revolutionary wing and the opportunist wing'.[34] The struggle against opportunism is a never-ending task, for opportunism can assume many shapes. It affects questions of organization, and thus the structure of the party itself. It affects 'the fundamental problems of our world conception' and the programme. It affects tactics. It emerges in new, disguised, hidden forms:

We must never forget a characteristic feature of present-day opportunism in every sphere, namely, its vagueness, amorphousness, elusiveness. An opportunist, by his very nature, will always evade taking a clear and decisive stand, he will always seek a middle course, he will always wriggle like a snake between two mutually exclusive points of view and try to "agree" with both and reduce his differences of opinion to petty amendments, doubts, innocent and pious suggestions, and so on and so forth.[35]

Some would agree on the programme and be opportunist in tactics: *reformist*. Others would be revolutionary in tactics, and opportunist in organization: *Menshevik*. Tracking down opportunism in all the nooks and crannies where it might be hiding is the principal spur to Lenin's intellectual activity. Sometimes opportunism manages to infiltrate its emissaries right up to the immediate environs of the centre. These groups reached the very height of perversity. There were two main species which undermined the twin columns on which the edifice of the party rested: the doctrine was undermined by the *revisionists*; the organization by the *liquidators*.

In concentric order, like the party's adversaries, but starting from the centre, the party's allies also have their place.

One must distinguish between those who depend directly or indirectly on the party, and occasional or tactical allies. The first form a hierarchy, in a 'gnostic' way, according to degrees of knowledge, and hence of organization and secrecy. These last criteria are enumerated by Lenin as follows: '1) organizations of revolutionaries; 2) organizations of workers, as broad and as varied as possible... These two categories constitute the Party. Further, 3) workers' organizations associated with the Party; 4) workers' organizations not associated with the Party but actually under its control and direction.'[36] Martov and the Mensheviks sought to confuse party and class, to suppress the hierarchy, and to consider all the categories as themselves forming the party. The list, which dates from 1904, can be extended indefinitely, with organizations of the masses, of youth, of women, etc., all controlled by the party and all distinct from it. They were the driving-belts of which Lenin later was to speak.

The party's essential role is to disseminate consciousness, and the correct knowledge, but in a manner commensurate with the ability to hear and understand of the milieu in which it is 'working'. 'The object of the practical activities of the Social-Democrats is', wrote Lenin in 1898, 'to lead the class struggle of the proletariat.'[37] It does this through *propaganda*, which consists in spreading among the workers a 'correct conception of modern society', and through *agitation*, which consists in participating in all the spontaneous manifestations of the working-class struggle, and by means of specific and limited slogans to develop their consciousness.[38] Within the working class there is a pre-established harmony between the tasks of the union and those of the party, although the former is not aware of it. Therefore, within the union there must be a section of the party to manifest this harmony which is guaranteed by the theory.

A small, compact core of the most reliable, experienced, and hardened workers, with responsible representatives in the principal districts and connected by all the rules of strict secrecy with the organization of revolutionaries, can, with the widest support of the masses and without any formal organization, perform *all* the functions of a trade-union organization, in a manner, moreover, desirable to Social-Democracy.[39]

The party can attain union aims, because they derive from the theory. But the union cannot attain socialist aims, because it has no theory. A nucleus within the union: that is infiltration. But Lenin was right to see nothing hypocritical in this. Looking back over his past actions and offering advice to the young opportunist parties of the West, Lenin wrote again, in 1920:

You must be capable of any sacrifice, of overcoming the greatest obstacles, in order to carry on agitation and propaganda systematically, perseveringly, persistently and patiently in those institutions — even the most reactionary — in which proletarian or semi-proletarian masses are to be found...We must... agree to make any sacrifice, and even — if need be — resort to various strategems, artifices and illegal methods, to evasions and subterfuges, as long as we get into the trade unions, remain in them, and carry on communist work within them at all costs.[40]

Agitation, propaganda, theory are the steps leading to *initiation*. Between what the party says in the 'mass organizations' and what it says within itself, lies all the difference between exoteric and esoteric teachings. It is the same teaching, but with leaps and reversals which make up so many stages towards the ultimate meaning. In the union, the Communist speaks a language opposite to the one he speaks within the cell. The non-Communist unionist does not have the intellectual equipment to understand that they are fundamentally the same language. The Communist is not 'tricking' him, but he is keeping the interpretation tucked behind his back.

It is not the same with tactical allies. Because of their social position, they are not ready to receive initiation; in fact, the theory condemns them and predicts their liquidation. None the less, because of their particular interests, they can travel some of the way with the party. The enemy camp is seen as a shifting, heterogeneous coalition, and at every moment the party has to determine which is the strong point, and which the weak point in the enemy's front, who is the principal adversary, and who is one who can be temporarily undermined. There are no other rules in the matter than the interests of the revolution and of the seizure of power.

In applying this rule, there was no one more rigorous than Lenin, and hence no one more flexible in the choice of alliances. Some are desirable: these are the ones which will lead directly to the revolution. Others are acceptable because they make possible some delicate step in the preparation of that revolution.

The Mensheviks, or at least those who had the courage to repudiate the term, aimed more or less clearly at the reinforcement of civil society and the integration of the working class within it. They thus tended towards liberal alliances. They feared the barbarism and violence hidden in the ocean of Russian villages, and were afraid that it would completely submerge the frail barque of civilization. Their policy towards the peasants sought to avoid the explosion, and the regression which they thought would follow. Lenin had no fear of that explosion — he desired it passionately. So the favoured ally of the proletariat was, according to him, the most backward and, he assumed, the most violent part of the peasantry. He even imagined a sort of class struggle within the peasantry, setting in opposition the 'poor', the 'average' and the 'rich'. This struggle did not exist, for the village was as a rule united. All the same, there certainly did exist poor peasants, and Lenin unreservedly supported their demands and their actions. In this he was returning to the most maximalist of the populist programmes of the past.

Another great disruptive force existed in the Russian Empire: the non-Russian nationalities. Lenin did not go into whether it would be better to think of a federative status for the foreign nationalities, nor whether, as Rosa Luxemburg dreamt, proletarian internationalism should not transcend and surpass nationalist demands: he supported these demands unconditionally, because they contributed to the breakdown of the political entity he sought to destroy.

But in the hurly-burly of political life, Lenin accepted, as well as these two alliances (which he considered natural because the ideology declared them to be so) many other alliances, which he considered to be against nature, but which were desirable for the good of the party and of the revolution. He several times allied himself with the liberals, and even more costly were the alliances with closely related enemies, the legitimate-Marxists, the opportunists, the Mensheviks... No doctrinal reason, let alone any personal feeling, seemed to Lenin worth considering once the alliance became politically expedient in terms of the immutable good of the revolution and the seizure of power.

We are here approaching the focal point of political Leninism. Between high politics and sectarian conspiracy, at the very point where it had been conceded that there existed a tension and even an opposition, Leninism created a close link and even constructed a bond. The party, as developed by Lenin in *What is to be done?* is at one and the same time a secret conspiratorial organization and a political organization, and the one must not be sacrificed to the other.[41] Even more than this, it is because there exists a stable, centralized organization, possessed of the absolute doctrine — in fact, constituted and possessed by it — because the party preserves its identity and specific nature towards and against everyone that it can establish the boldest, most extravagant and acrobatic alliances. 'Only those who have no confidence in themselves should fear temporary alliances, even with doubtful elements. No political party can exist without such alliances.'[42] But the Bolshevik Party, precisely because it is bound together by an infallible theory, with the discipline and centralized organization which follow from it, runs no risk in conducting dangerous political operations in which other parties would lose their cohesion.

Alliances, non-aggression pacts, sacrifice of an advantage, abandonment of a claim, temporary retreat, all these belong to the Leninist category of compromise. In September 1917, at the height of the struggle for power, Lenin wrote:

The task of a truly revolutionary party is not to declare that it is impossible to renounce all compromises, but to be able, *through all compromises*, when they are unavoidable, to remain true to its principles, to its class, to its revolutionary purpose, to its task of paving the way for revolution and educating the mass of the people for victory in the revolution.[43]

That is its duty, because in behaving thus the party maintains its own internal logic: 'Our Party, like any other political party, is striving after political domination *for itself*.'[44] The consistently voluntary policy of compromise is correctly applied when the party attacks and denounces its ally without giving up either the benefits of the alliance or its duty of theoretical enlightenment of the proletarian consciousness. Lenin wrote in 1902: 'An essential condition for such an alliance [with the bourgeois democrats] must be the full opportunity for the socialists to reveal to the working class that its interests are diametrically opposed to the interests of the bourgeoisie.'[45] Again, in 1920 he wrote: 'Between 1902 and 1912, there were periods of several years in which we were formally united with the Mensheviks in a single Social-Democratic Party, but *we never stopped* our ideological and political struggle against them as opportunists and vehicles of bourgeois influence on the proletariat.'[46] One must, he added, make use of the hesitation of one's allies to *unmask* them.[47]

One can go further: it is not only the choice of alliances, it is the whole political strategy which the party's particular structure makes possible. Because the starting-line, the party, and the finishing-line, power (or the revolution) have been fixed, it is possible to determine at every moment just what the political position is, to draw a line and work out the score to date. Around an optimal position, which constitutes the *correct* line, the party oscillates between two equally erroneous positions. One is right-deviationism, which is in danger of dragging the party off in tow to its natural or its temporary allies, leading it to *capitulationist* compromises. The party, directed by its alliances, a prisoner of its language and forgetful of its own interpretations, runs the risk of being dissipated in opportunism. The other deviation is *left-deviationism*, the infantile disorder of Communism. If opportunism can be seen as a forgetting of the principle (of the party), left-deviationism can be seen as a forgetting of the aim (of power). It is not politically coherent and 'does not measure up to the conditions and requirements of a consistently proletarian class struggle'.[48] The leftist is a man in revolt who has taken literally the great revolutionary refusal, wants everything straight away, and has misunderstood the austere disciplines of waiting, of the right moment, and of political manoeuvre. The opportunist does not want the revolution, the leftist misses it. The one wants nothing to do with the party, the other involuntarily leads it to ruin.

Where do these two antithetical deviations come from? From the same single hostile influence: bourgeois ideology. In Leninism, there is no other enemy. Lenin thus has a theory of the leftist as a 'petty-bourgeois revolutionary', a small producer, a small employer, seized with rage. Anarchism, he wrote, was the penalty of opportunist deviations: 'The two monstrosities complemented each other.' What should one do against left-deviationism? Explain and explain again. Show by example that the party has nothing against individual terrorism: 'It was, of course, only on grounds of expediency that we rejected individual terrorism'.[49] Show that denying the necessity for the party and for party discipline is to disarm the proletariat to the benefit of the bourgeoisie. So the small producer must be *re-educated*, and within the party, discipline and rigorous centralization must reign supreme.[50]

The rearrangement of alliances, changes in the programme, switching demands can all take on a brutal and sudden character if political circumstances require it. This is called a *shift*. A fundamental rule of the party is never to be a prisoner of the position adopted and to remain free to take up another position if political interest (understood as the seizure of power) requires it. A shift should be prepared politically, by ensuring that alliances are reversible, and theoretically, because one would have to explain it ideologically in order to maintain the unity of the party. Once again, it is the 'conspiratorial' structure of the party which makes possible this classic instrument of high politics, the volte-face and the shift of ground.

To generalize: in the Leninist mind, politics in all its aspects and at all times operates in two registers, the one common to all the forces present and the other particular to the party itself. But as Lenin said, they are related. The war between imperialism and the party is a total war and there is no event, or tendency, or even accident which cannot — which must not — be seen in terms of the final outcome. The theory embraces the totality of the real. The party, which is the incarnation of the theory, is pan-social. That is why the party can espouse so easily the specific causes of a village in the steppes, a group of fishermen, a discontented university, or a humiliated Jewish ghetto. In the party's analysis, all these unrelated facts converge and are given a coherent explanation. For each of these groups, as for each of its allies, even the most dubious, the party can speak in a language identical to theirs. This is not done to trick them. There exists, in fact, a plurality of meanings. The same slogan, the same demands are presented in a moderate light to liberals, in a romantic light to populist student circles, in a nationalist light to foreigners or to Russians, in an internationalist light to the International. But the meaning of meanings, the meaning which comprehends them all and can set them in their correct hierarchy, is worked out within the party, and in turn constitutes the party. What links the most conspiratorial aspect of the party with its most public, legal and normal aspect is this scale of interpretations, this chain of meanings of which the party holds one end and which would unravel completely if the party lost its cohesion, and the doctrine its certainty.

The hierarchized meanings which alter at a touch, which are unrecognizable from one stage to another, which are the same and different, can only be understood synoptically by the party, or rather by those or by the one in whom the spirit of the party resides. This forms the most important aspect of dialectics. The principal Communist intellectual effort is directed towards ensuring dialectical coherence both in terms of political action and in term of theory. Thus the two registers are brought together.

And it contributes even more to the shading of the frontier between conspiracy and regular politics that all these operations are carried on publicly. It could not be otherwise since knowledge had to be disseminated throughout the party, and the *work of explanation* had constantly to start all over again. Discussions within the party were carried on in fairly open congresses, with informers all over the place, and in journals which were barely clandestine and often legal. Between the exoteric interpretation and the esoteric interpretation there was no wall of secrecy. The Bolsheviks were not freemasons. But they knew from experience that the public enunciation of their ideology did not ensure its comprehension. The central vision which was theirs had to be attained and adhered to before one could accede to the universal understanding it provided. Without that it appeared a tissue of absurdities. The doctrine explains the phenomenon: it is not understood because of bourgeois ideology. But this phenomenon seemed to the Bolsheviks a fresh proof of the ideology and nourished an immovable contempt in Lenin. The inability of the enemy to understand the posters declaring his condemnation, which had been put up right in front of his nose, made him a 'mark' which the 'unscrupulous' Communist could 'con' at leisure. Whence Lenin's mockery when he speaks of the 'services' of the liberals or the aid given to the opportunist Henderson as 'enough rope for him to hang himself' — rope incidentally provided by the bourgeois themselves.[51]

14
Truth and Falsehood

Effective political action is dependent on the existence of the party, and the existence of the party is dependent on the existence of the ideology. The political impact of Leninism is contained in this equation. Stated in extreme terms, the formula would be: the more a militant is wedded to the ideology, the more he can act in a politically effective manner. It was Leninism's most brilliant innovation to have linked the idea of conspiracy and counter-conspiracy (an idea presented in the most coherent and detailed way, but an idea which seems quite mad when seen from the outside) to rational action aimed at the seizure of power. It is an innovation which combines Marat's *idée fixe* with Bismarck's logic in terms of the goal, his *Zweckrational.*

At this point, it would be a good idea to look more closely at the question of Lenin's Machiavellianism.

Machiavelli has commonly been credited with delineating the political sphere, and with demonstrating its logic, namely, the seizure and conservation of power. This could hardly be said to apply to the social democracy of the Second International, which denied the autonomy of politics and declared the desire of power for power's sake to be an empty ambition. And Lenin was suspected of practical Machiavellianism. But in fact Lenin did not set much store by Machiavelli. In a confidential letter to the People's Commissar for Justice on 20 February 1922, in which he drew up a programme of terror, he wrote: 'An intelligent writer has written with justice on questions of State, that if the attainment of a political goal means passing through a series of harsh measures, then this should be done in the most energetic way and in the shortest possible time, because the popular masses would not put up with a long-drawn out application of harsh measures.'[1] The intelligent writer, though Lenin does not name him, is Machiavelli, and the episode he had in mind, that of Caesar Borgia and the terror of Romagna, is described in Chapter VII of *The Prince*. So Lenin knew his Machiavelli and approved of him as a technician in questions of state. But this is not enough to make him a disciple of the Florentine secretary. Machiavelli justified trickery, lying and perjury by the Prince's inability to know the future. Events demanded that the Prince navigate solely by sight. As a man, he could not see far and therefore preserved his freedom of movement and did not feel bound by what he had said — all the while giving the impression of fidelity. But Lenin believed that he could see far. The necessity to which he submitted his actions was not blind: it had been penetrated by the revolutionary who understood its laws. The question of falsehood and duplicity is raised not in the context of human short-sightedness but in the context of the superhuman vision of ideology. The question of falsehood is a particular aspect of the problem which we have already looked at — that is. the public conspiracy and the new type of party.

In Tkachev's writings, the ideological rationale and the political rationale remained two clearly separate entities. Tkachev made an ideological analysis of the general situation, but the practical measures which he suggested rendered this analysis an abstraction and submitted everything to the specific rationale of the political dictate: the seizure of power. He juxtaposed the militant revolutionary and the Machiavellian Prince in a sort of modern Lorenzaccio, distinguishing their different characteristics, as one might draw an intellectual distinction in a robbery between the moral act of stealing and the technical act of opening the safe. On the one hand Tkachev wanted to establish Communism, and on the other he indicated the technique for a *coup d'état* in a cold and realistic way, without treating it in terms of the ideology. He described in advance the October Revolution as it appeared to non-Leninist historians. That is why those historians regard Tkachev as the precursor of Lenin, as though Lenin performed the same mental operations as they did, as historians, and as Tkachev also did. Which was, as I have said, a mistaken belief.

Lenin is not Machiavellian, not even in his methods. To be sure, the two rationales, the political and the ideological, can be distinguished for ease of analysis. But the intellectual task of the militant

Communist consists in conferring on each political step an ideological meaning, in such a way that the 'Machiavellian' logic of the seizure of power cannot be fulfilled unless it is covered over and rendered more or less unconscious by a second logic — the logic of the ideology.

Machiavellianism is aware of the disparity between the Prince's public pronouncements and what he says in his private councils or in the secrecy of his own heart. But Leninism is a sustained methodology specifically aimed at removing this disparity. There is no gulf of falsehood in the mind of the Communist between what he says in conversation with his provisional ally and what he maintains openly in the party's publications, publications which the provisional ally may read for himself. Mr Henderson is frankly shown the rope. If he cannot see it, that's his affair, and, incidentally, something which can easily be accounted for.

The multiplicity of meanings is a consequence of the duality of the world and of the constantly changing configurations taken in time and space by the struggle between the two principles. The way they are shut off so as to be indecipherable is a result of objective social conditions. Lack of consciousness is the lot of those who do not know the doctrine. But for those who do know it, who are in possession of proletarian science, the barriers have been broken down, language becomes transparent, and the same truth is seen to have its being in a variety of guises.

Machiavelli's ontological monism made possible the opposition of truth and falsehood within the same reality. Truth described common reality, while falsehood distorted and misled. There was thus a disparity of language. Truth and falsehood have their place in the heart of the same subject, and he can choose of his own free will either to speak the truth or to lie. If he lies, he is divided, because the knowledge of the truth still functions within him. There is thus only one meaning. Lenin's ontological dualism reverses the situation. There is no truth in itself, any more than there is freedom in itself. Whose truth? Freedom for whom? Those are the questions Lenin would immediately have asked. There is no common reality. There are two truths in mortal combat, each related to its objective *camp*, bourgeois truth for the bourgeois, and proletarian truth for the proletariat. But there is no symmetry, and still less equality between the two truths. In fact: (1) the truth of the proletariat is guaranteed by the future, while bourgeois truth belongs to the past and is swallowed up in it: it is false; (2) proletarian science can understand bourgeois science, but the reverse is not possible.

Truth and falsehood can no longer reside in the same subject unless he is for a time in error, and has not yet come into possession of the truth. The (true) proletarian ideology and the (false) bourgeois ideology contend for men's minds, just as the objective forces contend for the world. The work being achieved in the party is on the one hand to make manifest the proletarian truth in its quintessential purity, and on the other hand to eliminate in each militant, through education, explanation, criticism and self-criticism, the vestiges of the bourgeois truth. When the work has been well done, the consciousness thus purified no longer has to choose between the truth it can see and the error of which it has been cleansed. So the intellectual labour ends by unifying the language and making it denote the truth. The Communist does not lie, because his language coincides with the objective truth of one of the two conflicting realities, the proletarian reality.[2]

What then is falsehood in terms of this Leninist dualism? It is a question of knowing who is doing the lying, and who is being lied to. The class enemy lies all the time. He lies subjectively, because he wants to dupe the working class. He also lies objectively even when he thinks he has reached the truth, which, because of his social position, is not accessible to him. He is at best a bourgeois objectivist. It is easy to see through him when he lies, but he is more dangerously persuasive when he is sincere, because then it takes a full-scale explanation of the theory to reveal his so-called universal truth as a class truth.

The Communist, in making false statements, may lie from the point of view of proletarian science. If he is addressing other Communists then he is lying because he has fallen back into a bourgeois stance. Then he is a *renegade*. It is of small interest to determine whether, in so doing, he is sincere. There is always the presumption that he is, for this lie is nothing but a sudden reversal of the process of education. The 'gnostic' sin was an invasion of the consciousness by the hostile principle: that is precisely the *error* — the falsehood — of the renegade: a contamination by bourgeois ideology. It is up to the party to weigh whether it is worth the trouble of resuming the educational process — in which case the renegade is subject to criticism, then purged by self-criticism and finally re-educated — or whether, on the other hand, the renegade should be expelled from the ranks of the party. The party's decision on the matter is a political decision which, like all the others, is *Zweckrational* in relation to power.

If the Communist lies in the same way, in addressing a class enemy, this falsehood would be very close to the Machiavellian falsehood. He seeks to deceive the enemy by dissimulating his motives, his means and his aims. At that point it is possible to say that he has two languages, if he knows consciously that what he maintains publicly is the opposite of what be believes privately.

This type of lie is inevitable in a life devoted to politics. Lenin was good at manoeuvring, he was an expert in deflecting a deviation in a congress, in acquiring a majority, in blocking a hostile motion, or in taking over a journal. He was an expert at conspiracy. His daily life was filled to the brim, almost obsessively so, with such goings on. He was a past master at them, but this sort of behaviour was no different from what any *Octobrist* or liberal leader was engaged in at the time. This routine political Machiavellianism which he practised liberally within the ranks of social democracy was not something he was likely to forgo when dealing with the institutional class enemy. Some of this was plotting pure and simple, in the conspiratorial tradition of the sixties: Lenin supervised the *eks* from on high, which meant resorting to gangsterism to refill the party's coffers after the failure of the 1905 revolution. He did not reject the tortuous plots to seduce rich heiresses or other such highly specialized missions, but he himself considered this sort of thing to be minor and marginal. It remained confined to the conspiratorial extreme of the party. Such plots were in no way characteristic of Leninism, nor of Lenin himself, whatever his enemies might claim. Other cases are explained by the conduct of the battle at decisive moments. Lenin was not going to declare his insurrectionary plans. When a break or a switching of alliances was in the offing, one still had, while waiting to make them public, to defend the old line and to flatter the ally of the moment. But Lenin did not consider this to be of central importance either. What practical Machiavellianism there is in Lenin's conduct finds its application in the lower and middle echelons of political life. It is part of an unavoidable way of behaving, a technique with which one must be familiar, but which one does not have to be a Bolshevik to put into practice. There is reason to believe that one of the causes for Lenin's discontent with Stalin and Trotsky was their too ready reliance on methods of this kind.

Leninism, in fact, and in particular its conception of the party, kept this 'Machiavellianism' down to a bare minimum. It was subordinate, and thus, not being part of the serious concerns of the party, it could be carried out coldly and in the most detached manner, and with all the more skill and efficiency because of that.

Machiavellianism is a restricted Leninist practice, because it tends to contradict the prime task of the party: 'to lead the class struggle of the proletariat',[3] 'spreading among the workers a proper understanding of the present social and economic system',[4] 'to generalize all these manifestations and produce a single picture of ...capitalist exploitation',[5] '*to direct* the thoughts of those who are dissatisfied only with conditions at the university, or in the Zemstvo, etc., to the idea that the entire political system is worthless'.[6] The Machiavellianism of concealing one's intentions from certain categories of people hindered the universal explanation which the party desired to present to all categories. How could one dissimulate information and at the same time disseminate it by means of an 'all-Russia political newspaper', a newspaper which would be a 'collective organizer'?[7] That information is the doctrine. It is the meaning which it imposes on events, those 'political exposures'[8] which are, according to Lenin, the prime instrument of propaganda. Spreading the meaning abroad, placing oneself entirely at the disposal of that meaning, cannot be done by lying. A lie would block the party's influence on all the classes it was addressing. A multiplicity of interpretations within the party, due to some having access to the truth and some not, would compromise its unity and split it into several factions. Its unity rests only in this constant labour of explanation. The Leninist party's policy is thus fundamentally *explicit*.[9] There is a continuity running through Lenin's works, and a congruence between political programme and political conduct. There does, to be sure, appear to be a contradiction between the absolute democratism of *The state and the revolution*, and the practice of militant Communism. Yet there does exist a superior point of view, contained in Lenin's works, from which one is enabled to resolve this contradiction and perceive that it is more apparent than real.

The explanation is designed to lead the militant, whatever his rank, up to this superior point.

Lenin did not leave any memoirs. If, in writing his memoirs, the political man is animated by a desire to reveal the underlying intentions and secret strategy which dictated his conduct, then Lenin would have had no need to write them. He had declared his thinking and his aims right at the outset, and subsequently at various points during his career. Few political men have lied as infrequently as Lenin, if one takes lying in the Leninist meaning of the word.[10] He did not claim any moral virtue for this frankness, but saw it as a political virtue: it worked better in terms of seizing power.

One must ask the same question about truth, in the same dualist perspective, as about falsehood: who is speaking the truth and to whom?

Only the Communist speaks the truth. All the same, when he has made some politically 'correct' pronouncement, it cannot be certain that he will adhere to this pronouncement as he should. There are, in this regard, two deviations possible.

He may, in effect, understand this pronouncement not in the manner in which it is received within the party, but in the manner in which it is received by the class enemy. He appears formally to adhere to the party's position, but, as he does not understand it correctly, when the position changes, he suddenly appears to be outside the party.

For example, one of the most long-standing of all the opposition demands had been the call for a constituent assembly. The Bolshevik Party had adopted this demand, priding itself on pursuing it more energetically and single-mindedly than any other party. But when the Assembly was elected, and proved not to have a Bolshevik majority, it was dissolved on the very first day, challenged by a red sailor.

Let us imagine a Bolshevik who had campaigned for the setting up of the Constituent Assembly, and who had developed all the arguments there were in favour of it being set up — liberty, democracy, popular representation and so on — but who had taken these arguments literally, that is, in a 'formal', 'mechanical', and not a dialectical manner, that is, in a bourgeois manner. He would not have 'understood' that the party had to dissolve the assembly, and would have charged it with breaking its promises. But he would have been in the wrong. Lenin explained it all in advance in his *Theses on the Constituent Assembly*, drawn up a few days before it was dissolved. They went as follows:

1. The demand was 'legitimate'.
2. But the Soviets constitute a higher form of democracy than the Constituent Assembly.
3. The Assembly was not a faithful expression of the will of the people; besides which, this will had undoubtedly altered with the development of the October Revolution.
4. It was the class enemies who took as their slogan: all power to the Constituent Assembly.
5. The Assembly was in conflict with the interests and the will of the people. The interests of the revolution prevailed over the formal rights of the assembly. To consider the Assembly from a formally juridical point of view was equivalent to betraying the proletariat.
6. Either the Assembly should submit to the Soviets or else a crisis would ensue 'which can be settled only in a revolutionary way'.[11]

One can see that Lenin's dialectics do not contradict any of the arguments which had been put forward for setting up an assembly, but adjust the meaning of these arguments 'from a class point of view'. And from that point of view, given the circumstances, these same arguments — liberty, democracy and popular representation — dictated the revolutionary dissolution of the assembly.

This first deviation can be called 'naïve'. The other we can call 'cynical'. It consists in this: the party member makes a 'politically correct' pronouncement, but he does not understand it as the party understands it, because he gives it a purely instrumental meaning, simply as a design to dupe the class enemy, and without in any way taking it seriously. If we pursue the same example, we must imagine a Bolshevik who had campaigned for the setting up of the constituent assembly, and who had developed the arguments of liberty, democracy and popular representation. But instead of taking them literally, like the 'naïve' deviationist, he would have thought from the very beginning that these slogans were merely politically expedient, and that when the time came, the Assembly would be dissolved to give power to the Soviets, and then, after the Soviets had been set aside, to the Party. As this is in fact what happened, it is tempting to cast the Bolsheviks as cynics.

Cynicism goes under the same heading as Machiavellianism. The reasons which make the latter impossible make cynicism impossible too. Cynicism destroys the essential spirit of the party. It is no different from *naïveté* in so far as it too takes a bourgeois position: the cynic understands the party's slogans in the same way as the class enemy thinks the party understands them. He puts himself in a bourgeois position which has simply been given a negative aspect, and not in the reality within which the party thinks and acts.

Both the cynic and the naïve Communist accuse each other of cynicism and *naïveté*. But both positions must be denounced from the basis of the correct position. This is what Lenin did in his reply to Kautsky. Kautsky 'pretended' not to understand Lenin's irresistible demonstration about the constituent assembly. 'No-one', remarked Kautsky, 'had demanded the Assembly more vociferously than Lenin.' It was, he suggested, because the Bolsheviks had found themselves to be in a minority in that assembly that after the event they invented the 'higher kind of State'. So they had either been naïve in calling for the assembly, or, much more probably, cynical. 'Such an infamous lie could only have been uttered by a scoundrel who has sold himself to the bourgeoisie...'[12] In fact, as early as April 1917 Lenin had publicly announced theses in which he proclaimed the superiority of that sort of state (of that type: Paris Commune) over the bourgeois parliamentary republic and had frequently repeated them after that date. Kautsky presents the Bolsheviks as people 'without ideological principles'. He had, moreover, forgotten his Marxism because '*he refrains from putting the question*: the organ of what *class* was the constituent assembly of Russia?'[13]

The correct position is neither naïve nor cynical. Lenin had given in advance all the clarification on the limits which should be applied to the demand for the assembly. But this demand could appear either cynical or naïve if one considers with what complete sincerity Lenin had called for the setting up of this assembly and then for its dissolution. His first proposition refutes the charge of cynicism: 'The demand for the convocation of a constituent assembly was a perfectly legitimate part of the programme of revolutionary Social-Democracy.' But, he added, cutting short in advance any possible *naïveté* (which would at that point be called *opportunism* or *suivisme*), 'because in a bourgeois republic the Constituent Assembly represents the highest form of democracy'. This prepares the way for the dialectical leap of the immediate dissolution of that same assembly, since at the same moment there is conjured up the possibility of a régime superior to that of the bourgeois republic.

The party should tell the 'proletarian' truth, and stick completely and whole-heartedly to the correct interpretation which it can give it, because that is the only way of being believed by its allies and of beating the enemy. To the ally the party's sincerity is demonstrated: the demand for a constituent assembly is *legitimate* and the reasons given for it by the party are the same as it gives its own militants: liberty, democracy and popular representation. But each one receives the truth as best he may, according to his station. The close ally, 'the poor peasant' for instance, would have no difficulty in sensing the limits of the notion of 'liberty' or 'democracy'. It would not be impossible for him to side with the party's position, so long as he was told what it was. That is why the truth has to be public. Potential allies and neutrals will be deceived by these same notions, but they will not have been deliberately deceived. But not being able to convict the Party either of lying or of Machiavellianism will have a paralyzing effect on them. Indeed, what could they do? Oppose the assembly? Then they would be vigorously denounced as enemies of liberty and democracy. Oppose the meaning the Communist ascribed to these ideas? But it would be an unfounded criticism, since, so long as the assembly had not been set up and the situation remained the same, the Communists were quite prepared to accept the meaning ascribed to them by the 'bourgeoisie'. They simply enveloped it in a superior meaning, which transcended it but which did not cancel it out. In another political phase it was this new meaning which would take precedence, but not until conditions were ripe for a revolutionary solution of the conflict.

So it is not the party which is Machiavellian, but its ally. The party wants a constituent assembly, then, in the name of the same principles, more clearly understood; it wants to go beyond this assembly towards a higher stage which was to some extent ushered in by the red sailor. As for yesterday's ally, he wants to use the constituent assembly against the party and the proletariat. As a consequence, he betrays his own principles, since he shows that he is not aiming for a *true* liberty and a *true* democracy. He lies to his loyal ally, the party. So the party is the logical defender of the constituent assembly. Nor does it cease to be so, so long as it campaings to denounce the hypocrisy, the lies and the inconsistencies of its liberal allies who have sabotaged the demand right from the beginning. These the party places in the ranks of major enemies when, like Kautsky and Axelrod, they opposed the *Aufhebung*, the move to go beyond this same demand by negating it.

There is thus one crucial point on which Lenin is resolutely not in accord with Machiavelli: it is not falsehood which is effective in politics, but the truth. The truth misleads and disarms the enemy more than any falsehood.

This paradox can be explained by the fundamental lack of symmetry provoked by the introduction into a monist world of a dualist way of thinking. 'Bourgeois' politics sees in this a duplicity, a double-dealing, where in fact there is, in Leninist thinking, a double reality. That is why Leninism is not 'plotting' when it refuses to proceed by *sic et non*, Yea yea and Nay nay. It poses the yea and the nay as two moments in a process, whose law the Leninist knows, and which is called dialectics. Wholly in one and wholly in the other. Leninism's good faith is complete. Enlightened by the doctrine, trained in this way of thinking, it does not understand its ally's lack of understanding. So it taxes him with bad faith.

Machiavellian duplicity implies a sorry duplication within the subject. The Machiavellian world of pure politics is a sombre world, a fallen world, a robbers' cave, the most pessimistic Augustinian *latronicium*. A duplication of reality, on the other hand, resolves the internal conflict. The ideology allows the Leninist to project outside himself the evil he is combatting politically. He has no reason to question the ideology, since every step towards power verifies it, enriches it and consolidates it. The militant lives in a homogeneous sphere, enlightened by ideology, which political praxis extends little by little, by driving back the hostile elements, until it finally coincides with the universe. Within this sphere there prevails a system of articulate representation, and a differentiated language, which is none the less unitarian. Purified of any hostile vestiges, the militant feels filled with a new life which everything proves to be real life. A little more, and he would feel entirely good, omniscient and all-powerful. The militant is happy. *Eritis sicut dei.* It was at this point that Lenin seized power.

15
In Power

What an evocative picture Solzhenitsyn has conjured up of Lenin in the year before he seized power. There he was in Zurich, in neutral territory, an isolated oasis in the midst of a Europe at war. We can see him at home with his ugly wife, in his seedy apartment, with his little goatee beard and his shabby clothes. It was a mediocrity endured in order to set an example, and systematized because it was part of revolutionary asceticism. We can see Lenin involved in his public or pseudo-public activities, spending his days and nights in meetings, in planning insignificant manoeuvres in insignificant congresses, and fuming over press cuttings. His life was spent in discussions, reports, committees and meetings, all of them equally pointless. He carried about with him an aura of dust and stale tobacco, paper and ink. Lenin was meticulous, and wrapped in dreams. A Bolshevik, 'belonging to the majority', he was a man alone. The Swiss comrades drifted away from him after he declaimed against Swiss imperialism. His following? Zinoviev, a windbag, and Radek, an unreliable 'urchin'. There was no love lost between these, merely strict, ceremonious, punctilious political relations weighed down with reservations, badly patched-up quarrels and ill-digested disagreements. The party had foundered, but the style of relations characteristic of the party remained. Lenin spent his time in the library in Zurich, beavering away at God knows what, devouring the newspapers, though without that 'realist's morning prayer' offering him any comfort. He was plagued with migraines. His life was full of bustle, of tension and of continuous analysis. He dreamt up projects: fomenting a split in Swedish social democracy, making Switzerland the base for the world revolution... But from time to time he was gripped by *taedium vitae*, by a sudden nausea at the unreality of his life. Was it, to re-echo one of Dostoevsky's titles, nothing but *the dream of a ridiculous man?*

What remained of the party? Lenin himself. Through the methodical concentration of his life, he had conserved intact within himself the germinal seed of what would become Communism, half a century later, and spread over half the earth. In the spring, the 'sealed train' took him to St Petersburg and implanted this seed in Russia.

Neither Lenin nor the Bolshevik Party made the February Revolution. Indeed, the entire marvellously efficient and coherent system of Leninism, if one looks at it on the eve of the war, does not seem to have any effect at all. The Bolshevik's delight in feeling himself a unified, logical and efficient being, the master of history, was revealed as an illusion. An illusion from which even a good many party members were waking up.

According to what Lenin and Trotsky had laid down, the 'bourgeois revolution' and the 'proletarian' revolution were supposed to have succeeded each other, taking place one after another like a two-stage rocket going into orbit. That did not happen.

What there had been in Russia was the beginnings of a devolution of power from the monarchy by divine right to the civil society: a process which had occurred in England in the seventeenth century and in France in the eighteenth and nineteenth centuries, and which one may follow Malia in calling a 'great revolution'.[1] In each case the process took a very long time, extending over two or three generations. In Russia the revolution had only just begun. It had been in preparation since the abolition of serfdom, and had formally begun in 1905, but nothing had been in any way resolved by 1913. The monarchy was still standing, without having been able to achieve any Bismarckian compromise with the civil society. The latter had not proved strong enough to seize power (in the form of a representative parliament, for instance) on its own account, but the future seemed to belong to it. The maximalist parties had hindered its development but had not been able to interfere with it on any serious scale. They might, certainly, have been able to provoke accidents, probably along the lines of the Paris Commune – and destined, doubtless, to succumb to a similar fate. The archaic Russian sector (the village, the workers' suburbs, the semi-intelligentsia) had some chance of being absorbed without too many shocks into the still small but rapidly expanding modern sector. The peasant cooperatives, the workers' unions, despite the efforts of the Bolsheviks, already existed as a framework for future integration.

But instead of that, there was what a Russian poet has called 'accursed 1914'.[2]

The war transformed the balance of forces between the three parties who were contending for Russia. The revolutionary party, and first of all the Bolshevik section of it, initially disappeared in a unanimous wave of patriotism. Then the state of the Imperial régime became deeply undermined. It sank slowly under incompetence, coteries and neurosis. It seemed as if fate was on the side of the liberal (or social-democrat liberal) parties which represented civil society. But it was on the civil society that the weight of modern warfare bore most heavily, and it became clear that the burden was too great. Civil society was too slender, too young and too weak. It proved its vitality by improvising a powerful war industry, but it did not manage to stop the formation of scattered bottlenecks. The monetary and transport systems collapsed, which meant the danger of poverty and unrest in the rapidly growing major cities — as Tkachev had predicted. The organization of the masses and, in the first place, of the mobilized masses, the soldiers, proved every month less adequate and more fragile.

The war brought about a regression in the whole of Russian society. As war progressively exhausted the state and the economy, it brought back to the surface the primitive Russia which could never be further developed, but which could always be further exasperated and made even more savage. To such an extent was this so that when the decisive moment for a great revolution did occur with the fall of the monarchy, and the process, which had been temporarily halted, could resume, it was no longer able to evolve according to the classic French and English models.

What happened after February 1917 was only superficially the same as the Girondins' shift towards the Jacobins. Events in St Petersburg present a speeded-up version of the move to the left which characterized the Western revolutions. But the crucial point is that the civil society finally disappeared completely. The peasants returned to a natural economy. Inflation destroyed money and the exchanges. Industrial production came to a halt and the workers, abandoning the starving cities, went back to the villages. The deserting soldiers also returned to the villages. This completed the breaking up of the noble estates, and the destruction of the remnants of the nobility. The industrial bourgeoisie and the technical bourgeoisie were ruined and unemployed. The foreign nationals seceded and the Empire was broken up. It was an uninterrupted process. It began with the war, speeded up after February 1917, without the October Revolution marking any new departure, and was completed in 1918 and the years which came after.

It follows that the 'bourgeois revolution' could only be a shadow play. When the monarchy finally did relinquish its power to the civil society, civil society was no longer in a condition to hold it. The liberal parties believed that the revolution was over, and indeed, the devolution of power did appear to be complete. So they thought that their crucial task was to hang on, come what may, until the peace, and then they would take up the march interrupted in 1914. But what had been devolved to them was not power, but the task of attempting to contain the enormous thrust towards anarchy, which broke them down as it had broken down the monarchist state. Neither the right (as Kornilov's lamentable failure goes to show) nor the *Cadets*, nor Kerenski had the slightest chance. It was perhaps not inconceivable that, within the enormous Socialist-Revolutionary party, which though shapeless and unorganized was none the less in the majority in the nation, there might have arisen some sort of phenomenon of 'fascization', the kind of combination of populism, nationalism and militarism which carried Mussolini or − to take a less 'fascist' example and one nearer to home − Pilsudski to power. But it seems that the decomposition had gone so far that even this situation was impracticable. The outcome of the war ruled it out for good.

II

Lenin aimed for the destruction of the monarchical state. But this was something which could be predicted in terms of the normal development of a process already begun, and which no observer had any doubt about. Thus what Lenin was principally aiming for was the destruction of the civil society. This was the nub of his political activity, whether expressed in terms of doctrine, the party, the struggle against the Mensheviks, liberals, opportunists, *suivistes*, adventurists, *oztovists*, and so on. In 1913 he had failed completely. In 1917 he succeeded, but not because of anything that he had done. What he wanted and what happened coincided, without his wishes having played any part in events. The meeting of two independent causal series, the real series of the war and the imaginary series of Bolshevik politics, lent Bolshevism the reality which it had always lacked.

This coincidence conferred on Bolshevism a popularity it had never previously enjoyed. Lenin, for once, was going in 'the direction of history'. His politics coincided with the spontaneous movement of the workers, peasants and soldiers. But his politics had not changed. There was no new chapter to be added to the principles of Leninism as they had been fixed twenty years earlier. Lenin's genius, contrary to what most of the parties and most of the leaders of his own party did, lay in remaining faithful to his original doctrine despite the transformation of the political scene and the radical and total change in circumstances.

Lenin's policy during these nine months was twofold.

The first aspect of it was entirely contained in the first instructions he gave to his party in March and April 1917. Now that the monarchical state had been brought down, it was important to stop the state of the civil society from consolidating itself and from governing. In order to do that, the destruction of the civil society must be completed and all the initiatives of the masses which would lead to that destruction must be followed through. This was the anarchist plank of Leninism during the period of the revolution. This explains the revolutionary defeatism, the help given to the *prikaz* No. 1 and to the dissolution of the army, the slogans about the confiscation of land, peace now, the confiscation of the banks, and finally the support for the soviets. These last consisted in the strike committees and ill-defined permanent popular assemblies which were the embryos of direct democracy such as always spring up when the regular network of power has disappeared.[3] They were capable, not of governing, but of making government impossible. The political problem lay in the fact that the masses, in seeking to achieve their own particular interest were in danger of re-forming among themselves, and in association with the rest of the social and political élites, a society of the ordinary type. By which I mean a society Aristotle would have called *democratic*, that is, answering only to the particular needs of the poor, and thus a bad society, a bad government, but none the less a society and a government of a recognizable type, a type of which humanity had had historical experience and which political science was capable of classifying. The Russian Revolution would then have been limited to a revolution of the poor against the rich, such as had abounded in antiquity, and which would then have given rise to other good or bad governments ('republic', aristocracy or oligarchy, monarchy or tyranny, etc.) according to a cycle with which history was already well acquainted.[4] This was not what Lenin wanted: for him the revolution was supposed to consist in the overthrow of *capitalism* and the setting up of *socialism*.

What Lenin feared, what he wanted to break up, were the remnants of solidarity between the classes, and what lingering notions might persist of the common good and even of the particular good. It was this fear which was expressed in the absurd assertion that 'Russia is the most petty-bourgeois of all European countries. A gigantic petty-bourgeois wave has swept over everything and overwhelmed the class-conscious proletariat, not only by force of numbers but also ideologically; that is, it has infected and imbued very wide circles of workers with the petty-bourgeois political outlook.'[5] The anarchist leanings of Leninist politics were not easily distinguishable from the politics of radical democracy, a simple displacement or catastrophic extension of civil society, finally leading to definitive consolidation with it. That is why Lenin wrote: 'We studiously avoid the words "revolutionary democracy". We may use them when there is a question of an attack by the government, but at the present moment they are highly deceptive, for it is very difficult to distinguish the classes which have mingled in this chaos.'[6] So when Lenin applies democratization (distribution of land, parliamentary representation, peace without annexation or indemnity), he also develops a 'dialectically' superior, that is, opposite thesis: the superiority of the great model exploitation, superiority of a state of 'the Paris Commune type', and the transformation of the imperialist war into a civil war.[7] Although this thesis was not in step with contemporary political feeling, it none the less had to be put forward, in order to prepare the future, 'to raise' the level of consciousness 'within the Party and its natural allies'. In the state of confusion and chaos which characterized the revolution, two principles and two lines had to be set down: 'The party must concentrate all its efforts and all its attention on winning over the mass of workers and soldiers, and must draw a line between the policy of the proletariat and that of the petty bourgeoisie, between the internationalist policy and the defencist policy, between the revolutionary and the opportunist policy.'[8]

The second aspect of Lenin's policy worked in exactly the opposite direction to the first. It consisted in forging the instrument he had been dreaming of for twenty years, but which, reeling from schism to schism, had never been able to become operational — the Party. In February 1917 there were perhaps 17,000 Bolsheviks scattered throughout the Russias, Europe and the United States. By October, there were about 200,000. They were still far from possessing the discipline and the unity of thought of the reflexes of the party mind which they were to acquire during the civil war and the purges and purifications which followed. But Lenin had managed to keep them apart from the process of breakdown which was at that time affecting the whole of society and the majority of political bodies. The party was now sufficiently powerful and united to take on two separate functions.

The first was to constitute in the eyes of all of society and, more particularly, in the eyes of what remained of civil society and of those elements in the masses which were resisting the anarchist breakdown, an alternative to the impotence of the provisional government. Since Lenin's aim was to separate the masses as far as possible from their traditional setting, he posited, in opposition to the first method of doing so (that is, anarchism), another, totally different method: a restoration of the state, but this time, around the Bolsheviks. He thus set up a potential pole for the reconstitution of society, perhaps a society not desired by many, but none the less still preferable to no society at all. He thus laid the foundations for the recovery of a large part of the old administrative machine, the police and military of the erstwhile monarchical state, as well as the collaboration of the technical and scientific sector of civil society, the skilled bourgeoisie. This explains the social nature of his recruitment: not the 'people', but junior officers, foremen and NCOs.

The second function was to prepare to take over the power of the state. The means: the infiltration and domination of the soviets from within. These assemblies were by nature unstable, lacking the organization and method of the unions — which incidentally hardly existed — and were thus vulnerable to Bolshevik penetration. As early as September Lenin was writing that 'the Bolsheviks, having obtained a majority in the Soviets of Workers' and Soldiers' Deputies of both capitals, can and *must* take state power into their own hands'. He added: 'It would be naïve to wait for a "formal" majority for the Bolsheviks. No revolution ever waits for *that*.'[9]

Moreover, one should ensure certain alliances. Fighting against leftism, Lenin defended the spirit of compromise. 'Our Party, like any other political party, is striving after political domination *for itself.*' To this end, 'we, as a party may offer a voluntary compromise — true, not to our direct and main class enemy, the bourgeoisie, but to our nearest adversaries'.[10] The allies — and rarely does Lenin formulate this so clearly — are not friends, but essentially the 'nearest adversaries'. In September 1917 he was thinking of the Mensheviks and the Socialist-Revolutionaries, and although he did not in fact dispose of more than a 'leftist' fraction of the Socialist-Revolutionaries, this hardly mattered in the event. 'Since the 1905 revolution', he wrote, 'Russia has been governed by 130,000 landowners...yet we are told that the 240,000 members of the Bolshevik Party will not be able to govern Russia...'[11]

'The crisis has matured', wrote Lenin. To let slip the present opportunity would either be 'utter idiocy, or sheer treachery'.[12] In effect, there was no crisis, in the sense of class warfare, but there was certainly an opportunity. There was no crisis because anarchism had finally prevailed over the activism of the masses, by sending the workers and soldiers in pursuit of the engrossing daily tasks of fuel and provisions. The popular wave which carried the Bolsheviks to the forefront was beginning to ebb away, leaving them up in the air quite as much as what was left of the provisional government. The day of 7 November 1917 was a phantom conflict between Kerenski's 'regiment of death' and a few detachments of Red Guards, both factions indescribably disorganized and very quickly (in the victors' case at least) dead drunk.[13]

III

Lenin, unlike many of his lieutenants, faced the insurrection without a qualm. Besides, according to him it was 'inevitable'.[14] It was, in fact, basically a defensive measure against the imperialist plot, and the bourgeois onslaught of the Kornilovites.[15] It was above all a counter-plot.

Lenin rested his confidence in the doctrine. This showed society as, so to speak, pregnant with self-organization, although this potential could not be fulfilled within the framework of a capitalist state, but would take its natural form as soon as that capitalist state had been shattered and the socialist state established. There would be no need to destroy the capitalist state entirely. In fact, he wrote a few days before the rising, there existed in the contemporary state, apart from the machinery of oppression (the army and police) machinery very closely linked with the banks and the cartels, machinery involved in a huge undertaking of statistics and records. This machinery neither could nor should be disturbed. 'It must be wrested from the control of the capitalists; the capitalists and the wires they pull must be *cut off, lopped off, chopped away from* this apparatus; it must be *subordinated* to the proletarian Soviets; it must be expanded, made more comprehensive, and nation-wide.'[16]

The tasks of the state, once it had become proletarian, would be easily performed, because there would be no reason why the huge majority of the population, in whose interests it was founded, should not collaborate in the communal work. That is why the state would not be reduced but rather immeasurably extended. It would not be a state which could be wagged about like a tail on the dog of bourgeois liberalism, but the omnipresent, omnipotent state of the liberated workers, liberated through the very fact of this strengthening of the state: 'Our task here is merely to *lop off* what *capitalistically mutilates* this excellent apparatus, to make it *even bigger*, even more democratic, even more comprehensive... This will be country-wide *book-keeping*, country-wide *accounting* of the production and distribution of goods, this will be, so to speak, something in the nature of the *skeleton* of socialist society.'[17] Lenin envisaged various additional methods: the monopoly of cereals, bread rationing, a general obligation to work, and, finally, work-books, for the 'rich' to begin with, but afterwards progressively extending to all the population. All this would apparently come about of itself, because it was included in the self-movement of the social matter. Governing would be easy: it would be sufficient simply to go along with the natural emergence of socialism. The uprising was the curtain-raiser for a familiar drama which was at last going to have the opportunity to be acted out.

The curtain went up and the stage was empty. Nothing happened, or nothing happened as Lenin expected it to. That day in October had so little effect on the course of events that a good many foreign observers did not even notice it, everyone had become so inured to the daily round of riots and gunfire. The new government legislated in the void, while the nation went on breaking down. The Ukraine, the countries of the Caucasus, Siberia, the Upper Volga all formally escaped from the central power. The Russian Empire had contracted back to the boundaries of the old Grand-Duchy of Muscovy. The peasants, no longer able to buy anything in the towns, had no reason to sell anything any more. The proletariat, who for months had been more concerned with forming queues outside the empty shops rather than with making strikes or the revolution, was going down rapidly. Hyper-inflation had abolished money, and Russia had to take up barter. On the frontiers anti-Bolshevik armies were mustering, and in any event, the Germans could sweep away the self-styled government in St Petersburg in a simple police operation, whenever they so wished. The rabble of disbanded soldiers no longer made up an army, let alone a red army, capable of stopping them.

Up to this point Lenin had had no reason to question the ideology which had carried him to power. Faced with a reality that contradicted it, he still saw no reason to question the ideology, because it allowed an interpretation which salvaged not the phenomenon, but the ideology itself, and, by that token, the party and the power, albeit at the price of destroying the reality. The same interpretation applies equally well in explaining why the experiment succeeded or why it failed. The spontaneous setting-up of socialism would have verified the ideology. But failure to establish socialism verified it even more.

Lenin preserved his analysis and saw his methods intact. If it is a characteristic of great statesmen to bow to circumstances, and to make a fresh analysis at every instant, then Lenin is not of their number. Leninism is a block. It had failed for twenty years. It had succeeded in taking power in the midst of a revolution, all the while believing that it was thus controlling that revolution. Leninism was kept intact up to the last weeks of its creator's life, and because of that, power was maintained.

Within the framework of an unchanging dualist analysis, there took place an extensive reshuffling of allies and adversaries. At the time of taking power, Lenin believed that almost all of Russia, and soon Europe, would be on his side, and that only a tiny majority, made up of capitalists and the great landowners, would be on the other side. So the struggle between the two principles would not have been an equal one: the greater part of the social body had passed or would pass to the Bolsheviks. But when power had been seized, one saw, by contrast, a vast transference from one camp to the other as time went on. Assumed friends became enemies. Natural allies, those whom the ideology had declared to be so, were revealed as enemies. In short, the process of treachery and defection which had existed before the war on the scale of tiny groups and small parties began again, but this time throughout Russia. And the response was the same: splits and purges. But as Lenin was in power, the splits, the exclusions, the purges, slowly affecting all of the people, assumed another form and another name: repression.

Lenin did not forget the prime task, the destruction of civil society: 'The bourgeoisie in our country has been conquered, but it has not yet been uprooted, not yet destroyed, and not even utterly broken', he wrote in April 1918. But conditions must be created in which 'it will be impossible for the bourgeoisie to exist, or for a new bourgeoisie to arise'.[18] That was the aim of the programmatic decrees, as yet inapplicable for lack of real power, which he made after October, with as their target not only the annihilation of 'the bourgeoisie' but of all that engendered it — markets, the exchanges, individual contracts and finally private ownership. Gradually he came to see, with horror, that the bourgeoisie finally amounted to the whole of the population.

'The question of ownership having been settled in practice, the domination of the [working] class will have been ensured.' But how? By accounting and control. These should be carried out by the Soviets, as the supreme power of the state, or — and everything was to depend on the other term of the alternative — 'on the instructions, on the authority, of this power'. 'Widespread, general, universal accounting and control, the accounting and control of the amount of labour performed and of the distribution of products — is the *essence* of socialist transformation.'[19]

These are phrases which recur obsessively in every speech and every comment. On the basis of this vision, he constructed for himself a whole mythology of the German war economy, as if he had transferred his old admiration for German social democracy to the powerful organizing cartels of that nation. The *mimetic* law of conspiracy and counter-conspiracy, and of identification with an imaginary adversary, can be applied here too. 'The organization of accounting, the control of large enterprises, the transformation of the whole of the state economic mechanism into a single huge machine, into an economic organism that will work in such a way as to enable hundreds of millions of people to be guided by a single plan — such was the enormous organizational problem that rested on our shoulders.'[20]

But there was no relationship between the vision and actual reality. There was nothing to account, nothing to control in the unbelievable collapse of production, and the devastation of the economic body. So Lenin sought those responsible, and found them immediately, for the enemy was always the same. In December 1917: 'The bourgeoisie was spoiling everything, sabotaging everything...'[21] 'We wanted to take the line of agreement with the banks ...but they carried out sabotage on an unprecedented scale.'[22] In the spring of 1918: 'The famine is not due to the fact that there is no grain in Russia, but to the fact that the bourgeoisie and the rich generally are putting up a last decisive fight...'[23] Only the bourgeoisie? Already we are being presented with a picture of 'the rural rich, the kulak, the parasite',[24] 'the rich peasants, who have battened on the war'.[25] But in 1919, any landed peasant was potentially a bourgeois, and one must distinguish the working peasant from the landed peasant who by that very token is a 'peasant huckster', a 'peasant who profiteers'.[26] Even the workers themselves entered into the fatal process of reconstituting the bourgeoisie. They changed class and became *petit-bourgeois*: 'They are obliged to rob or else to carry out private commissions in the socialist factory...as a speculator or small producer' (1921).[27] So were they still workers?

'Very often the word "workers" is taken to mean the factory proletariat. But it does not mean that at all. During the war people who were by no means proletarians went into the factories; they went into the factories to dodge the war.'[28] These were not proletarians, but 'casual elements of every description', or in other words, the bourgeoisie again.

There was a bourgeoisie as soon as there was exchange, and that is why the bourgeoisie had not been extirpated, but on the contrary flourished everywhere. The freedom of exchange, wrote Lenin, was the freedom of trade. But 'free exchange and freedom of trade' mean 'turning back towards capitalism'; they mean 'circulation of commodities between petty proprietors'.[29] So the peasant pushing his plough, with his cow or his wife fastened to it, or the worker doing some tiny private job, were petty proprietors. There was in Moscow in Sukharevskaya Square a sort of souk where miserable exchanges of this sort were carried. It was closed down. But, wrote Lenin, it was not difficult to close the black market, 'the sinister thing is the "Sukharevka" that resides in the heart and behaviour of every petty proprietor. That is the "Sukharevka" that must be closed down.'[30]

The hostile principle is in the structures. Chased out of the structures, it infiltrated men's hearts. The enemy was everywhere.

This was the real surprise: the class struggle was not over, it had got worse. 'I cannot recall the work of a single socialist or the opinion of a single prominent socialist on future socialist society, which pointed to this concrete, practical difficulty that would confront the working class when it took power.'[31] The way that it was belied by the reality did not, however, lead to abandoning the theory of the class struggle, but to its being reaffirmed up to the hilt: the class war does not disappear, but 'merely changes its forms'[32] and becomes 'incomparably more bitter'[33] because the exploiters' power of resistance 'has increased a hundred- and a thousandfold' precisely 'because they have been defeated',[34] because the whole of the population fell under their influence and perhaps soon under their power.

What was to be done? Nothing other than extend the principles of *What is to be done?* to this situation of the *faithlessness* of the working class and of the people in general, by applying to it the same remedy, namely the party, which should at this juncture take on the furthest possible extension as the situation demanded. It was the same evil, and the same remedy, but on an unprecedented scale. 'The revolution demands…that the people *unquestioningly obey the single will* of the leaders of labour',[35] meaning the party, wrote Lenin in May 1918. He was more specific: 'unquestioning obedience …to the one-man decisions of Soviet directors, of the dictators elected or appointed by Soviet institutions', once more naming the party.[36] 'Iron discipline in our party',[37] 'the tenet that the Party rectifies, prescribes and builds according to a single principle',[38] this was the basis of socialism. Now that capitalism was running out of every pore and infiltrating all society, invading the proletariat, the party became a repository for the proletariat, just as it had been before the revolution.

The party thus underwent an intensification, with its discipline strengthened along military lines, and an expansion, with its membership increasing from 200,000 to around 600,000 by 1920. It became identified with the state. That is why, as well as junior officers, NCOs, schoolteachers and foremen, it began to attract those who were drawn to the party through a repudiation of anarchy. 'We have a large section of such bourgeois doctors, engineers, agronomists, and co-operators' who are entering the state apparatus under surveillance and who will, by that fact, 'be conquered *morally*'. 'They will then of themselves be drawn into our apparatus and become part of it.'[39]

But it was crucially important that this developing party—state should not become consciously autonomous, but should act and believe itself to be acting in the name of the proletariat. Lenin provided the guarantee of that. He watched ceaselessly to be sure that the party retained 'the confidence of the masses' which it was busy dominating and crushing. And Lenin, the dictator, in the Kremlin just as in Zurich, never conceived that he was anything other than the focal point of the proletariat and of the good part of the universe working out its self-movement towards salvation.

The party's political activity was conducted according to principles laid down before the revolution. It merged with military activity, since politics is the continuation of war by other means. Foreseeing annihilation, it divided itself between an attack, which was more of an assault, and a defensive which as usual took the form of a provisional compromise.

The assault was simultaneously both civil and military. The organization of the Red Army, of the *Cheka*, of the detachments which went into the country pillaging the villages and breaking down their solidarity, all this went on at the same time. They met with very varied success. In the military arena, the Red Army just managed to prevail over the armies which successively opposed it. The forced requisitions did succeed in stopping what remained of the cities from dying of starvation, but set the villages against the Bolsheviks, and brought about famines the like of which had not been known in Europe or in Russia for centuries. The *Cheka* and the police, the first organs created by the government, were also the first to function properly.

The particular difficulty facing any police force lies in identifying and tracing offenders. Leninism rendered this task infinitely easier by giving such a general description of an offender as to make it cover anybody who might have been arrested by the police. 'War to the death against the rich and their hangers-on, the bourgeois intellectuals; war on the rogues, the idlers and the rowdies!' If one reads this text of 27 December 1917 in the light of the commentary which follows it, one can see that the whole of the population can be put either under the heading of *rich* and *bourgeois intellectual* (the old civil society), or under the heading of *rogues, idlers and rowdies* (that part of the people which does not lend itself to accounting and control). Lenin gives himself up to an excess of sadistic fury about them at a rather unusual pitch, about which Solzhenitsyn has written some unforgettable lines which are well worth recalling:

> V. I. Lenin proclaimed the common, united purpose of 'purging the Russian land of all kinds of harmful insect'. And under the term *insects* he included not only all class enemies but also 'workers malingering at their work' − for example, the typesetters of the Petrograd Party printing shops... True, the forms of insect-purging which Lenin conceived of in this essay were most varied: in some places they would be placed under arrest, in other places set to clean latrines, 'after having served their time in punishment cells, they would be handed yellow tickets'; in others, *parasites would be shot.*[40]

Going into detail, Lenin advised the *Cheka* on police techniques and particularly on carrying out night arrests.[41] Modern scholarship − Medvedev again recently − has had no difficulty in showing that what is understood as Stalinism, a repression which can strike anybody who can be set in any ideological category − 'opportunist', 'enemy of the people' and simply 'rowdy' − derives directly from the principles of Leninism.

Indeed, one is hardly going to abandon at the height of the battle the ontological division between those to be destroyed and those to be saved, when it is in the name of that division that the battle has been carried on since the dawn of time. 'Human history these days is making a momentous and most difficult turn, a turn, one might say without the least exaggeration, of immense significance for the emancipation of the world. A turn from war to peace... a turn from an abyss of suffering, anguish, starvation and degradation to the bright future of communist society, universal prosperity and enduring peace.'[42] One must go even faster than Peter the Great, and 'not hesitate to use barbarous methods in fighting barbarism'. 'Our government is excessively mild.'[43] But how can one carry out this purge, this cleansing of the harmful insects? Force alone is not enough. Pure coercion must be accompanied by a development of consciousness. The people's leaning towards the 'rich', the 'bourgeois intellectuals' or the 'parasites' took political forms. They became 'Cadets' or 'quasi-Cadets'.[44] The place for Mensheviks and Socialist-Revolutionaries was obviously in prison. But there were also those who, without belonging to their party, followed them, who might follow them, or whose attitude amounted to following them: 'The Mensheviks and the Socialist-Revolutionaries have now learned to don the "non-party" disguise.'[45] Their place is in prison too. That is why, if one wants repression to play a part in raising the level of consciousness, one must explain it to the people so that they can be associated with it. That is the role of the court, which does not deliver justice in a formal, juridical, abstract sense, but which discriminates from a class point of view: 'As the fundamental task of the government becomes, not military suppression, but administration, the typical manifestation of suppression and compulsion will be, not shooting on the spot, but trial by court.' But the people's courts were still 'extremely, incredibly weak'. That was because of their lack of consciousness: 'It is not yet sufficiently realized that the courts are an organ which enlists precisely the poor, every one of them, in the work of state administration,...that the courts are *an organ of the power* of the proletariat and of the poor peasants, that the courts are an instrument for *inculcating discipline.*'[46]

So the courts and revolutionary jurisdiction worked out a net of offences so fine that in principle no one could bank on slipping through the mesh, but a net which was at the same time full of revolutionary instruction, since the categories of offences mapped out the political front and designated the sectors on which the party was making an attack. Thus simultaneously one of the two camps withered away while the other grew stronger.

The assault involved the whole world. The world revolution had begun in Russia. In that country, all that the party had done was to take 'advantage of the setback of international imperialism; the engine that was supposed to bear down on us with the force of a railway train bearing down on a wheelbarrow and smashing it to splinters, was temporarily stalled — and the engine was stalled because the two groups of predators had clashed'.[47] The greatest difficulty awaiting the Russian revolution was 'the need to evoke a world revolution, to effect the transition from our strictly national revolution to the world revolution'.[48]

But once the principle had been established, the assault could come to rest temporarily. So long as the forces at one point cancelled each other out, it was useless to risk defeat. One should disengage, gain time and establish a *compromise*. In the domain of foreign policy, the most substantial compromise was the Treaty of Brest-Litovsk, which surrendered to Germany the most useful and prosperous half of the country. It was nationalism which had ruined the Second International. The patriotic reaction had scattered most of the Bolshevik forces in 1914. This patriotism — which was a feeling of once more belonging to a community, and of the existence of a common good between classes — reappeared in the party when faced with the severe conditions demanded by the Germans. The feeling was disguised in the phrase 'leftist' in the revolutionary war. Lenin himself felt it was 'impermissible tactics to stake the fate of the socialist revolution, which has already begun in Russia'[49] by putting all one's faith in an imminent German revolution. That would have been *adventurism*.

'How the socialist revolution can be most firmly and reliably ensured the possibility of consolidating itself, or, at least, of maintaining itself in one country'[50] meant keeping one portion of territory, however much diminished, which had the form and status of a state. The revolution, for Lenin, had always meant the conquest of the state, and its success was measured in the extent and solidity of the state thus conquered. Brest-Litovsk also gave Lenin a motive for despising imperialism, which might be fierce and fearsome, but is also, because it lacks consciousness, stupid. Ultimately, the German High Command, merely in order to ensure a wheat harvest for the army to tide them over the difficult spring of 1918, saved the Bolshevik government, which was entirely at its mercy. Another example of imperialist idiocy was the Hoover mission. Without demanding any sort of political concession, American imperialism distributed millions of tons of wheat to the starving, saving about eight million men, women and children from death, and also perhaps indirectly and *gratuitously* saving the Bolshevik government. Lenin, as ever in any *compromise*, pocketed the profits, and continued mercilessly to attack and unmask this *close adversary*.

The assault was also directed against the totality of social groups which found themselves within the boundaries of the Bolshevik state. But there came a moment when the Soviet government was endangered by its very victory, just as a fire might go out for lack of anything more to burn. The terrorized, cowed peasantry, pillaged disastrously in a 'military campaign',[51] and long since ravaged of any surplus, no longer had anything left with which to feed itself. The country was dying of hunger and disease, in a state of shock and physiological distress probably unsurpassed even by the effects of the Mongol invasion. The government, losing its foundations, was threatened.

Lenin, against the advice of one section of his party, then made the same sort of compromise with the internal adversaries as he had made with those abroad, a compromise which was called the New Economic Policy. Within certain limits, which had to be meticulously laid down, free exchange, trade, money circulation and the market were to be tolerated. The reason given was not to ease the suffering of the masses. The party did not set itself that goal, because the masses would reach it spontaneously, although by non-Communist routes. The party's aim was to build socialism, whence, by definition, all prosperity and every good would flow. If that good could be attained by other means, it became hostile to socialism, and thus harmful to those same masses the party had undertaken to save. In their interests, the prime objective was thus to safeguard the party, and that was why an easing of the distress became desirable. That is why Lenin temporarily renounced militant Communism: 'We went further than we needed from the theoretical and political point of view. We can allow to a notable extent local free exchanges without harming the political power of the proletariat, but, on the contrary, consolidating it. How to do so, is a technical problem.'[52]

As usual, the compromise was not made on an equal basis. It was, as Lenin said, a 'ransom' paid to capitalism in order to strengthen the Soviet government.[53] It was a provisional retreat. Drawing the most general lesson from the compromise, he wrote in November 1921:

Before the victory of the proletariat, reforms are a by-product of the revolutionary class struggle. After the victory...they are, in addition, for the country in which the victory has been achieved, a necessary and legitimate breathing space when, after the utmost exertion of effort, it becomes obvious that sufficient strength is lacking for the revolutionary accomplishment of some transition or another. Victory creates such a 'reserve of strength' that it is possible to hold out even in a forced retreat, hold out both materially and morally...Holding out morally means not allowing oneself to become demoralized and disorganized, keeping a sober view of the situation, preserving vigour and firmness of spirit... even retreating a long way, but not too far, and in such a way as to stop the retreat in time and revert to the offensive.[54]

So the assault had not been in vain, nor the offensive too bold, since it left a lot of room for manoeuvre in which to retreat. 'The more conscious, the more unanimous, the more free from prejudice we are in carrying out this necessary retreat, the sooner shall we be able to stop it, and the more lasting, speedy and extensive will be our subsequent victorious advance.'[55]

IV

After March 1923, Lenin no longer played any part in affairs. It is an open question whether he did not, in the last months of his life, consider extending the NEP further than he had previously anticipated, and whether he was not beginning to look at what had happened in the five years previously with a fresh eye. In any event, all he proposed was supervision of the party's activities by inquiries set up within the party, and entrusting to the police the responsibility for correcting police abuses. Leninism remained intact. Lenin died on 21 January 1924. Let us take that date as a point at which to pause and cast an eye over the situation in which the Soviet government then found itself.

In geographical terms, the government had resumed control of the old Russian Empire, with the exception of Poland, Finland, the Baltic countries and some Ukrainian and Bielorussian territories. Leninism had been formally implanted in a certain number of European nations and was beginning to explore the rich possibilities offered by the beginnings of the crisis of European colonialism. But there was no question of world or European revolution for a long time yet.

In terms of intensity, it had had to concede another limitation. The frontal assault against the peasantry had failed. The party did not have the political means of encompassing the village and breaking down its traditional structure so as to control its daily life. Therefore, since it was impossible to enclose, so to speak, each peasant, what it did was to enclose the peasantry as a whole. But within that vast enclosure, the peasantry still enjoyed a certain freedom of movement.

So the Soviet government's actual domain was still fairly restricted. It controlled the cities. The working class no longer had any say following the Bolshevization of the Soviets. Any return to syndicalism was considered a form of *economism*. Now, wrote Lenin, 'politics must take precedence over economics'.[56] The state being 'a sphere of coercion', 'the administrative approach and "steerage" are indispensable'.[57] What then are the unions? They 'are a reservoir of state power, a school of communism and a school of management'.[58] Strikes are only possible in the case of a malfunction in the driving belt linking the masses to the government of the state. They should immediately go to the arbitration of a higher authority, the party. That was the narrow margin allowed to the workers by the NEP when the idea of the complete militarization of industrial labour had been abandoned after Kronstadt.

More important than the control of the cities and of the proletariat was the control of free speech, of the press and education. This was the index of ideological power. The decree on the press was passed three days after the October victory. It was sufficient in its provisions: the passage of sixty years has not seen the need to add anything.

The worker–peasant government draw the attention of the populace to the fact that in our society this liberal screen [of the freedom of the press] in reality masks the freedom of the propertied classes, who have the lion's share of all the press, to poison people's minds with impunity and to trouble the consciousness of the masses. Everyone knows that the bourgeois press is one of the most powerful weapons of the bourgeoisie... It is impossible to leave this weapon entirely in the hands of the enemy when, at this time, it is a weapon more dangerous than bombs and machine-guns.[59]

So this 'weapon' was entirely taken away from it. The institution of a monopoly of information was the easiest, the most complete and the most definitive monopoly ever achieved by the Soviet government.

The government had passed a good deal of legislation about educational matters from the moment it was set up. It nationalized the schools, and started to root out the old bourgeois knowledge and the old way of teaching, and to introduce Communist education. About half the school teachers and teachers of higher education were eliminated, and the other half brought into line. To Lenin, the educational *front* was no less important than the military front, because the struggle between the two principles involved the spiritual arena quite as much as the material, and the former in the end decides the latter. We must 'combat the bourgeoisie in the military sense and still more by means of our ideology through education.'[60] 'The working masses, the masses of peasants and workers, must oust the old intellectualist habits and re-educate themselves for the work of building communism.'[61] Lenin saw this spiritual struggle as being analogous in its methods to the military struggle. It was a red army of education which he wanted to let loose on the country.

We must put hundreds of thousands of useful people to work in the service of communist education. That is a task that was accomplished at the front, in our Red Army, into which tens of thousands of representatives of the old army were incorporated. In the lengthy process of re-education, they became welded with the Red Army...This is an example that we must follow in our cultural and educational work. True, this work is not so spectacular, but it is even more important.[62]

On his death, this work had not yet been completed, but it had been begun, and the principles had been laid down.[63]

The literary and artistic intelligentsia was gone or divided, often fellow-travelling, sometimes begging for its bread. Early in 1920, Krupskaya had removed from the public libraries all 'forbidden literature'. Under the heading of forbidden Western philosophers were Descartes, Kant, Plato, Schopenhauer, Nietzsche and William James. Mach, of course, was not overlooked.[64] In effect, the destruction of the old culture was a cheap and easy way of disorienting and weakening the adversary without serious material or political consequences. At the same time as Lenin gave up the idea of supervising the way in which the peasant sowed and planted, he was destroying at a blow the heart of village culture by annihilating the Church. In the same way, when he destroyed the synagogue and the network of Jewish schools, he deprived a significant number of craftsmen and of the working class of their frame of reference and support. He found the support of a section of the Orthodox clergy and the Jewish people for these two tasks. Those whom the NEP had put 'in reserve' were able to contribute to the maintenance of the Soviet government, but, cut off from their cultural models, and reduced by the loss of their spiritual framework, they lost a good part of their capacity to resist future assaults.

The Communist Party was preparing itself for such assaults, but it did not yet have the numbers, nor the unity, nor the impetus to undertake them immediately. Lenin's succession was not settled, although the most promising candidate, Joseph Stalin, was rising fast. The party—state had been sketched out, but not yet completely finished off. It would not be completed until the whole of the Soviet population had been brought under its control, through collectivization; until the party itself had been entirely renewed, which was the object of the purges of the 1930s; and until Stalin's succession had been settled, which would take ten years more, from 1953 until the fall of Khrushchev. So it was only in 1964 that one could say that the Bolshevik Revolution had been completed and that the process begun on 7 November 1917 had come to an end and established itself as stable and lasting.

In 1924, however, the party was sure of itself and knew that its founder had set it on the right road. It had considerably strengthened its capacity for repression. Lenin had shown the particular need for it in a period of retreat or of a halt in the offensive. 'Discipline must be more conscious and is a hundred times more necessary...the slightest breach of discipline must be punished severely, sternly, ruthlessly.'[65] In the area in which it was completely dominant, the party had taken every possible measure. On Lenin's death, the police had been perfected and the *Gulag* had long been opened.

Lenin had won. The English Diggers, the Jacobins, the *communards* had none of them lasted more than a few months. Lenin, after six years, left a consolidated situation behind him.

Among the reasons which ensured the success of the party, one must stress the one emphasized by the official historiography – Lenin enjoyed the support of the masses. Of course this support was never lent by the majority, and it is not possible to see how it could ever have been more than about 25 per cent of the vote, which is what the Bolsheviks polled in the elections to the Constituent Assembly. But is equally impossible to see how the party could have reconquered almost all of its territory if it had not been able to rely on a significant section of the 'people', of the peasants and workers, and also of the old ruling class of the country. Witnesses agree that the masses, after some hesitation, and often after having rallied to the White armies, had finally abandoned the White cause, and had rallied or resigned themselves to the Soviet government.

The reason for this is that for the main body of the Russian people – the military reconquest of the foreign territories is a separate question – the Soviet government represented a hope of restoring the civil society. The peasant wanted land: he had it. The worker wanted better living conditions and more dignity. Living conditions had collapsed, but the public exaltation of 'the proletariat' could pass as compensation for a syndicalist autonomy whose loss he scarcely felt, never having been able to enjoy it. The officers and the nationalists delighted in the apparent re-establishment of the Empire, Doctors, engineers, teachers, all hastened to get to work. The elimination of the greater part of the old administrative and economic personnel had left room for a renewal of élites, for social movement and competition for positions. There were a good many who would profit or who hoped soon to profit from what they conceived to be a radical democratization of Russian society.

Notable within the party were those who shared this hope or who encouraged it in those not of the party. That was, one might say, a sound application of cynicism and *naïveté*. From the Communist point of view these were deviations, but as such they could prove useful in rallying provisional allies to the party. A good many joined the party in the hope of a career, like those terrorist but well-established Jacobins who later turned up as Prefects or wealthy landowners. Cynicism within the party consisted in the introduction of private enterprise, and in the intention to deal with anybody at the level of the diverse transactions which constitute civil society. One could always, so ran the thinking, reach an understanding with that sort of Communist.

The political effects of *naïveté*, which was much more widespread under Lenin than at any later date, were different but equivalent. The naïve Communists more or less confused the conceptual proletariat with the real proletariat, the 'poor peasant' with the poor peasant, and class justice with justice. They conceived an idea of socialism which mingled with the idea of a common good to the extent that the two became identical. The 'spirit of the Party', 'class consciousness', all the separating discipline of Leninist dualism had been to a great extent wiped out in them.[66] Useless for other tasks, these 'naïve' Communists could at least be employed to encourage hopes of a 'return to normal', with more justice, more freedom and more dignity in reward for their great labours. This, it was thought, would happen with the victory of Bolshevism over its enemies and the definitive consolidation of the régime. After that, there would be no need for terror. Were not the NEP and peace on the frontiers the first steps? That was how the reasoning went in France, in England, in Germany and in the United States. They hoped for a return to normal. They helped the Bolshevik government because they thought they were helping it to 'normalize' itself. The policy of the West was even then what it would always like it to be — a policy of *détente*.[67]

One of the causes of the Bolshevik success lies in the falseness of the political analysis to which it has been subjected, as much on behalf of the foreign powers as of Russian society itself. It was widely believed that the party was either going to dissolve into a civil society in the process of reconstitution, or else was going to form a civil society itself, purely and simply replacing what it had just destroyed. But this was mistaken. The party had effectively substituted itself for the old civil society, but it was quite incapable of constituting another one in turn. And this was because of the relationship it maintained with the ideology.

16

The Dominion of the False

The survivors of the Slavophile tradition, such as Blok, Rozanov and Berdiaev, saw the revolution as an apocalypse. The fire of destruction heralded the Last Days.

The apocalyptic spirit created an absolute divide between the two realities, or as they put it, between the two ages. The apocalyptic revelation heralded the new age, but as something which came from elsewhere, and for which one had to be prepared to wait. Blok and Berdiaev reacted to the revolution like the Old Believers in the seventeenth century who saw, in the upheavals of Peter the Great, the imminence of the End and the work of Anti-Christ. They were mistaken. The new era was not the beginning of a new age but the product of a gnosis in power. The gnostic mind saw the new reality as being contained in its entirety in the present reality, not as transcendant but as immanent. The revolutionary was not in *expectation* but in the *great work*. He tried to break down the thin partition which was concealing the future age behind the present age. Lenin was the midwife of socialism, and there often recur in texts of the time images of violent birth and Caesarians. But for six years the mother's belly had been opened and ransacked, and still there was no baby. Lenin can also be compared to a treasure hunter. He had demolished the castle where he thought the treasure was hidden, from the cellar to the attic. But no treasure. Lenin had acted according to the magic formula which Bakunin thought he had found in Hegel: the spirit of destruction is the spirit of creation. He had certainly demolished 'capitalism'. But where was socialism? Nowhere. Contrary to the predictions, it did not manifest itself spontaneously. It had to be built.

In 1920, Lenin began to envisage the *building of socialism*. 'In our struggle two aspects of the matter stand out: on the one hand, there is the task of destroying the heritage of the bourgeois system, of foiling the repeated attempts of the whole of the bourgeoisie to crush the Soviet state. This task has absorbed most of our attention hitherto and has prevented us from proceeding to the other task, that of construction.' Destruction, added Lenin, had taken up 'nine-tenths of our time'.[1]

But how to build socialism? Lenin was hostile to any form of utopia. The small amount of imaginary projection he allowed himself conjured up a transcapitalist landscape with plenty of large machines, electricity and organized industry, in which the masses and the party competed in harmony: in short, the setting up of 'accounting and control' in the Hall of Machines of some universal exhibition. It was Chernyshevski's 'Crystal Palace' brought up to date by the memories of a man deeply marked by Wilhelmine Germany. One can already glimpse the future slogan: 'Catch up and overtake.'

But the whole of the real Russia slipped away from this task of construction, workers and cadres, writers and painters alike. The peasantry, which made up the vast majority of the population, had officially retreated to its private fields, surrounded by its livestock, on its own *property*. What could be the explanation?

Since nothing exists except socialism and capitalism, and since there is no evidence of socialism, it must be that capitalism is more rife in Russia than ever. 'The corpse of capitalism is decaying and disintegrating in our midst, polluting the air and poisoning our lives, enmeshing that which is new, fresh, young and virile.'[2] The gnostic spirit remained intact, but it was working in reverse. Under capitalism, Lenin had perceived the imminent socialism. Now the deeper reality of socialism, its ulterior world, its hidden face, was capitalism. All the revolution had achieved was to install capitalism in impregnable fortresses.

As a result, one could not seriously hope to build so long as the work of destruction had not been properly finished off. *Everything* had to be destroyed. The respite of the NEP had only concerned the social forces with which it had been necessary to come to terms. Those with whom the respite thus achieved made it possible to deal seriously, experienced an increase in the terror brought to bear on them. That is why the instruments of the future assault, the party, the police, the army, all experienced an enormous expansion, thanks to the NEP and to the great surprise both of foreign observers and of the Russian people. The treasure had not been found: that was because a few sections of the castle walls were still standing.

In the end the solution to the problem was political. Lenin had thus not abandoned, and did not in any way abandon, the politicism of his youth. If nothing worked, it was occasionally said, that was because Russia lacked culture. 'If a definite level of culture is required for the building of socialism...why cannot we begin by first achieving the prerequisites for that definite level of culture in a revolutionary way, and *then*, with the aid of the workers' and peasants' government and the Soviet system, proceed to overtake the other nations?'[3] In order to send Russia back to school, in order to remould people's souls, in order to uproot capitalism, in order to destroy, what was needed was power, and yet more power, always power. And, as Lenin said, 'we have quite enough political power'.[4]

And along comes the ideology again. It has not been contradicted by events, since the explanation which would have covered success did equally well to explain the apparent failure. But there was one area in which the theory had been directly verified and in the most striking way, and that was in the domain of political power. In short, it was politics which tested the validity of the ideology, and political success, that is to say, taking and keeping power, which proved it beyond challenge. It was clearly because the ideology, circulating within the party, constituted it and maintained it, that it emerged victorious from a deadly struggle, in which it had skirted irremediable disaster time and time again. The only thing which had worked properly throughout the whole affair was the party, and that was because it had remained faithful to the ideological principles which had set it up.

The legitimacy of the Communist Party lay in Communism. So far as the workers and peasants were concerned, the party did not represent anything other than the glowing future towards which it was leading them, while they remained blind to their fate. In 1924, they were more blind than ever. All the farsightedness of the ideology was sheltering within the party, and that is why, while universal doubt and disillusion demonstrated the power of the bourgeois ideology, it was necessary for the party to become more than ever the guardian of certainty. On Lenin's death, Leninism became canonized. Leninism seen in these terms gave the party the solidity and monolithic quality which it needed to preserve deep within it the Communist idea, and thus its legitimacy and the absolute monopoly of power. The baby had not been born, the treasure had not been found — not true, because the party *was* the baby and the treasure. Where the party is, there is socialism.

A gap had opened between reality and the Bolshevik perception of reality. Materialism entailed losing touch with matter, and substituting for it the schema which had been projected onto it. The proletarian character of the party was not conceivable without breaking with the reality of the working class. Socialism can only exist so long as society keeps well away.

But this gap did not stop the Bolsheviks staying in power. On the contrary, they stayed in power because of it. This enormous complex of false analyses, these imaginary class struggles between ghostly adversaries, these inconsistent notions of imperialism, this fabulous interpretation of events, none of this did any harm. The theorization without relation to reality was certainly costly politically (the cost in human terms was not taken into account), but it did, on the other hand, make possible the maintenance of that excellent and supreme instrument of Leninist policies, the party. The political balance of the ideological *unreality* was *really* positive. The cynics of the party were the first to recognize that this was so.

That is what makes Lenin's genius appear so baffling to an outsider. Sometimes he seems to function with a marvellous efficiency, with the same impersonal dedication as a termite defending its anthill. At such a time his professional superiority shines out over muddlers like Zinoviev, thugs like Stalin and amateurs like Trotsky. At other times, though, as if the instinct had become deranged and was pursuing its programme in the void, one sees him relentlessly refuting, in the drained and exhausted Russia of 1919, obscure German social democrats; labelling class struggle the struggle between parties; calling militant communism, poverty, famine and typhoid; and dictatorship of the proletariat, his own power. And just like the termite, he is condemned never to know what he is doing. This is a fresh reason for not seeing Leninism as a kind of Machiavellianism. Whereas the Prince was clear-headed, and knew what the truth was, Lenin, blinded by ideology, perceived only a falsified version of the truth. He did not deceive the enemy, but he deceived himself. The dualism of the two irreconcilable truths is sufficient to suggest the cause for this apparent paradox. He gave the enemy the Communist truth as far as he could be expected to understand it. He gave it to himself too, and remained entirely deaf to the commonly-held truth.

Everything happened as though Communism could not retain power unless it managed to ignore the reality it was supposed to control. The vast body of information gathered throughout the country by the bureaucracy and the police, both swollen well over the numbers employed under the old régime, had to pass through an ideological filter, a linguistic coding, a distorting mirror before reaching the leaders of the party, so that, when it came out the other side, it was no longer information.

Once in power, the duplication of truths became, or rather sought to become, a duplication of realities. 'Proletarian' truth *was* the party, 'bourgeois' truth *was* the society which resisted the party. That is why the government could only act on the real in a destructive way, since it was that real which had to be destroyed before the reality of which the party was the repository could manifest itself. It could not compromise with society on the level of interests in common, nor even govern in its own private interest, because the party only exists in the fiction of the total dedication of its own private interests to the common interest which nobody wants, called Communism. And it was in the name of that Communist common interest that it took power.

But Communism is not a moral ideal. It is scientific, that is, it must impose on itself by virtue of natural laws a necessary relation deriving from the nature of things which the action of the party goes along with but does not create. The duplication of realities, the yawning gulf between the party and society, between the world as seen by the party and the world which society knows, is a constant threat to the legitimacy of the government's power which rests on the verification of the theory.

The gulf was one which the party prepared itself to remove in fact; in the meantime it removed it magically. In fact, because as far as it could, it was melting the social matter down and pouring it into the mould prepared for it, which would give it the form for which the party provided the example. That is what coercion was for. That was what the new moulds were being prepared for, so that soon the peasants would be poured into them, and, once again, the workers and the intellectuals and other city types, because the first casting had not taken, and they had come out of the mould just as they had gone in: full of *bourgeois vestiges*. All the same, it would not be enough for the subjects merely to accept socialism, nor even hope for it: they must actually assent to the belief that the law of development has been proved and that socialism exists. In other words, Communist education consists not in persuading the subjects to *want* socialism, but to *see* it. The party did not simply devote its energies to building socialism, but also giving credence to the fiction that it was already working, that it was embodied there and then, and obtaining recognition of this fiction from its subjects. Coercion was enough to enforce obedience, but to gain assent, smiles, gaiety and enthusiasm, with gratitude being expressed to the party for imaginary benefits, this needed a terror of an order never seen before.

This terror was a result, not of the real, but of the fictional building of socialism, the magical removal of the unbridgeable gulf. This was achieved through language, and on a secondary level, through art.

At the time of Lenin's death, the language of Communism was fully formed. It had been forming since the 1860s, but Lenin fixed it and generalized it. It is the outward sign of the party's communion with the ideology. The progress of the militant, and his level of Communist education, are judged by his capacity to deal with the outside world by using canonical methods of analysis, the same logical leaps, the same turns of style, and by setting himself within it in such a way that it comes to merge with his own vision.

In this way, the correct use of the ideological language is a sign of the identification of the person who employs it with its model. As a means of communication, it is a sign that agreement on the central vision exists between the speakers, and evidence of the growth and establishment of the ideological reality between them at the time of speaking. It is thus a sacrament of unity. In the Communist world, the curse of Babel has been lifted because the variety of languages has been overcome by the uniformity of style, and because each individual tongue has given up uttering any sounds other than those belonging to what soon came to be called the 'wooden language'.

In the party congresses, the report of the secretary general was presented as being an exemplary analysis of the state of the universe and of the two forces fighting over it. It had to be lengthy so that no important aspect might escape from the business of the ideological reconstitution of reality. Others afterwards spoke up, not in order to contradict, but to round off this reconstitution. Thus the aim of the ceremony was to demonstrate, through the carefully maintained harmony of linguistic rules, the harmony of the ideological world within the doctrine which unified it.

It is in an analysis of this language that one comes to perceive more clearly than anywhere else the nature of the ideology as the confusion of a debased religion with a debased science.[5]

Like the language of ideology, the language of liturgy is transpersonal. It manifests the presence of a reality other than empirical reality. The celebrant moves out of his subjectivity, and with him moves the participant assembly. Liturgical language must be rigorous because the reality being described must be described accurately or risk being seriously altered. Not a word can be changed, and that is why a liturgy always develops very slowly. The tone is not that of ordinary language. There is a distinctive diction, a distinctive psalmody. Finally, liturgy also promises to lift the curse of Babel, since binding all the participants is an image of the One. On quite another level, that of phenomenal reality, scientific language possesses the same attributes as the language of liturgy; it is transpersonal, not dependent on common intelligibility, objective, rigorous and unificatory.

The language of ideology is a fusion of liturgical and scientific language. Of course, it would like to be entirely scientific. But ideological 'science' does not restrict itself to the phenomenon. It penetrates Being, and relates its laws. Ideological language is thus the single liturgy of the single reality, which draws its ontological substance not from a transcendental Being but from matter subject to determinism.

This language becomes magical as its powerlessness becomes apparent. Incapable of modifying the real according to its ends, unable to create another reality which conforms to what it has promised, its function is to *evoke*, in the magical meaning of the word, that is, to suggest the non-existent reality. In order to do so, it borrows from the two magics which have traditionally grafted themselves into religion and science, that is, the black mass and quackery. It is formulary, because its power is linked to the letter, and it is incantatory. Dedicated to suggesting through words an illusory reality, side by side with and transcending real reality, it is the medium for that reality's necessary transfiguration. The propagandist who descends on the countryside with his armed bands and seizes the wheat has not come to persuade the peasant, but to enthrone the ideological reality. This reality makes its entry by breaking into the village reality, with all its apparatus of banners and 'elections', 'full discussions' and 'Soviet democracy'. It arrives, installs itself, and its reign begins.

Based on this linguistic magic, there developed an aesthetic magic. One of Lenin's last bequests, and by no means the least important, was to promote it and to facilitate its establishment. Its aim was to give visual substance to the other reality, to make it visible by making it apprehensible to the senses. So it mobilized in its service the representational techniques which had been worked out during the centuries when art had attempted to 'compete with nature' and which were, at the time of Lenin's death, on the point of being abandoned in the West, and among the *avant-garde* in Russia itself. This aesthetic called itself *socialist realism*. It gave a clear picture of the reality it was supposed to represent: beloved leaders, eager people, fertile fields and model factories. In traditional painting, to compete with nature meant using techniques of representation, of colour and perspective in order to attain a reality deeper than that visible to the eye of the non-artist. In this way art acted as an intermediary between the sensible world and the intelligible world, with the latter being even more real than the former. Socialist realism would like to mirror a non-existent reality. So, far from being able to distance itself to some extent from the techniques of visual illusion, as 'classical' realism was able to do, socialist realism depended on these techniques absolutely. Since unreality must be affirmed to be the only reality, it was a question of applying all the tricks of photographic illusion. Pictures were made up like nineteenth-century panoramas, to give the spectator the feeling of actually *being there*. In the same way, in literature, the techniques of evocation developed by the great classical novelists were made use of, but turned to different ends, and put to the service of illusion. Art became unreal through the development of its 'realism', and its spell was reduced to the summary technique of some Hollywood scene-setter. The spectator never gets the feeling of being there, because he knows he is not. He does, though, undergo the most brutal form of assault by the false, like a counterfeit bill which the state had guaranteed to be legal currency. So perfectly did socialist realism and the party symbolize each other — the aesthetic acting by political methods and the party acting aesthetically — that it has never been possible to separate them.

The only point of contact between the two realities came down to the government itself. But, unless it falls into cynicism, the government has no legitimacy except in acting as a link between the two existing realities, both the 'old' and the 'new', and ensuring the transition from the one to the other. But can it do so? Real reality is the only reality. Ideological reality exists only as language (or decoration). It is made of words. The party cannot act on the real reality except by means of words belonging to the ideological reality and the subsequent transformation of the former can only be described in terms taken from the latter, which are by definition inadequate. It is thus crucially necessary that the transcendance of the duplication of the world should finish by entirely depriving the real reality of speech, and creating, next to it, another reality which exists only in speech. Once this has been done, there need be no limit to the proliferation of pronouncements, *reports* can extend to infinity, multiplied still further in the press, and language, encountering no resistance in reality, but itself constituting its only simulacrum, 'runs riot' like a prisoner just set free from jail. The immoderate inflation of empty words is thus the exact (but reverse) counterpart of the real reality, which, reduced to silence, flows away indefinitely in the opposite direction, in a flood whose dimensions are measured, on the other side of the watershed of power, by verbal inflation. The ideology expends its powers in a cult which is crushing in its weight and in its detail, and its speech, unrelated to the phenomenon, and still less to the Being, presents a species of liturgy of the void.

This magic has as its aim the abolition of the chasm between the two orders of reality. The dualism will, in the end, be resolved into a monism, since the real reality will merge with the other in Communism. The naïve Communist will not accept the *initial* separation of the two orders of reality. 'If it was to treat people like that', he thinks, 'it was not worth making the revolution.' The cynic will not believe in the *final* coincidence of the two realities. He would make use of the internal duplication for his own profit. But the Communist who held the correct position would reject both these temptations, and live entirely within the ideological reality, in order to be the *advance guard*, the forerunner of the future reconciled world.

Through coercion, socialism is built; through linguistic magic, it is endowed with a pre-existing reality. What the party discovered is that the two methods combine marvellously, in such a way that the magic facilitates the coercion, and the coercion sets the scene for the magic. No one is going to resist the *Cheka*, if the man coming to arrest your father is *by that token* bringing you true freedom. On the other hand, police are necessary if you do not want the banners torn down and if you want everybody to participate in the elections. It is in this combination that there resides the efficiency of the Soviet government, the quality of its enchantment, the tonality of its terror. It is not the tyranny of Lenin, but, as Pasternak has said, the far worse tyranny of the phrase and 'the spell of the dead letter'.[6] The disorientation of the reason, the removal of any point of reference, the confidence of the ideological assertion, the absolute separation between what it says and how things are, reveal themselves incomparable aids to the Soviet government. And since it is the ideology which makes possible the increase of this power and, by that token, brings nearer the moment of its fulfilment, then it must be that it is true. The omnipotence of the 'falsehood' is proof once again of the truth of the ideology. It is through the ideology that one enters the Dominion of the False.

Having arrived at this point, the ideology undergoes a radical change. At the beginning of this book, it appeared to be a belief of a certain kind, a doctrine. It is no longer that except incidentally or in a secondary capacity.

The substance of the ideology, when it is in power, is that power itself. It is the form of that power, and that power has no other content than itself. It is the new reality, which, emancipated from the common reality, sets itself to transform it to fit its own model, and meanwhile, it claims to be the only reality.

It follows that the ideology no longer needs to be believed, not even in the form of the false evidence and gnostic pseudo-empiricism under which it had earlier gripped revolutionary consciousnesses. It was fact: it was power. It did not thus need to be carried out. Since the ideology had foreseen democratic elections and the unanimity of the electors in favour of socialism, all that was needed was to organize these elections carefully, so as to consolidate the ideology not in its mode of belief but in its mode of power. It is the same with the huge army of propagandists and the printers where all the books are printed, in editions of hundreds of millions: their aim is not to convince, but to make manifest the fact of the power of the ideology.

When Stalin proclaimed the most democratic constitution in the world, when in his speeches he opposed false Western democracy to the true democracy, he was not seeking to persuade, but to intimidate by falsehood, a falsehood so enormous and so crushing that it drew its amazing force from the daring improbability with which it was imposed, because that showed just what the government was capable of.[7] The ideology is the sign, the emblem, of the power. It is no longer a question of adhering to the ideology by free choice, nor even of entering into the intellectual operations which constitute it. It is enough simply to obey it. It must be *spoken*, because language is a social institution and that particular language is the institution of the society which is supposed to exist.[8] But hardly has one spoken it, even at first in all innocence, in simple social conformity and full consciousness of its lack of meaning, than one can see it take shape. In fact, speaking it means that the government has scored, and that the ideology, which is one with it, has begun to take shape. So it must be true. Whoever speaks it gives it his own truth and his own substance. As soon as the subject of the ideology has taken the first step, which remains as yet a lie, he is drained of his substance, which is conferred on the lie: given that weight, the lie is no longer a lie, but a sort of fact to which one will soon be able to commit one's sincerity, and perhaps even one's belief. By then the subject can no longer recall the initial step which opened the way to his dispossession — or perhaps one should say, his possession.

It took until 1974 to find a man who, as a result of his sufferings and private meditation, was able to find a formula which could lift the spell. 'Violence does not always necessarily take you physically by the throat and strangle you! More often it merely demands of its subjects that they declare allegiance to the lie, become accomplices in the lie. And the simple step of a simple, courageous man is not to take part in the lie, not to support deceit. Let the lie come into the world, even dominate the world, but not through me.'[9] The impersonal sway of the ideological word is swept away by the eruption of the personal word, the *me*. 'For when men turn their backs on the lie, the lie simply ceases to exist. Like a contagious disease, it can only exist in a crowd.'

There is a fundamental distinction drawn in the USSR between *Them*, the party members, and *Us*, the passive subjects of the party's power. But it does not follow that the party is more free than its subjects with regard to the ideology.

Departing from us, Comrade Lenin adjured us to hold high and guard the purity of the great title of member of the Party. We vow to you, Comrade Lenin, that we will fulfil your behest with credit!...Departing from us, Comrade Lenin adjured us to guard the unity of our Party as the apple of our eye. We vow to you, Comrade Lenin, that this behest, too, we will fulfil with credit![10]

What makes Stalin's 'sermon' comprehensible is the fact that the sequence of ideology–party–power, which the party inherited from Lenin, could no longer be separated. Lenin had formulated it freely. It had become a necessity. It was to be endured. In Lenin's time, it was the first term of the sequence which had absorbed his attention. He had forged the second, and seized the last. For his successors, the sequence should be taken in the reverse order. If they wanted to keep power, they had to take care of the unity of the party, and preserve its immaterial soul, the ideology to that end. At the point where Russia now finds itself, to lose power means to lose one's life. It is a question of life and death to preserve the ideology, whether alive or dead hardly matters.

There is one incontestable fact about the Leninist régime: it is in power, and well able to extend its dominion even further. All the reality of the ideology is concentrated in the exercise of power. Only at that level does there exist rational, instrumental conduct, neutral in relation to the ideology, but enveloped in it and endowed by it with an effectiveness lacking in the most cold-blooded Machiavellianism of the past. At this level, too, there exist the traditional human passions of governing, of dominating, and, in a general way, of acting, which must be transcended by the ideology, but which are also, thanks to it, amply satisfied. Leninist power, like any other, has a hold on the real, attacks and devours the real, and thus may appear to be nourished by it. The lust for power which is sanctioned by the ideology is a way of escaping from the unreality of the ideology. Power represents for the ideologist the perpetual hope of a cure.

But it is a hope doomed to disappointment. For the power, existing only through the ideology, is taken over and enslaved by it. It can only act according to the scheme which the ideology imposes, which is necessarily unrealizable, but which cannot be changed. The price paid by the party to the ideology in order to retain power is a radical impotence to act on reality *as it is*. The ideology claimed to embrace the whole of the real. But the real lies hidden in the shadow cast on it by the ideology. Never has the rift between the ideology and the real been so great as since the ideology has had the real in its power. It cannot even recognize the grain of reality which it does actually possess, that is, power itself, for what it is. The ideology is the consciousness of the party, but it is unconscious, and the form remains hollow. The party must seek to build socialism, but at the same time it insists that socialism exists — meanwhile, the real reality is seeping through every crack, and remains, however weakened, however cut about, the only reality. Thus the power of the party demands to be extended indefinitely in impotent compensation for its fundamental powerlessness. It is a power without content and the desire for socialism, so long as it is not realized, is a desire for the void. The indefinite extension of power (which is also an indefinite extension of the ideology) is like *painting over* an entire picture, without being able to stop the figures from coming through again from underneath, so that it soon needs a fresh coat of whitewash.

We need not pursue this history further, since the history itself stopped at this point. What evolved is the reality. It has done what it could, in a permanent compromise between its essential demands and the role imposed upon it. But the Leninist régime has remained immobile, fixed in the ideology which preceded it, shaped it and maintained it — and maintains it still — in place. It is the strange fate of this chronolatry to have removed from the historical time to which it claimed to submit everything, the very régime established to bring it to fulfilment.

This power does keep a sort of reality on its main front, the shifting line dividing what it controls from what it does not yet control. It conquers in order to live, but no sooner has it conquered than its conquest dies and slips away from it, and cannot be assimilated. It remains a disembodied force, rather like an angel whose eternal fate it is forever to desire that what is, should not be, and what is not, should be.

The gulf which opened, first in one man's mind, and then in a city, on 7 November 1917, has thus not closed again, but has continued to widen, to the whole world's cost. In its void, the ideology is both all and nothing, depending on whether one considers its visible omnipresence or its invisible impotence. The party cannot be rid of it, however moribund in thought and belief it might be, without destroying itself. Its torment, and that of its subjects, is like that which, according to Virgil, a certain Etruscan king inflicted on his prisoners, in binding them to a corpse.[11]

The corpse is on public view. It is in the mausoleum raised to it by the government once it realized that the corpse could not be buried. Since then, a queue longer than anything seen in Orthodox Russia during the Easter Procession has built up at the entrance. Men, women and children enter the sepulchre to look upon the body still lying there — or the wax figure which has perhaps replaced it — whence escaped the *ideological soul* which has taken possession of them.

Notes

Translator's Note: Where an English edition of a work is available the original note has been changed to refer to that. Only in those cases where a marked difference was found between the French and English versions has a reference to the French edition been retained.

CHAPTER 1: *The Ideology*

1. Solzhenitsyn, 1974, p. 47.
2. Zamyatin, 1970; Orwell, 1949, 1970. To which one should also add Milosz, 1953.
3. And in fact, after taking power, ideology ceases to be a belief. One could say that it is only effective so long as it is not believed. Solzhenitsyn: 'We who have had a taste of it are only pretending willy-nilly...', 1970, p. 43. Making believe to believe what one does not believe destroys the spirit and so accomplishes one of the aims of the ideology. See below, Chapter 16. But that is no reason to think, as Sakharov does, that Soviet society is characterized by its 'ideological indifference and by pragmatic use of ideology as a convenient façade'. Sakharov, 1975, p. 00. The link between society and ideology is a closer one than mere pragmatism might suggest.
4. Lenin, 1977, vol. I, pp. 121–2. *What is to be done?*
5. *Petit dictionnaire philosophique*, 1955, p. 262. [*Translator's Note*: The English edition, *A dictionary of philosophy*, Progress Publishers, Moscow, 1967, is not identical.]
6. *Diamat*: colloquial abbreviation of *dialektitcheskii materializm*.
7. Boukharine and Preobrajenski, 1971.
8. Published as Paragraph 2 of Chapter IV of the *History of the Communist Party of the Soviet Union (Bolsheviks)*, 1939. It does not matter that, as seems more than likely, Stalin is not the author.
9. Mannheim, 1936.
10. Baechler, 1976. Cf. his definition of ideology, p. 60.

11. There are other groups as well. In particular, there is one committed to describing the ideological phenomenon in psychological terms. This is what Gabel did, 1952, 1962, 1974, though he did, it is true, mingle with the psychiatry certain Lukàcsian sociological considerations which did not make things any easier. I will not be regarding things from this point of view in the present study.

12. Cf. Shils, 1968.

13. Lenin, 1977, vol. I, p. 44. *The three sources and the three component parts of Marxism*.

14. Lenin, 1947, vol. I, p. 84. *What the 'friends of the people' are*.

15. Losski, 1951; Zenkovsky, 1953.

16. Chambre, 1955. Timidly amended in his new book, 1974.

17. There is the same error of perspective in Wetter, 1966.

18. Papaioannou, 1967.

19. Cf. V. Soloviev, 1947. Soloviev recanted later.

20. Monnerot, 1953.

21. Aron, 1957, chap. IV. Cf. also: Aron, 1955, p. 80.

22. Mandelstam, 1974, p. 20.

23. Doresse, 1972, p. 380.

24. Augustine, 1961, p. 513.

25. Plotinus, *Enneads*, tr. A. H. Armstrong, Heinemann, London, 1966, II, 9, 15.

26. Puech, 1972, p. 538.

27. There is thus identity between the known and the knowing, and it is one and the same act to agree with gnosticism and to be converted to gnosticism.

28. Puech, 1972, p. 575.

29. *Letter from Secundinus to Augustine*: 'It is not to virtue that the masses turn.' Augustine, 1961, p. 519.

30. *Contra Fortunatum*, 20, 21, Augustine, 1961, p. 167.

31. *Letter from Secundinus to Augustine*, Augustine, 1961, p. 513.

32. A. Solignac, Preface to the *Confessions* of Saint Augustine. Augustine, 1962, p. 125.

33. Plotinus found this shocking: 'By giving names to a multitude of intelligible realities they think they will appear to have discovered the exact truth, though by this very multiplicity they bring the intelligible nature into the likeness of the sense-world, the inferior world, when one ought there in the intelligible to aim at the smallest possible number, (II, 9). In other words, the explanation becomes just as impenetrable as the complexity of the real, to which it finally comes to form an imaginary and useless double. It is an elucubration.

34. Rudolph, 1972.

35. *Petit dictionnaire philosophique*, 1955, p. 487. [*Translator's Note*: The English edition, *A dictionary of philosophy*, Progress Publishers, Moscow, 1967, is not identical.]

36. *Ibid.*, p. 548.

37. There is a very widespread school of historical thought, perhaps even the dominant one, which maintains that there is a continuity between Tsarist and Soviet Russia. Thus, recently, such acute historians as Pipes, 1974, and Szamuely, 1974. But ideology, which is responsible for having fixed Russia in itself and for having exacerbated some of the more extreme characteristics of the Tsarist régime, is also responsible for a radical break with that régime, a far more complete break than the normal distance between past and present prevailing in modern nations. I have already written briefly about this paradox (Besançon, 1974). This point of view runs the risk of making it possible to believe that an ideological régime could only arise in the localized terrain of Russia and that it could not be transposed elsewhere. Which goes against the evidence of contemporary history.

CHAPTER 2: *The French Cycle*

1. I am indebted to Lenoble, 1957, 1969, 1971, throughout this passage.
2. Alquié, 1966, p. 233.
3. Lenoble, 1971, p. 350.
4. Tests to which P. Chaunu has rightly drawn attention: Chaunu, 1966, chap. XIV.
5. Hazard, 1953.
6. Armogathe, 1973, p. 97.
7. Quotation and commentary in Koyré, 1958, p. 228.
8. Quoted and commented on by Alquié, 1974.
9. Koyré, 1958, p. 276.
10. Notably by Plekhanov, see below, Chapter 10.
11. Here, too, I owe a debt to Lenoble, 1969.
12. D'Alembert, 1965, p. 111.
13. *Traité des animaux*. Quoted by Cassirer, 1951, p. 104.
14. Cf. Lenoble, 1969, p. 343.
15. D'Alembert, 1965, p. 111.
16. Lenoble, 1969, p. 344.
17. La Mettrie, 1960, p. 202.
18. La Mettrie, 1954, p. 186.
19. *Cit.* Cassirer, 1951, p. 67.
20. Gouhier, 1933, vol. II, pp. 200-14.
21. Sade, 1968, pp. 1188–9.
22. Diderot, 1951, p. 1247.
23. Groethuysen, 1966, p. 162.
24. *Ibid.*, p. 188.
25. Helvétius, 1973, p. 492.
26. Morelly, 1970, p. 40.

27. This paragraph relies on Cochin, 1921.
28. See the figures given by Tulard in Gaxotte and Tulard, 1975, p. 321.
29. Cochin, *Le patriotisme humanitaire*, in Cochin, 1921, p. 292.

CHAPTER 3: *The German Cycle*

1. Cf. the analyses by Jaeger, 1965.
2. Koyré, 1971a and 1971b.
3. Jaeger, 1965, 1977. Gusdorf, 1972, pp. 59–142. Gusdorf, 1976, pp. 244–313. As his investigations proceed, Gusdorf appears to accord Pietism an increasingly important position.
4. Benz, 1968. In particular, chap. III, 'Eschatologie et philosophie dans l'histoire'.
5. Yates, 1966, pp. 379–89.
6. Leibnitz, 1952, pp. 251–3, *Theodicy*, § 200 and 201. Cf. Martin, 1964, p. 23.
7. Kant, 1963, p. 83.
8. *Ibid.*, p. 84.
9. Kant, 1953, p. 154.
10. Vancourt, 1971, p. 8, pp. 107–23.
11. McClellan, 1969, p. 64.
12. *Cit.* McClellan, pp. 65–6.
13. *Aus früherer Zeit*, IV, p. 570, *cit.* Löwith, 1965, p. 91.
14. *Ludwig Feuerbach*, in Marx and Engels, 1947, p. 41.
15. Maritain, 1964. Cf. chapter entitled 'The Marxist dialectic', pp. 220–9.
16. *Ludwig Feuerbach*, in Marx and Engels, 1947, p. 41.
17. Engels, 1977.
18. Graham, 1973, p. 58.
19. *Theses on Feuerbach*, in Marx and Engels, 1947, pp. 57 and 59.
20. *Cit.* Löwith, 1965, pp. 43–4.
21. Bernstein, 1974, p. 67.

CHAPTER 4: *The Religious Education of Russia*

1. The best history, and the least affected by this kind of working over, remains Florovsky, 1937. Milyukov, 1942, is also still very useful.
2. Florovsky, 1970, p. 132.
3. Ross, 1973.
4. On the other hand, the Orthodox liturgy makes more room for the Old Testament than the Roman liturgy does.
5. Cherniavsky, 1970, p. 65 *et seq.*

6. Cf. Stremooukhoff, 1970.

7. Dvornik, 1970, p. 730.

8. It would, in fact, be wrong to attribute Muscovite Caesaro-Papism purely and simply to Byzantium. Cf. Obolensky, 1970, pp. 21–3.

9. Cf. the excellent chapter in Treadgold, 1973: 'Russia's quasi-Reformation', pp. 84–115. On the Kiev-West links, Rupp, 1970.

10. Cf. the article on Russia in the *Dictionnaire de théologie catholique*, which is amazingly erudite on the subject.

11. On the relations between Leibnitz and Peter the Great, Baruzi, 1907, chap. III. On relations between Halle University and Russia, M. Raeff, 1967b and 1966, chap. V.

12. Treadgold, 1973, p. 125. Faivre, 1973, p. 168.

13. It was published in English in 1912.

14. Faivre, 1973, p. 96.

15. Rouet de Journel, 1922.

16. Treadgold, 1973, chap. V: 'Rationalism and sentimentalism'.

17. Text in Ley, 1975, p. 56.

18. Koyré, 1929, p. 99.

19. *Ibid.*

20. Works on Slavophilism should be divided into two groups. In the first are those who adhere to Slavophilism. They are the great majority. Notably: Gratieux, 1939 and 1953. Christoff, 1961. In the second group, there are to my knowledge only two works, both of them remarkable: Rouleau, 1972, unfortunately as yet unpublished, and Walicki, 1975. To which one can add the more specialized approach of P. Baron, 1940.

21. Kireevski, 1911. For theological works, Khomiakoff, 1872, covers the main ground.

22. 'On the necessity and possibility of new principles in philosophy', 1856.

23. Zenkovsky, 1953, vol. I, p. 237 *et seq.*

24. Walicki, 1975, p. 154.

25. *Ibid.*, p. 161.

26. E. Susini, *Lettres inédites de Franz von Baader*, Paris, 1942, pp. 456–61. *Cit.* Walicki, 1975, p. 164.

27. Translation by R. Tandonnet in the appendix to Gratieux, 1953.

28. Walicki, 1975, p. 193.

29. *Ibid.*, p. 316.

30. In 1831.

31. *Le XIXe siècle.*

32. Kireevski, 1911, vol. I, pp. 153–4.

33. *Ibid.*, vol. I, pp. 214–15.

34. *Ibid.*, vol. I, p. 203 *et seq.*

35. *Ibid.*, vol. I, p. 184 *et seq.*

36. As noted by Walicki, 1975, p. 209.

37. *Mémoires sur l'histoire universelle*, 1,500 pages without a single reference! Cf. Gratieux, 1939, vol. II, p. 51 *et seq.* and Walicki, 1975, pp. 208–30.

38. Walicki, 1975, p. 222.

39. P. Baron, 1940, p. 116.

40. Walicki, 1975, p. 250.

CHAPTER 5: *Liberalism or Revolution*

1. Michelet, 1968, pp. 203 and 205.

2. *Ibid.*, p. 36.

3. *Ibid.*, p. 16.

4. Marx, 1954, p. 207.

5. Even de Tocqueville. Cf. Starr, 1972, p. 71 *et seq.*

6. Herzen, 1968, vol. II, p. 511.

7. *Letter to Gogol*, 1847, Biélinski, 1948, p. 535.

8. *Ibid.*, p. 539.

9. Letter to Granovski, 29 September 1836. *Cit.* Koyré, 1950, p. 123.

10. He immediately felt the gnostic sense of 'depersonalization': 'My personal self has been wiped out for over; it seeks nothing for itself any longer; its life will be henceforward the life of the absolute in which my personal self has found more than it has lost.' (Letter to his brothers, 4 February 1837.)

11. Koyré, 1950, p. 138.

12. In the *Deutsche Jahrbücher*, too, Bakunin has similarities with Ruge.

13. *Ibid.*, p. 140.

14. *Ibid.*, p. 139.

15. *Ibid.*, p. 140.

16. *Ibid.*

17. *Ibid.*, p. 144.

18. Blok, 1974, p. 165.

19. *Cit.* Koyré, 1950, p. 163.

20. Malia, 1961, p. 197, and Labry, 1928, p. 202.

21. Cieszkowski, 1979, p. 55.

22. *Ibid.*

23. *Ibid.*, p. 56.

24. Cieszkowski, 1973, p. 50.

25. Cieszkowski, 1979, pp. 77–8.

26. Herzen, 1968, vol. II, p. 403.

27. Labry, 1928, p. 241.

28. Malia, 1961, chaps. XIV and XV.

29. Michelet, 1968, p. 97.

30. One can see him at this point castigating 'ordinary' science in exactly the same terms as the Slavophiles: it is 'unilateral' and 'abstract', it is not full, etc.

Dilettantism in science in Herzen, 1956, pp. 97 *et seq.* Equally note this para-Marxist phrase: 'The history of thought is the continuation of the history of nature.' *Ibid.*, p. 135.
31. Herzen, 1956, pp. 105–6.
32. 'The task of science is the elevation of the whole being in thought. Thought tends to comprehend, to absorb the external, other object which is opposed to thought; that is to say, it denies the immediacy of the object, generalizes it, and deals with it as a universal', etc. Herzen, 1956.

CHAPTER 6: *The Intelligentsia*

1. The most recent books on this subject: Brower, 1975; Besançon, 1974.
2. W. Weidlé, 1952, pp. 66–7.
3. Nicholas Obruchev, a redoubtable conspirator in the sixties, ended up as a general and Chief of the General Staff. The case is typical. Ulam, 1977, p. 71.
4. Ivanov-Razumnik, 1908.
5. Nomad, 1958: B. Souvarine, 1939, p. 565; Avrich, 1967, p. 102 *et seq.*; M. Heller, 1974, p. 17.
6. *Vekhi*, 1909, p. 25.
7. Cf. the collection edited by Pipes, 1961, with the indispensable article by M. Malia, 'What is the intelligentsia?', and articles by Pipes, Schapiro, Labedz *et al.* Cf. also Raeff, 1966, and Confino, 1972.

CHAPTER 7: *The New Man*

1. In all the vast literature on Chernyshevski, I take the best to be the portrait given of him by Nabokov in Chapter IV of *The gift*, 1963.
2. *Le principe anthropologique en philosophie*, 1860, in Chernyshevski, 1957, pp. 49–137.
3. *Ibid.*, p. 68.
4. *Ibid.*, p. 70.
5. *Ibid.*, p. 78.
6. *Ibid.*, p. 84.
7. *Ibid.*
8. *Ibid.*
9. Chernyshevski, 1967, p. 319.
10. Chernyshevski, 1957, p. 85.
11. *Ibid.*, p. 92.
12. *Ibid.*, p. 96.
13. *Ibid.*, p. 122.
14. *Ibid.*, p. 124.

15. *Ibid.*, p. 98.
16. *Ibid.*, p. 113.
17. Chernyshevsky, 1967, p. 271.
18. Chernyshevski, 1957, p. 132.
19. Chernyshevski, 1967, p. 306.
20. *Ibid.*, p. 312.
21. *Ibid.*, p. 315.
22. *Ibid.*, p. 313.
23. *Ibid.*, p. 427.
24. *Ibid.*, p. 282.
25. *Ibid.*, p. 328.
26. Walicki, 1969, p. 16.

CHAPTER 8: *A Dream of the Party*

1. Lenin, 1975, vol. I, p. 225. *What is to be done?*
2. Confino, 1973, p. 13.
3. *Ibid.*, p. 109.
4. The text was established by Confino, 1973, pp. 97–105.
5. Cf. for example Brown, 1966; Raeff, 1967a; Koyré, 1929.
6. Besançon, 1974a, chap. III and IV.
7. Besançon, 1967, p. 217.
8. Besançon, 1974c.
9. Confino, 1973, p. 15; Venturi, 1972, p. 12.
10. Cf. the analyses by Girard, 1961, 1963 and Besançon, 1974c.
11. Confino, 1973, p. 18.
12. Works on Dostoevsky, like works on Slavophilism, can be divided into two groups, the 'Dostoevskyites' and the rest. Amongst the 'Dostoevskyites', Mochulsky, 1967, is undoubtedly the best. Amongst those who keep their distance, Drouilly, 1971, and Pascal, 1969 and 1970.
13. Chestov, 1972.
14. *The possessed*, Part II, I, 7.
15. Papaioannou, 1962, p. 33; Besançon, 1972, 1975.
16. *Letter to Nathalie von Vizine*, 15 February 1854, Dostoevsky, 1949–61, t.I, p. 157.
17. There is no need to look for direct influences, though Dostoevsky's relations with Swedenborg, cf. Milosz, 1975, might be worth noting.
18. The other source being his Russian messianism, which was thus in competition with the people of Israel. Cf. Goldstein, 1976.
19. Thus at the end of the century there appeared a progressive Christianity through a move to the left of the themes dear to the Slavophiles, but this time without any loss of religious fervour. This progressive Christianity invaded the

clergy, recruiting members of what would be, after the revolution, 'the living Church', a schism fomented by the Bolshevik government. It was at the turn of the century that Slavophilism, which was originally an entirely lay movement, began to make its way into clerical circles. The move leftward, in France, of Marrassism, as a lay and then a clerical movement, giving rise to a progressive Christianity deriving from the Front Populaire, gives a fairly close picture of what happened in Russia. On this phenomenon, cf. Scherrer, 1973, 1976, 1977.

CHAPTER 9: *A Sketch of the Party*

1. Confino, 1973, p. 68.
2. *Ibid.*
3. Venturi, 1960, p. 450.
4. Lavrov, 1903, pp. 67–81.
5. Kuljabo-Koreckij, *Iz davnykh let*, p. 24, *cit.* Venturi, 1960, p. 450.
6. Lavrov, 1903, p. 80.
7. *Filosofija i Sociologija*, p. 54, *cit.* Walicki, 1969, p. 34.
8. Karpovich, 1963.
9. For this passage, I have followed Walicki, 1969, pp. 46–80. Cf. also Ivanov-Razumnik, 1908, vol. II, pp. 135–206.
10. This question of the entry of Marxism into Russia was taken up again by Walicki, 1969. Cf. Chap. III, 'Populism and Marxism', p. 132 *et seq.*
11. Walicki, 1969, p. 132.
12. *Ibid.*, p. 137.
13. Koz'min, 1922, p. 19. Koz'min's monograph remains the essential work. Completed by Koz'min, 1961, reproducing the preface to Tkachev's Selected Works, edited by the same author, in 1932–1937.
14. Tkachev, 1932, vol. I, p. 427.
15. *Ibid.*, vol. II, p. 205.
16. *Ibid.*, vol. I, p. 326.
17. *Ibid.*, vol. I, p. 174.
18. *Ibid.*, vol. I, p. 415.
19. *Ibid.*, vol. III, pp. 69–70.
20. *Cit.* Papaioannou, 1972, p. 265.
21. *Ibid.*
22. Tkachev, vol. III, p. 224. *Cit.* Venturi, 1960, p. 419.
23. *Ibid.*, vol. III, p. 65. *Cit.* Venturi, 1960, p. 414.
24. *Cit.* Venturi, 1960, p. 406.
25. Tkachev, 1932, vol. I, p. 282. *Cit.* Venturi, 1960, p. 406.
26. *Ibid.*
27. Venturi, 1960, p. 426.
28. Tkachev, 1932, vol. I, pp. 348–9.

29. Venturi, 1960, p. 414.
30. Tkachev, 1933, vol. III, p. 310. *Cit.* Venturi, 1960, p. 422.
31. *Ibid.*, vol. III, p. 286. *Cit.* Venturi, 1960, p. 419.
32. *Ibid.*, vol. III, p. 266. *Cit.* Venturi, 1960, p. 423.
33. *Ibid.*, vol. III, p. 327. *Cit.* Venturi, 1960, p. 420.
34. On relations between Lenin and Tkachev, *see* L. Schapiro, 1970, p. 26. On the parallel with Lenin, Szamuely, 1974, pp. 287–319.
35. Cf. Mathieu, 1974, chaps. IV and V.
36. On *Zemlia i Volia*, two accounts suffice: Venturi, 1960, and Ulam, 1977.
37. Venturi, 1960, p. 565.
38. *Ibid.*, p. 566.
39. Mathieu, 1974, p. 81.
40. Venturi, 1960, p. 586.
41. On the opposition between revolt and revolution, cf. the fine analysis made by Mathieu, 1974, p. 181 *et seq.*
42. Venturi, 1960, p. 590.
43. *Ibid.*, p. 609.
44. *Ibid.*, p. 615.

CHAPTER 10. *Social Democracy*

1. Plekhanov, vol. I, p. 7, *Socialisme et lutte politique*, 1883.
2. Walicki, 1969, p. 154.
3. Plekhanov, n. d., vol. I, p. 58, 'Socialisme et lutte politique', (written in 1883).
4. Walicki, 1969, p. 164.
5. Pipes, 1963, particularly chap. VI.
6. On the sort of sound papers which Marx could have read before he died, Walicki, 1969, p. 166.
7. Pipes, 1970, p. 101 *et seq.*
8. Keep, 1963, p. 58 *et seq.*
9. *Cit.* Papaioannou, 1972, p. 248, *Socialisme théorique et social-démocratie pratique*, 1899.
10. Bernstein, 1974, p. 13. *Lettre au congrès...*
11. *Cit.* Papaioannou, 1972, p. 252, *Socialisme théorique et social-démocratie pratique*, 1899.
12. Bernstein, 1974, p. 222.
13. *Cit.* Papaioannou, 1972, p. 247, *Socialisme théorique et social-démocratie pratique*, 1899.
14. Bernstein, 1974, p. 16.
15. *Cit.* Papaioannou, 1972, p. 248, *Sozialistische Controversen*, 1904.
16. *Cit.* Papaioannou, 1972, p. 251, *Réforme ou Révolution*, 1899.

17. Walicki, 1969, p. 170.
18. Ulam, 1964, p. 104. Seton-Watson, 1967, p. 511.
19. Pipes, 1970, p. 221 *et seq.*
20. Baron, 1963, p. 173.
21. Plekhanov, vol. II, p. 390.
22. The hardy can read them in Plekhanov, vol. II.
23. Plekhanov, vol. II, p. 11.
24. *Ibid.*, p. 264.
25. *Ibid.*, p. 370.
26. *Ibid.*, p. 376.
27. *Ibid.*, p. 462.
28. *Ibid.*
29. *Ibid.*, p. 467.
30. Ulam, 1966, pp. 161–3, p. 168.
31. *Cit.* Baron, 1962, p. 50.
32. Ulam, 1974, p. 50.
33. Reported by Kuskova, 'Davno Minuvshee', *Novyj Zhurnal*, LVI, 1958, p. 139. Baron, 1962, pp. 50–1.
34. Baron, 1963, pp. 353–4.

CHAPTER 11: *Lenin*

1. Plekhanov, vol. II, p. 334, *A propos du rôle de l'individu dans l'histoire*, 1898.
2. Wolfe, 1955; Fischer, 1965; Ulam, 1966.
3. Valentinov, 1968, pp. 51–2. On 6 May 1921, Lenin sent Lunacharski the following telegram: 'Aren't you ashamed to vote for printing 5,000 copies of Mayakovsky's "150,000,000"? It is nonsense, stupidity, double-dyed stupidity and affectation. I believe such things should be published one in ten, and *not more than 1,500 copies*, for libraries and cranks. As for Lunacharsky, he should be flogged for his futurism.' Lenin, 1970 (*Collected works*), vol. 45, pp. 138–9.
4. Valentinov, 1968, p. 50.
5. *Ibid.*, p. 182.
6. *Ibid.*
7. Fischer, 1965, pp. 78–9.
8. Valentinov, 1968, p. 238.
9. Lenin, 1977, vol. I, p. 626, *On the national pride of the Great Russians*.
10. 'The *their*', commented Trotsky (*Lenine*, Paris, 1925, p. 137), 'referred, of course, not to the English, but to the enemy.' Fischer, 1965, p. 51.
11. Letter to his mother, July 1911. *Cit.* Fischer, 1965, p. 72.

CHAPTER 12: *Metaphysical Leninism*

1. Engels, 1935, p. 28.
2. Engels, 1977, p. 24.
3. Lenin, 1960—78, vol. 38, p. 141, *Conspectus of Hegel's 'Science of logic'*.
4. *Ibid.*, p. 147.
5. *Ibid.*, p. 359, *On the question of dialectics*.
6. Lenin, 1960—78, vol. 14, p. 155, *Materialism and empirio-criticism*.
7. Lenin, 1947, vol. I, p. 98, *What the 'friends of the people' are*.
8. Lenin, 1960—78, vol. 14, pp. 189—90, *Materialism and empirio-criticism*.
9. *Ibid.*, p. 55.
10. *Ibid.*, p. 130.
11. *Ibid.*, p. 136.
12. *Ibid.*
13. *Ibid.*, p. 138.
14. *Ibid.*, p. 42.
15. *Ibid.*, p. 32.
16. *Ibid.*, p. 335—6.
17. *Ibid.*, pp. 336—45.
18. *Ibid.*, p. 342.
19. *Ibid.*, p. 292.
20. Lenin, 1947, vol. I, p. 79, *What the 'friends of the people' are*.
21. *Ibid.*, p. 84.
22. Lenin, 1962—78, vol. 14, p. 98, *Materialism and empirio-criticism*.
23. Lenin, 1947, vol. I, pp. 84—5, *What the 'friends of the people' are*.
24. Lenin, 1977, vol. I, p. 45, *The three sources and three component parts of Marxism*.
25. *Ibid.*, p. 48.
26. Stalin, *On the death of Lenin*, in Lenin, 1947, vol. I, p. 33.
27. Lenin, 1977, vol. I, pp. 49—53, *Marxism and revisionism*.
28. *Ibid.*, p. 55.
29. Lenin, 1977, vol. III, pp. 416—18, *The tasks of the youth leagues*.
30. *Ibid.*, p. 425, *On proletarian culture*.
31. *Ibid.*, p. 412, *The tasks of the youth leagues*.
32. *Ibid.*, p. 427, *Speech at the conference of political education workers*.
33. *Ibid.*, p. 428.
34. *Ibid.*, p. 413, *The tasks of the youth leagues*.
35. *Ibid.*, vol. II, p. 312, *The state and the revolution*.
36. *Ibid.*
37. Lenin, 1947, vol. I, p. 559, *Two utopias*.

CHAPTER 13: *Political Leninism*

1. Aristotle, *Politics*, tr. H. Rackham, London, Heinemann, 1932, III, v, 14.
2. Aron, 1976, t. II, pp. 61—8.
3. Lenin, 1977, vol. I, p. 459, *Two tactics of the social democrats in the democratic revolution.*
4. *Ibid.*, p. 530, *Lessons of the Moscow uprising.*
5. Lenin, 1977, vol. II, p. 591, *The immediate tasks of the Soviet government.*
6. Lenin, 1960—78, vol. 24, p. 432, *People from another world.*
7. Lenin, 1977, vol. II, p. 710, *Letter to American workers.*
8. *Ibid.*, p. 34, *The dual power.*
9. *Ibid.*, vol. III, p. 206—8, *The state.*
10. 'If a definite level of culture is required for the building of socialism (although nobody can say just what that definite "level of culture" is, for it differs in every West-European country), why cannot we begin by first achieving the prerequisites for that definite level of culture in a revolutionary way, and *then*, with the aid of the workers' and peasants' government and the Soviet system, proceed to overtake the other nations?' *Ibid.*, p. 707.
11. *Ibid.*
12. Lenin, 1977, vol. I, p. 97, *What is to be done?*
13. *Ibid.*, p. 196.
14. *Ibid.*, pp. 226—7.
15. Cf. Chapter 5 above; on the party against society, Kriegel, 1972, p. 136 *et seq.*
16. Lenin, 1977, vol. I, p. 135, *What is to be done?*
17. *Ibid.*, p. 145.
18. *Ibid.*, p. 148.
19. Cf. Papaioannou, 1964.
20. Lenin, 1977, vol. I, p. 114, *What is to be done?*
21. *Ibid.*
22. Papaioannou, 1964.
23. Lenin, 1977, vol. I, p. 120, *What is to be done?*
24. *Ibid.*, p. 201.
25. *Ibid.*, p. 189.
26. *Ibid.*, p. 178.
27. *Ibid.*, p. 201.
28. *Ibid.*, p. 97.
29. *Ibid.*
30. *Ibid.*, p. 190.
31. *Ibid.*, p. 546, *In memory of Herzen.*
32. Lenin, 1947, vol. I, p. 556, *Two utopias.*
33. *Ibid.*, p. 558.
34. Lenin, 1948, p. 404.

35. Lenin, 1977, vol. I, p. 404, *One step forward, two steps back.*
36. *Ibid.*, p. 291.
37. Lenin, 1947, vol. I, p. 132, *Tasks of the Russian social-democrats.*
38. *Ibid.*, pp. 132–3.
39. Lenin, 1977, vol. I, p. 183, *What is to be done?*
40. *Ibid.*, vol. III, pp. 318–19, *'Left-wing communism' – an infantile disorder.*
41. *Ibid.*, vol. I, p. 177 *et seq.*, *What is to be done?*
42. Lenin, 1948, t. I, p. 224.
43. Lenin, 1977, vol. II, p. 171, *On compromises.*
44. *Ibid.*
45. *Ibid.*, vol. I, p. 103, *What is to be done?*
46. *Ibid.*, vol. III, p. 333, *'Left-wing communism' – an infantile disorder.*
47. *Ibid.*, vol. I, p. 106, *What is to be done?*
48. *Ibid.*, vol. III, p. 300, *'Left-wing communism' – an infantile disorder.*
49. *Ibid.*, p. 301.
50. *Ibid.*, p. 293.
51. *Ibid.*, p. 346.

CHAPTER 14: *Truth and Falsehood*

1. *Cit.* Heller, 1974.
2. Cf. by analogy, Kriegel, 1971.
3. Lenin, 1946, vol. I, p. 132, *Tasks of the Russian social-democrats.*
4. *Ibid.*
5. Lenin, 1977, vol. I, p. 154, *What is to be done?*
6. *Ibid.*, p. 157.
7. *Ibid.*, pp. 216–18.
8. *Ibid.*, p. 159.
9. Which none the less goes with the *secrecy* of the party: cf. Kriegel, 1972, p. 171 *et seq.*
10. The same can be said of Stalin and Hitler: both always declared precisely what they were going to do, while a selective deafness afflicted their future victims.
11. Lenin, 1977, vol. II, pp. 456–9, *Theses on the constituent assembly.*
12. *Ibid.*, vol. III, p. 47, *The proletarian revolution and the renegade Kautsky.*
13. *Ibid.*, p. 49.

CHAPTER 15: *In Power*

1. I refer here, and in other passages, to a memorable course of lectures given by M. Malia at the École des Hautes Études.

2. Khodassevich.

3. On the Soviets: Anweiler, 1972.

4. On the nature of the Soviet régime: Besançon, 1976a.

5. Lenin, 1977, vol. II, p. 41, *The tasks of the proletariat in our revolution.*

6. *Ibid.,* p. 68, *7th (April) all-Russian conference of the RSDLP (B).*

7. *Ibid.,* pp. 46–8, *The tasks of the proletariat in our revolution.*

8. *Ibid.,* p. 105, *7th (April) all-Russian conference of the RSDLP (B).*

9. *Ibid.,* p. 329, *The Bolsheviks must assume power.*

10. *Ibid.,* p. 172, *On compromises.*

11. *Ibid.,* p. 369, *Can the Bolsheviks retain state power?*

12. *Ibid.,* p. 348, *The crisis has matured.*

13. Daniels, 1967. Especially chap. XI, 'The myth and the reality'.

14. Lenin, 1977, vol. II, p. 405, *Meeting of C. C. RSDLP (B), 16 (29) October 1917.*

15. *Ibid.,* p. 415, *Letter to central committee, 24 October (4 November), 1917.*

16. *Ibid.,* p. 365, *Can the Bolsheviks retain state power?*

17. *Ibid.*

18. *Ibid.,* p. 591, *The immediate tasks of the Soviet government.*

19. *Ibid.,* p. 470, *How to organize competition?*

20. *Ibid.,* p. 529, *Extraordinary 7th congress of the RCP (B).*

21. *Ibid.,* p. 455, *Report on the economic condition of the Petrograd workers.*

22. *Ibid.,* p. 462, *Speech on the nationalization of the banks.*

23. *Ibid.,* p. 651, *On the famine.*

24. *Ibid.,* p. 653.

25. *Ibid.,* p. 693, *Speech at a joint session of All-Russia CEC, 29 July 1918.*

26. *Ibid.,* vol. III, p. 235, *Economics and politics in the era of the dictatorship of the proletariat.*

27. *Cit.* Papaioannou, 1964, p. 439.

28. Lenin, 1977, vol. III, p. 636, *11th Congress of the RCP (B).*

29. *Ibid.,* p. 510, *10th congress of the RCP (B).*

30. *Ibid.,* p. 460, *8th All-Russia congress of Soviets.*

31. *Ibid.,* vol. II, p. 661, *Speech at the first all-Russia Congress of economic councils.*

32. *Ibid.,* vol. III, p. 162, *Greetings to the Hungarian workers;* and p. 236, *Economics and politics in the era of the dictatorship of the proletariat.*

33. *Ibid.,* p. 237, *Economics and politics in the era of the dictatorship of the proletariat.*

34. *Ibid.*

35. *Ibid.,* vol. II, *The immediate tasks of the Soviet government.*

36. *Ibid.,* p. 622, *Six theses on the immediate tasks of the Soviet government.*

37. *Ibid.,* vol. III, p. 293, *'Left-wing communism' — an infantile disorder.*

38. *Ibid.,* p. 430, *Speech at a conference on the political education of the workers.*

39. *Ibid.*, p. 125, *8th congress of the RCP (B), 1919.*
40. *Ibid.*, vol. II, p. 474; Solzhenitsyn, 1974, p. 27.
41. Heller, 1976, p. 183 *et seq.*
42. Lenin, 1977, vol. II, p. 565, *The chief task of our day.*
43. *Ibid.*, p. 608, *The immediate tasks of the Soviet government.*
44. *Okolokadety, cit.* Solzhenitsyn, 1974, p. 31.
45. Lenin, 1977, vol. III, p. 553, *The tax in kind.*
46. *Ibid.*, vol. II, p. 609, *The immediate tasks of the Soviet government*; on the educational function of trials in the USSR, Kriegel, 1971.
47. The predators: the two coalitions engaged in the Great War. *Ibid.*, p. 531, *Extraordinary 7th congress of the RCP (B).*
48. *Ibid.*, p. 530.
49. *Ibid.*, p. 485, *On the history of the question of the unfortunate peace.*
50. *Ibid.*, p. 483.
51. *Ibid.*, vol. III, p. 451, *8th all-Russian congress of Soviets.*
52. Lenin, 1975, t. III, p. 662.
53. Lenin, 1977, vol. III, p. 541, *The tax in kind.*
54. *Ibid.*, p. 593, *The importance of gold.*
55. *Ibid.*
56. *Ibid.*, p. 476, *Once again on the trade unions.*
57. *Ibid.*, p. 488.
58. *Ibid.*
59. 'Pour le centenaire de Lénine', 1970, p. 28.
60. Lenin, 1977, vol. III, p. 428, *Speech at a conference of political education workers.*
61. *Ibid.*, p. 429.
62. *Ibid.*, p. 431.
63. Berelowitch, 1977.
64. 'Pour le centenaire de Lénine', 1970, p. 34.
65. Lenin, 1977, vol. III, p. 622, *11th congress of the RCP (B).*
66. Platonov, the writer, seems to me an excellent example of the 'naïve' Communist.
67. On this concept, Besançon, 1976a.

CHAPTER 16: *The Dominion of the False*

1. Lenin, 1977, vol. III, p. 432, *Speech at a conference of political education workers.*
2. *Ibid.*, vol. II, p. 712, *Letter to American workers.*
3. *Ibid.*, vol. III, p. 707, *Our revolution.*
4. *Ibid.*, p. 627, *11th congress of the RCP (B).*
5. The question of language under an ideological régime is undoubtedly

crucial. But up until now it has been more sensed than fully explored. There are ideas on the subject in Bod, 1975; Glazov, 1974; in Orwell, of course, throughout his work, and in Milosz, 1953.

6. Pasternak, 1958, p. 453.

7. Cf., too long to be quoted here, Stalin, 1936.

8. The uniformity of the *wooden language*, which meant, before the seizure of power, communion in the central vision, represents, after the seizure of power, submission to that power. Linguistic conformity is in fact the prime test of allegiance. Heteroglossy is the first sign of rebellion.

9. Solzhenitsyn, 1972.

10. Stalin, *On the death of Lenin*, in Lenin, 1947, vol. I, p. 21.

11. *Aeneid*, tr. W. F. Jackson Knight, Penguin Books, 1958, VIII, lines 485—8.

Bibliography

This is neither a general nor a comprehensive bibliography. It gives the references for all the works quoted, and, among the ones which I consulted, those which provided me with information or ideas immediately relevant to the subject.

Alembert, J. le Rond d', 1965, *Discours préliminaire de l'Encyclopédie*, Gonthier, 'Médiations', Paris.

Alquié, F., 1966, *La découverte métaphysique de l'homme chez Descartes*, PUF, Paris.

Alquié, F., 1974, *Le cartésianisme de Malebranche*, Vrin, Paris.

Anweiler, O., 1972, *Les Soviets en Russie*, Gallimard, Paris.

Armogathe, J. R., 1973, *Le quiétisme*, PUF, Paris.

Aron, Raymond, 1955, *Polémiques*, Gallimard, Paris.

Aron, Raymond, 1957, *The opium of the intellectuals*, tr. T. Kilmartin, Secker and Warburg, London.

Aron, Raymond, 1968, *Democracy and totalitarianism*, tr. V. Ionescu, Weidenfeld and Nicolson, London.

Aron, Raymond, 1976, *Penser la guerre, Clausewitz*, Gallimard, Paris, t. I and II.

Augustine, Saint, 1961, *Six traités antimanichéens, Oeuvres*, t. 13, Desclée de Brouwer, Bruges.

Augustine, Saint, 1962, *Confessions, Oeuvres*, t. 13, Desclée de Brouwer, Bruges.

Avrich, P., 1967, *The Russian anarchists*, Princeton UP, Princeton, NJ.

Baechler, J., 1976, *Qu'est-ce que l'idéologie*, Gallimard, Paris.

Baron, P., 1940, *Alexis Stepanovitch Khomiakov*, Pont. Inst. Orientalum Studiorum, Rome.

Baron, S. H., 1962, 'Between Marx and Lenin, George Plekhanov', in *Revisionism, Essays on the history of Marxist ideas*, ed. L. Labedz, Allen and Unwin, London.

Baron, S. H., 1963, *Plekhanov, the father of Russian Marxism*, Stanford UP, Stanford, Cal.

Baruzi, J., 1907, *Leibniz et l'organisation religieuse de la terre*, Alcan, Paris.

Benz, E., 1968, *Les sources mystiques de la philosophie romantique allemande*, Vrin, Paris.

Berelowitch, W., 1977, 'Ecole et idéologie dans la Russie soviétique des années vingt', unpublished thesis, EHESS.

Bernstein, E., 1974, *Les présupposés du socialisme*, Seuil, Paris.

Besançon, A., 1967, *Le tsarévitch immolé*, Plon, Paris.

Besançon, A., 1972, *L'Idiot* (Preface), Gallimard, Paris.

Besançon, A., 1974a, *Education et société en Russie dans le second tiers du XIXᵉ siècle*, Mouton, Paris and the Hague.

Besançon, A., 1974b, 'Présent soviétique et passé russe', *Contrepoint*, no. 14, pp. 21–7.

Besançon, A., 1974c, 'L'inconscient: l'épisode de la prostituée dans *Que faire?* et dans le *Sous sol*', in *Faire de l'histoire*, eds J. Le Goff and P. Nora, Gallimard, Paris, t. III, pp. 31–55.

Besançon, A., 1975, 'Michelet, Dostoïevski, l'Histoire', *Contrepoint*, no. 19, pp. 87–101.

Besançon, A., 1976a, 'De la difficulté de définir le régime soviétique', *Contrepoint*, no. 20, pp. 115–28.

Besançon, A., 1976b, *Court traité de soviétologie*, Preface by Raymond Aron, Hachette, Paris.

Biélinski, V., 1948, *Textes philosophiques choisis*, Moscow.

Blok, A., 1974, *Oeuvres en prose*, L'Age d'Homme, Lausanne.

Bod, L., 1975, 'Langage et pouvoir politique', *Etudes*, February, pp. 177–215.

Boukharine, N. and E. Preobrajenski, 1971, *ABC du communisme*, F. Maspero, Paris.

Brower, D. R., 1975, *Training the nihilists*, Cornell UP, Ithaca and London.

Brown, E. J., 1966, *Stankevich and his Moscow circle*, Stanford UP, Stanford, Cal.

Bukharin, N. and Preobrazhenski, E. *see* Boukharine, N. and E. Preobrajenski.

Byelinski, V. *see* Biélinski, V.

Cassirer, Ernst, 1951, *The philosophy of the Enlightenment*, tr. F. C. A. Koelln and J. P. Pettegrove, Princeton UP, Princeton, NJ.

Chambre, H., 1955, *Le marxisme en Union soviétique, idéologie et institutions*, Seuil, Paris.

Chambre, H., 1974, *L'évolution du marxisme soviétique*, Seuil, Paris.

Chaunu, P., 1966, *La civilisation de l'Europe classique*, Arthaud, Paris.

Cherniavsky, M., 1970, 'Khan or Basileus' in *The structure of Russian history*, ed. M. Cherniavsky, Random House, New York, pp. 64–79.

Chernyshevski, N. *see* Tchernychevski, N.

Chestov, L., 1972, 'Kierkegaard et Dostoïevski', in *Kierkegaard et la philosophie existentielle*, Vrin, Paris.

Christoff, P. K., 1961, *An introduction to nineteenth-century Russian Slavo-philism: a study in ideas*, Mouton, 's-Gravenhage, (vols. 1 and 2), 1. *A. Xomjakov.*

Cieszkowski, A. D. von, 1973, *Prolégomènes à l'historiosophie*, Champ libre, Paris.

Cieszkowski, A. D. von, 1979, *Selected writings*, tr. and ed. A. Liebich, Cambridge.

Cochin, A., 1921, *Les sociétés de pensée et la démocratie moderne*, Plon, Paris.

Confino, M., 1972, 'On intellectuals and intellectual traditions in eighteenth and nineteenth-century Russia', *Daedalus*, Spring, vol. 101, no. 1, pp. 117–49.

Confino, M., 1973, *Violence dans la violence, le débat Bakounine-Necaev*, F. Maspero, Paris.

Daniels, R. V., 1967, *Red October*, Scribner and Sons, New York.

Diderot, D., 1951, 'Entretiens sur le fils naturel' in D. Diderot, *Oeuvres Choisies*, Gallimard, 'Pléiade', Paris.

Doresse, J., 1972, 'La gnose' in *Histoire des religions*, Encyclopédie de la pléiade, Gallimard, Paris, pp. 364–430.

Dostoevsky, F. M., 1949–61, *Correspondance*, Calmann-Lévy, Paris, t. I–IV.

Drouilly, J., 1971, *La pensée politique et religieuse de Dostoïevski*, Les cinq continents, Paris.

Dvornik, F., 1970, *Les slaves*, Seuil, Paris.

Engels, F., 1935a, *Herr Eugen Dühring's revolution in science* [*Anti-Dühring*], Martin Lawrence, London.

Engels, F., 1935b, *Ludwig Feuerbach and the outcome of classical German philosophy*, Martin Lawrence, London.

Engels, F., 1977, *Dialectics of nature*, tr. and ed. C. Dutt, Laurence and Wishart, London.

Faivre, A., 1973, *L'ésotérisme au XVIIIe siècle*, Seghers, Paris.

Fejto, F., 1973, *L'héritage de Lénine*, Casterman, Paris.

Fischer, L., 1965, *The life of Lenin*, Weidenfeld and Nicolson, London.

Florovsky, G., 1937, *Puti russkago bogoslovija*, Paris.

Florovsky, G., 1970, 'The problem of old Russian culture' in *The structure of Russian history*, ed. M. Cherniavsky, Random House, New York, pp. 126–39.

Gabel, J., 1952, 'Délire politique chez un paranoïde', *Evolution psychiatrique*, Paris.

Gabel, J., 1962, *La fausse conscience*, Editions de Minuit, Paris.

Gabel, J., 1974, *Idéologies*, Ed. Anthropos, Paris.

Gaxotte, P. and J. Tulard, 1975, *La Révolution française*, Fayard, Paris.

Girard, R., 1961, *Mensonge romantique et vérité romanesque*, Grasset, Paris.

Girard, R., 1963, *Dostoïevski, du double à l'unité*, Plon, Paris.

Glazov, Y., 1974, 'Le double langage dans la littérature et la société soviétique', *Plamia*, Easter, no. 38, pp. 24–36.

Goldstein, D. I., 1976, *Dostoïevski et les Juifs*, Gallimard, 'Idées', Paris.

Gouhier, H., 1933, *La jeunesse d'Auguste Comte et la formation du positivisme*, Vrin, Paris, t. I–III.

Graham, L. R., 1973, *Science and philosophy in the Soviet Union*, Allen Lane, London.

Gratieux, A., 1939, *A. S. Khomiakov et le mouvement slavophile*, t. I and II, Editions du Cerf, Paris.

Gratieux, A., 1953, *Le mouvement slavophile à la veille de la Révolution*, Editions du Cerf, Paris.

Groethuysen, B., 1966, *Philosophie de la Révolution française*, Gonthier, 'Médiations', Paris.

Gusdorf, G., 1972, *Dieu, la nature et l'homme au siècle des lumières*, Payot, Paris.

Gusdorf, G., 1976, *Naissance de la conscience romantique au siècle des Lumières*, Payot, Paris.

Hazard, P., 1953, *The European mind*, tr. J. L. May, Hollis and Carter, London.

Heller, M., 1974, *Le monde concentrationnaire et la littérature soviétique*. L'Age d'Homme, Lausanne.

Heller, M., 1976, 'Lenin i Veceka', *Vestnik*, no. 119, Paris, pp. 183–205.

Helvétius, *De l'Esprit*, Marabout Université, Verviers, 1973.

Herzen, A., 1956, *Selected philosophical works*, tr. L. Navrozov, Foreign Languages Publishing House, Moscow.

Herzen, A., 1968, *My past and thoughts: memoirs*, tr. C. Garnett, rev. H. Higgens, vols. I–IV, Chatto and Windus, London.

History of the Communist Party of the Soviet Union (Bolsheviks), 1939, ed. by a Committee of the CPSU (B), Moscow.

Ivanov-Razumnik, R. V., 1908, *Istorija Russkoi obshchestvennoi mysli*, St Petersburg, vols. I and II.

Jaeger, H., 1965, 'La mystique protestante et anglicane' in A. Ravier, *La mystique et les mystiques*, Desclée de Brouwer, Bruges, pp. 256–407.

Jaeger, H., 1977, *Le Piétisme*, Plamia, no. 47. pp. 15–20.

Kant, I., 1953, *Prolegomena to any future metaphysic*, tr. P. G. Lucas, Manchester UP, Manchester.

Kant, I., 1963, *Dreams of a spirit-seer*, tr. E. F. Goerwitz, in *Kant*, sel. and trans. G. Rabel, OUP, London.

Karpovich, M. M., 1963, 'P. L. Lavrov and Russian socialism', *California slavic studies*, vol. II, pp. 21–38.

Keep, J. L. H., 1963, *The rise of social democracy in Russia*, Clarendon Press, Oxford.

Khomiakoff, A. S., 1872, *L'Eglise latine et le protestantisme au point de vue de l'Eglise d'Orient*, Vevey, Lausanne.

Kireevski, I. V., 1911, *Polnoe sobranie sochinenii*, Moscow, vols. I and II.

Koyré, A., 1929, *La philosophie et le problème national en Russie au début du XIXe siècle*, Honoré Champion, Paris.

Koyré, A., 1950, *Etudes sur l'histoire de la pensée philosophique en Russie*, Vrin, Paris.

Koyré, A., 1958, *From the closed world to the infinite universe*, Harper Torchbooks, New York.

Koyré, A., 1971a, *La philosophie de Jacob Boehme*, Vrin, Paris.

Koyré, A., 1971b, *Mystiques spirituels et alchimiques du XVIe siècle allemand*, Gallimard, 'Idées', Paris.

Koz'min, B. P., 1922, *P. B. Tkacev i revoljucionnoe dvizenie 1860kh godov*, Moscow.

Koz'min, B. P., 1961, 'P. N. Tkacev' in *Iz Istorii revoljucionnoj mysli v Rossii*, Moscow.

Kriegel, A., 1971a, 'Les procès ou la pédagogie infernale dans le système stalinien', in *Mélanges en l'honneur de Raymond Aron*, Calmann-Lévy, Paris, t. I, pp. 500–46.

Kriegel, A., 1971b, 'Notes sur l'idéologie dans le Partie communiste français', *Contrepoint*, Spring, no. 3, pp. 95–104.

Kriegel, A., 1972, *The French Communists*, tr. E. P. Halperin, Chicago UP, Chicago.

Labedz, L. (ed.), 1962, *Revisionism: essays on the history of Marxist ideas*, Allen and Unwin, London.

Labry, R., 1928, *Alexandre Ivanovic Herzen*, Bossard, Paris.

Laloy, J., 1967, *Le socialisme de Lénine*, Desclée de Brouwer, Paris.

La Mettrie, J. O. de, 1954, *Textes choisis*, Editions sociales, Paris.

La Mettrie, J. O. de, 1960, *L'homme machine*, ed. A. Vartanian, Princeton UP, Princeton, NJ.

Lavroff, P., 1903, *Lettres historiques*, Schleicher frères, Paris.

Leibnitz, G. W. F. von, 1952, *Theodicy: essays on the goodness of God, freedom of man and the origins of evil*, tr. E. M. Huggard, Routledge, London.

Lenin, V. I., 1934, *Marx, Engels, Marxism*, ed. J. Finenberg, Martin Lawrence, London.

Lenin, V. I., 1947, *Selected works*, 2 vols., Foreign Languages Publishing House, Moscow.

Lenin, V. I., 1948, *Oeuvres choisis en deux volumes*, Moscow.

Lenin, V. I., 1960–78, *Collected works*, 46 vols. (in progress), Moscow and London: Laurence and Wishart.

Lenin, V. I., 1975, *Oeuvres choisis en trois volumes*, Moscow.

Lenin, V. I., 1977, *Selected works*, 3 vols., Progress Publishers, Moscow.

Lenoble, R., 1957, 'Origines de la pensée scientifique moderne' in *Histoire de la Science*, Encyclopédie de la Pléiade, Gallimard, Paris.

Lenoble, R., 1969, *Histoire de l'idée de Nature*, Albin Michel, Paris.

Lenoble, R., 1971, *Mersenne ou la naissance du mécanisme*, Vrin, Paris.

Ley, F., 1975, *Alexandre Ier et sa Sainte Alliance*, Fischbacher, Paris.

Lopukin, I. V., 1912, *Some characteristics of the interior church*, London.

Losski, N. O., 1951, *History of Russian philosophy*, Allen and Unwin, London.

Löwith, Karl, 1965, *From Hegel to Nietzsche*, tr. D. E. Green, Constable, London.

McClellan, D. T., 1969, *The young Hegelians and Karl Marx*, Macmillan, London.

Malia, M. E., 1961, *Alexander Herzen and the birth of Russian socialism, 1812–1855*, Harvard UP, Cambridge, Mass.

Mandelstam, Nadezhda, 1974, *Hope abandoned*, tr. M. Hayward, Collins, London.

Mannheim, Karl, 1936, *Ideology and utopia*, Kegan Paul, London.

Maritain, J., 1964, *Moral philosophy*, tr. M. Suther *et al.*, Geoffrey Bles, London.

Martin, G., 1964, *Leibniz: logic and metaphysics*, tr. K. J. Northcott and P. G. Lucas, Manchester UP, Manchester.

Marx, K. and F. Engels, 1947, *Etudes philosophiques*, Editions Sociales, Paris.

Marx, K., 1954, *La Russie et l'Europe*, Gallimard, Paris.

Mathieu, V., 1974, *Phénoménologie de l'esprit révolutionnaire*, Calmann-Levy, Paris.

Michelet, J., 1968, *Légendes démocratiques du Nord*, PUF, Paris.

Milosz, C., 1953, *The captive mind*, tr. J. Zichonko, Secker and Warburg, London.

Milosz, C., 1975, 'Dostoyevsky and Swedenborg', *Slavic Review*, June, vol. 34, pp. 302–18.

Milyukov, P. N., 1942, *Outlines of Russian culture*, tr. V. Ughet and E. Davis, 3 parts, Univ. of Pennsylvania Press, Philadelphia.

Mochulsky, K. V., 1967, *Dostoevsky: his life and work*, tr. M. A. Minihan, Princeton UP, Princeton, NJ.

Monnerot, J., 1953, *Sociology of communism*, tr. J. Degras and R. Rees, Allen and Unwin, London.

Morelly, 1970, *Le code de la nature*, Editions sociales, Paris.

Nabokov, V., 1963, *The gift*, tr. M. Scammell, Weidenfeld and Nicolson, London.

Nomad, M., 1958, 'Machaiski', *Contrat Social*, vol. II, no. 5.

Obolensky, D., 1970, 'Russia's Byzantine heritage', in *The structure of Russian history*, ed. M. Cherniavsky, Random House, New York, pp. 43—72.

Orwell, G., 1949, *1984*, Secker and Warburg, London.

Orwell, G., 1970, *The collected essays, journalism and letters*, Penguin Books, Harmondsworth, vols. I—IV.

Papaioannou, K., 1962, *Hegel*, Seghers, Paris.

Papaioannou, K., 1964, 'Classe et partie', *Contrat Social*, vol. VIII, nos. 4 and 5.

Papaioannou, K., 1967, *L'idéologie froide*, J. -J. Pauvert, Paris.

Papaioannou, K., 1972, *Marx et les marxistes*, Flammarion, Paris.

Pascal, P., 1969, *Dostoïevski*, Desclée de Brouwer, Bruges.

Pascal, P., 1970, *Dostoïevski, l'homme et l'oeuvre*, L'Age d'Homme, Lausanne.

Pasternak, B., 1958, *Doctor Zhivago*, tr. M. Hayward and R. Harari, Collins, London.

Petit dictionnaire philosophique, 1961, eds. M. Rosenthal and P. Ioudine, Moscow.

Pipes, R., ed., 1961, *The Russian intelligentsia*, Columbia UP, New York.

Pipes, R., 1963, *Social democracy and the St Petersburg labor movement, 1885—1897*, Harvard UP, Cambridge, Mass.

Pipes, R., 1970, *Struve, liberal on the left, 1870—1905*, Harvard UP, Cambridge, Mass.

Pipes, R., 1974, *Russia under the old régime*, Weidenfeld and Nicolson, London.

Plekhanov, G., 1926, *Introduction à l'histoire sociale de la Russie*, Bossard, Paris.

Plekhanov, G., n. d., *Oeuvres philosophiques*, Moscow, t. I and III.

'Pour le centenaire de Lénine', 1970, special number of *Est-Ouest*, 1—30 April, Paris, nos. 444—5.

Puech, H.-C., 1972, 'Le manichéisme', in *Histoire des religions*, 'Encyclopédie de la Pléiade', Gallimard, Paris, t. II, pp. 523—696.

Raeff, M., 1966, *Origins of the Russian intelligentsia, the eighteenth century nobility*, Harcourt Brace, New York.

Raeff, M., 1967a, 'La jeunesse russe à l'aube du XIXᵉ siècle, André Turgenev et ses amis', *Cahiers du monde russe et soviétique*, Paris, vol. VIII, no. 4, pp. 560—86.

Raeff, M., 1967b, 'Les slaves, les allemands et les lumières', *Canadian Slavic Studies*, vol. I, no. 4, pp. 521—51.

Ross, N., 1973, 'La conception du monde, l'image de l'homme et de la nature en Russie à l'epoque d'André Roublev', unpublished thesis, Paris.

Rouet de Journel, M. J., 1922, *Un collège de Jésuites à Saint-Pétersbourg, 1800—1806*, Librarie académique Perrin, Paris.

Rouleau, F., 1972, 'Ivan Kireevski et sa place dans la pensée russe', unpublished thesis, Ecoles des Hautes Etudes, t. I and II.

Rudolph, K., 1972, 'La religion mandenne' in *Histoire des Religions*, 'Encyclopédie de la Pléiade', Gallimard, Paris, t. II, pp. 498—522.

Rupp, J., 1970, 'Les théologiens de Kiev trait d'union paradoxal entre l'Est et l'Ouest à l'âge de Sobieski', *Arbeits- und Fordderungsgemeinschaft der Ukrainischen Wissenschaft Mitteilungen*, nos. 6—7, Munich, pp. 37—53.

Sade, D. A. F., Marquis de, 1968, *Juliette (ou les prosperités du vice)*, tr. A. Wainhouse, Grove Press, New York.

Sakharov, A., 1975, *My country and the world*, tr. G. V. Daniels, Harvill Press, London.

Schapiro, L., 1970, *The Communist Party of the Soviet Union*, Eyre and Spottiswoode, London.

Scherrer, J., 1973, *Die Petersburger religios-philosophischen vereinigungen*, Osteuropa Institut, Berlin.

Scherrer, J., 1976—7, 'Intelligentsia, religion, révolution', *Cahiers du Monde russe et soviétique*, vol. XVII, no. 4, Oct.—Dec., pp. 427—66 and vol. XVIII, nos. 1—2, Jan.—June, pp. 5—32.

Seton-Watson, H., 1967, *The Russian Empire, 1801—1917*, Clarendon Press, Oxford.

Shils, E., 1968, 'The concept and function of ideology', *International encyclopedia of the social sciences*, vol. VII, pp. 66—76.

Soloviev, V., 1947, *La crise de la philosophie occidentale*, Aubier, Paris.

Solzhenitsyn, A., 1972, *One word of truth…*, Bodley Head, London.

Solzhenitsyn, A., 1974, *Letter to Soviet leaders*, tr. H. Sternberg, Collins, London.

Solzhenitsyn, A., 1974—8, *The Gulag Archipelago*, tr. T. P. Whitney and H. T. Willetts, 2 vols., Collins, London.

Solzhenitsyn, A., 1976, *Lenin in Zurich*, tr. H. T. Willetts, Bodley Head, London.

Souvarine, B., 1939, *Stalin*, tr. C. L. R. James, Secker and Warburg, London.

Stalin, J., 1936, *The new democracy, speech on the new constitution, 14th November 1936*, Laurence and Wishart, London.

Stalin, J., 1940, *Leninism*, Allen and Unwin, London.

Starr, S. F., 1972, *Decentralisation and self-government in Russia, 1830—1870*, Princeton UP, Princeton NJ.

Stremoukhoff, D., 1970, 'Moscow the third Rome: sources of the doctrine', in *The structure of Russian history*, ed. M. Cherniavsky, Random House, New York, p. 108—24.

Szamuely, T., 1974, *The Russian tradition*, Secker and Warburg, London.

Talmon, J. L., 1952, *The origins of totalitarian democracy*, Secker and Warburg, London.

Tchernychevski, N., 1957, *Textes philosophiques choisis*, Moscow.

Tchernychevski, N., 1967, *Que Faire? (What's to be done?)*, Moscow.

Tkachev, P. N. (Tkacev), 1932—7, *Izbrannye sochinenija na social'no politi-cheskie temy v chetyrekh tomakh*, Moscow.

Treadgold, D. W., 1973, *The West in Russia and China*, vol. I, 1472—1917, Cambridge UP, Cambridge.

Ulam, A., 1964, *The unfinished revolution*, Vintage Books, New York.

Ulam, A., 1966, *Lenin and the Bolsheviks*, Collins, London.

Ulam, A., 1974, *Stalin: the man and his era*, Allen Lane, London.

Ulam, A., 1977, *In the name of the people*, Viking Press, New York.

Valentinov, N., 1968, *Encounters with Lenin*, tr. P. Rosta and B. Pearce, OUP, London.

Vancourt, R., 1971, *La pensée religieuse de Hegel*, PUF, Paris.

Vekhi, Sbornik Staej o Russkoj Intelligencii, Moscow, 1909.

Venturi, F., 1960, *Roots of revolution*, tr. F. Haskell, Weidenfeld and Nicolson, London.

Venturi, F., 1972, *Les intellectuels, le peuple et la révolution*, Gallimard, Paris.

Walicki, A., 1969, *The controversy of capitalism, studies in the social philosophy of the Russian populists*, Clarendon Press, Oxford.

Walicki, A., 1975, *The Slavophile controversy*, Clarendon Press, Oxford.

Weidlé, Wladimir, 1952, *Russia: absent and present*, tr. A. Gordon Smith, Hollis and Carter, London.

Wetter, G. A., 1966, *Soviet ideology today*, tr. P. Heath, Heinemann Educational, London.

Wolfe, B. D., 1955, *Three who made a revolution (Lenin, Trotsky, Stalin)*, Boston, Mass.

Yates, F. A., 1966, *The art of memory*, Routledge, London.

Zamyatin, E. I., 1970, *We*, tr. B. G. Guerney, Cape, London.

Zenkovsky, V. V., 1953, *A history of Russian philosophy*, tr. G. L. Kline, Routledge, London, vols. I and II.

Index